Richard Critchfield has been covering war, revolution and politics in Asia since 1959. Since 1962 he has been a correspondent of *The Washington Star* in New Delhi, Hong Kong and Saigon. He first visited Saigon during the Diem government's administration in 1959, then lived in Vietnam for three years, from May 1964. He was awarded the Overseas Press Club award for best daily newspaper or wire-service reporting from abroad for his Vietnam coverage in 1965.

Mr. Critchfield served as a sergeant in the Army Engineers in the Korean war. Born in Minneapolis, Minnesota, he received a B.A. degree in Far Eastern Studies from the University of Washington in 1953, an M.S. from the Graduate School of Journalism at Columbia University in 1957 and did graduate work at Northwestern University and the universities of Innsbruck and Vienna in Austria.

In 1960–61, Mr. Critchfield was a lecturer in journalism at the University of Nagpur, India. He has been a contributor to *The Reporter* and *The New York Times Magazine*.

The Long Charade

The Long Charade

Political Subversion

in the Vietnam War

by Richard Critchfield

 HARCOURT, BRACE & WORLD, INC.
NEW YORK

Copyright © 1968 by Richard Critchfield

First edition

Library of Congress Catalog Card Number: 68-28815

Printed in the United States of America

The lines quoted on pp. xv, 61, 361 and 362 are from "Charade,"
copyright © 1963 by Southdale Music Corp. & Northern Music
Corp., music by Henry Mancini, words by Johnny Mercer.

To
Tran Van Van,
Marguerite Higgins,
and all the others who tried to expose the charade

Preface

This book was begun in a thatched hut on the island of
Bali in December 1967, mostly written on a Virginia farm near
Washington, and finished at the University Club on the island of
Manhattan. In October 1965, the historically gentle Balinese rose
up to kill nearly 30,000 island Communists, because, as one fisherman told me, "they are cursed by the gods"; the greatest renais-
sance of Balinese art, culture and religion in living memory
followed. It is an ironic commentary on our times that nowhere
have I found more sympathy and understanding of the predica-
ment of the Vietnamese people than on this South Sea island
paradise, and it was in this environment that I reached the
decision to return to the United States to put my ideas and
experiences in Vietnam together in the form of a book.

These experiences center on the three and a half years I
covered the Vietnam war, from May 1964 to November 1967, as

the correspondent of the Washington evening *Star*. I have also drawn upon a short visit to Saigon in 1959, a year with the U.S. army engineers in South Korea in 1953, and other experiences in my nine years as a journalist in Asia. I have endeavored to set out, as I saw it unfold, the story of political subversion in South Vietnam in the past five years. The book is not complete. The first draft of the manuscript came to nearly 300,000 words; for the sake of clarity and reducing the story to readable length, I have excluded most of the battle scenes, as well as the diplomatic conflict and the air war against North Vietnam. And the struggle is still going on.

A word about recent Vietnamese history and the Vietnamese language. For place names of the three pre-1954 Vietnamese political entities, I have used the more precise French names of *Annam, Tonkin* and *Cochinchina*, rather than the current Vietnamese use of *North, Center* and *South*. This is to reduce confusion, since the geographical areas involved are different from the North and South of the 1954 partition. Annam extends along the central coast, roughly from Thanh Hoa to Nha Trang; Cochinchina covers Saigon and the Mekong Delta; Tonkin includes Hanoi and the Red River Delta.

Until 1947, Annam was a semiautonomous Buddhist kingdom, Tonkin a self-governing French protectorate, and Cochinchina a direct French colony. Under the 1945 Potsdam agreement, Chinese and British forces were allocated the reoccupation of former French Indochina. Before they arrived, Ho Chi Minh's Viet Minh guerrillas seized power, but the Chinese and British refused to negotiate with representatives of Ho's self-styled "Democratic Republic of Vietnam." Ho Chi Minh initially formed a coalition popular front government; the last emperor of Annam, Bao Dai, supported Ho in the status of a political adviser. At the Fountainebleau Conference in 1946, the French refused to give Ho Cochinchina and he walked out. At this point, Bao Dai and the traditional nationalists left the Viet Minh, who attacked Hanoi, starting the war which has gone on in one form or another to the present day. In 1947, the French, whose forces now held the towns, sought to form an autonomous single state of Vietnam out of Annam, Tonkin and Cochinchina. Bao Dai agreed and formed a shaky Saigon-based provisional government in 1949, although Annam and Tonkin remained largely self-administered and Saigon was literally run by a gangster army, the Binh Xuyen. By mid-1952, the French transferred all powers and functions to Bao Dai's largely phantom government and created a Vietnamese national army; its first officers class graduated in 1952 from newly opened schools at Nam Dinh in Tonkin and Thu Duc in Cochinchina. In 1954, the Geneva agreement partitioned the country into North Vietnam, divided into the twenty-nine provinces of Tonkin and four of northern Annam, and South Vietnam, consisting of the twenty-four provinces of former Cochinchina and seventeen provinces of Annam (eventually subdivided into a total forty-four provinces). Tonkin, Annam and Cochinchina are separated from one another by natural hill barriers, and each has had a distinct separate history and political development; this has left most Vietnamese with a stronger sense of regional than national identity.

The Vietnamese language reflects these regional distinctions: its accents are as different from one another as are those of American English. Indeed, peasants along the coastal strip from Vinh to Hue are not easily understood by many Vietnamese. Although Ngo Dinh Diem became the south's first president, after Bao Dai was deposed by national referendum in 1955, and ruled South Vietnam for nine years, he himself pronounced his name "Ziem," as in Annamite or Tonkinese dialect, while he is still referred to by Mekong Delta peasants as "Yiem."

There is also good reason why Vietnamese names are considered so unpronounceable in this country. Although the Vietnamese language is not a Chinese dialect, 50% of the words in conversational speech and 90% in some literary texts are Chinese derivatives. Yet in Vietnamese there are six tones and verbs are timeless and voiceless, although these are usually specified by modifiers. Moreover, Vietnamese do not use Chinese characters or the English romanized system employed in China, but have a system of writing devised in the seventeenth century by a Portuguese Catholic, Alexander de Rhodes, which was first published in Rome as a dictionary and catechism and indicates the spelling peculiarities of the Portuguese and Italian languages. To further complicate matters, the Vatican publishers used a complex system of diacritics, which represented the language well and made it easy for native speakers to learn but left it all but incomprehensible in foreign printing.

Yet the names themselves, once heard correctly, are easy to pronounce. Nguyen Cao Ky becomes three English words, Win Cow Key. Since an *a* in Vietnamese is pronounced *ah*, as in *fawn* and *dawn*, and the letter *u* is sounded as *oo*, Tran Van Huong becomes Trahn Vahn Hoong, and Dang Van Suong becomes Dahng Vahn Soong. Tonkinese and Annamites give some *s* sounds a *sh* pronunciation, so that Sung becomes Shoong and Suu becomes Shoo, but this is not done in the south. The names of both Le Duan and Vo Nguyen Giap make use of the *zh* sound, as in Doctor Zhivago. Le Duan is pronounced Lay (rhymes with *day*) Zhooan; Vo Nguyen Giap becomes Vo Win Zhaap. More difficult is Nguyen Van Thieu, which is really a Chinese-sounding name, Win Vahn Tyao. Hue is the same as curds and *whey;* Laos, louse; Thich Tri Quang, Tick Tree Kwong; Truong Dinh Dzu, Truong Dinn Zoo; and Mrs. Quach, Mrs. Kwock (to rhyme with Dr. *Spock*). Other names such as Ho Chi Minh and Dien Bien Phu sound as written. As in China or Korea, personal names usually have three syllables, of which the first is the family name. But unlike the Chinese, the Vietnamese use the last (given) name except in very formal circumstances, when the entire name is cited. Thus it is correct both to say President Diem and the Ngo family. If President Thieu had equally well-known relatives, they would be the Nguyen family.

Had there been a bibliography, Sir Robert Thompson's *Defeating Communist Insurgency* (Praeger, 1966) would have led it. His book is the best theoretical study of insurgency and counterinsurgency ever written. As will be self-evident, I owe a great debt of gratitude to Sir Robert, who headed the British advisory mission in Vietnam from 1961 to 1965, and to Dennis J. Duncanson, a member of the Thompson mission who stayed on until 1966 as a counselor in the British Embassy and is the author of *Government and Revolution in Vietnam* (Oxford University Press, 1968.) Without their many hours of patient analysis and interpretation, I would not have begun exploring political subversion in Vietnam—although both may be startled to discover where it has led me. I am also indebted to my friends Edward Lansdale and Douglas Pike, whose *Viet Cong* (M.I.T. Press, 1966) would be high on any Vietnam bibliography. So would the late Marguerite Higgins' *Our Vietnam Nightmare* (Harper & Row, 1965), the indispensable work on the 1963 *coup d'état* against Ngo Dinh Diem. I am indebted, too, to Mrs. Jean Miller for devoting so much time and effort to typing the full manuscript, and to my twelve-year-old nephew, Tommy, for some pointers on chess. I am also very grateful to the editors of the Washington *Star* for giving me leave to finish the book, and to the staff of the *Star's* library for their interested and enthusiastic help; the views and opinions expressed in the book are, of course, my own and not necessarily those of the newspaper with which I have been associated.

Finally, it is to the Vietnamese whose help I cannot now acknowledge by name that my deepest gratitude is owed. Much of the story does not lie in the public record but in the intangible opinion and personal memories of these Vietnamese, who someday, I hope, can tell their story for themselves. The peculiar nature of this book is that the sources on which I have most depended cannot be identified until the situation is resolved in Vietnam. In this sense, its confirmation must await events and the voices of witnesses who for now must remain silent.

R.C.

New York, August 1968

Contents

Preface   vii

The Players   3

1 Tran Van Van's Last Testament   11

2 Le Duan's Most Clever Tactic   30

3 Thich Tri Quang Sets the Stage   62

4 The Northerners Seize Power   82

5 The Killing at Tan Buu   103

6 Near Defeat   129

7 The Search for a Counterinsurgency Doctrine   156

8 Judo   171

9 Land to the Tiller   187

10 To Honolulu and Back   209

11 Revolt in Annam   226

12 To Pacify a Countryside   268

13 The Voice of the People   292

14 Toward Negotiations   321

15 A Choice Denied   342

16 The End of the Charade   364

Index of Persons   395

*It is possible to defeat a stronger enemy only through display-
ing great effort and under the necessary condition of taking
advantage very minutely, very attentively, very carefully and
very cleverly to any rift, even the smallest one, among the enemy; any contradiction, even the smallest one, among the interests of the bourgeoisie of various countries and among the various bourgeoisie groups and factions in each country. . . .*

—*Lenin*

*When we played our charade,
We were like children posing.
Playing at games,
Acting out names,
Guessing the parts we played.*

*Oh, what a hit we made
We came on next to closing . . .* *

—*Saigon's favorite ballad*

---

* From "Charade," copyright © 1963 by Southdale Music Corp. &
Northern Music Corp., music by Henry Mancini, words by Johnny
Mercer.

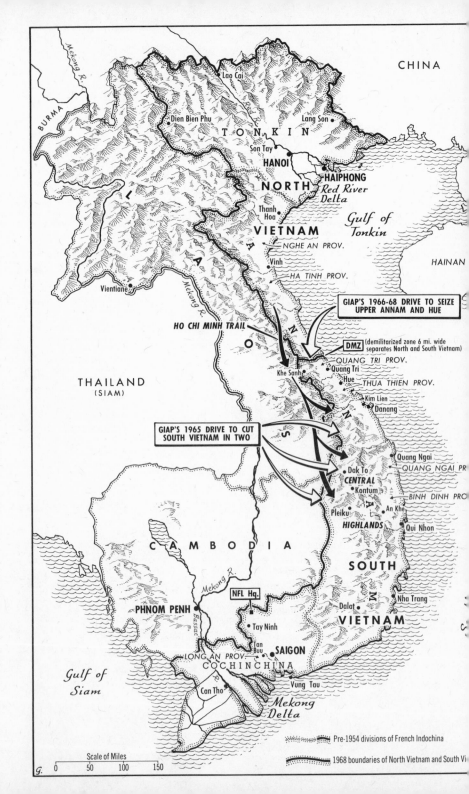

CHINA

Mekong R.

BURMA

Lao Cai •

T O N K I N

Dien Bien Phu •

Lang Son •

Son Tay •

HANOI

NORTH

HAIPHONG

*Red River
Delta*

Thanh
Hoa •

*Gulf of
Tonkin*

VIETNAM

• NGHE AN PROV.

HAINAN

• Vinh

• HA TINH PROV.

Vientiane •

Mekong R.

L

A

O

S

HO CHI MINH TRAIL

**GIAP'S 1966-68 DRIVE TO SEIZE
UPPER ANNAM AND HUE**

DMZ (demilitarized zone 6 mi. wide
separates North and South Vietnam)

QUANG TRI PROV.

• Quang Tri

THAILAND
(SIAM)

Khe Sanh •

• Hue

THUA THIEN PROV.

• Kim Lien
• Danang

**GIAP'S 1965 DRIVE TO CUT
SOUTH VIETNAM IN TWO**

• Quang Ngai

QUANG NGAI PR

• Dak To

CENTRAL

• Kontum

BINH DINH PRO

• Pleiku

• An Khe

HIGHLANDS

• Qui Nhon

C A M B O D I A

SOUTH

Mekong R.

PHNOM PENH

NFL Hq. ▪

• Tay Ninh

Dalat •

• Nha Trang

VIETNAM

Tan
Buu •

SAIGON

Bassac

LONG AN PROV.

COCHINCHINA

*Gulf of
Siam*

Can Tho •

• Vung Tau

*Mekong
Delta*

Pre-1954 divisions of French Indochina

1968 boundaries of North Vietnam and South Vi

Scale of Miles

G.   0   50   100   150

The Players

North Vietnamese

The Politburo

Ho Chi Minh, 78, Annamite, native of Nghe An Province; went to sea as a ship's steward; was in Europe by about 1910, did not return to Vietnam until 1944; founder of expatriate Vietnamese Communist party in 1925, expanded movement by absorbing other nationalist factions in 1930 to form the Indochinese Communist party, as the story goes, in the bleachers at a soccer game in Hong Kong; seized Hanoi with a band of guerrillas in August 1945; declared provisional government of the "Democratic Republic of Vietnam" during the administrative vacuum and anarchy after Japanese surrender in World War II; attacked Hanoi with Viet Minh troops in 1946, after French rejected his claims to Cochinchina at Fountainebleau Conference, starting hostilities which continue to this day; North Vietnam's party chairman and head of state, Asia's senior Communist; reported in 1968 to be ailing and senile

Le Duan, 61, Annamite from Quang Tri Province; first secretary of Lao Dong Vietnam, or Vietnamese Workers (Communist) party, which claims to uphold Marxism, Leninism and Stalinism, aims at creating a "people's democracy" closely allied with Russia and China; founding member of Indochinese Communist party in 1930; led purge of party leaders in Cochinchina in early fifties; avoided publicity but is believed to have been in charge of clandestine operations and internal party organization for past twenty years; since 1960 has emerged as Vietnamese Communists' supreme ideologue and political strategist; the director of the charade

General Vo Nguyen Giap, 56, Annamite, native of Vuang Binh Province, the Communist military commander since 1941

The Mandarin Dai Viets

Dr. Phan Quang Dan, 50, Annamite, native of Nghe An Province; Harvard-educated physician and South Vietnam's leading Western-style liberal; newspaper editor, Hanoi, 1945; adviser for youth affairs, Bao Dai government, 1945; doctor in Chinese public hospital in Shanghai, 1946–47; minister of information and political adviser to Emperor Bao Dai, 1947–48; practicing physician in Saigon since 1954; arrested by Diem government, 1955–56 and 1960–63; member of Constituent Assembly, 1966–67; vicepresidential candidate, 1967 election; despite Dai Viet "loyalty unto death" oath, claimed in 1966 he left the organization twenty years before; appointed minister of state in Huong government, May 1968; dismissed within days for advocating negotiations with the National Liberation Front in a speech in San Francisco

Bui Diem, 47, Tonkinese, Paris-educated; Cabinet secretary in Defense Ministry, Bao Dai government, 1950, again in 1953; newspaper publisher in Hanoi, 1951; publisher of Saigon *Post* since 1964; secretary of state to Premier Phan Huy Quat, February to June 1965; secretary of state and later deputy foreign minister to Premier Nguyen Cao Ky, June 1965 to December 1966; appointed ambassador to Washington, January 1967; father once ran Viet Minh in Tonkin, uncle was first Vietnamese premier in 1945; leader of unofficial South Vietnamese delegation to Paris conference, 1968; Dr. Sung's chief lieutenant

General Le Nguyen Khang, 38, Tonkinese; member Son Tay "revolutionary group"; 1952 graduate Nam Dinh Reserve Officers School; commander of Vietnamese Marine Corps since 1964; Saigon military governor since 1965; Third Corps commander of Saigon region since 1966; 25th Division commander since January 1968; all commands held concurrently; forced to resign as Saigon military governor, June 1968

Air Vice-Marshal Nguyen Cao Ky, 38, Tonkinese, native of Son Tay Province; reportedly failed examinations at Hanoi's Chu Van An High School, 1948; joined Dai Viet "revolutionary group" in 1949; 1952 graduate in first French-sponsored reserve officers school with branches at Nam Dinh and Thu Duc; joined Vietnamese Air Force at its creation in 1953; commander of South Vietnamese Air Force since August 1964; married foster daughter of Le Van Thai, a Dai Viet leader, 1964; premier of South Vietnam, June 1965 to October 1967; vice president since October 31, 1967; president of alumni association, Nam Dinh-Thu Duc Reserve Officers School, first class of 1952; forced to resign extra-constitutional posts, June 1968

Colonel Pham Van Lieu, 40, Annamite; recruited Ky, Khang, Bao Tri and others into Dai Viet "revolutionary group" in Son Tay Province, 1949; national police chief, February 1965 to May 1966; since then director of Vietnamese Army's national noncommissioned officers training center

General Nguyen Ngoc Loan, 38, Tonkinese; 1952 graduate Thu Duc Reserve Officers School; joined Vietnamese Air Force when created in 1953; appointed chief of national police and internal security apparatus, May 1966; wounded in Saigon firefight, May 1968; forced to resign, June 1968

Dr. Phan Huy Quat, 59, Annamite, native of Ha Tinh Province; education and later defense minister in French-sponsored Bao Dai government, 1949–53; jailed by Diem government, 1960–63; foreign minister of South Vietnam, 1964; premier of South Vietnam, February to June 1965, when withdrew from active politics

Dr. Dang Van Sung, 53, Annamite, native of Nghe An Province; joined the clandestine Dai Viet organization in 1940, supported in part by the Japanese occupation forces and composed of remnants of the old Vietnamese Quoc Dan Dang party, or Vietnamese Kuomintang, the most important non-Communist nationalist organization in Vietnam, which today survives in only a few provinces of Annam; exiled in China, 1945–47; elected secretary-general of Mandarin (Tonkinese) Dai Viet faction in Hanoi, 1951; reported leader of Dai Viet youth organizations in Tonkin, 1949–51; went underground during Diem's nine-year rule; editor of *Chinh Luan,* Saigon's most influential newspaper, since 1964; "grey eminence" of Quat government, 1965; member of Constituent Assembly, 1966–67; elected to Senate, 1967; the presumed leader of the secret brotherhood

General Nguyen Duc Thang, 39, Tonkinese, attended Hanoi University; 1952 graduate Thu Duc Reserve Officers School; chief of South Vietnamese Army's operations and later intelligence branches 1964–65; chief of pacification, 1966–67; in charge of 1966 and 1967 national elections; appointed commander of Fourth Corps in Mekong Delta, February 1968; forced to resign, June 1968

General Bao Tri, 38, Tonkinese; member Son Tay "revolutionary group"; 1952 graduate Nam Dinh Reserve Officers School; Third Corps commander, 1966; appointed minister of information and amnesty in 1966; forced to resign, May 1968

Others of Origin above the 17th Parallel

General Pham Van Dong, age unknown, Tonkinese, native of North Vietnam's Nung mountain tribal region; second highest-ranking officer in French Army, 1947–54; military governor of Saigon, 1964–65; a staunch anti-Communist retired since May 1965, when Premier Quat brought charges against him of graft and corruption, never proven; regarded as South Vietnamese Army's leading tactician

Thich Tri Quang, 45, Annamite, native of Ha Tinh Province; Buddhist bonze long resident in Hue; arrested twice and once denied visa by French Sûreté as suspected Communist agent, 1947–54; led the 1963 agitation against Diem government for alleged "religious persecution" of Buddhist faith that resulted in "sacrificial suicides" by a number of Buddhist monks, nuns and laymen, who burned themselves alive; founder and secretary-general of the "Unified Buddhist Congregation," 1964; accused of being Communist by Ky in June 1966; placed under house arrest for sedition after leading insurrection in Annam in March–June 1966; arrested after 1968 Tet offensive and charged with collaborating in Viet Cong attack on Saigon; subsequently released and rearrested; given amnesty by President Thieu, July 1968

South Vietnamese

The Cochinchinese National Leadership

Tran Van Huong, 64, Cochinchinese, schoolteacher of peasant origin; led students in anti-French resistance in jungle fighting in 1946, but soon returned to private life after refusing to join Viet Minh government; mayor of Saigon, 1955 and again in 1964; premier of South Vietnam, October 31, 1964 to January 27, 1965; presidential candidate in September 1967 election; South Vietnam's most authentic popular leader and a respected Confucian; reappointed by Thieu as prime minister, May 1968

Phan Khac Suu, 63, Cochinchinese, native of Mekong Delta; Paris-educated in agricultural engineering; imprisoned in 1941 and property confiscated by French for anticolonial role; released in 1945 but rearrested and jailed until 1947; visited China, 1948; carried out Ngo Dinh Diem's land-reform program as director general of agrarian reform in early fifties; imprisoned by Diem government, 1960–63; appointed president of South Vietnam, October 1964 to June 1965; chairman of the Constituent Assembly, October 1966, until he resigned, October 1967, to protest Assembly's ratification of Thieu's election; presidential candidate in 1967 election

Tran Van Van, Cochinchinese; Paris-educated millionaire murdered at age fifty-nine on December 7, 1966; economics minister in Bao Dai government, 1949; led Cochinchinese delegation to 1954 Geneva Conference to oppose Ho Chi Minh's claims to the south; led "Caravelle group" critical of Diem government in 1960, arrested for four months; elected president of provisional legislature, Council of Notables, under first post-Diem government; secretary-general of High National Council, a body of seventeen formed in September 1964 to supervise the transition from a military to civilian government; was instrumental in installing Tran Van Huong government in late 1964; chairman of People's Army Council, a quasi-legislative advisory body to Ky government, 1966; elected September 11, 1966 to Assembly charged with drafting a constitution within six months; announced candidate for 1967 presidential elections; the most effective leader of the Cochinchinese opposition

The Dai Viets' Southern Collaborators

Truong Dinh Dzu, 51, Annamite, Saigon lawyer; director of Rotary Club for Southeast Asia, 1961; arrested and jailed for four months by Diem government for passing bad check, 1963; surprise runner-up in 1967 presidential elections after campaigning against military rule and for instant peace; arrested and sentenced for embezzlement and fined $40,000, October 1967; rearrested after 1968 Tet offensive for publicly endorsing a coalition government with the Viet Cong

General Nguyen Khanh, 40, Cochinchinese; overthrew first post-Diem government of General Duong Van Minh, January 30, 1964 after accusing Minh and his colleagues of supporting France's proposal for a "neutralist" solution of war; resigned both premiership and presidency, the latter assumed nine days before, in August 1964; in December 1964, led coup against the Huong government, confirming stay of Huong and Suu in office but dissolving the provisional legislature and arresting Tran Van Van; led second coup against Huong January 27, 1965, in which the northern Dai Viets seized power in Saigon, themselves purging and then exiling Khanh within ten days; since then has been living in exile in New York, then Paris

Nguyen Van Loc, 44, Cochinchinese; educated in criminal law in France; vice-chairman of Ky's electoral law drafting commission, 1966; author of *Social Classes* (1948), *Rebellion* (1949) and *Liberation Tide* (1949); Viet Minh propagandist, 1945–47; appointed by Thieu as prime minister of South Vietnam, October 31, 1967; removed from office May 1968

Au Truong Thanh, 48, half-Chinese Marxist professor of economics, Saigon University; economics minister in Ky government, February to October 1966; disqualified from 1967 presidential elections on the grounds of holding pro-Communist sympathies; arrested after 1968 Tet offensive

Nguyen Van Thieu, 45, Annamite, native of Phan Thiet Province; Viet Minh district chief, 1945–46; enlisted in French Army, 1947; rose to commander of Mekong Delta by 1964; in June 1965 led National Leadership Committee, a military triumvirate later expanded to ten, in taking over government and installing Nguyen Cao Ky as premier, himself assuming position of chief of state; remained ruling junta's chairman until October 31, 1967, when he became president of South Vietnam; the charade's most enigmatic figure

Professor Ho Huu Tuong, 58, Annamite, retired teacher, Trotskyite; elected October 1967 to House of Representatives

Others

Mrs. Le Thi Quach, 41, Annamite; accused Communist spy in Danang

General Nguyen Chanh Thi, 45, Annamite; military governor of Annam and First Corps commander, 1964–66; exiled to Washington in June 1966

Madame Tran Van Van, 47, Cochinchinese; defeated senatorial candidate in 1967 election, when she ran in the place of her dead husband

Ta Vinh, 38, executed Chinese importer

The Americans

Ellsworth G. Bunker, 74, ambassador in Saigon since April 1967; America's most accomplished diplomat and a firm believer in popular civil government

Philip Habib, 48; counselor for political affairs, American mission to South Korea, 1962–66; served as political chief to Ambassador Lodge from early 1966 to early 1967; in mid-1967 became deputy assistant secretary of state in charge of the State Department's Vietnam Task Force; third highest ranking diplomat and chief drafter U.S. political position papers at 1968 Paris conference

Lyndon B. Johnson, 60, President of the United States from November 1963

Robert W. Komer, 45, White House aide on Vietnam nonmilitary effort who became deputy ambassador in charge of pacification (nominally under Westmoreland) in April 1967

Edward Lansdale, 60, adviser to President Roman Magsaysay in the Philippines, 1951–54; first visited Vietnam in 1953; returned as aide to President Ngo Dinh Diem, 1954–56; returned as pacification adviser to Ambassador Lodge, July 1965; stayed on as political adviser to Ambassador Bunker, April 1967 to June 1968

Henry Cabot Lodge, 66, ambassador in Saigon, August 1963 to July 1964 and again from July 1965 to April 1967; supported South Korean-type military rule and social reform

Maxwell D. Taylor, 67, principal architect of American counterinsurgency strategy and doctrine of combatting Communist "wars of national liberation"; ambassador in Saigon, July 1964 to July 1965

General William C. Westmoreland, 54, the American military commander, May 1964 to June 1968

Barry Zorthian, 47, U. S. information chief in Saigon, May 1964 to June 1968

The British

Dennis Duncanson, member of Thompson advisory mission, 1961–65; counselor for aid in the British Embassy, 1965–66

Sir Robert Thompson, 53, the world's greatest counterinsurgency expert; deputy secretary and secretary for the defense of Malaya, 1957–61; head of the British advisory mission in Vietnam, 1961–65

One

Tran Van Van's Last Testament

A charade, like any theatrical performance, never looks quite the same to anyone once he has watched it backstage. The players posture and grimace as before, fighting their mock battles before the footlights. But the illusion of reality is gone.

Looking back on those years in Vietnam is, I find, like remembering it all as seen from the wings, where everything is quieter and darker. The performance out front goes on as before —the horror shows of fiery suicides and flaming villages, the stage-managed riots and rebellions, even the last bloody battles of the cities—but now I can see Le Duan in the shadows above, jerking the strings. I try to imagine how it once was, sitting in the audience. And yet, when I do, the players' words and actions seem so caricatured and grotesque I wonder how any of us ever thought they were real.

I sometimes wonder if things would have gone any differently if I had not been home that morning in mid-November 1966, when a servant brought a message to my room at the Continental Palace Hotel. It was a brief note from the war government's most bitter civilian critic, urgently summoning me to his home. Tran Van Van was an aristocratic landowner and a member of the two-month-old Constituent Assembly whom in those days I regarded unsympathetically as a rich reactionary trying to stem the inevitable tides of social revolution. Still, he led the only remaining civilian opposition to the military junta of Nguyen Cao Ky.

I remember how hot it was that day; the cooling rains had ended in the southern Delta. Saigon's main streets and cafés were full of people, the women with their silk gowns and parasols, and the men in loose trousers and cheap open-necked shirts, and a haze of exhaust fumes already hung over the downtown traffic. Old men with stringy beards sipped tea at little stands along the Saigon River, fortune tellers squatted with their soiled packs of cards, and the smell of food from little portable kitchens that burned and bubbled in the steamy sunshine mixed with the stench of fermented fish and stale urine. Only the bustle among the cargo freighters, grey navy boats and clusters of sampans along the quay suggested that there was a war on. Van's house was on the edge of the city in the old residential quarter of Dakow behind the Zoological Gardens. The quarter was off Hai Ba Truong Boulevard, five quiet streets lined with dusty tamarind trees and square stucco houses, each isolated within its own courtyard by a high wall and a small wooden gate. The spaces between the houses formed narrow lanes, used as footpaths to hidden courtyards and rows of tenements and small shops behind.

A man in sunglasses sat straddling a motor bike in the shadow of a tamarind tree near Van's gate. He turned and stared as I approached. I nodded, but he did not respond. I pushed the buzzer and a bell sounded inside the courtyard. After some minutes, the gate opened a few inches and a girl looked out. "I would like to see Monsieur Van," I said in French, giving her a card. She went away again and returned with an older woman, who asked through a crack in the gate what I wanted. I explained why I had come and the two disappeared. Several minutes passed before they came back to open the gate.

The wall of the courtyard was about twelve feet high; pieces of broken glass were stuck in the mortar on top below strands of barbed wire. Inside, the wall was concealed by straw matting and rows of potted bamboo trees. The floor was paved with irregular flagstones. Out in a square space set into the stones was a miniature Japanese garden; there was a red and golden temple and a teahouse in the midst of a woods of twisted dwarf pine trees; tiny painted figures with parasols stood on pathways of white sand and rocks, and patches of vivid green moss bordered a pool where live fishes swam.

The front of the house was about fifteen feet from the wall, a brown façade of very old, weathered teak, with an elaborately carved door framed with dragons and snakes. The door was open and I could see a dim passageway running the length of the house, lined with enormous glassed-in cabinets and white and blue crockery vases as tall as a man. Motioning me to follow, the woman entered the house.

The drawing room was a cavernous place, supported by pillars hewn from single teak trees. A pale yellow half-light filtered through gauze stretched across a tall unshuttered window overlooking the courtyard. It was all very clean and smelled of incense. The room was filled with teak furniture of the kind made centuries ago for the palaces of Chinese mandarins. The walls were paneled with black lacquer set with semiprecious stones. Some were hung with long bamboo scroll paintings of misty mountain landscapes and medieval warriors in armor. Most of the floor space was covered with massive tables and cabinets displaying Ming Dynasty porcelain, cloisonné vases and large artificial bouquets of jade flowers. At one end of the room was a red altar some twenty feet high with burning joss sticks and oil portraits of the family's wispy-bearded mandarin ancestors.

As I came into the room, Van, who had been sitting on a divan by the courtyard window, rose to his feet. He had once been the richest landowner in the Mekong Delta and looked it. He was an extremely thin, bony-faced man, with sunken cheeks, sleek black hair only slightly touched by grey, and bushy black eyebrows that curled prominently outward at the corners. His forehead was broad and high, and he had grey intelligent eyes that wrinkled into crow's feet when he was amused, giving him an ironic, Gallic air. There was unusual vitality in the brightness of his eyes and the impatient, almost arrogant, directness of his speech. He spoke English with the Parisian accent peculiar to the French-educated Cochinchinese aristocracy. As always, he wore an incongruous grey American slack suit.

He smiled politely as he greeted me. "It was kind of you to come. May I introduce my wife?" I was surprised to learn that the woman who had let me in was Madame Van. She was pale and slight and dressed in a severe black *ao dai*, but I saw now that she had a pleasant smile.

"Please sit down." He sat down himself. He was holding a sheaf of papers, which he fingered nervously. "My wife speaks no English. I am sorry you were kept waiting." Madame Van remained standing and said something in rapid and angry Vietnamese to her husband. He listened and then asked her to bring tea.

When she had gone, Van said, "My wife has been pleading with me to leave politics, to resign from the Assembly. The past week I have received two assassination threats. They were, of course, anonymous, but I believe they came from the government. A number of the deputies have received them. Unfortunately my wife does not share my concern with politics. She would prefer to take our son and go to Paris, where my two older children are studying.

Madame Van returned, placed a delicate tea set before us, and left the room with an angry glance at her husband. Van began pouring the tea himself; his hand trembled slightly and some of the tea spilled onto the saucers.

"You see, I have a reason for inviting you here today." He handed me a cup of tea. It was green and bitter. "The situation is very delicate and we must be cautious. This regime is capable of anything. But you have been friendly toward us in the Assembly." Behind his usual façade of extreme courtesy with a hint of arrogance, Van seemed tense and uncertain how to proceed. "A mysterious hand is at work to insult the Assembly and lessen its authority. I am afraid one must reach the conclu-

sion the government is doing all it can to humiliate and intimi-
date us. The police have offered a pistol to each deputy. It is
an insult. The government knows we have no defense against
kidnaping and assassination. And now these anonymous letters
I have received. They could be threats from the Communists or
any other sphere."

"Have you gone to the Americans?"

Van gestured impatiently. "The blunt truth is that the American Embassy is backing Ky. He wants a constitution something
like South Korea's, with a puppet parliament. Lodge lives on the
fiction he does not interfere in our internal affairs. Yet you
Americans make pressure, every day you do, just as you would
on any satellite country."

He picked up his tea reflectively. "Now the situation has
become very serious. This government cannot stay in power if it
carries out American policy and we have free elections. Ky
understands what Lodge does not, that a northerner could never
be elected in the south. That is why Ky is trying to foment
trouble between northerners and southerners to prevent us from
finishing the constitution. Yesterday when Madame Xa warned
the Assembly we must stop wasting time and finish the constitution by February as a gift for the people at Tet, Ky's men
shouted her down."

"I've seen that happen to you. You know they are trying to
discredit you. The line is you are a very rich man who exploits
the poor."

Van nodded. I sensed why he was afraid. The Viet Cong
almost never killed anyone of prominence without first trying to
destroy his reputation. "It isn't a crime to be a rich man," Van said
defiantly. "In some countries, men enter politics to become rich.
I prefer my politicians to have their fortunes first; then they have
the education and leisure. The poor, except when stirred up by
the Viet Cong, care little for politics."

"Some of your opponents say there are too many rich landowners in Vietnam who have kept their land when they would
have been lucky just to keep their heads."

"Those who say such things are demagogues. Naturally, everybody is happy to keep his head on his shoulders when the Viet
Cong pass by. But promising things is easy. I defy such men to

come up with a workable plan for the economy and commerce of this country. Actually, we landowners are poorer than the people in the towns who are getting rich from the war. We are the new poor. We must create new wealth through industry and the modernization of agriculture through fertilizer and canals."

He paused and I asked if he thought there would really be elections. He looked at me sharply, as if I had interrupted a train of thought. "Yes," he said, "in the end Ky must accept what the Assembly does. We must have a civilian government; military men have no popular backing in this country."

"Will you run for president?" (Ambassador Lodge had told me he considered Van one of the four or five probable contenders. Lodge had called Van "a civilized and amusing, decent man" but doubted any civilian could win. "There really are no civilian politicians in this country," Lodge had said, "just survivors of conspiracies against Diem and the French.")

"Yes, I hope to run," Van answered. "We need the leadership of civilians, to shorten the war through a healthier, more efficient regime. Only one civilian should run against the military." I assumed he meant to avoid splitting the civilian vote.

"Do you think Ky will really be willing to take a back seat when the time comes?"

"Nobody, humanly speaking, will give up something unless he is forced to, unless you fight for it." He leaned forward, lowering his voice. "We have started a dialogue to create a schism in the National Liberation Front, to appeal to its middle-class wing. The NLF is a front of southerners; Hanoi runs things from behind. Just like Ky and the northerners do in Saigon. With some of the Catholic priests, we are working to get these people in the NLF to come back on condition no neo-colonialist is elected as president."

"What do you mean by neo-colonialist?" I asked.

"I mean a Tonkinese like Ky coming down and trying to run our country as the French did. We must end this northern domination!"

"But Ky says he wants to invade the north."

Van smiled bitterly. "That is the only way he can stay in power. To convince the Americans he has the will to defeat the Communists." His voice turned scornful. "When Ky told me he wanted to invade the north, I asked him, 'Who will allow you?' This is not a Vietnamese war. It is an international war. We must never invade the north. I would never do it. It would be absolute folly unless the Chinese had come in. Emperor Gia Long lost in the south; the Germans lost the battle of Verdun. No, never! Lengthen Hanoi's route of communications and supply and then you can beat it." He paused for a moment and put down his tea.

"I have asked you here today because I have written an article I wish to have published in the American press. Will you read it and tell me if you think your newspaper would print it?" He seemed almost apologetic. "I have written many articles and letters for newspapers here, and the government's censors bar them from publication. Yesterday I warned the information minister, General Bao Tri, 'I will give you two weeks and then I will publish abroad. You cannot stop me.'" Van handed me the sheaf of notes and poured more tea. "Read it and take notes if you wish," he said. "I will return when you have finished."

The article was written on yellow legal paper and must have run to several thousand words, page after page of spidery longhand. But the message was clear enough. It began: "I am now a man nearing sixty, but someone must make the effort to find honest and dedicated people who can save the country. In the face of this task, I consider it my duty to expose the north-south cancer, something no one has ever dared to do. I am not so mad as to blame everyone, to arouse the antagonism of all northerners and create hatred in this nation. But it remains my firm belief that a man who loves his country should not be concerned over his own future. . . ."

Van wrote that before beginning his article he had sought the advice of Father Tran Du and Father Hoang Quynh, the two most prominent leaders of some 700,000 Roman Catholic Tonkinese who had come south in 1954; he said he had found them in accord with his belief that South Vietnam could only survive with an indigenous civil government.

Yet, he went on, the United States, since early 1965, had supported a government almost wholly dominated by refugees from the north, most of them non-Catholics. He believed this was political folly, because regional feeling was deeply ingrained in most Vietnamese. He argued that American policy was defying the most fundamental force in Vietnamese history: the resistance of northern aggression, whether Tonkinese or Chinese, by the southern rice-growing peasants of Cochinchina. Vietnamese regionalism, he wrote, was as strong as "Austrian resentment of Prussians, or southerners against the Yankees during the American Civil War."

Van warned that for more than a century preceding the 1954 partition, the history of Vietnam had been that of three separate political entities: Annam, from Thanh Hoa to Nha Trang along the Chaîne Annamitique, Cochinchina in the south, and Tonkin in the north. In all its history, he continued, Vietnam had been united as a single nation state for only fifty-six years, under the Emperor Gia Long in the early nineteenth century. From 111 B.C. until the ninth century, Vietnam was a colony of the Han dynasty in China. In 1630, Van's Nguyen ancestors built two walls across the plains of Quang Tri just a few miles north of the present 17th parallel dividing North and South Vietnam; the walls kept out the feudal Tonkinese Trinh warlords for a hundred and fifty years. The French in 1884 divided Vietnam into the colony of Cochinchina (Saigon and the Mekong Delta), the semiautonomous imperial kingdom of Annam, with its Buddhist capital in Hue, and the self-governing protectorate of Tonkin (Hanoi and the Red River Delta). Each had a different constitution and each developed its own brand of nationalism. Conspiracy, anarchy, and revolution, such as the development of the Indochinese Communist party, flowered in Tonkin in the north, while in Cochinchina in the south there was a movement toward religious sects and more conventional Western-style politics.

During a period of anarchy, after the Japanese occupation forces in World War II had turned against the French, Ho Chi Minh—a then-obscure agitator who had spent nearly thirty-five years, or most of his adult life, in Europe, Russia and China— seized Hanoi with a small band of fellow Communists. At first, the French were willing to recognize Ho's self-declared "Democratic Republic of Vietnam" as an autonomous socialist republic within a French union of all five former Indochinese states. Instead, Ho insisted on laying claim to rice-rich Cochinchina, and in 1947 the long war began. (Although Van merely touched on it, he seemed to regard the early Ho Chi Minh not so much as a Vietnamese nationalist but rather as a foreign-supported expatriate whose initial activity in Tonkin was as agent for Soviet Russia.)

When Vietnam was partitioned in 1954, its southern population was divided into the native Cochinchinese majority, the Annamite inhabitants of the southern half of the old kingdom, and around 860,000 mostly Catholic Tonkinese who had fled Ho's suppression of religion. The south also had large minorities of Montagnards, Chinese and Cambodians.

Van wrote that Cochinchina's problem of self-determination had grown acute only after World War II, since the French had ruled largely through a Cochinchinese civil service. He asserted that the first wave of Tonkinese who came south were chiefly Ho Chi Minh's agents. Their job was to penetrate the anti-French resistance movement in the late forties and early fifties. Then came the 860,000 Tonkinese refugees in 1954. Although Ngo Dinh Diem, the son of an old mandarin family serving in the Annamite imperial court in Hue, formed a predominantly Cochinchinese government during his first few years in office (almost all Diem's top army commanders were southerners), once the Viet Cong insurgency began he turned increasingly to the rigidly anti-Communist Catholics from the north.

My interest quickened as Van began then to relate the history of an elite secret brotherhood called the Mandarin Dai Viets. Originally, it seemed, its members had belonged to an anticolonialist organization called the Greater Vietnam Nationalist party. The Dai Viets were sponsored by the Japanese occupation forces in 1939 under an anti-French northern nationalist leader who was assassinated by the Communists in 1946.

According to Van, while the original Dai Viet party largely disintegrated, the remaining members in Tonkin formed, by the early fifties, a secret brotherhood of reactionary extremists who, despite holding senior posts in the French protectorate's army and government, were responsible for a rash of political murders and terrorism. These Tonkinese dominated the last Hanoi administration from 1949 to 1954; a few held key Cabinet posts in Emperor Bao Dai's shaky French-sponsored national government, and most of them fled south with their families after the 1954 Geneva accords. The brotherhood was never thought to number more than a few hundred men at most.

Although he provided no evidence, Van held the view that the Mandarin Dai Viet influence in Tonkin and the Bao Dai regime had helped hasten the French defeat. He said the leader of the brotherhood since the early fifties was a Dr. Dang Van Sung, a well-known Saigon political figure who was perhaps the capital's most influential newspaper editor and a member of the Constituent Assembly. According to Van, the brotherhood was secretly collaborating with an Annam-based Buddhist militant organization led by Thich Tri Quang, the monk who had been a prime mover in Diem's overthrow. This strange alliance of Buddhists and brotherhood members, he went on, by working secretly together had been able to convince the world there was religious persecution under Diem, had stage-managed the overthrow of the government, then risen to power by toppling a rapid succession of post-Diem governments. Together, they had jointly seized power in January 1965 and installed predominantly Tonkinese governments of their choice, first with a civilian premier, Phan Huy Quat, one of the few overt Dai Viet members, who had been a Cabinet minister under Bao Dai, and then five months later, with Nguyen Cao Ky.

On the next page came Van's main allegation.

He said that at least seven leaders in the present government, including Prime Minister Ky himself, were in fact members of the·secret Dai Viet brotherhood and had been for seventeen years. Besides the premier, Van named four generals who ran the national pacification program, the Saigon military region, the police and internal security apparatus and the information ministry, as well as two civilians, one serving as deputy foreign minister, the other as secretary of state in the premier's office. Of the five generals, he said, two were high school classmates of Ky and were from the same native province of Son Tay near Hanoi, while all five were fellow alumni of the first French-sponsored Vietnamese army reserve officers' class of 1952.

After they seized power in February 1965, Van wrote, the Dai Viet northerners soon entrenched themselves enough to begin systematically replacing the leading southerners in the govern-

ment, army, press and business with their own handpicked
fellow northerners. "I believe," he concluded, "the same alien-
ation of the Cochinchinese majority as befell the Diem regime
will inevitably follow."

I turned to the last page. "Without a southern civilian government," Van wrote, "Saigon can never rally the vast population of
the Mekong Delta to the anti-Communist side. Many Cochinchinese are anti-Communist simply because they oppose northern
or Chinese domination. I believe the popularity of General
Duong Van Minh [leader of the first post-Diem government] lay
in his image as a Cochinchinese hero who threw off the yoke of
Annamite and Tonkinese domination as symbolized by the Diem
regime in its final years. General Nguyen Khanh, while a
Cochinchinese, alienated the people by overthrowing Minh.
Khanh, as the leader of an unpopular war regime, had to rely on
Tonkinese Buddhists, since the Catholics were being purged for
having served Diem."

"In the present situation, calls for unity are but an echo in the
desert. A southern government could split Hanoi from the Viet
Cong and itself make a separate peace in the Delta. Instead, we
are driving the southern masses into the arms of the Viet
Cong."

I put down the article and for some minutes sipped my tea.
My mind was racing. The allegations would seem incredible if
they suddenly appeared in print in the United States, but to me
they explained everything and confirmed much that I had long
suspected.

In the field with the American troops in Vietnam you often
heard the old platitude that if you can hear a mortar shell
whistling, it's going to miss you. You won't hear the one that
matters coming. There were always rumors and gossip in Saigon
that the same rule held for South Vietnam's invisible war of
subversion, that beneath the surface political confusion a really
dangerous fifth column had been patiently and silently assem-
bling all the levers of power in its hands.

Sometimes the subversives were described as agents of Hanoi,
sometimes as sinister Buddhists, sometimes as a cabal of fascist
opportunists who aimed to get rich, jump the sinking ship and
leave the Americans to walk the plank. Van's extraordinary docu-

ment provided me with the essential information linking Ky and his fellow northern generals with Dr. Sung and the Dai Viets. I began to see how subversion in South Vietnam could indeed be a combination of all three elements.

At the same time I realized that no American newspaper would publish what I was now almost sure was the truth without the kind of documentation neither Van nor I could provide. If he was right, the United States had supported a government for nearly two years that was run by a secret fascist brotherhood of North Vietnamese which by its very nature was undermining the entire U.S. anti-Communist effort in Southeast Asia. We were fighting to ensure the right of self-determination of a people for whom it had already been effectively denied.

I had heard about the secret brotherhood before, though never such specific information of its fascist character, nor that so many of its members held positions of power in the government and that the generals had been allied together since the late forties. But I had long sensed an odd staginess and artificiality about the behavior of these men, as if little they ever did was really genuine or spontaneous. And for nearly two years, I had had my own suspicions about Ky, Dr. Sung and a few of the others.

Ever since they had come to power, in early 1965, one had the strange feeling of being involved in a guessing game, in which everything could be understood if only you watched all the spoken or acted clues. It had been like a long charade, with Saigon as the theatrical setting: a drama enacted in the bright lights of the streets, with crowds of extras playing bonzes, soldiers, students, police, citizens and foreign newsmen. What happened on this stage was being headlined throughout the world: the bodies of the Ngo family littering the stage like the final scene of a Shakespeare tragedy; the old southerners as dignified and ineffectual as Polonius; Ky and the young northern soldiers, the reckless desperadoes of the piece; Tri Quang, as malevolent as any Richard the Third. Battles were fought and riots rampaged through the streets that, while real enough in themselves, had an aura of unreality about them, like a performance staged for an audience. President Johnson was in that audience, as were the American people. The players in the charade had an extraordinary sense of theater and, in their macabre way, seemed to enjoy it so, especially with the world press intoning predictions of doom from the sidelines, like an electronic-age Greek chorus.

The immediate problem was that if Van's story were true, as I was almost certain it was, he was in extreme danger and needed protection from the Americans.

Van came back into the room and I looked at him with relief. Whatever he was, he seemed to me genuine and not part of the charade. He sat down and waited attentively. I decided to put the question at once.

"Do you think Ky is working for the Communists?"

My question disappointed him. "From the Vietnamese viewpoint, this is a civil war, between north and south. For you Americans this is an ideological war. But you must win our war first."

He went on calmly. "Do you know Le Duan? He is a southerner, an Annamite from near Hue. But he is also a very intelligent dialectical Communist. He is in charge of Hanoi's secret political activities, of the Viet Cong's political underground. I have long suspected that some of the older Dai Viets are subject to his manipulation. But how can it be proved? The most important point about the present government is that it is the Quat government without Quat. And Quat and Dr. Sung wanted to sue for peace at a time when it would have meant a Communist victory. This government is run by a secret society of Mandarin Dai Viets who include the most senior administrative officials, some ministers and at least five generals. They lost the war for the French in the north, and now they have come here to lose it for us in the south. Ky has the air force; Bao Tri, the Information Ministry; Thang, the Interior Ministry; Khang, the troops around Saigon; Loan, the police and security; Bui Diem, foreign affairs. They are the hard core."

He paused and smiled. "Why do they do it? Sixteen years ago Ky was the son of poor parents in North Vietnam. He had failed his high school examinations and was working as a conductor on his uncle's country bus. He had a peasant wife and a baby son in his village. Probably they are still there. Such men have been made into generals. The Mandarin Dai Viets are the richest, most opportunistic group of men in this country. And Dr. Sung is their real leader. He is the most dangerous man in South Vietnam."

I told him I would write my editor, but that he should also try other publications since the article was very long. "Perhaps if we could use excerpts . . ."

"No," Van interrupted. "I want it published in full. If your newspaper will not accept it, I will wait until another foreign publication agrees."

He took the article back and rose to his feet. I got up to go. Somehow we would have to get documentation.

On the way out we passed some Ming porcelain and I told Van how much I admired it. He smiled and said the seventeenth century had produced much finer workmanship. He ran his fingers gently across a small yellow vase and said, "This was the apogee. Is that what you Americans say—apogee?" For a moment we were back in a civilized world. We walked out into the courtyard and shook hands. In the harsh sunlight, Van look tired and frail. "Perhaps I have said too much," he said. "You must be very careful."

"If people like you with convictions are silent, how can the war ever be won? If you say it, I'll write it," I said at the gate, not realizing how deeply I would later regret my flippant tone.

He shrugged. "What can the generals do to me?" His voice had a touch of the old arrogance. We said goodbye.

The man on the motor bike was still there under the tamarind tree and this time he smiled grimly. I assumed he was a bodyguard.

At some time or other, I suppose, most newspaper correspondents living in an Asian world of intrigue and conspiracy indulge in the notion that, should the occasion arise, they could brilliantly influence the course of events. Some of them in Vietnam had done so. My experience after my meeting with Van was different. With a determination that now seems pathetic, I urged the American mission to come to Van's rescue. I felt that if only his message got to the right people, the war in Vietnam might take a vastly different direction.

Oddly, I did learn one thing: each of the important Americans

I talked to, first in Saigon and later in Washington, saw Van's plight—and even the Vietnamese political struggle itself—through the prism of his own experience and commitments. Everyone listened politely—with varying degrees of sympathy and excitement—but, in the end, the American establishment involved with Vietnam did not accept Van's allegations to the point of acting on them. Nothing happened.

That first day I went directly to Edward Lansdale, the legendary Asian hand who had tried unsuccessfully, behind the scenes, to launch the Ky regime on a program of social reform. Lansdale heard me out but said he had complete trust in Dr. Sung, whom he had long valued as a close adviser and friend. Lansdale knew he was a Dai Viet, but believed in Dr. Sung's reformist protestations. "I can't explain why," he said, "but I can assure you I am positive Dr. Sung would never do anything he thought would serve the interests of the Communists. Sung's just a very sincere guy who really wants to serve his country. He's maneuvering with the farm and labor groups to try and build a mass-based political organization that will ensure the Dai Viets' survival." Lansdale said he could not go to see Van personally because Ambassador Lodge had formally forbidden him further contact with members of the Vietnamese civilian opposition. He suggested that I approach the Embassy's political section.

Philip Habib, the Embassy's political chief, shrugged off Van's allegations entirely. Habib, a swarthy, chain-smoking career foreign-service officer of Lebanese descent, had been brought to Saigon by Lodge after scoring a major success in supporting the legitimatization of South Korean President Park Chung Hee's regime. Lodge wished to have this feat repeated with the Ky government and chose Habib to succeed Lansdale as the chief American political adviser to Ky and the ruling generals.

"I don't care what some disgruntled politician says," Habib told me. "We've got all that in the generals' dossiers. Don't you think the United States government has access to a lot more information than an old southern separatist like Van? I can assure you, I see no sign whatsoever that any North Vietnamese conspiracy is underfoot with Dai Viet involvement."

I attempted to see Van several times during the next three weeks, but he kept putting me off. My interpreter, who delivered my messages to Van's house, suggested that Van was either angry or afraid. On the afternoon of December 6th I flew to Hong Kong on my way to Washington for a holiday.

On the morning of December 7th, Van left his house in his black De Soto, instructing his chauffeur to drive to the old French opera house for a session of the Constituent Assembly. Three blocks from home, his car was blocked by a brown Mercedes and quickly caught in a traffic jam. Two men who had been following the car on a red-and-white Honda motor bike roared up alongside and shot Van four times in the back with a Walther .32 automatic pistol. He died on the way to the hospital without regaining consciousness.

Eight hours later, the government's police chief, Nguyen Ngoc Loan, called a press conference. He produced a man who told the foreign and Vietnamese press he had been sent by the Viet Cong to murder Van. The man was blind in his left eye, which was covered with a white glaucous film and turned up in its socket. He gave his name as Vo Van Em and his age as twenty. He said he had been a member for three years of the Viet Cong's Capital Liberation Regiment operating around Saigon and had been brought from the nearby small town of Cu Chi for the express purpose of killing Van. He insisted he only drove the scooter while the second member of the assassination team did the shooting. The other man had escaped. Vo Van Em also insisted he was unaware of the victim's identity. A policeman said he chased the two terrorists on foot after their motor scooter crashed and that Em fired two shots at the police before he was caught.

"I am satisfied," the self-confessed terrorist told the press. "I am resigned to die if I receive the death sentence."

The Viet Cong's clandestine Liberation Radio broadcast an unprecedented denial that the insurgents had ordered the assassination. The Vietnamese *Guardian*, Saigon's last independent English-language newspaper, published two photographs on its front page. One was of the alleged culprit, taken at the press conference. The second, taken at the scene of the shooting, showed the police apprehending two gunmen, neither of whom was the man produced by the police. The newspaper was permanently closed by the government the next day.

Three days later, in a graveside oration before 3,000 mourners, Madame Van appealed for clemency for the arrested man. She made no condemnation of the Viet Cong. In a television interview broadcast in the United States, she was quoted by her interpreter as saying, "Ky killed my husband." The man arrested by the police was not executed, and interest in this aspect of the affair soon faded.

The day after Van's murder I learned of it from a Hong Kong newspaper headline. I immediately cabled my newspaper, the Washington *Star*, a full account of our last conversation, omitting only Van's suspicion that Dr. Sung was collaborating with Le Duan in the Hanoi Politburo. The article was published on page one, but its impact, if any, was not evident when I arrived in Washington.

The attempted assassination of a second prominent opposition leader, Dr. Phan Quang Dan, on December 27th aroused my foreign editor sufficiently to fly out to Saigon himself a few days later. Once again, no one in the American mission would confirm Van's allegations, and he was unable to see Van's widow. But the elderly Cochinchinese chairman of the Assembly thought that Van's assassination had been intended "to sow dissension within the ranks of the nationalists." My newspaper naturally sought some official confirmation before pursuing the matter further. None was forthcoming. I advised my editor it would be enough to support early national elections, since I did not see how the brotherhood's hold on the Saigon government could possibly survive them.

Few senior American government officials seemed aware that the Ky regime was wholly dominated by northerners. Almost no one was familiar with the true nature of the Dai Viet society. Convinced that the Vietnamese Army was the only source of real power and stability, the State Department was pursuing the course it had followed in South Korea. Some officials were still defending past commitments to a mistaken belief that Tri Quang's Buddhists represented an authentic nationalist force in South Vietnam. Only at the White House were Van's allegations taken seriously. Robert Komer, then President Johnson's special aide on Vietnam, said that Ambassador Lodge had told the President he suspected Ky's economics minister of collaborating with the Communists. "Stay with it," was Komer's advice. "That's not what the CIA is telling us, but we can't afford to leave any flank unprotected."

I told Walter Lippmann about my meeting with Van before his death, and said that it suggested to me that Ky and the generals might be working for their fellow northerners in Hanoi. "It's sensational," Lippmann said, considering the possibility with visible relish. "But no newspaper would print it without documentation. It's too incredible. The generals are too anti-Communist. The Johnson administration has been supporting them for two years." A few days later Lippmann did write a column describing Ky as "a northern adventurer who is not at home in the south" and calling for an indigenous civilian government to end the "civil war."

Senator Eugene McCarthy, whom I met at a dinner party, asked me to relate Van's allegations to an executive session of the Senate Foreign Relations Committee. McCarthy caught cold and did not attend. Senator Fulbright led the questioning. None of the senators had ever heard of the Dai Viet society. A stenographer asked me to spell it. When I described Van's suspicions that some of its members were influenced by Hanoi, Fulbright said, "I have wondered about that myself for some time."

The session began cordially. But the tone of the questioning suggested that while most of the senators present were critics of American policy in Vietnam, they still believed that the South Vietnamese people supported the Communists and that the government supported us. When I tried to tell them I believed the reverse was true, that the people supported us while the government itself did not, the committee-room atmosphere grew perceptibly cooler. One got the feeling that the senators had made up their minds and wanted no new information. When I attempted to defend President Johnson's overall policy, Fulbright slumped back and shut his eyes. None of the senators seemed to care much about Tran Van Van's fate or what he represented in South Vietnamese society. They especially did not seem eager to hear that I believed most of the ordinary South Vietnamese were fighting valiantly for their freedom and were naturally opposed to a Viet Cong victory.

Yet a few days later, on "Meet the Press," Senator Fulbright declared, "If the present government won't do what we tell them to do, we should get a new government." He described Ky as a creation of the Johnson administration. "He's only there because we put him in. He wouldn't last two weeks, I don't think, without our support. I don't think he has any choice but to follow U.S. wishes." Fulbright said Ky had "neither a political base of his own, nor any military support except ours." If Ky refused to negotiate with the Viet Cong, Fulbright thought he should be replaced.

In New Zealand, where he was making a good-will tour in hopes of being invited to Washington, Ky lashed back at Fulbright. His voice trembling with indignation, Ky retorted, "I am no puppet of the United States or anyone else. That is my answer to Senator Fulbright. He's a colonialist."

The day I left Washington, a new South Vietnamese ambassador presented his credentials to President Johnson. After the ceremony Ambassador Bui Diem told newsmen that Fulbright's remarks "clearly overstepped the bounds of serious discussion. . . . Let us remind him that the United States also adheres to that fundamental principle of self-determination." I read the new ambassador's remarks with interest. Bui Diem had resigned as deputy foreign minister to come to Washington. He was one of the seven men Van had listed as the hard core of the Dai Viet brotherhood.

Two

Le Duan's Most Clever Tactic

Marxism-Leninism, this truth, the very highest summit of human reason.

—Le Duan, November 1967

In Saigon in early February of 1967 it was as if nothing had changed. The Hotel Continental Palace, where I lived during most of my three and a half years in Vietnam, was one of those old, stately places where footsteps echoed and only the sudden, silent appearances of elderly barefoot servants reminded you others were present. The entrance had a certain seedy elegance— potted palms, faded posters of Paris and a hydraulic lift in a wrought-iron cage that creaked and shuddered ominously if it ran at all. There was a lot of soiled red plush in the foyer.

The inner gardens, ballroom and restaurant were dark and empty after ten o'clock, but the terrace bar usually stayed full until curfew; it was popular, being the only bar in town not caged in against terrorist grenades. A young Frenchman and his Chinese wife owned and managed the Continental. It was generally believed that most of the servants were on both the

30

police and Communist payrolls. While the staff spoke little English, their smiles were always gracious and they held ready for me the same third-floor room with its wrought-iron balcony and bougainvillea vines overlooking the opera house and Lam Son Square.

The war went on. Men died. And yet, because of my piece in the newspaper, the brotherhood now knew Van had shown me his article before he was murdered. They could not know just how much he had said. I remembered Van's remark that Saigon afforded no protection against murder and kidnaping, especially the casually thrown grenade; for the first time I began bolting my door at night.

Van's death had left me with many things to investigate and confirm. In the days that followed, I discovered that the origin and history of the secret Mandarin Dai Viet brotherhood, its relationship with the Vietnamese Communist movement, its past and present membership, and even its very nature were wrapped in mystery and a fantastic confusion of conflicting claims. Much of this confusion seemed intentionally generated as camouflage by the Dai Viets themselves, especially after their seizure of the Saigon government's propaganda apparatus and much of the Saigon press in 1964 and 1965.

I found my most reliable sources in this investigation were Cochinchinese political leaders of national standing and Tonkinese who fled south after partition in 1954, most of them men who could stand on non-Dai Viet, non-Communist records going back many years. They included academics and professional men from Hanoi, peasants from North Vietnam's Son Tay Province, others who lived in Hue during the thirties, Vietnamese army officers who fought in Tonkin during the Indochina war, and a number of priests from the two former Tonkin dioceses of Phat Diem and Bui Chu who had bitterly resisted Dai Viet attempts at domination from 1949 to 1954. I discovered that some French citizens with a financial stake in Vietnam's future and opposed to President de Gaulle's Vietnam policy were anxious to tell what they knew. I also made the acquaintance of Japanese intelligence operatives in Saigon who were themselves investigating the Dai Viets. One of these, whom I used to think of as "Mr. Moto," had connections high in the Japanese government and got to know the Dai Viets well, playing mah jong and gambling with some of Ky's fellow generals and Cabinet ministers and their wives. Eventually he reached a similar conclusion to Van's, that the Dai Viets were ruthless opportunists who cared little for South Vietnam's fate and were possibly conscious instruments of Hanoi's policies. Other Japanese who were close to Tri Quang's Buddhists provided valuable information. The American Embassy's political section was at this time influenced by Dai Viet thinking, but it made its unclassified dossiers on the personalities involved readily available. The British Embassy was especially informative. Several fragments of information, based on his research of the old Office of Strategic Services files from Hanoi in the forties for his book *Viet Cong* (M.I.T. Press, 1966), also came from Douglas Pike, who was then in his sixth year with the American mission's information office. Pike, for instance, named Dr. Phan Quang Dan—the country's Harvard-educated Western-style liberal and the friend of mine who had just escaped death in the December terrorist explosion—as a Dai Viet. I was astonished to discover this but found that the Embassy's biography of Dan also carried him as a current Dai Viet member. When I asked Dan about this, he heatedly denied it and said he had left the brotherhood twenty years before. Similarly, Robert Shaplen in his *The Lost Revolution* (Harper & Row, 1965) repeatedly referred to Dr. Dang Van Sung as a Dai Viet; Sung himself, in conversation with me, was evasive on this point.

Few Vietnamese openly declared their Dai Viet affiliation, although with some, such as Sung, it was such common knowledge that the American press regularly called several politicians Dai Viets in their news reports from Saigon. This generated a certain amount of confusion about the Dai Viets in the United States, since press dispatches often referred to a "Dai Viet party," with northern, southern and *centriste* factions, as if it were a conventional overt organization of people united in a political cause—what Americans think of as a political "party." I began using the more precise term "brotherhood" because the Dai Viet organization, since the forties, had been a secret, elite society of civil servants, professional men and military officers bound together by fraternal ties for mutual protection, financial help and advancement. Among themselves the Dai Viets called one another "brother" or "comrade." Based primarily on his research in the OSS records and personal observation in Vietnam, Douglas Pike in *Viet Cong* describes the Dai Viets as "ultranationalistic, totally clandestine and at one time the most influential political group in Vietnam. . . . The organization never made any particular obeisance either to democracy or to the rank-and-file Vietnamese. It probably never numbered more than 1,000 members and did not consider itself a mass-based organization. It turned away from Western liberalism, although its economic orientation was basically socialist, in favor of authoritarianism and blind obedience."

Dennis Duncanson, who spent five years in Saigon with Sir Robert Thompson's British advisory mission, told me the Dai Viets had a "loyalty unto death" oath. Later, discussing the Dai Viets' status in 1964, Duncanson was to write in *Government and Revolution in Vietnam* (Oxford University Press, 1968): "The Dai Viet at this time . . . consisted in fact only of its half-dozen leaders and their personal clients, and these divided broadly into two ways: firstly into Tonkinese, Annamite and Cochinchinese, and secondly into émigrés and those who stayed at home. . . ." My own research led me to conclude that there were about fifty key Dai Viets in Saigon, of whom I could confirm the membership of about two dozen, plus another dozen prominent Vietnamese who had either been converted, deceived or intimidated into working for them. Military officers who were members were concentrated in the secret police, the Vietnamese Army's operations and intelligence branches and military departments concerned with personnel and training.

The origin of the Mandarin Dai Viets was extremely murky. Again based on the OSS records, Pike says that the organization was "formed in 1939, by Truong Tan Anh, who was assassinated by the Communists in 1964." Duncanson, in discussing the Japanese occupation in 1939, gives a less flattering version:

> Many ephemeral patriotic associations, vaguely presided over by Cuong De [a royal prince] from Tokyo, were set up with Japanese funds in different parts of the country, although they probably lost their attraction whenever the money ran out; two of them nevertheless were destined to become permanent, the Dai Viet Quoc Dan Hoi (Greater Vietnam Republic Asso-

ciation) and the Dai Viet Cach Menh Dang (Greater Vietnam Revolutionary party), later fused with it. Various political leaders were given Kempeitai [Japanese secret police] protection against possible arrest by the French. . . .

(It will be remembered that the Vichy government's colonial administration in Indochina collaborated with the Japanese occupation forces.)

Later, writing about Ho Chi Minh's seizure of Hanoi in 1945 and attempt to gain French recognition of his self-styled "Democratic Republic of Vietnam," Duncanson says: "Ho Chi Minh's statesmanship was ill received in Tonkin, and the VNQDD, with the Japanese-sponsored Dai Viet, in league with a group of bandits, tried to 'liberate' their own base areas along the Chinese frontier. Vo Nguyen Giap's elimination of these pockets during the summer of 1946 was a rehearsal for the bigger tussle with the French army. . . ." Duncanson, describing how the French attempted to create a national Vietnamese government out of Cochinchina, Annam and Tonkin in the late forties, confirms Van's statement that the Dai Viets dominated Tonkin from 1949 to 1954. (This, of course, is also confirmed in official U.S. records.) Duncanson says:

> In Tonkin . . . the Dai Viet party was allowed a free hand in almost any locality of which it could gain control, on condition there were no Vietminh incidents in it. . . . Provincial government fared no better. Tonkin had had no central administration for several years. . . . It was too far away to be governed effectively under present circumstances—the railway was interrupted, shipping was erratic, and air travel still expensive—as an integral part of the new Saigon-based state; but the head of the Dai Viet, Nguyen Huu Tri, declared his support for Bao Dai and in return was appointed Governor—by accession, as it were, rather than appointment. He presided, however, only over the municipalities and his own party machine, for there was not in reality any administration in the countryside, even inside the security perimeter. . . .

As Pike adds, "Dai Viet membership included leading Vietnamese figures and government officials who viewed Japan as a suitable model for Vietnam."

Duncanson also provides insight on the state of the French-supported first national government under Bao Dai, in which, as we shall soon see, Dai Viets occupied key ministries:

> The tone was set by the Head of State; no drama or excitement over this historical moment [i.e., the fusion of Tonkin, Annam and Cochinchina into a unified nationalist state of Vietnam] for which, the world had been led to believe, the Vietnamese people had waited eighty years. Instead, His Majesty retired to his establishment in the mists and pinewoods of Dalat to hunt, to meditate, and to hold court in the most paltry of senses—not to reign over, still less inspire, progressive government or to grapple with the appalling crisis of civil war, but to bestow remunerative office, much as his forefathers had been content to issue patents for tutelary spirits. Under him, and answerable only to him in the absence of either legislature or political parties, came the Prime Minister and a Cabinet of other Ministers who, working without any clear principle of responsibility, nevertheless represented the extension to Annam and Tonkin of the writ of the former Cochinchinese Provisional Government rather than the setting up of an administration with a nationwide horizon. . . .

Duncanson also says the creation of the first national Vietnamese Army in 1953, which was to be important in the Dai Viets' rise to power, necessitated the opening of new officers' training schools, since the existing Vietnamese officer corps trained by the French Army was "insufficient for the imposing conventional army most Vietnamese politicians pictured themselves reviewing on parade." Such were the Dai Viet origins.

With the Geneva agreement of 1954 and the replacement of Bao Dai's shaky constitutional monarchy with Ngo Dinh Diem's republic by national referendum in 1955, the Dai Viets appeared to go underground. But I found that most Vietnamese regarded their resurgence in 1963 and control of the Saigon governments since January 1965 as a well-established fact.

Gradually, I decided to label Vietnamese as Dai Viets only if cited as such by Van and subsequently confirmed to be so by a spectrum of Vietnamese political leaders and official records in Saigon and Washington. The basic nature of my investigation was to gather information from separate sources, then put the mutually confirmed pieces together. It was essentially a task of correlation, which no one, at least in the unclassified files available to me, ever seemed to have done.

To illustrate how I went about this, take, for example, Van's charge that aside from Dr. Sung, seven members of the Saigon government in mid-November 1966 were secret Dai Viets. Van named Nguyen Cao Ky, the premier and air force commander; General Nguyen Duc Thang, the pacification chief; General Nguyen Bao Tri, the information minister and head of the amnesty (Chieu Hoi) program; Dinh Trinh Chinh, Ky's top civilian aide; Bui Diem, who had just been made ambassador to Washington; General Nguyen Ngoc Loan, the police chief; and General Le Nguyen Khang, the commander of the Third Corps, the military region around Saigon. In terms of preventing a Cochinchinese-Catholic countercoup, as was twice attempted in 1964 and 1965, Khang controlled the Saigon troops; Loan, the police; and Ky, the skies.

To establish the Dai Viet affiliation of Sung, Chinh and Bui Diem was easy since they were so labeled in all the official records. The problem with the generals was more complex. Of some twenty to thirty Vietnamese leaders interviewed, almost all of them shared Van's contention that Thang, Loan, Khang and Bao Tri were Dai Viets. Most of them, but not all, included Ky. A good many also named General Nguyen Van Thieu, then the junta's chairman and nominal head of government, as a Dai Viet; others took the position that Thieu himself was not a member but his two brothers were. There was near unanimity that Thieu's closest political adviser, Nguyen Van Huong (no relation to the former Cochinchinese premier) was a hard-core Dai Viet. Other names frequently mentioned as Dai Viets were Colonel Pham Van Lieu, an ex-police chief; Le Van Tien, a Saigon writer who used the *nom de plume* Nhu Phong; Le Van Thai, Ky's foster father-in-law and a close associate of Dr. Sung; Dang Duc Khoi, a press spokesman for Ky; Mai Van Dai, General Loan's brother-in-law and the deputy information minister; Ha Thuc Ky, the Dai Viet boss in Annam and an ex-Communist.

Of these Dr. Sung and Colonel Lieu turned out to be the most interesting figures.

Sung was born in 1905 in Nghe An Province in North Vietnam,

where Vietnamese Communism had first got its start. Like most of the older Dai Viets, he was a descendant of mandarins who served the imperial Vietnam's dynasties at Hue. He attended the University of Hanoi and was a classmate of Dr. Dan and Vo Nguyen Giap, whom he knew personally. He went to Hue and lived there from 1937 to 1943, earning a medical degree although he would never practice medicine. In 1940, Dr. Sung joined what the records called the "Dai Viet Dan Chinh, a clandestine anticolonialist organization persecuted by the French." He appeared to play no prominent role for some years and in 1945 fled to Shanghai after Ho Chi Minh's guerrillas seized Hanoi. Some sources said that he went on to Tokyo. Others said he was accompanied by Dr. Dan, who stayed on to work in a public hospital in Shanghai.

Sung returned to Hanoi in 1947, where his record becomes ambiguous indeed. The official U.S. file in Washington said that he "acted as the leader of the Tonkin Committee of the Dai Viet Youth Group, the Thanh Nien Bao Quoc Doan, from 1949 to August 1951, when it was dissolved by government decree." (Reason not stated.) He was elected secretary-general of the Mandarin Dai Viets in 1951, after having already been chosen secretary-general of the National Popular Front in Tonkin, which, the record said, was "an outgrowth of the Dai Viet opposed both to French rule and the Communists." Yet the American Embassy files in Saigon reported that Sung "advocated a degree of cooperation with the French-supported government of Bao Dai (1947–51)."

Vietnamese who knew him at the time say Sung, who had returned from China just as Mao Tse-tung's Communists were defeating Chiang Kai-shek's Kuomintang forces, did switch from anticolonialism to a pro-French position. Under his leadership, they say, the Dai Viets quickly became an extremely reactionary secret society, which, although its small elite membership of civil and military officers held many key posts in the Bao Dai national government, practiced assassination and terrorist tactics. While Duncanson says the government was "Saigon-based," Dr. Dan told me most of the ministries were physically located in Hanoi. Sung fled south in 1954, and although some sources claimed he was on the CIA payroll for a time, he dropped out of the political limelight until he re-emerged as a liberal critic of Diem in 1963 and, after Diem's fall, began editing Saigon's most influential newspaper, *Chinh Luan.*

But it was Sung's past that now interested me. Especially his 1945–47 exile in China, his switch from anticolonialism to a pro-French position on his return, and the entry in his official U.S. file that said "Sung acted as leader of the Tonkin Committee of the Dai Viet Youth Group, the Thanh Nien Bao Quoc Doan, from 1949 to August 1951, when it was dissolved by government decree." In Colonel Lieu's biography I had found a link. Lieu, a native of North Vietnam's Nam Dinh Province next to Nghe Anh in the Annamite panhandle, is first mentioned as affiliated with the old nationalist Vietnam Quoc Dan Dang party's "youth training program" in 1945, later "becoming a Dai Viet." In 1949 Lieu went to North Vietnam's Son Tay Province and "recruited" Nguyen Cao Ky, Nguyen Bao Tri and Le Nguyen Khang into what was variously described as a Dai Viet "revolutionary group" and as a "military training program." All three were natives of Son Tay and had finished their studies at Hanoi's Chu Van An high school in 1948. Ky's official biography, to be published in *Who's Who in Vietnam* in July 1967 by Vietnam Press, the government news agency (also run by a Tonkinese Dai Viet, Nguyen Ngoc Linh), stated that Ky graduated from high school. Vietnamese sources from Son Tay and the official U.S. record contradicted this, indicating that Ky had failed his examinations and in 1949 (confirming Van's story) was working on his uncle's country bus, was married to a local peasant girl and had a baby boy. (No one knew what happened to Ky's wife and son; they were completely written out of the official record.)

Lieu faded out of the picture in Tonkin in 1951, when he went south to enter the Dalat Military Academy. He rose to the rank of major by 1954, became a well-established Dai Viet leader and South Vietnam's police chief when the Dai Viets seized effective power in Saigon in January 1965. After he was replaced as police chief by Loan the following year, Lieu became the national director of the training of noncommissioned officers for the Vietnamese Army, possibly recruiting more Dai Viets.

Now, in the official biography of another Dai Viet and close associate of Dr. Sung, Dr. Phan Huy Quat, I learned that Quat served first as education minister and then as defense minister in the Bao Dai government. But Quat also acted as secretary-general of the reportedly anti-French, anti-Communist National Popular Front in 1952, succeeding Dr. Sung. Quat, like Sung and Lieu, was flatly described as a Dai Viet. His personal Cabinet secretary in both ministries was Bui Diem, also termed a Dai Viet. (The record notes that Bui Diem's father ran Tonkin for a time for Ho Chi Minh and that his uncle was "Vietnam's first premier," in an abortive 1945 government set up with Japanese support.) Dinh Trinh Chinh, the other civilian named by Van, was shown during this period, 1951–54, to have been working as an "information representative" for the American mission in Hanoi. Chinh was also officially described as a Dai Viet by then.

These fragments piece together in 1951 when the French commander in Indochina, Marshal de Lattre de Tassigny, in an effort to harness the forces of Vietnamese nationalism by creating a Vietnamese army, opened a new reserve officers training school, with branches at Nam Dinh in the north and Thu Duc in the south. The defense and education ministries in Hanoi, under the influence of Quat and Bui Diem, were in charge of selecting applicants. Ky, Khang and Bao Tri, from Lieu's Son Tay Province "revolutionary group," were admitted at Nam Dinh and the two other generals named by Van, Nguyen Ngoc Loan and Nguyen Duc Thang, at Thu Duc. In his official 1967 biography, Ky was to list his only "association" as "President, Association of Alumni of the First Class of Nam Dinh and Thu Duc Reserve Officers Schools." Investigation showed that the requirement for admission was high school graduation, which should have made Ky ineligible if his fellow Tonkinese refugees from Son Tay Province and U.S. records are right about his failure. The implication, based entirely on the public record, is that Ky and the others were Dai Viet protégés since 1949. And their careers were marked by rapid advancement and promotion over a large number of far more senior and experienced men.

In recent Vietnamese history, the Communists used similar tactics to recruit and train cadres. Duncanson notes in his book:

> Since his rise to power, Ho Chi Minh has told us that, although it was patriotism that first led him to Lenin and the Third International, once caught up in the "struggle" he became

a thorough-going Marxist-Leninist vowed to "emancipating workers and downtrodden people all over the world." Not surprisingly, however, his biggest success in spreading Communist influence in this period [the thirties and forties] lay not in his activities among Asians of other nationalities so much as in the subversion of young Vietnamese being sent to Canton . . . for training at the Whampao Military Academy. By the time of Chiang Kai-shek's break with the Communists, Ho Chi Minh had subverted some 200 *can bo* (cadres) and either sent them to Moscow with the Chinese Communist contingent for further training, alongside Vietnamese arriving via Paris, or straight back to Vietnam, as members of the "Brotherhood of Revolutionary Youth. . . ." These were the first Communists working in Vietnam to establish, by a process they called "bead-stringing," a conspiratorial "people's network" (*luoi nhan dan*) to be used, at a suitable moment, for "masses activation." . . . It was already plain at this stage that the purpose the Communists had in mind was to lay the foundations of an organ for seizing power, rather than to advance any definite ideology. . . .

The Dai Viets, too, wanted to "lay the foundations of an organ for seizing power," which they were to achieve in Saigon in 1965. It seemed reasonably possible that they would follow Ho's example. Once the French started the Nam Dinh and Thu Duc training schools to create an indigenous Vietnamese army in 1953, the Dai Viets had a small-scale Whampao made to order for them.

Another curiosity about the Dai Viets' history, I found, was the way they kept splintering into factions with long imposing names. According to Pike, again based on the old OSS records:

> The major Dai Viet organization was the Dai Viet Quoc Dan Dang (Greater Vietnam Nationalist Party, sometimes translated as the Greater Vietnam National People's Party). . . . Later the Dai Viet fragmented into four major Dai Viet parties. In addition to the original there were the Dai Viet Duy Dan (Greater Vietnam Association for Advancement of the People) headed by Phan Huy Quat and attorney Le Thang; the Dai Viet Dan Chinh (Greater Vietnam People's Political Association) led by Nguyen Tuong Tam, Dr. Phan Quang Dan, Dr. Dang Van Sung and Dr. Nguyen Ton Hoan and the Dai Viet Quoc Xa (Greater Vietnam National Socialism Association).

By 1967 the Dai Viets had again split three ways, this time regionally with the Tonkinese Mandarin Dai Viets, the Annamite Revolutionary Dai Viets and the Cochinchinese Tan Dai Viets. My own feeling was that all these splits were primarily tactical; there was only one Dai Viet organization and Dr. Sung and the North Vietnamese around him were its leaders.

Despite the record, Dr. Sung enjoyed the respect and confidence of some key American officials in Saigon such as Lansdale and some of the senior CIA men. By the time I started to investigate Van's charges in February 1967, Sung's position as a reasonable and moderate anti-Communist who was perhaps the most well-informed man in Saigon was almost unassailable.

Anyone who questioned his credibility as an anti-Communist was likely to be reassured by an incident that occurred in late 1965. In June of that year, Sung, who had been under fire for suspected maneuvers toward a compromise peace with Hanoi, published an announcement that he and his chief editor, Tu Chung, were on the Viet Cong's assassination list. Sung claimed that a letter had arrived at his newspaper's offices accusing *Chinh Luan* of "serving American bosses" and threatening to kill the two men. The letter was published with a signature: "Vo Cong Minh, Commander of Detachment 628, Liberation Armed Forces of the Saigon-Gia Dinh area." Sung played on this theme for months and finally, in mid-December, he published a story saying a "last warning" had arrived that threatened to dispose of "two scabby sheep." Dr. Sung replied with a ringing declaration: his newspaper sought to serve only one master, truth, and it intended to continue to fight the Communists ideologically and politically. The editorial concluded: "We love the life that God has breathed into our bodies, as all men love life. But we will look straight into the gun barrel held by the murderer who comes against us and will say: You can kill us but our spirit will live on."

This would have been merely a bizarre little episode had not two unidentified gunmen fired four bullets into Tu Chung as he stepped from his car one day in late December. He died instantly and the killers escaped on a motor bike. The murder caused much speculation in Saigon because it did not fit the established pattern of Viet Cong terror. Those who had been in

Hanoi in the late forties and early fifties said it reminded them of the old Dai Viet assassinations. (Frank Scotton, one of the co-founders of the pacification program and a veteran official in Vietnam, later told me in Washington in 1968 that the Embassy had strong suspicions of Sung's involvement but ascribed whatever motives he might have had to personal jealousy.) It was, of course, exactly the same method that was used to kill Tran Van Van.

From then on, Dr. Sung kept a life-size photograph of the victim on the wall behind his desk; visitors sat facing it just above Sung's head. It was always garlanded with dried, wilted flowers, and sometimes joss sticks were burning. Tu Chung had been a thin, apprehensive-looking intellectual who wore steel-rimmed glasses; his eyes were staring directly at the camera; you couldn't avoid looking into them. The effect was chilling.

The view many Americans held of Dr. Sung is perhaps best illustrated in passages from Robert Shaplen's *The Lost Revolution*. Shaplen, *The New Yorker* correspondent in Southeast Asia, wrote: "Two opposition political leaders I knew in 1962 were Dr. Dang Van Sung, the head of the Front for Democracy [another Dai Viet phantom organization], and Dr. Phan Huy Quat. . . . Dr. Sung, who was operating more clandestinely than Dr. Quat, had also unavailingly sought Diem's permission for opposition political parties to exist freely and to be allowed to contribute to the democratic process. In a long talk I had with him, he emphasized that 'there are no political leaders here, there is no political class as such.'" Shaplen does not mention, as few Americans in Saigon did, that Dr. Sung was the head of a conspiratorial North Vietnamese refugee faction which was claiming to speak for the indigenous Cochinchinese and Annamite population. Later, Shaplen writes: "As expressed to me by my previously quoted friend, Dr. Dang Van Sung, one of the most astute of the Dai Viet leaders who went underground during the Diem regime and who, in mid-1964, was seeking a fresh approach with a mixed group of intellectuals, 'Out of sheer irresolution, the anti-and-non-Communists allowed the Vietminh to seize the initiative and take command of the resistance movement, and this proved to be the Communists' greatest victory.'" Again no mention that from 1945 on, rather than taking part in the anti-French resistance, Sung was either in China, or on his return, *advocating collaboration* with the French.

Shaplen quotes Sung as saying, "The past party groupings are no longer useful. They were part of the clandestine revolutionary underground, but things are different now. We need something more appropriate to build toward a proper democracy. . . ." This was a line I had heard Sung voice again and again—it actually had cropped up, almost verbatim, in an interview with Sung in the late forties from the old OSS files from Hanoi. Vietnamese sources claimed Sung had been telling Americans for twenty years that conspiratorial societies were outdated and that he hoped to build a mass-based organization. But there was no indication that he had ever seriously tried.

Shaplen's final passage on Dr. Sung suggests how the Dai Viet leader came to have such persuasive influence on the American mission in Saigon:

> Dr. Sung, for example, whom I had known since his under-ground days of the Diem regime, and who was regarded as one of the best informed men around, asked me one day if I would introduce him "to someone at the Embassy." He had never met anyone there, he said, either since Diem's over-throw or before. No one had ever sought him out. . . . It was a simple matter to arrange to have him meet a top man at the Embassy, but to the best of my knowledge, until he subsequently came to hold an important position in the gov-ernment [presumably Shaplen means as the grey eminence in Quat's regime, since Sung held no official position until elected to the Constituent Assembly in 1966], I do not believe the opening was ever followed up. Nor was Dr. Sung the only one I introduced to the Embassy. . . .

It is true that Shaplen introduced Sung to a number of American officials, such as John Hart, the CIA chief in Saigon in 1967, whom Shaplen invited to dinner to meet the Dai Viet leader. But in actuality, Sung already knew Lansdale and several senior CIA men.

Van had voiced suspicions of a Dai Viet link with Le Duan, the first secretary of the North Vietnamese Communist party, and I turned now to learning what I could about him. The first thing that struck me from reading the American Embassy's biographical files, from other official government files and from Vietnamese who had known him before the 1954 partition, was how little information existed about the man. Until the previous summer, when he had been forced to publicly defend his policies against Communist Chinese criticism, Le Duan had been a mysterious figure. Little was written about him in the press, although for the past six years he had ranked second to Ho Chi Minh in the eleven-man Politburo. If Ho at seventy-six was as senile and infirm as some visitors to Hanoi claimed, then Le Duan was the most powerful man in North Vietnam, since he controlled the policy-making Politburo as well as the Viet Cong's political underground in the south. The much more famous General Vo Nguyen Giap, for instance, stood only fifth in party standing.

Vietnamese sources stressed that, alone in the Politburo, Le Duan was of peasant origin. He was born in 1907, in a small village in South Vietnam's northernmost province of Quang Tri, not far from Hue and Khe Sanh. According to the Embassy's biography, he was recruited by Ho Chi Minh himself into an anti-French organization, the "Revolutionary Youth Force" at the age of twenty-two and a year later became a founding member of the Indochinese Communist party. Although Le Duan spent five of the next six years serving a sentence of hard labor on Poulo Condore, the French administration's Hell's Island off the Cochinchinese coast, he rose rapidly in party ranks. When he was released in 1936 in a general amnesty of 7,000 Vietnamese political prisoners that was rammed through by Léon Blum's left-wing Popular Front government in Paris, Le Duan became the top Communist for the old kingdom of Annam.

For the next two years, from 1937 to 1939, Le Duan lived in Hue. Vietnamese described the old city at the time, with its antiquated court ceremonial and musty royal house subject to the whims of a *résident supérieur* from Paris, as seething with revolutionary ferment. Spengler had written his *Decline of the West;* Nazi Germany and a fascist Japan were on the march. Ho Chi Minh was in northwest China and Mao Tse-tung was writing his thesis on "the people's revolutionary war" and proph-esying, "When the Chinese revolution comes into full power, the

masses of many colonial countries will follow the example of
China and win a similar victory of their own." All over Asia the
lights were going out for the white man after a century of
colonialism.

In such a political climate, it seems reasonable that Le Duan,
as the foremost revolutionary in Annam, would be well known.
Although thirty years later, Hue's population had doubled to
120,000 people, it still remained in spirit a small university town
and most educated people knew one another. It then occurred to
me that Le Duan and Dr. Sung had lived in Hue at the same
time; Sung arrived in 1937, to stay five years as a medical
student, a twenty-two-year-old from a prosperous Annamite
mandarin family. Sung must have been active in politics, since
midway through his studies he joined the just-founded Dai Viet
nationalist party, which was extremely anti-French. Tri Quang,
whom Van had accused of working with the Dai Viet brotherhood to overthrow Diem and the post-Diem governments, was
also in Hue at this time, having arrived as a thirteen-year-old
boy in 1936. Sung was from the Annamite province of Nghe An,
and Tri Quang from its neighboring province of Ha Tinh. This
region had also been the birthplace of Giap and Ho Chi Minh. A
generation later, at the fiftieth anniversary celebration of the
Russian Revolution in Moscow, Le Duan was to say: "The apex
of [the Vietnamese Communist] revolutionary movement was in
1930–31 in the Nghe An and Ha Tinh soviets. . . ." Was it
possible Le Duan, Tri Quang and Dr. Sung had all known each
other?

In September 1939, as the Nazis carved up Poland in their
joint aggression with the Russians, the Communists in Hue, as in
all French dominions, were outlawed. Le Duan was rearrested
and placed in prison, where he remained until Ho's Communist
guerrillas seized power in 1945. Le Duan immediately went to
Hanoi, where he became a member of the standing bureau of
the party's Central Committee. That same year Dr. Sung and Tri
Quang also moved—Sung to China, Tri Quang to Hanoi, although the Communists had already begun their systematic
liquidation of the non-Communist leadership there and many
people were trying to get out.

The next episode in Le Duan's life that I learned about from the files came in 1950. By then Le Duan was already regarded by the knowledgeable as a grim Marxist dialectician. His ideology, unlike that of many other North Vietnamese leaders, was untempered by nationalism. His special talent seemed to be for organization and conspiracy. Although he was said to be a forceful speaker, his cold logic made him the prototype of the scientific political commissar; he was a man who lacked the charisma to kindle the peasant imagination as Ho Chi Minh had.

He was sent to Cochinchina to arrange the execution in 1951 of Nguyen Binh—a Tonkinese sailor trained in China who had become the popular commander of the Viet Minh troops in the Mekong Delta—by betraying him into the hands of a French-commanded patrol of Cambodian light infantry. They shot Nguyen Binh in the belief he was a common guerrilla. In a diary found on his body, Nguyen Binh had written: "I had reached the stage where the only alternatives were to yield and do what was asked of me, thus ensuring my own destruction and the victory of the Party, or else to resist, going over to Bao Dai. But if I had changed sides I could never have persuaded myself that I had not been a traitor. It would have been treachery towards my comrades in the Resistance, the living and the dead; and the next day they would have become my enemies. I belong on their side, and on their side I stay; for a battle fought together for years supplies the place of conviction."

Nguyen Binh had been ordered by Hanoi to launch a suicidal "general offensive" against the French in the Delta; it had failed, the French pacification effort was beginning to take hold, and many of the Viet Minh leaders in Cochinchina were soon to be purged, either by betrayal into the hands of the French or by Le Duan's men from Hanoi. Some authorities believe it was Ho Chi Minh's deliberate aim to have Le Duan weaken the Viet Minh leadership in the south. Ho's Tongbo party committee in the north was about to begin a large-scale conventional war in Tonkin; they appeared ready to sacrifice the Cochinchinese Communists rather than risk having a victorious rival in Saigon. This purge was to become important three years later. Faced with an unexpected partition of Vietnam after the Geneva agreement, Ho and Le Duan had to build their subversive apparatus in the south almost entirely from men sent down as refugees in 1954.

In 1959, Hanoi ordered the Viet Cong uprising in the Mekong Delta against Ngo Dinh Diem's five-year-old government. As an Annamite who had fought with the Communist-led Viet Minh resistance against the French in Cochinchina, Le Duan had some claim to be a South Vietnamese. It was he who appealed to his "fellow southerners" to join the newly formed Viet Cong guerrilla movement. He made the first speech urging this course at the third Lao Dong, or Communist party, conference in September 1960, more than three months before the National Liberation Front came into existence.

From then on Le Duan identified himself with the Viet Cong in the south. He well understood the importance of appealing to southern regional feelings. Sixty-three of the Front's sixty-four Central Committee members were native-born southerners. The single exception, Nguyen Van Tien, although born in Tonkin, had spent most of his adult life as a Saigon schoolteacher and laid claim to being an adopted southerner. A veteran of Le Duan's team of commissars, Tien was eventually named as permanent NLF representative in Hanoi. Asked by a foreign newsman why the NLF had quasi-diplomatic representation in Hanoi, Tien replied, "The North cannot speak for the South."

Others saw Le Duan's hand in the choice of NLF leaders. The president, Nguyen Huu Tho, once a prominent lawyer, was largely a figurehead. Many Saigonese regarded the two most important political figures to be Huynh Tan Phat, a rich Saigon architect with many friends in the old Cochinchinese landed gentry, who served as Tho's nominal deputy, and Tran Buu Kiem, a convinced Marxist-Leninist who was put in charge of the NLF's external-affairs committee and the subversive network in Saigon. Most Vietnamese sources and such Americans as Douglas Pike believed Kiem was Le Duan's key operative in the south. This view was shared by Dr. Sung, of all people. Once when I asked him if General Nguyen Chi Thanh (who, Westmoreland's headquarters maintained, was the top Viet Cong commander) was Le Duan's man, Sung was contemptuous: "He would like to be, but he can never belong to Le Duan's group." (It occurred to me, of course, to question how Dr. Sung could speak so authoritatively about the power rivalries in Hanoi.)

Another Vietnamese who believed that Kiem was Le Duan's chief lieutenant in the south was Professor Ho Huu Tuong, a Trotskyite who was unusually knowledgeable about the Viet Cong. Tuong claimed that Kiem and Phat spent most of their time living clandestinely in Saigon itself. He said the two men moved in and out of the city through Tan Son Nhut Airbase, using official government passports.

In March 1963, Kiem's wife, Pham Thi Yen, a veteran Communist party member herself, was arrested and sentenced to life imprisonment by the Saigon Military Court of the Diem government. The court convicted Mrs. Kiem on the charge she had been running the capital's secret agitprop network to win support for the NLF among Saigon's intellectuals. Arrested with her were three senior bonzes (Buddhist monks) from Tri Quang's organization and a professor at Saigon's respected Lycée Petrus-Ky. Mrs. Phat was also held in protective custody, although no charge was brought against her.

In early 1965, soon after the Dai Viets seized power in Saigon, their first premier, Dr. Phan Huy Quat, released Mrs. Phat without informing the American mission. In the course of my investigation of Le Duan, I came across the information that Ky had released Mrs. Kiem from Saigon's Chi Hoa prison in January 1967. According to Vietnamese sources, he had paid her convalescence bill at an expensive private clinic on Cong Ly Street and arranged her transportation as far as the Cambodian border. She reportedly proceeded to the French-owned Mimoo plantation just across the frontier from the Viet Cong's national headquarters in the jungle of Tay Ninh Province. There she was joined by her husband. The director of the plantation, Henri Say, was a former military attaché at the French Embassy in Saigon, whom many people suspected of running the Deuxième Bureau's operations in Vietnam. The French government in Cambodia, although not the French population, was fairly open in its help and sympathy to the Viet Cong.

After my newspaper published a dispatch to this effect, I received a visit from an American Embassy official who wanted to know where I had got the information. I could not as a newspaperman divulge the source, but fortunately the Embassy was able to confirm Mrs. Kiem's release elsewhere. Ky had not informed them.

Now, in my research, I found one thing was certain: Since the creation of the Viet Cong and its political arm, the NLF, Le Duan had always taken credit for its successes. Most authorities felt that should the Communists win, Le Duan's position as the leader of all Vietnam and Ho Chi Minh's heir apparent would be unchallengeable.

Conversely, it was felt that defeat would end Le Duan's career and he would face the same kind of Communist punishment for failure he had dealt out to Nguyen Binh. Le Duan was inextricably bound to a policy of continuing and uncompromising support for the Viet Cong campaign in the south, and able to uphold this policy by virtue of the majority commanded by him and his fellow ideologists in the Politburo.

Many Vietnamese who had known them before the war felt that such leaders in Hanoi as Premier Pham Van Dong or General Giap shared the traditional Vietnamese antipathy toward China, and were probably questioning the wisdom of fighting to the bitter end as victory became more remote and bomb damage increasingly disrupted the life and economy of the north. But they also thought that such men were powerless against Le Duan as long as he held the levers of organizational power.

By now I had gained the impression of Le Duan as a dialectical machine, standing astride a political network that crisscrossed the whole of Vietnam. One French authority said that Le Duan extended this control through highly developed propaganda techniques, to achieve what he called "total psychological mobilization of the masses." Building the network required supreme Oriental patience. At the slightest error, the process stopped. The situation was then analyzed, there was autocriticism, the fault committed was corrected and a better approach and tactics worked out. It was an extremely slow process—hence the need to protract the struggle that had begun in 1947 and had certainly not ended when the French left in 1954. Despite countless reversals and fresh starts, its advance, at least in terms of controlling human minds, seemed to be relentless.

Still, Le Duan faced great, perhaps insurmountable, problems.

From 1954 onwards, he had to find enough skillful and dedicated political cadres to make the system work, to penetrate and organize all of South Vietnam's myriad religious and ethnic groups, and overcome the extreme parochialism of the Vietnamese village. His objective was the seemingly impossible one of developing the revolutionary consciousness of the Vietnamese people in the more than 14,000 individual southern hamlets to the point of a spontaneous uprising.

Until late 1964, Le Duan appeared to be willing to follow the Chinese Communist revolutionary model. He had a disciplined Communist party, and, in the NLF, he had a broad united front to conduct a protracted guerrilla struggle, with a rural base of armed peasantry. The peasants, of course, were led to believe that they were part of a genuinely indigenous movement for land and independence. The movement would actually be controlled by the Communists from the outset.

To carry out his plans, it was important that Le Duan and his foreign supporters, the Russians and the Chinese, maintain some semblance of unity. And, until 1964, the differences between the Chinese and Soviet prescriptions for power were not very great. China's President Liu Shao-chi, Peking Mayor Peng Chen and General Party Secretary Teng Hsaio-ping, who were in charge of China's subversive effort abroad, were, contrary to Mao himself, not unlike such Russians as the hard-line Soviet theoretician Mikhail Suslov. In Indonesia, for instance, the Chinese had sponsored the same sort of Communist seizure of state power through subversion alone, as Russia had done in Eastern Europe, without an armed peasant uprising on Mao's classic model.

Any real difference was one of semantics, at least until Liu's subversive efforts in Africa and Indonesia backfired and Mao became strong enough to begin his crusade to bring pure Marxism to China. Until then, it was not so much that the Soviet theorists had dropped violence while China stuck to it. Instead, the Russians had simply conceded that "socialism" could, in certain areas, be achieved through nonviolent and constitutional methods, while the Chinese held to the line that violence was, "generally speaking," inevitable.

In January 1961, Nikita Khrushchev had reaffirmed that while the Soviet Union would follow a policy of "peaceful coexistence," it would also fully support "just wars of national liberation." This was to become the basis of Russia's involvement in the Vietnam war:

> . . . Liberation wars will continue to exist as long as imperialism exists, as long as colonialism exists. These are revolutionary wars. Such wars are not only admissible but inevitable, since the colonialists do not grant independence voluntarily. Therefore, the peoples can attain their freedom and independence only by struggle, including armed struggle. . . . It is a liberation war of a people for its independence, it is a sacred war. We recognize such wars, we help and will help the peoples striving for their independence. . . . The Communists fully support such just wars and march in the front rank with the peoples in waging liberation struggles.

Khrushchev made this harshly plain to President Kennedy when they met in Vienna. In a televised review of his first two years in office in January 1963, Kennedy described this policy as the only insurmountable obstacle to *détente*. Kennedy said he believed the strategic-weapons question was manageable but that Russia's policies of sponsoring revolutionary movements and its consolidation of its relationship with the United States were incompatible.

The Russian commitment to the specific Vietnamese "war of national liberation" appeared to be cemented by the fall of the Ngo Dinh Diem government in November 1963. In September of that year, Peking for the first time published excerpts from a secret memorandum addressed to the Russians by the Chinese Communist party in November 1957, soon after the Sino-Soviet split began. The 1957 memorandum was designed to bring the Soviet party back to what the Chinese considered orthodoxy, despite the reality of nuclear bombs and intercontinental ballistic missiles. The memorandum declared: "It is advantageous from the point of view of tactics to refer to the desire for peaceful transition [of a Communist party to power]. But . . . they [the people and the Communist party] must be prepared at all times to repulse counter-revolutionary attacks and, at the critical juncture of the revolution when the working class is seizing state power, to overthrow the bourgeoisie by armed force if it uses armed force to suppress the people's revolution: generally speaking, it is inevitable that the bourgeoisie will do so."

The message of the Chinese was plain: reference to "peaceful transition," a phrase pointedly quoted from Khrushchev's report to the Twentieth Congress of the Soviet Communist party in February 1956, could be made, but only with the object of misleading non-Communists.

At the same time in Hanoi, Truong Chinh, the third-ranking and most fanatically pro-Peking member of Hanoi's Politburo, made a speech to the party laying an official theoretical basis for the "liberation" of South Vietnam. The speech first appeared in *Hoc Tap*, the party theoretical journal, and was at once reprinted in the Peking *People's Daily*. Truong Chinh maintained it was sheer illusion to suppose that the Communists in the south could seize power through a parliamentary majority or any other means that required popular support. Power, he said, could come only by "direct extra-parliamentary actions of the masses. In a colonial and agrarian state like Vietnam . . . an armed uprising may be launched by steps, and guerrilla bases or even liberated areas may be set up, and then, in accordance with the situation, the uprising may be expanded into a national one for the seizure of state power."

In late October, on the eve of Diem's overthrow, Moscow indicated that it was ready to support Hanoi's "war of national liberation" in South Vietnam. The Russians sponsored an international trade-union conference in Hanoi to underline this, both to the North Vietnamese and their Chinese supporters. The conference, with delegates from all Communist bloc countries, promised to channel funds and matériel to the NLF, use Russian and East European agitprop networks to push globally for an American withdrawal from Vietnam and gain diplomatic recognition of the NLF by various bloc and Afro-Asian countries.

In December, a month after Diem's fall, *Pravda* published a lengthy treatise again recognizing that "peaceful coexistence" did not extend to the national liberation movement. Indeed, the duty of the Soviet Communist party, said *Pravda*, was to give all support—political, economic, "and if necessary support by arms" to the national liberation struggle. This was only marginally different from Peking's approach, which said the same thing more frankly. This firm promise of Russian material and diplomatic support appeared to be Le Duan's main justification for departing so radically from Maoist principles of protracted revolutionary warfare a year later in the fall of 1964.

At this time there were only 12,000 Americans in an already-reeling South Vietnam. In August 1964, the government had nearly collapsed and Saigon was near anarchy. Le Duan and his Politburo allies made the strategic decision of throwing regular North Vietnamese units into the battle in expectation of a quick killing and to ensure political control over the indigenous southern Viet Cong forces at the moment of victory. Hanoi calculated quite incorrectly that President Johnson would fear international opinion too much to commit American combat troops to the struggle. After all, Le Duan could reason, Kennedy had not militarily intervened in Cuba, which was practically on the United States' doorstep.

Until then, North Vietnam's strategic doctrine had found its principal expression in General Giap's thesis on *The People's War, the People's Army*. Giap, the onetime history teacher and guerrilla commander who defeated the French at Dien Bien Phu, earnestly subscribed to the guerrilla-warfare tenets of Mao Tse-tung and Mao's own primary inspiration, the theories of General Sun Tzu, a Chinese warrior who lived about 500 years before Christ.

In his thesis, Giap had explained that revolutionary military operations must always pass through three phases: first, the defensive, during which the population is taken in hand, while leaving the enemy in control of the main centers; second, offensive guerrilla warfare, which obliges the enemy to split up his forces while the organization of the Communist regular and local units is actively continued on a battalion and regimental scale; finally, the third phase, the "general counter-offensive," whose object is to crush the enemy's main forces in preparation for seizure of the cities.

Giap adhered strictly to the principles that provided Mao Tse-tung with his own blueprint for Communist victory in China. In a "people's war," the soldiers are drawn from the supporting masses of the people around them, so that they may move flexibly and secretly in their own familiar element, as a fish swims in water. The revolution must come from the people, and the revolution must therefore be self-reliant, not heavily dependent on foreign help. Moreover, since a people's war must usually be fought by lightly armed guerrillas against regular army units with modern weapons and air support, their creed must be that man

in the mass can overcome the machine gun; as Mao had indicated, outnumbered in general, they must always concentrate a
local superiority of forces against the well-equipped enemy
before engaging him in battle.

Now Le Duan, with Ho Chi Minh's backing, broke the rules.
The North Vietnamese Army's 325th Division, in September
1964, began training to infiltrate the south. In October, General
Nguyen Chi Thanh, a rival of General Giap, was sent south—
ostensibly to oversee the movement of troops across the 17th
parallel and along the Ho Chi Minh trail through Laos. Some
Vietnamese sources held that General Thanh, who was the only
four-star general in North Vietnam besides Giap and had been
pro-Chinese in the past, was actually being exiled from the
center of power and decision-making in Hanoi.

In Peking, Mao Tse-tung bitterly disapproved. For one thing,
the Viet Cong should be conducting a classical, long-drawn-out
guerrilla campaign to produce a victory that would vindicate
Mao's revolutionary methods throughout the underdog world.
For another, the bigger and the more conventional the forces
engaged, the more North Vietnam and the Viet Cong would
have to depend on Russia for scientific modern weapons, and the
more Hanoi would have to shift toward Moscow in the Sino-
Soviet rivalry for leadership of the world Communist movement.
Worst of all, it might give Russia a foothold in a country China
had traditionally considered little more than a tributary state.
Peking's propagandists warned, "Acting contrary to Mao's theory
will lead only to defeat." And in September 1965, Peking went
much farther. Defense Minister Lin Piao published his famous
article "Long Live the Victory of People's War." Lin's thesis
postulated the nations of Asia, Africa and Latin America as the
"countryside of the world" and the industrialized West as the
"cities of the world." The "cities" according to Marshal Lin,
would inevitably be isolated and eventually captured by the
revolutionary forces of the "countryside."

The New York *Times* described it as "Mao Tse-tung's nightmare blueprint for the world's future," but to Le Duan it must
have had special meaning. While Marshal Lin stated unequivo-
cally that a "people's war" would receive encouragement and
support from Peking, he also made it clear that each people

must fight its own battles. Thus the principle of "self-reliance" could be invoked by the Chinese to withdraw their support from Vietnam any time they found themselves inconveniently embroiled.

Even more significantly, Marshal Lin's thesis followed the publication of major military articles by two rival senior generals in the Chinese army who soon disappeared from public view. They were later identified as purge victims of the Cultural Revolution of 1966. Both had presented thinly veiled "revisionist" arguments, putting more faith in missiles than citizens' armies and calling for a rapprochement with Russia before direct Chinese military intervention in Vietnam to match the growing American involvement. The purge of the two generals was eventually followed by the arrests and vilification of President Liu, Party Chief Teng and Peking Mayor Peng Chen, thus depriving Le Duan of his three major Chinese allies. The Chinese also moved 40,000 troops across the North Vietnamese frontier, ostensibly to repair the two rail links into China and build supply depots.

Meanwhile, Le Duan ordered the discontinuation of public abuse of "revisionists." In late 1964, following the fall of Nikita Khrushchev, he personally led a good-will mission to Moscow to build Hanoi's links with the Soviet party. This was followed by Premier Kosygin's state visit to Hanoi in February 1965. When daily American bombings began that month, Russian surface-to-air missiles versus Chinese rifles made Le Duan's shift toward Moscow a necessity. Yet it was not until early 1966 that the dispute between Le Duan and the Maoists in Peking became open and acrimonious. A senior unidentified Politburo member in Hanoi attacked "those of conservative spirit" who "mechanically copy the past experience of foreign countries." Coming out into the open against Mao's revolutionary warfare formula, he derided the guerrilla thesis that revolutionaries must outnumber the enemy locally by two to one, or even nine to one, before giving battle, calling it unscientific "divination" masquerading as military arithmetic. Most authorities assumed that Le Duan was the speaker, since the attack contradicted Vo Nguyen Giap's own theories as well.

Finally in July 1966, Le Duan appeared in public to challenge

Mao's favorite dictum: "Man, not weapons, decides the issue of war." Man in the mass was important, Le Duan said, but so was technology. Besides, he went on, the Vietnamese Communists had evolved "unique tactical methods" which enabled them to confidently predict success in their struggle with the United States. Then came Le Duan's detailed analysis of these methods in the September 1966 issue of *Hoc Tap*, the party journal. In effect, this was his blueprint for defeating the United States in Vietnam.

"We can be proud," he began, "that during 36 years of leadership . . . our party has not committed any error . . . in applying Marxism-Leninism to the concrete conditions of our country." The two main slogans of the Vietnamese revolution, Le Duan said, were "national independence" and "land to the tiller." (This confirmed what I had already seen in the Mekong Delta. There, Le Duan's political commissars told the Cochinchinese peasantry, "The regime in Saigon is not working for Vietnam but for the Americans; we are struggling to get rid of the Americans for you. They are coming here to replace the French. You have been working in the rice fields for the benefit of rich landowners who have fled to take refuge in the cities. Now you no longer have to pay rents to them or taxes to the Saigon government. The land is yours, we will protect you. In exchange you must give us your undivided assistance.")

Le Duan insisted that the Vietnamese war was a class struggle but said that the "anti-feudal" task should be postponed until the "anti-imperialist" task was completed; the Communists should first enlist the help of all elements of Cochinchinese society—rich and poor, landowners and tenant alike—to drive out the Americans. Residual feudal remnants of South Vietnamese society could be exterminated later; Hanoi must defeat one enemy at a time. He denied that the war in Vietnam was a civil war; "our party is a part of the international Communist movement," he said, and victory would be "useful to the revolutionary struggle of the people of the world." But, declaring Hanoi's ideological independence of both great Communist powers, he warned that while Soviet "revisionism" was the "principal danger," with Chinese "dogmatism" the "revolution will [also] fail."

Le Duan explained that he was trying to "provide timely,

theoretical solutions to the problems arising from reality" in the Vietnam struggle, "specifically the problems of people's war strategy and tactics . . . and the problem of coordinating political struggle with armed struggle, the problem of fighting the enemy's war of destruction and psychological warfare, and so forth." Instead of "learning solely from foreign experience," he said, Hanoi had worked out its own "unique and clever tactic" against the United States, drawing directly from Lenin's principle of "exploiting internal contradictions in the enemy camp." "On the basis of keeping firm in strategy," he went on, "our party cleverly applied its tactics: on the one hand, it cleverly took advantage of the *regional and temporary contradictions* of the enemy to sow division among him. On the other hand, it united with anyone who could be united, won over anyone who could be won over, neutralized anyone who should be neutralized, completely isolated the imperialists and their most dangerous lackeys, and concentrated the spearheads of the attacks on them to overthrow them."

He cited as "typical examples of the clever application" of Lenin's principle the founding of four seemingly nationalist but covertly Communist-led popular front movements since 1936, including the Viet Minh against the French and the National Liberation Front against the Americans. He gave as another example "the present NLF policy of upholding the mottoes of independence, democracy, peace and neutrality."

Le Duan then quoted the instruction of Lenin on which he based his most clever tactic: "It is possible to defeat a stronger enemy only through displaying great effort and under the necessary condition of taking advantage very minutely, very attentively, very carefully, and very cleverly to any rift, even the smallest one, among the enemy; any contradiction, even the smallest one, among the interests of the bourgeoisie of various countries and among the interests of various bourgeois groups and factions in each country." He described "culture and ideology" and "regional and temporary contradictions" as the most fruitful fields for applying Lenin's principle, adding, "Anyone who does not understand this truth understands neither Marxism nor scientific, modern socialism in general."

Le Duan said that he was applying his tactic to the present

"protracted war," using "combined armed struggle with the political, military and military-proselytizing fields . . . to build rural areas while building forces in the cities," and "to conduct partial uprisings in advancing toward the use of both political and military forces to defeat the enemy completely."

Further amplification of Le Duan's tactic was contained in a twenty-six-page letter he wrote in March 1966 to General Nguyen Chi Thanh, who was then inspecting Viet Cong forces in the south. The authenticity of the letter, captured when an American military operation overran an important Viet Cong headquarters near the Cambodian border, was established beyond any doubt. He seemed supremely confident of his own command of the situation, and was subtly patronizing in tone toward the Russians and somewhat defiant—with perhaps a touch of apprehension—toward the Chinese. His underlying view seemed to be that the Russians were now committed and would continue to support North Vietnam no matter what future course he followed. He implied that the Soviet leaders could be manipulated without much difficulty and that Russia itself was riven with internal contradictions.

Le Duan admitted to General Thanh that Peking wanted the Viet Cong to refrain from conventional big battles and instead concentrate mainly on protracted guerrilla warfare along Maoist lines. The object, he quoted the Chinese as saying, would be to bog down the United States for as many as seven years, or until 1973, when Peking would be strong enough to launch an armed offensive across Southeast Asia in support of Hanoi. He conceded that China was sustaining half of Hanoi's budget, but he spoke contemptuously of China's technological inferiority to Russia, and of its ideological extremism. The general tone suggested that Le Duan did not trust the men controlling China.

Le Duan's attitude toward peace negotiations seemed to me to reflect the thinking of a man whose career depended on a successful outcome of the struggle. "Our strategy on negotiations," he wrote, "must serve in a practical manner our political aims." He believed it would be possible for North Vietnam to exact concessions from President Johnson in return for its acceptance of talks, and that, aided by such concessions, the Viet Cong must struggle harder than ever, both politically and militarily, while talks dragged on. Ultimately, Le Duan foresaw, an American president's bargaining position could be made so weak that he would be obliged to accept the Communist peace conditions.

That was the story on Le Duan. For several evenings I sat in the silent hotel reading through the mass of material I had collected on the man. Sometimes I studied past curfew and then stared across the flat roofs and the tops of tamarind trees at the desolate city, as still as the landscape of a dead world. Some nights the silence was broken by the dull boom of artillery or the distant spatter of machine-gun fire. Nowhere had Le Duan spelled out what he meant by internal contradictions. Yet he had referred several times to "reality." Obviously, there were numerous contradictions to exploit in a country that so profoundly resented foreign control and where such strong regional feelings had developed out of Vietnam's historic territorial divisions—the kingdom of Annam in the center, the protectorate of Tonkin in the north and the French colony of Cochinchina in the south. By applying his tactic, Le Duan had claimed in his *Hoc Tap* analysis, the Communists had "united with," "won over" and "neutralized" whoever stood in their way, had "completely isolated" the Americans and the "most dangerous" South Vietnamese leaders, and then "concentrated . . . attacks on them to overthrow them."

Overthrow whom? Ngo Dinh Diem? South Vietnam had been artificially created in 1954 with a predominantly Confucian Cochinchinese population and a Roman Catholic president from the southern half of divided Annam. Plenty of contradictions there. Diem had lasted nine years; after him General Duong Van Minh fell in three months; Harvard-educated banker Nguyen Xoan Oanh, six days; General Nguyen Khanh, eight months; Tran Van Huong, the only Cochinchinese civilian in the lot, three months; then Khanh again for thirty days until, as Van had said, the Dai Viet brotherhood seized power in February 1965. Their first premier, Phan Huy Quat lasted only five months, but he had voluntarily handed back power to the army, which chose Ky as prime minister.

Since then the brotherhood had ruled the country through a handful of young Tonkinese military officers. Was not this monopoly of power by northerners an ultimate internal contradiction? The United States' aim in fighting the war was to allow the South Vietnamese, most of whom were Cochinchinese, the right to choose their own government. But their government had in fact come to be dominated by Tonkinese, although Cochinchina had fought throughout its history against northern hegemony.

Moreover, there was a further contradiction Le Duan could exploit in that the continuation of Tonkinese political domination in Saigon—embodied as it was in a small militaristic faction that controlled the army—was highly dependent on continuation of a big military war. They had nothing to gain from an appreciable advance in pacification or social reform that might create a rival political base among the Cochinchinese peasantry.

I began to see the north-south struggle described by Van in a new light. Le Duan wasn't talking about some abstraction, he was talking about South Vietnam, here and now, populated by real people. He and his political commissars couldn't exploit internal contradictions, or sow division among the South Vietnamese, by sitting idly in Hanoi or out in the jungles. If that was the kind of political chess game Le Duan was playing, he had to have kings, bishops, knights and pawns in the south, people of some apparent standing in the non-Communist camp. People who were trusted. People he had "united with," "won over" or "neutralized." The secret of the long charade would then be found not so much in what the players said as in their associations, their performance and the effect of their actions over a prolonged period of time, perhaps going back many years. The answer would be found in the lives of those Vietnamese who were intelligent enough to be responsible for the effects of their actions and yet who consistently damaged or disrupted the war effort.

The evening this came to me, I suddenly didn't want to be alone in my room any longer and went down to a bar behind the Continental on the Rue Catinat. I ordered a scotch. It was late and only two or three of the tables were still occupied. The bar, however, was crowded: most of the men were slick young Vietnamese in air force uniforms, though there were a couple of American civilians. The pianist, a fat Chinese with haggard eyes

and untidy hair, seemed a little drunk. One of the Vietnamese
pilots asked him to play. I recognized the song; it was nostalgic
and bittersweet, but the way the Saigonese played it, it always
sounded vaguely sinister.

> *When we played our charade,*
> *We were like children posing . . .*

Le Duan's charade would go on. There was nothing to stop it
now. I thought of Van. "I am now a man nearing sixty . . . but
a man who loves his country should not be concerned over his
own future." He never had a chance. I saw that now. These men
were out to build a power structure and had no intention of
letting anyone or anything stand in their way. I ordered another
scotch.

Le Duan's likeliest instrument in the charade, of course, aside
from the Dai Viets, was the Buddhist monk, Thich Tri Quang,
South Vietnam's most experienced overthrower of governments.
Some said he only sought personal power, but I wondered. I
asked Gio, one of the girls behind the bar, what she thought
about Tri Quang. Gio shrugged at first, then leaned forward, her
head close to mine. "I am Buddhist," she said. "But I don't like
what they do. When the Buddhists make trouble, I go home and
lock my door."

She smiled professionally and straightened up again, her face
a rouged mask of boredom and indifference. I looked around,
but the Vietnamese pilots were listening raptly to the music.

> *Playing at games,*
> *Acting out names,*
> *Guessing the parts we played . . .*

Three

Thich Tri Quang Sets the Stage

With correct and flexible revolutionary methods the South Vietnamese people have overthrown the Ngo Dinh Diem fascist regime, plunged the puppet administration into endless crises, and the Americans into a tunnel with no end in sight . . . a very atrocious war of aggression, waged by 1.2 million men with barbarous weapons, which has consumed 50 billion dollars.

—Le Duan, November 1967

Few Vietnamese have captured the world's imagination as much as Thich Tri Quang.

His sympathizers described him as a passionate Buddhist, pacifist and nationalist; his detractors maintained he was a crypto-Communist. Everyone agreed he was one of the most powerful men in South Vietnam. For years speculation centered on his real motives. Was he merely seeking to dominate the Saigon government, or did he want to make peace with Hanoi at the Communist price? It occurred to none of us in the first year or two after Diem's fall that Tri Quang's role, as I now suspected, might be much more secondary, something similar to that of a bishop in chess who moves diagonally to set up plays for the kings and rooks.

I first saw Tri Quang at one of the many Buddhist victory celebrations that seemed to follow each of the dizzying succession of *coup d'états* against the post-Diem governments. Although Tri Quang was a prime mover in each of the coups, he rarely made a public appearance until after the rioting and turmoil were over. I drove out on one of these occasions to Tri Quang's Saigon suburban headquarters, the Buddhist Institute, or Vien Hoa Dao. It was in the cool of evening and girls in white silk trousers bicycled home down the Rue Catinat. Hefty military police from the American plains cruised past the neon-lit bars, and elderly pimps along the curb held out their soiled portfolios of watercolors and quaint French pornography. The streets and cafés were full of people buying flowers, sipping drinks, listening to music as if nothing had happened. As I drove, I thought how indifferent and aloof the Saigonese seemed to be to a change of government.

The Buddhist Institute grounds resembled a military garrison: wooden barracks, coils of concertina wire along the walls, a tent encampment of Boy Scouts. At an open stall women were buying colored pictures of an old bonze sitting in the middle of a Saigon street, burning to death. The flames were a dull orange.

The bonzes in the jerry-built pagoda were kneeling in prayer, chanting in high-pitched, birdlike voices. Press photographers swarmed around an altar under an enormous pink plaster Buddha with a neon halo. In the back, crowds of old women, their hair coiled on top in the Tonkinese manner, were praying for peace.

Excitement rose as a bearded bonze, the senile patriarch of the Annamite church, made a ceremonial entrance supported by two young novices. As the patriarch kneeled to light three joss sticks at the altar, Tri Quang came in through a side door and flashbulbs began popping. In the heat of television lights, the air was steamy and cloying with the smell of incense, tightly packed bodies, and rotting offerings of fruit and flowers on the altar. My shirt was already soaked with sweat, but I saw there was not a bead of perspiration on Tri Quang's face.

He was a slim little monk in his early forties with the flat features and high cheekbones of the northern Annamite and a wide mouth. His head was too large for his body; deep, intelligent eyes stared out from an enormous forehead. In triumph, he remained silent and mysterious but shot sudden glances at the press as he went through the mechanics of the Buddhist ritual. He kept pursing his lips with satisfaction; he seemed to be enjoying himself.

An English correspondent behind me whispered, "Yul Brynner playing Dracula." The pagoda, with its corrugated tin roof, cheap painted Buddha and cameramen scrambling over the altar platform for closeups, did have the air of a movie soundstage. Strangely the 3,000,000 Saigonese in the city outside seemed to take no notice of the performance here. This drama was for the world television audience.

There is little doubt that Tri Quang was a spellbinder with a real theatrical flair. A remarkable amount of biographical material on him was available at the American mission; yet little of this ever found its way into the world press. His name was an alias; Tri Quang means "brilliant mind," and he had chosen it for himself as an adult. He was born Pham Van Bong on December 31, 1923, in Diem Dien village in North Vietnam's Ha Tinh Province. One of the three sons of a prosperous farmer, Tri Quang was encouraged to enter the Buddhist priesthood from the age of nine. His father was a genuinely religious man, who became a Buddhist bonze himself late in life. At the age of thirteen, Tri Quang was sent to Bao Quoc Pagoda in Hue to train for the monkhood. Wild and unruly at first, he was expelled a year later in 1937. But instead of being sent home in disgrace, Tri Quang was given a second chance and picked to come under the personal tutelage of Thich Tri Do, who would later head the Buddhist church of North Vietnam and become a member of Ho Chi Minh's rubber-stamp parliament. Another of three such chosen novices was Thien Minh, also an Annamite peasant boy, who was to remain Tri Quang's chief lieutenant over the next thirty years. I could not establish whether Thich Tri Do knew Le Duan in Hue; but it seemed likely.

In 1945, soon after Ho Chi Minh seized power in Hanoi, Tri Quang's mother died. Shortly afterward an aunt protested Communist confiscation of the family property by setting fire to the ancestral home and throwing herself into the flames. Tri Quang was twenty-three then, and this act may have suggested the later Buddhist "self-immolations" which were alien to Vietnamese Confucianist tradition. (But not to Mahayana Buddhism elsewhere. There is a reference to suicide by fire in Mahayana scripture as the "most sublime worship of Buddha.")

After Ho Chi Minh seized Hanoi in 1945, Tri Quang, carrying nothing but his begging bowl, saffron robe and a pair of rubber sandals, went with Tri Do to the Tonkinese capital, where, as he later told friends, he "studied Marxism." At the outbreak of the French Indochinese war in 1947, Tri Quang fled from Hanoi with Ho Chi Minh's Viet Minh guerrillas to a jungle hideout. According to Vietnamese there who later broke with the Viet Minh, Tri Quang's friends in the guerrilla force included two men named Nguyen Dang and Hoang Trong Ba, who seventeen years later were to figure significantly in Tri Quang's rise to power. The years Tri Quang spent with the Viet Minh remained the murkiest period of his life, and he himself divulged few details of it. In mid-1965, he was to tell the American Embassy in Saigon he had "passively collaborated with the Viet Minh" as chairman of the United Vietnamese Association, a Communist front in North Vietnam's Quang Binh Province. According to the French colonial archives in Paris, Pham Van Bong alias Tri Quang was twice arrested on suspicion he was a Communist. Once he spent ten days in jail, but the Sûreté could not prove the charges against him and he was released.

In my investigation I discovered that Tri Quang appeared to move back and forth from Hue to Hanoi several times between 1947 and his permanent return to the south in 1961, but it was difficult to pin down the exact dates. Some Vietnamese sources remembered he was in Hue at the fall of Dien Bien Phu in 1954. They thought he went north immediately after the Geneva agreement and stayed about two years. If true, this was highly significant, since only Viet Minh troops were known to have gone north for regrouping. Certainly, Tri Quang seemed to have training in Marxist-Leninist dialectics, law and English and French, which he presumably picked up in his Hanoi years.

What is firmly established is that by the early sixties Tri Quang had mysteriously emerged as the dominant monk at Hue's Tu Dam Pagoda, a beautiful old temple set in a grove of ancient fig trees in the city's French quarter. Some Vietnamese claimed Tri Quang reached this position through coercion and intimidation. To me it appeared highly relevant that Tri Quang's rise exactly paralleled in time a Chinese movement to use Buddhism as Communism's partner in subversion in Southeast Asia. Philosophically, this was possible because Buddhism was an ethical religion without a single, personal god. Many Asian monks, while rejecting Communism for its material interpretation of life, were inclined to see it as an ally in the older, more familiar struggle against Western theism. In so far as a Communist society was atheistic, it could be argued that such a society would not attempt to force a personalist theology upon Buddhists, as French missionaries had, or, in a less direct fashion, the Ngo Dinh Diem government. Throughout the years, Tri Quang consistently stressed to his supporters that Vietnam had been a Buddhist theocracy before the French priests and soldiers came.

Until the early fifties both the Vietnamese and Chinese Communists dealt harshly with Buddhists. In Tonkin, where the Roman Catholics fared comparatively well, pagodas in Communist-held zones were either destroyed or turned over to local party committees and hundreds of monks were summarily executed. In China itself, it has been authoritatively estimated that few of the 130,000 Buddhist pagodas survived the revolution. Mao Tse-tung, with dialectical reasoning, was trying to release the Chinese people from a restrictive, feudal Confucianist past as well as an intrusive Western "imperialist" present. (Le Duan himself, by drawing the fire of American artillery and bombers on the old imperial palace in Hue in early 1968, accomplished the master stroke of getting one of his two enemies to destroy the other.)

Around 1954, Chinese Buddhism had been transformed into a kind of religious museum under state supervision. Peking had begun to flood the rest of Asia with propaganda representing China as the champion of Buddhist tradition, in an effort to penetrate and subvert Asia's post-colonial Buddhist revival. A towering Seven Jewel Golden Pagoda was erected on a prominent Peking boulevard to house a two-inch molar believed to be one of Buddha's two enshrined teeth; the other was in Ceylon. Fortunately for Peking, the Chinese holy tooth's history was wrapped in anticolonial resentment; its original shrine had been destroyed by European artillery during the Boxer Rebellion in 1900. In the mid-1950's the tooth was exhibited on tours of Ceylon and Burma to the accompaniment of Communist Chinese propaganda claiming Peking to be the protector of Buddhism against past wrongs committed by Western colonial powers.

In 1953, Peking established an official government-supported Chinese Buddhist Association. Its president, Shirob Gyaltso, was a former Communist party official of eastern Tibetan origin. He subsequently functioned as a kind of Buddhist ambassador-at-large, lavishly hosting visiting Buddhist delegations, attending international conferences and dutifully issuing statements on political issues. A typical Gyaltso utterance: "Buddhists all over China are deeply indebted to the party's policy of religious freedom, which has brought new life to Buddhism; they uphold the Communist party wholeheartedly and resolutely follow the road to socialism together with their compatriots." In early 1952, Tri Quang was invited to join Gyaltso at an international Buddhist conference in Cambodia. According to official American sources, he was denied a visa by the Sûreté on grounds of being a suspected Communist.

In Hue, Tri Quang appeared to live the life of an authentic bonze. Abstaining from meat, cigarettes and liquor, he lived in a bare room furnished only with a typewriter, a bed, a steel lockbox, where he kept his records, and a large and startling oil portrait of himself. He rose with the other monks at dawn, spent a third of the day in prayer and another third in contemplation. This allowed only a few hours for other activities. He attained the honorific title Thich, a Vietnamese derivative of Gautama Buddha's own name, and was addressed by other monks as the venerable Thich Tri Quang.

According to French sources, one of Tri Quang's two brothers joined North Vietnam's Interior Ministry after the Communist takeover. By the late fifties he was reported to be a senior official involved in internal security, which indicated he was a party member of some standing. A second younger brother, a Buddhist monk in the north, was believed to have visited Tri Quang in Saigon in May 1964, reportedly accompanied by a political spokesman from the National Liberation Front.

One of Tri Quang's prolonged absences from Hue coincided

with the first outbreak of the Viet Cong armed insurgency in the southern Delta in 1959. After it gradually extended over the whole of South Vietnam the next three years, the Diem government, in early 1962, began its attempt to counter the insurgency by establishing a strategic-hamlet program, based on a model used in Malaya, in which rural peasants were regrouped into self-defending villages.

The aim of the program was to provide protection to the peasantry, unite the people in a positive action on the government's side and develop the Vietnamese villages socially, economically and politically. The program was run by Ngo Dinh Nhu, the president's younger brother. Nhu appreciated that if the effort was successful, he would be able to build up the peasantry as a political counterbalance to the 150,000-man Vietnamese Army, created with American aid to prevent an invasion from the north. Nhu, however, attempted to impose political control from the top instead of relying upon winning voluntary political support from the bottom. He also depended too much on youth, in the process alienating village elders. Another and perhaps Nhu's most important failure was to underestimate the extent of Communist political penetration, both in the countryside and within the Diem government itself. But most responsible and authoritative Westerners in Vietnam at the time believed these mistakes had a reasonable chance of being remedied.

Then came the incident in Hue.

The occasion was the celebration of the 2,507th anniversary of Buddha's birth on May 8, 1963. By then, Tri Quang's two previously mentioned associates in the Viet Minh guerrillas in the forties had come south as refugees (in 1954) and risen to positions of prominence in Hue. Hoang Trong Ba was a close adviser of Diem's brother Can, the governor of Hue. Nguyen Dang was the chief of surrounding Thua Thien Province. The see of Archbishop Thuc, another of Diem's brothers, was also in Hue. The Buddhist celebration had overlapped a Catholic one commemorating the twenty-fifth anniversary of Archbishop Thuc's consecration as a bishop. Although during Thuc's celebration the Vatican flag was displayed along with the national flag all over Hue, Dang, as province chief, gave orders for strict enforcement of a two-year-old ban against flying religious flags. Tri Quang defiantly ordered his Buddhist organization to show flags and banners three days before Buddha's birthday and announced that a mass meeting would be held to protest religious persecution.

In the morning Tri Quang led a demonstration to Hue's radio station. After he delivered an incendiary speech, the crowd surged toward the station. The provincial troops guarding it at first responded with fire hoses, blank shells and tear gas. Then Dang ordered his Roman Catholic deputy to tell the troops to use live ammunition and grenades. Still the provincial soldiers hesitated, until a grenade was thrown at them from the crowd, which had grown to nearly 8,000 people. In the confused rioting that followed, twelve persons, including three children, were killed. The Diem government issued a statement blaming the deaths on Communist plastic grenades. Eyewitnesses could be found who blamed the troops for firing on the crowd. Tri Quang's organization blamed Dang's Catholic deputy province chief, Major Dang Sy, and demanded that he be severely punished.

The incident gave Tri Quang the martyrs and the momentum he needed. On June 11, 1963, Thich Quang Duc, the first of seven monks to eventually burn themselves alive in protest against Diem, sat down in the middle of a downtown Saigon street surrounded by American newsmen and, after other monks soaked him with gasoline, set himself aflame. Although these "self-immolations" (there were to be more than forty by 1968) were shocking spectacles, I gradually became suspicious of them. They may or may not have been suicides, if by suicides we mean conscious acts determined on by men in full control of their senses. Most of the later ones took place in isolated places, before dawn or late at night, without reliable witnesses and with nearly identical suicide notes written in the stereotyped anti-American jargon heard on Communist propaganda broadcasts. But world opinion, shocked by the grisly spectacle, accepted Duc's "self-burning" at face value and became increasingly critical of the government's handling of the Buddhist opposition.

Tri Quang also deceptively claimed that Buddhists comprised 80% of the South Vietnamese population and asserted himself as their authentic spokesman. This, too, was generally accepted by the world audience, although less than a third of the South Vietnamese were, indeed, practicing Buddhists, and few of these in 1963 had ever heard of Tri Quang. From official U.S. sources I discovered that most of the 16,000,000 South Vietnamese were ancestor-worshiping Confucians, including many who nominally adhered to other religions. There were also 1,500,000 Roman Catholics, about half of them refugees from Tonkin; 500,000 Protestants, including Baptists, Methodists, Seventh-day Adventists and others; roughly 800,000 Montagnard animists, who worship gods of the soil, river, weather; around a million Cao Dai, who believe in a synthetic religion combining Buddhism, Confucianism, Taoism and Christianity and worship as saints such figures as Victor Hugo, Sun Yat-sen and Joan of Arc; 2,000,000 Hoa Hao, a reformist Buddhist movement in the Mekong Delta which rejected pagodas and a formal clerical hierarchy; 500,000 Taoists; 500,000 Hindus and Moslems, many of them Cham tribals, human relics of the defeated medieval empire; and a million Theravada Buddhists in the Delta, most of them of Cambodian descent. The majority of orthodox Vietnamese Buddhists were Cochinchinese who rejected Tri Quang both as an alien Annamite and out of the conviction that religion should be kept separate from politics.

At best, Tri Quang probably never had an active following of more than a tiny minority. What following he had was ephemeral. As Duncanson once told me, it "could be 20,000 people one day if the issue was a burning one and two alley cats the next." Throughout my years in Vietnam I never met a single peasant or country bonze who had ever heard of him. Tri Quang's real strength lay in a formidable propaganda apparatus, its signal effect on the American press, and his ability to exploit the existing internal contradiction of a Catholic president trying to rule a predominantly Confucian people.

At the same time that Tri Quang was mounting his campaign, a much subtler offensive to isolate and destroy the Ngo family on straight political grounds was launched by Dr. Sung, then known only as a former nationalist leader from the north who had retired from active politics since coming south in 1954 as a refugee. In January 1963, Dr. Sung published a seventy-eight-page manifesto analyzing what he called the American failure in Vietnam. He wrote that "with its negative anti-Communist cause and its negative posture of nonintervention in South Vietnamese internal affairs, the United States sees no necessity to acquire a thorough knowledge of the country beyond the military situation. Nor does it try to win popular support. . . . In its aid to the underdeveloped world in the midst of revolution for political and economic emancipation, the United States has never yet fought against the Communists with ideas of freedom and justice but only with bombs and dollars."

Dr. Sung attacked the Diem regime as incapable of realizing needed reform. This was echoed by Dr. Phan Huy Quat, the Saigon physician, who sent an open letter to American Ambassador Frederick E. Nolting, Jr. saying "large-scale and sincere" reforms were needed before Diem could command popular support. In February, Nguyen Ton Hoan, an exiled politician, declared from Paris in a letter to President Kennedy, that Diem was "incapable of leadership and unamenable to reform." (All three men—Sung, Quat and Hoan—were listed as Dai Viets in the official U.S. records.) Others in the brotherhood picked up the line and pushed it with their American contacts.

In July 1963, just two months after the Hue incident, Viet Cong guerrillas throughout the country launched a strong campaign to destroy Diem's strategic-hamlet program. In retrospect, it is remarkable to see how well Diem himself understood what Le Duan, three years later, was to describe as his most "clever tactic." That July, he said in a press interview: "The government has never practiced a policy of religious discrimination. Thus I believe that fully all the political campaigns waged from within, as well as from without the country, under this false pretext will fail by themselves simply in view of the government's sincerity. . . . Hypocritical people attack us, just like the Pharisees. In addition to the hot war, I have to deal with a cold war. . . . In classic tradition, the Communists seek to isolate the president. Their tactics seek to cut off from the president all the people around him who are valuable. They charge that this is a family government, a corrupt government. There are those who charge this government has lost the support of the people. But what counts fundamentally is this: How can they claim there is inept leadership when people without pay die for their country every day? . . . If ever there were Vietnamese politicians who would propose a kind of protectorate of the United States over Vietnam in exchange for support of their intrigues, such actions would not fail to harm the friendship between the two countries. . . . All the problems I have faced since 1954 are problems of underdevelopment—technical, economic and social backwardness—with the feeling of humiliation attached to that miserable condition, and the desire to rapidly emerge from it. Then there is disunity, with extremely virulent passions which do not exist any more in advanced countries, and finally the Communist subversive war. . . . The American people should obtain a more penetrating knowledge of Communist subversive war . . . which refuses actual combat but seeks instead the moral attrition of the opponent."

To me, this was no authoritarian divorced from reality; it was the voice of an intelligent and perceptive man desperately trying to tell a naïve world what was happening. As it turned out, in 1963, the year Diem was overthrown, South Vietnam's export earnings rose to an all-time high of $76,670,000, $20,000,000 higher than the year before. The Mekong Delta had its biggest crop since World War II and was able to export 322,500 tons of rice. (Within three years it would have to import three times this amount.) Whatever Diem's shortcomings may have been, anyone who believes he had lost popular support might ponder the meaning of these figures.

Diem was firmly supported by his British pacification adviser, Sir Robert Thompson; CIA Chief John Richardson; and Ambassador Nolting, who declared: "The trouble with this damn thing [the Buddhist dispute], if I may speak frankly, is that everybody focuses on a tiny aspect of it . . . I myself, I say this frankly after almost two and a half years, have never seen any evidence of religious persecution." Diem's brother Nhu, who did toward the end arrest hundreds of Buddhist sympathizers, asked, "Why overthrow my brother? This would lead to anarchy."

Certainly, an inherent religious problem existed. During eighty years of French rule, Catholicism had been nurtured at the expense of Buddhism, and Catholic churches occupied choice sites in every major town, just as Anglican churches still do today in

India. As was universally true in Asia, from Japan to India, Catholic schools provided an education no indigenous religion could match. Catholic merchants, soldiers and civil servants, thus better equipped, inevitably prospered. But the country's richest men, such as Tran Van Van, were authentic, orthodox Buddhists who detested Tri Quang as an impostor who debased their religion.

Tri Quang tried to portray Diem as an extension of the worst aspects of French colonial rule. While the Vietnamese people knew better, Diem himself became increasingly aware that Tri Quang might achieve his aims if he got a sympathetic American press. In late 1962, Diem told Sir Robert Thompson, "This war can only be lost by the American press." By late September 1963, Diem had almost given up hope and quoted to Sir Robert the famous phrase attributed to Louis XV, "*Après nous, le déluge.*"

Oddly enough, it was a fairly low-ranking official in Washington, Roger Hilsman, the Assistant Secretary of State for Far Eastern Affairs, who first described the Buddhist crisis as affecting the war effort, which he said "none of the Vietnamese want, either the government or the Buddhists." He was, I believe, unwittingly deceiving the American people, since damaging the war effort seemed precisely Tri Quang's aim.

In many ways, the fall of 1963 is one of the most dismal chapters in modern American history. Such eminent newspapers as the New York *Herald Tribune* wrote of Tri Quang that "far from being a Communist, he is so fiercely nationalist in outlook he distrust all foreigners." When Tri Quang sought refuge from Diem's police after the August pagoda raids, Ambassador Henry Cabot Lodge gave him protection in the American Embassy's conference room for ten weeks. On September 2nd, President Kennedy told Walter Cronkite of CBS that the United States was prepared to continue to assist South Vietnam, "but I don't think the war can be won unless the people support the effort and, in my opinion, in the last two months, the government has gotten out of touch with the people. In the final analysis, it's their war. They're the ones who have to win it or lose it." Kennedy called the "repression" of the Buddhists "very unwise" and said the South Vietnamese government could win popular support only if there were "changes in policy and perhaps with personnel." In

Saigon, a spokesman for the Diem government replied with a short statement: "We feel President Kennedy's information is inadequate and his judgment quite wrong."

But the ordeal for Diem and his family went on; the tragic Madame Nhu was visibly hysterical toward the end. When the New York *Times* called her "Lucretia Borgia Nhu," she seethed back, "I would clap hands at seeing another monk barbecue show, for one cannot be responsible for the madness of others. But what else is there to say when the world, under a mad spell about the so-called 'Buddhist affair'—and much thanks to the good offices of papers like yours—needs an electro-shock to resume its senses and come better to understand the reality of the situation."

Sometime in September, Diem's brother Nhu had met with the French delegate general from Hanoi, who visited Saigon with a Polish member of the International Control Commission. The new tactic of those opposing Diem was to spread the impression through gossip and innuendo that Nhu was flirting with the Communist regime in Hanoi, although no proof was ever established. Dr. Sung and his associates told their American friends of a remark made by a French priest in 1959 who was said to have known Nhu well: "Nhu is perfectly capable of making an arrangement with the Communists and will do so when he sees himself cornered." This propaganda campaign received an assist when Charles de Gaulle in Paris declared that peace between north and south was possible, and that a neutral Vietnam would receive economic and cultural aid from France. The rumor campaign was so effective that after the November *coup d'état*, the London *Times* suggested that overtures by Nhu to Hanoi had stirred the Vietnamese army commanders into action.

Ambassador Lodge was apparently affected. Still harboring Tri Quang at the Embassy, he demanded that Diem get rid of Nhu or face a cutoff in military and economic aid. In Washington Senator Frank Church declared, "To persist in the support of such a regime can only serve to identify the United States with the cause of religious persecution, undermining our moral position throughout the world." At the United Nations, fourteen Afro-Asian countries demanded a debate on the "ruthless suppression" of Vietnamese Buddhists. In Saigon, a military mission led by General Maxwell D. Taylor and Defense Secretary Robert S. McNamara summed up their visit by stating that "the major part of the U.S. military task can be completed by the end of 1965." There were 685 American military advisers in Vietnam when the Kennedy administration assumed office; there were 14,000 when Diem fell.

In early October, CIA Chief Richardson was sent home at the insistence of Lodge and relegated to an obscure position. Within days the United States cut off a $250,000 regular monthly payment to support 2,000 Vietnamese special-forces troops who served, in effect, as Diem's praetorian guard. This was a green light for the young, ambitious Vietnamese army generals to stage their *coup d'état*. On November 1st, Diem was overthrown and he and his brother Nhu were beaten and shot to death in the back of an army truck.

But the crucial act that set these events in motion was a cable drawn up at a meeting on August 24, 1963 called by Undersecretary of State Averell Harriman and Roger Hilsman, who then headed the Vietnam Task Force. The cable instructed Lodge to make an effort to persuade Diem to fire Nhu, release jailed Buddhist rebels, end press censorship and restore other civil liberties suspended by Diem. If, as the cable anticipated, Diem refused, then the Embassy was to contact the Vietnamese generals and tell them that the United States would not stand in the way of a *coup d'état*. The cable was sent without the knowledge of Defense Secretary McNamara, CIA Director John McCone, Secretary of State Rusk, President Kennedy or General Taylor.

The most authoritative and detailed account of Diem's overthrow and murder and the inside story of what went on within the Kennedy administration at the time can be found in *Our Vietnam Nightmare* (Harper & Row, 1965), by the late Marguerite Higgins, who first disclosed the existence of the Hilsman-Harriman cable. Miss Higgins, a Pulitzer-prizewinning columnist, was the first American journalist to recognize and publicize the true subversive nature of Tri Quang and his artificially contrived Buddhist movement. Miss Higgins, who died in January 1966 of a rare tropical illness she had contracted on her tenth visit to

Vietnam, was also the closest American correspondent at the time to former Premier Tran Van Huong. In her book she quotes Huong's view on Diem's overthrow: "The top generals who decided to murder President Diem and his brother were scared to death. The generals knew very well that having no talent, nor moral virtues, and no popular support whatsoever, they could not prevent a spectacular comeback of the President and Mr. Nhu if they were alive."

Our Vietnam Nightmare was a revelation to me. Although I never met Marguerite Higgins and seldom saw her column in Saigon, we had independently reached the same conclusion about Tri Quang and his systematic attempt to subvert the American war effort.

After the coup, Diem's brother Can, the governor of Hue, was promised safe-conduct out of the country by Ambassador Lodge, but was seized at Saigon airport and later executed by firing squad. Madame Nhu was in California and Archbishop Thuc in Rome. In the United States, government policy was temporarily paralyzed by the assassination of President Kennedy on November 22nd. Vice President Lyndon B. Johnson had not been brought into the picture during the Diem crisis; when he assumed the presidency, just three weeks after Diem's murder, Johnson had little firsthand knowledge about the handling of Vietnam within the Kennedy administration in the weeks just before the coup in Saigon.

Tri Quang moved immediately to consolidate his gains. He demanded a wholesale purge of senior military officers and civil servants who had served Diem, regardless of their political views. Under this pressure, the new government led by General Duong Van Minh dismissed twenty-two high-ranking army officers on November 22nd, and 500 others, including many career civil servants, soon afterward.

The immediate post-Diem military junta, led by Cochinchinese generals trained in the French Army, lasted less than three months before it was overthrown in late January 1964 by General Nguyen Khanh, the plump goateed soldier who provided the United States with one of the most frustrating years of the war. Khanh kept on General Minh, Diem's popular former armed forces commander, as a figurehead chief of state but arrested four other senior generals in the junta on charges of secretly collaborating with the French to force a neutralist, Gaullist solution of the war. The charges were eventually dropped. Khanh, although a native southerner, came to power with no popular support except from a shortsighted element in the Vietnamese Army that wanted to seize control of the provincial administrations from Diem's old civil service. Largely because of Khanh's role in the coups against the Diem and Minh governments, he had bitterly alienated the all-important Cochinchinese educated middle class as well as the Roman Catholic refugees from Tonkin. Thus, in order to form a government, he had to fall back on a coalition of Tri Quang's Buddhists and the secret Dai Viet brotherhood, whose subsequent actions suggested to me that they jointly viewed Khanh as a transitional figure while preparing for an eventual seizure of power.

In early January, Tri Quang, given a free hand and the money he needed by Khanh, began strengthening his position. He invited leaders of eleven major Buddhist sects to a four-day convention in Saigon. A national Buddhist organization was established, the Unified Buddhist Church, which—contrary to the implications of its name—was largely an artificial and contrived organization from the start. The southern, or Cochinchinese, Buddhist sects, led by Dr. Mai Tho Truyen, a rich retired civil servant who ran Saigon's big Xa Loi Pagoda, withdrew from the organization and severed relations with Tri Quang in late 1964. Truyen barred Tri Quang's supporters from Xa Loi. This left the Unified Buddhist Church pretty much a paper organization with few actual members except in the Annamite cities of Hue and Danang and among a small Tonkinese refugee community in Saigon.

The Dai Viets also moved rapidly. Dr. Sung opened up *Chinh Luan,* which, helped by a generous issue of newsprint from other Dai Viets in the Khanh regime, quickly became the most influential Vietnamese daily. Sung's chief lieutenant, Bui Diem, began publishing the biggest English-language newspaper, the Saigon *Post.* Nguyen Cao Ky, an obscure air force colonel who had been running Saigon's relatively small city airport under Diem, was promoted to commander of the air force in January 1964; he gave himself the title of "Air Commodore," which he later changed to "Air Vice-Marshal." The previous air force commander, a colonel, fled to France. Other members of the brotherhood named by Van similarly moved up the ladder toward key positions of power in the army and civil service.

Having formalized his claim to be South Vietnam's No. 1 Buddhist leader, Tri Quang began moving on many fronts. He laid plans for a new Buddhist Van Hanh University in Saigon, to be financed by the Khanh regime. When it eventually opened in a pagoda near the Buddhist Institute, it attracted a thousand students by giving 80% of them passing marks in examinations, as compared with an average 20% at Saigon University. Van Hanh University soon became Tri Quang's second agitational center in the capital.

Tri Quang's seizure of Hue University was more elaborate. He first brought pressure on Khanh to appoint one of Tri Quang's own men as education minister. Then, after an agitational movement was launched among the students in Hue, Tri Quang had the minister order the rector to Saigon and force his resignation. The education minister then appointed himself rector and resigned from the government. Tri Quang's most important ally in this maneuver and his chief lay lieutenant in Hue was Dr. Le Khac Quyen, the dean of the medical faculty. Very soon after the highly respected Catholic rector was fired, university enrollment sharply declined as alarmed students transferred elsewhere.

Moving on another front, Tri Quang formed a "People's Revolutionary Committee" in Hue, which loudly professed to be anti-Communist. The committee then formed a new quasi-religious popular front called "the Popular Salvation Movement to Save Buddhism." Under the banner of a Buddhist religious revival, groups of militant youth were organized to storm through the villages of the five northernmost Annamite provinces, demanding that every district and village official who served under Diem be sacked. Using intimidation and threats, the movement managed to replace dozens of qualified and competent local officials by late 1964. When it became obvious to everyone that the movement was heavily penetrated with Viet Cong political cadres, Tri Quang disavowed it.

In the spring of 1964, Tri Quang also started a new weekly magazine in Hue that became progressively more critical of

General Khanh. Dealing in trade unionism as well, he pressed Khanh to arrest and try Tran Quoc Buu, the leader of the country's non-Communist Vietnamese Confederation of Labor, but the American Embassy intervened after pressure was brought by the AFL-CIO in Washington.

In midsummer, Tri Quang began a campaign to stir up religious strife between Buddhists and Catholics. Khanh's Military Court in Saigon sentenced Major Dang Sy, the Catholic deputy province chief during the Hue incident, to life imprisonment. Four other senior officials of the Diem government were given the same sentence without right of appeal. The offense: "persecution and killing of Buddhists." The next day, 35,000 Catholics staged a protest demonstration in Saigon.

The anti-Catholic trials suggested to many of us in Saigon that Khanh was now almost completely under Tri Quang's domination. But merely using Khanh as an instrument to carry out his designs apparently did not satisfy Tri Quang. In July, he threw his student agitators into the streets to demand that Khanh make good his pledges to establish a "more broadly based civilian government," conveniently ignoring the fact that Khanh's purges of Catholics and southerners from the government, at Tri Quang's insistence, had effectively alienated the majority of educated South Vietnamese.

It began to look as if Tri Quang were seeking Khanh's overthrow. The general reacted by trying to assume absolute power. Khanh made a ringing speech in downtown Saigon calling for a ground invasion of North Vietnam. *"Bac Tien!"* he shouted to the applause of a small claque of student supporters. "March to the north!" Then, using the Tonkin Gulf incident of August 2, 1964 as a pretext, Khanh placed the country under a state of emergency, including a curfew, ban on strikes and public meetings, press censorship, military trials without right of appeal, and arrests without warrant. A week later Khanh issued a new provisional constitution giving himself dictatorial powers. A military council of generals, which included a number of Dai Viets, approved the charter and made Khanh president. General Minh's post as chief of state was abolished.

Tri Quang then sprang his trap. He charged Khanh with being "a fascist dictator" and once again threw student mobs into the streets. Within nine days Khanh capitulated, quit the government, and fled to Dalat in a state of physical and mental collapse. This left South Vietnam between August 25th and November 1st in a state of anarchy. Organized government almost completely collapsed.

The most agonizing days came the last week of August as mobs of Buddhist and Catholic youths, carrying knives and clubs, roamed Saigon's streets. Thirteen died in riots one day, four more the next. Perhaps the most gruesome moment occurred when a Buddhist mob paraded a captured Catholic boy through the downtown streets and ritually murdered him in the central marketplace as unarmed police and troops stood by watching. Repeatedly stabbed with butcher knives by a group of maniacal little boys, the victim broke away and stumbled for a few steps on a broken leg, then fell. A bicycle was thrown on top of him and he was trampled to death. That same day I collapsed with hepatitis, which had abruptly reached the acute stage while I was running through the streets after the rioters. An American doctor insisted I fly out of Vietnam for hospitalization; rioters had seized several patients in Danang hospital that week and hanged them from trees with barbed wire. As I was paying my bill at the Caravelle Hotel the following morning, the entire fifth floor was blasted out by a terrorist bomb. I remember driving to Tan Son Nhut Airbase in a semidelirious state, past teen-age mobs and buses full of young men pouring in from the countryside. It seemed that all South Vietnam was going to pieces.

Three years later I was to ask Lieutenant Colonel Le Xuan Chuyen, the Tonkinese commander of the Viet Cong forces around Saigon at that time and later a defector, why he had not attacked the city that day. Chuyen replied, "The Viet Cong are very similar to good businessmen. Everything must be based on detailed calculations. We might have occupied Saigon, but what about the other provinces? Would they have followed? What if we failed? What if the Saigon people had not supported us? Our utmost secrets would have been known by the people and all our agents exposed. That would have been no good at all. Le Duan didn't want to gamble. He wanted to be sure of success."

As Le Duan was to later confirm, Hanoi was surprised by the

sudden and almost complete collapse of government in Saigon. But the South Vietnamese Army remained intact. In any event, Tri Quang abruptly called off his rioters and wrote General Khanh a letter pledging unity and support. In an interview, he told Robert Shaplen of *The New Yorker* magazine, "The revolution is not yet complete." Through September and October, the country was ruled by a troika of generals: Khanh, whom the Americans persuaded to return, Minh and a Roman Catholic, Tran Thien Khiem.

On September 13th, two Catholic generals, Lam Van Phat and Duong Van Duc, the Cochinchinese commander of the Mekong Delta forces, staged a bloodless coup. It collapsed within twenty-four hours when Khanh was backed by Ky's air force and paratroops loyal to Thi, the warlord of Annam. Two weeks later a High National Council, composed of seventeen elderly professional men, was installed to draft a provisional constitution and convene a constituent assembly. Its chairman was Tran Van Van, whom I then knew only as a Cochinchinese aristocrat and one of the six biggest landowners in the country.

Van miraculously pulled the country together. Under his influence, the council selected Phan Khac Suu, a respected snowy-haired agricultural engineer who had carried out Diem's land-reform program, as chief of state. At Van's behest, Suu named as his premier a former Saigon mayor named Tran Van Huong.

The American Embassy was embarrassed to find it had no biographical file on the new premier and no one had ever heard of him. Finally a Vietnamese switchboard operator could be found who remembered Huong. She described him as a plump, grey-haired old man with a fat stomach and the weathered face of a dock laborer. He was a common coolie's son, she said, from somewhere in the southern Delta, and had been the laughing stock of Saigon because when he was mayor he always rode to the prefecture on a bicycle.

No one knew it then, but here was the one man who still had a chance to save the country. Le Duan would learn not to underestimate him.

Four

The Northerners Seize Power

It was obvious that the situation of the war developed more rapidly than we had anticipated . . . we were not fully capable of making the puppet army disintegrate, really disintegrate, to an irretrievable extent.

—Le Duan, March 1966

Unlike the subtle sophisticates in Saigon, the Vietnamese peasant was plain, straight and conservative, a man with traditional and material drives. He wanted to own a few acres of rice land near his ancestral burial ground, build his house and rear his family. Once he had experienced Viet Cong rule, he knew what Communism meant to his wants and to the peasant as an individual.

Tran Van Huong was such a man. Much of the Dai Viets' power lay in their skillful exploitation of the Kennedy administration's belief that the wave of the future in Afro-Asia lay with the new revolutionary leadership. This was the philosophy put forward by such diverse men as Edward Lansdale, Bernard Fall, Roger Hilsman, the CIA's George Carver, Walt Rostow, Robert Shaplen. Most Americans in Vietnam were influenced by such ideas. We were troubled by the feeling that the United States refused to face up to the fact of the revolution itself, that, in Dr. Sung's phrase, the United States had indeed "never fought against the Communists with ideas of freedom and justice but only with bombs and dollars." But Huong saw the humbug in much of this thinking; the Vietnamese peasant did not want revolution so much as he wanted law and order, government that governed responsibly and a decent, normal life.

Huong's first public utterance as premier of South Vietnam attempted to demolish all such cant on revolution with a phrase; "I have never been a revolutionary," he said. "I am a law-abiding citizen." With a humility that was one of his enduring traits, this apostle of common sense told the press, "I'm not sure whether I should be congratulated or offered condolences. I promise my government will not indulge too much in politics but will try to stabilize the situation."

Tran Van Huong, then sixty, was the first Cochinchinese of peasant origin to come to power in Saigon. He had been born in a village in the Mekong Delta province of Vinh Long, the son of a day laborer and coolie; the family had no land. Huong was to remain poor all his life; at the time he assumed the premiership he had been living on a $60-a-month teacher's pension. Like all Asian peasantry, his father had great respect for education, and he was able to save enough to send his son to a small French *lycée* in Saigon, where Huong received a primary teacher's certificate in 1921. After two years as a teacher in his native province, Huong studied at a teacher's college in Hanoi, which then provided the only higher education in Vietnam. For the next twenty years he was an instructor in the French and Vietnamese languages and for a time was government inspector of primary schools in the upper Mekong Delta.

As with most Vietnamese, Huong's sense of nationalism was sharpened by World War II and the Japanese occupation. When the French returned after 1945, he refused all government teaching offers and took a succession of clerical and tutorial jobs to support his wife and two young sons. In 1945, Huong joined the National Party for Vietnamese Independence. Leading 150 young guerrillas, including many of his former students, he went to the Plain of Reeds outside Saigon to battle the French. When he learned that the Communist-led Viet Minh had seized control of his party and had jailed its leader, Huong withdrew his troops from the plain.

One of his sons remained with the Viet Minh guerrillas. He disappeared in 1946 and Huong never saw him again. The father assumed he was dead, but reports filtered back over the years, first that his son was living in Russia and then that he was a colonel with the Viet Cong forces. A second son developed tuberculosis and was sent to France. Huong himself was working in a Saigon pharmacy as a clerk when Ngo Dinh Diem chose him to be prefect, or mayor, of Saigon in 1954. Huong was later embarrassed by the legend of the bicycle-riding prefect. "It was a tale," he would say. "President Diem gave me a small car for my official transportation. I only used the bicycle to make private errands." After Huong's resignation as prefect, "because of my different political views from those of the president," in 1959 he joined, along with his Cochinchinese friends, Tran Van Van and Phan Khac Suu, what was called the Caravelle group. This was a band of eighteen eminent civilians who met in Saigon's then new and luxurious Caravelle Hotel to draft a protest to Diem against his autocratic policies. Most of its members had earlier served Diem as Cabinet ministers and advisers, and much of the criticism was constructive. The eighteen also included at least three well-known Dai Viets.

Signing this document led to Huong's arrest. When Diem brought the Caravelle group to trial in July 1963, Huong and the others were acquitted. Huong was working as a typist for the Vietnamese Dental Association when General Khanh again named him prefect of Saigon to restore order from the anarchy of August 1964. A few months later, Huong became premier of South Vietnam.

Huong made his maiden radio speech as premier on Halloween night 1964, startling many Saigonese with his tough tone. "Our youth have been driven to terrible degradation," he said, "and we ought to put an end to this. The government will not hesitate to take the necessary measures . . . in order to make young men realize their responsibility in taking part in this general struggle against the Communists." He vowed to break up the thriving Saigon black market and keep religion out of politics, an implicit warning to Tri Quang. But the main emphasis of his speech was on getting the Saigon government to govern: "We must improve and clean up government machinery, simplifying administrative procedure and cutting through red tape, giving local officials enough power to solve emergency problems."

That same night the Viet Cong launched their most destructive attack of the war thus far. Using six American-manufactured 81-mm. mortars to fire more than eighty shells, in thirty minutes they completely destroyed six B-57 bombers and severely damaged eight more at the big Binh Hoa Airbase near Saigon, killing four Americans and injuring seventy-two.

Huong assumed office just at the moment Hanoi had come close to achieving most of its military and political aims in General Giap's second "offensive guerrilla-warfare" phase. Militarily, as the villages began to encircle the towns, the South Vietnamese Army was being forced back to defend vital installations and communications, including bridges, oil depots, power lines and airfields. More and more troops were being deployed to garrison the forty-four provincial capitals and more than 200 district towns. After the Bien Hoa attack, General William C. Westmoreland, then chief of the U.S. Military Advisory Mission, spoke of "gaps in security"; static defense was becoming the rule, providing easier targets for guerrilla attacks and neutralizing the Vietnamese Army's offensive capacity. In many provincial and district towns, the government forces were unable to go outside defensive perimeters; as the Viet Cong's reaction to the August anarchy in Saigon suggested, Hanoi was not yet ready to march on the population centers. In government hands, these were still a useful source of supply to the Viet Cong, since they, too, lived off the national economy. Militarily, the guerrilla strategy of using the villages to encircle the towns was achieving its aim of making the still undefeated Vietnamese Army powerless to save the country. Politically, trade was slowing down in the countryside and prices of basic foods were beginning to rise in Saigon, causing the first signs of unrest in the slums. With the fall of Diem and the successive political crises of 1964, there had already been a severe loss of confidence in the Saigon government.

Thus Huong had come to power just as the critical strategic decision of the war faced the Politburo in North Vietnam. This may explain Hanoi's curious lack of effort to prevent the gradual formation of a Cochinchinese government in Saigon in September–October 1964, compared with the all-out Communist attempt to destroy Huong's regime that was to follow in November–December.

Hanoi, acting on the unforeseen sudden collapse of government in South Vietnam the previous August, had to decide whether to keep to classical Maoist principles of protracted war or throw in more troops in hopes of a quick kill. Once the decision was reached to reinforce the Viet Cong with regular northern combat units, as most authorities believe it was in October, Huong's government posed serious problems for Le Duan.

First, Huong was both a Cochinchinese and a stern Confucian moralist; there were no internal contradictions to exploit, and the man was almost impossible to discredit. Huong was also a tough-minded anti-Communist who would never allow his government to be induced to negotiate a ceasefire and accept a "neutralist" solution to end the war. He was believed to have some following within the Cochinchinese Viet Cong ranks in the Mekong Delta; at that time, the Viet Cong had a full-time standing army of around 30,000, but only some 10,000 soldiers and political commissars were reliable North Vietnamese who had been infiltrated south. When the moment of victory came, Hanoi would have to be absolutely sure it could control the Viet Cong; it would not want a popular and respected Cochinchinese leading the Saigon government then. I think it is fair to assume that Le Duan regarded Huong as a major obstacle to his plans and that in using Leninist tactics against him, he was taking a calculated risk of exposing his agents and their methods. Le Duan was to succeed, but just barely.

Two days after Huong formed a fifteen-member civilian Cabinet composed predominantly of Cochinchinese professional men who had remained aloof from politics since 1954, both the Saigon *Post* and *Chinh Luan,* as well as other Dai Viet and Buddhist-controlled newspapers, attacked Huong for excluding "politicians" from his government. It was the flimsiest issue they had yet come up with, but the New York *Times* reported it: "Most of the criticism centers on the feeling that Mr. Huong intentionally excluded leading spokesmen of movements, mostly

Buddhist. . . . In insisting on a separation between religion and politics, Premier Huong appears to have aroused those Buddhist groups which feel they should have a major role in government." The State Department, however, hailed the new Huong government as one genuinely "representative" of the South Vietnamese people and said the "way is now clear . . . to defeat the Viet Cong."

One of Tri Quang's supporters on the High National Council, the provisional legislature that had named Huong premier only a week before, now resigned in protest against the new Cabinet. He declared its members were divorced from "political realities" in that they were technicians, not politicians, and that a number had held posts under Diem. Such a government, he warned, "cannot win the confidence of the population." On this pretext, Tri Quang's student agitators took to the streets demanding that Huong's government step down.

Only six days after he had been sworn in, Huong had to announce a ban on street demonstrations and warn that his government would use force to put them down if necessary. The same day, General Khanh, who had remained as commander in chief of the armed forces, declared qualified support for Huong. Khanh said, "Only working in union can we defeat the danger of Communist dictatorship and the colonialists and foreigners who oppress our people and hinder us from becoming prosperous." But despite his August fall from power at Tri Quang's hands, Khanh appeared once again willing to cooperate with the Buddhists and Dai Viets. Sir Robert told me he thought Khanh still believed he could outsmart Tri Quang. "The man is an unmitigated disaster for South Vietnam," Sir Robert said, noting that Khanh's statement appeared to be a veiled attack on the United States. Tri Quang's student agitators continued their fitful street demonstrations, but they had no apparent popular support. Huong warned that students who broke the law would lose their two-year draft exemptions.

Meanwhile, Huong was diverted by the damage from heavy monsoon rains in Annam. The second week of November, floods inundated cities and hamlets in ten provinces along the central coast, killing an estimated 7,000 persons and leaving as many as 100,000 homeless. Communications were destroyed, the rice crop wiped out, and the armed junk fleet that patrolled the coast was severely damaged. This natural catastrophe was a bonanza to Hanoi. It created an enduring refugee problem and was exploited by Viet Cong propagandists who first attacked relief operations and then told the Annamite peasant victims they could expect no help from a Cochinchinese premier in Saigon.

On November 22, 1964, nearly 3,000 demonstrators, most of them destitute old women and street children, marched into downtown Saigon protesting the Huong government. They were led by Tri Quang's force of young agitators. General Pham Van Dong, the military governor of Saigon and a staunchly anti-Communist Tonkinese, ordered his troops to disperse the crowd with tear-gas bombs. The next day, in a veiled allusion, Huong accused "unscrupulous politicians" of instigating the demonstration.

Tri Quang then instigated child riots at several of Saigon's Buddhist-run schools. Hundreds of children would barricade themselves in their school buildings and throw stones at the police, or, in one instance, at American housewives shopping at Saigon's big American navy commissary. Covering these child riots was rather like watching an "Our Gang" film where the children suddenly run amok with stones and broken bottles. In one of these, I arrived at the school, reached by a narrow alleyway, just after both press and police had left. A mob of young Buddhist agitators was rampaging through the four-story school building, throwing books out windows and punching boys, while hundreds of students stood out on balconies which ringed the building, screaming for help at the top of their lungs. I had never heard anything like it. A teacher shouted down at me, *"Partez, monsieur, partez!"* He said the street urchins were trying to get the students to take out a protest demonstration against Huong and he had telephoned for troops. Before I could make it back to a taxi, a mob of boys came charging out of the school. A housewife riding along in a cycle-rickshaw provided a brief diversion; the mob chalked abuse of Huong on its canvas roof as the woman screamed hysterically and clung to her groceries. Then they came charging toward my taxi. We gained a moment or two when a jeepload of policemen turned into the alley, and the mob, howling with excitement, rushed toward them. The police jeep sped in reverse and shot back down the alley. The boys returned and pounded the taxi with their fists. My protests of *"Bao chi* [newsman]!" inspired one baleful child to throw a rock, which thudded against the roof. At that moment, a truckload of Vietnamese marines appeared at the end of the alleyway and the boys scattered in every direction. It was ludicrous, preposterous and dangerous. But hardly a threat to the state. Yet such riots were seriously reported on the world's front pages and were eventually to be used by General Khanh as a pretext to oust Huong's government on the grounds it could not preserve law and order.

There was only one serious demonstration against Huong's government. On Sunday night, November 29th, the Buddhists held a funeral procession for a fifteen-year-old youth whom Tri Quang claimed had been shot by troops breaking up a street demonstration. The government claimed that the youth was shot from behind by a Buddhist agitator. A truck in the procession was found to contain knives, clubs and grenades and was seized by the police. Most of the mourners were Tri Quang's professional agitators, whose faces were by now familiar to us. When the funeral procession refused to heed orders to disperse, paratroopers swung into the crowd with rifle butts and fired two shots in the air. The soldiers then put the victim's family inside the hearse and escorted them to the cemetery, much to their relief. An hour later General Dong announced in a communiqué that he had conclusive evidence the Viet Cong were involved in the funeral procession. Huong went on the air to appeal for public support in putting down demonstrations inspired by the Communists.

In an interview with Marguerite Higgins in early 1965, Huong spelled this out: "Thich Tri Quang is very clever. One has to be very careful with him. He acts like a Communist. He talks like a Communist. The things he does help the Communists. But you Americans want absolute proof. And evidence is not the same as absolute proof. We can prove that Thich Tri Quang held a secret meeting with Viet Cong leaders near Cap Saint Jacques [also known as Vung Tau]. But Thich Tri Quang is capable of saying that he was down there trying to convert the Communists to Buddhism—and some people will believe him. He has convinced some of the more naïve of our young generals that he is merely trying to advance the cause of militant Buddhism. He intrigues very skillfully with the more ambitious young generals, setting one against the other and inciting them against me. Indeed, many Vietnamese generals court Thich Tri Quang's favors because they imagine him to have some special power over the Americans. Thich Tri Quang owes a great deal to the Americans. In 1963 in the drive against Diem, he fooled the Americans into thinking he could speak for a lot more Vietnamese than was the case. Thich Tri Quang's followers number no more than a few thousand, and they are mostly Buddhist youth. But the mere fact that the American Embassy convinced itself that his power was real gave him stature.

"Sometimes the Americans act as if Thich Tri Quang was a shadow government. Some of your officials are forever pressuring me into making concessions to him to gain his favor. The fact that one-sided concessions to Thich Tri Quang will only generate counterdemands from other groups seems to escape these Americans. Some at the Embassy are disillusioned now with Thich Tri Quang but fear to say so out loud; they do not want to be called anti-Buddhist. Would they support me if I had Thich Tri Quang arrested on charges of treason? In any case, it is not just a simple matter of dealing with Thich Tri Quang. It is a matter of dealing with world opinion, the American Embassy, and some Vietnamese generals who seek to enhance their position by gaining this monk's favor. He works in the shadows. He is not easy to deal with."

In late November, Huong declared a state of siege in Saigon, closing all schools, prohibiting all public' meetings and giving wide powers to General Dong to search and arrest without warrant. In this, Huong appeared to have wide support from the Saigonese, who on other occasions were angered by such measures. Lacking any genuine grievance, Tri Quang's Buddhists were unable to produce any manifestation of popular support. By his firm behavior, Huong had come close to showing, at least in Saigon, what an unrepresentative and sinister minority the Tri Quang Buddhists really were. I believe that had they continued to demonstrate against Huong alone, the Buddhists would have found themselves increasingly isolated. And Huong was not vulnerable to character assassination, as the Ngo family had been. The line the Dai Viets took, spread in conversations with American officials and journalists, was that Huong was too old and not very bright. It was repeated more than once by some senior American officials, including Barry Zorthian, the mission's chief press spokesman. But it was not convincing to anyone who had ever met Huong.

So, instead, the forces against Huong turned to a more politically vulnerable target, the American ambassador, Maxwell Davenport Taylor, who had replaced Henry Cabot Lodge in July. Taylor had just returned from Washington, where he had urged President Johnson to begin bombing North Vietnam without further delay. Tri Quang, who appeared to have calculated that Taylor had a great stake in the survival of the Huong government (Johnson had made stability in Saigon a precondition for northern air strikes), at once issued a communiqué demanding that the United States withdraw support from Huong if it "still wants to be trusted by the Vietnamese people."

President Johnson's appointment of Taylor had had a certain inevitability. Taylor had already played a part in shaping American strategy in Vietnam. As Army Chief of Staff in 1959, he had opposed President Eisenhower's plan to reduce army strength and rely primarily on nuclear weapons. Taylor resigned and wrote the highly polemical book *The Uncertain Trumpet,* outlining his strategy of "flexible response" as opposed to the Eisenhower doctrine of "massive retaliation." This paralleled the great debate in the Communist world over "peaceful coexistence" and support for "wars of national liberation."

Taylor's views impressed Senator John F. Kennedy, and after Kennedy was elected president he appointed Taylor to work with his brother, Attorney General Robert Kennedy, and CIA Chief Allen Dulles in an investigation of the April 1961 Bay of Pigs disaster. The following June, Taylor joined the White House staff as Kennedy's special military adviser; he was a strong advocate of substantially increasing the role of the Pentagon and downgrading that of such civilian agencies as the State Department and Central Intelligence Agency in future U.S. counterinsurgency efforts.

In November 1961, Taylor made his first trip to Saigon. His

recommendations led to a significant curtailment of civilian countersubversion operations in Saigon and to Kennedy's decision to commit large numbers of American military advisers into the battle against the Viet Cong guerrillas, which then had an officially estimated strength of around 5,000. (By the end of 1964, midway through Taylor's year-long tour as ambassador, this had grown to an estimated 30,000 hard-core Viet Cong, another 80,000 farmer-guerrillas and a force of about 25,000 political cadres. By then there were roughly 25,000 American military personnel in Vietnam, of whom around twenty were of general's rank. The bulk of these Americans were professional soldiers. But as 1964 ended, some draftees were beginning to appear, including those in such hazardous assignments as helicopter gunners.) Taylor also recommended in 1961 a broad military, economic and political counterinsurgency drive, largely to be directed by the Pentagon and sustained with U.S. manpower, money and weapons, and helicopters to provide mobility. Taylor's basic strategy, although expanded and adapted by Defense Secretary McNamara in Washington and General Westmoreland in the field, was, in the main, followed in Vietnam for the next seven years. Then, in January 1962, President Kennedy appointed Taylor to head a special group to develop American doctrine to counter Communist "wars of national liberation" anywhere in the world. The doctrine that emerged, with its emphasis on the military rather than political aspects of counterinsurgency, bore Taylor's personal stamp.

Thus, after the collapse of the Diem government, when it seemed to Washington that a fresh start could be made, Taylor appeared eminently qualified to be ambassador. Taylor's original 1961 program, which had been combined with Diem's British-advised strategic-hamlet program, badly needed reorganization; moreover, General Khanh seemed to have few positive plans for running the government or waging the war.

When he arrived in Saigon in July 1964, Taylor told the Vietnamese, "I'm here to assure you of our unstinting support. There is no time limit to our commitment. I have great respect for General Khanh." From the first Taylor tried to follow a dignified, hands-off policy toward Vietnamese politics. He was not demonstrative, and in only a short time a personal coolness between himself and Khanh developed into open hostility over U.S. policy, especially after Khanh called for a march north and tried to assume dictatorial powers. Taylor established more cordial relations with Huong, but, as an Embassy aide was to tell me toward the end of Taylor's tour, there were few occasions when the ambassador asked Huong "what his problems really were and how he could help him." But with Huong in the saddle, Taylor felt confident he could at last give his attention to pacifying the countryside.

In Washington that November, Taylor had found President Johnson worried about the "consequences of getting American troops into a war with 700,000,000 Chinese." But the President had agreed "in principle" to a limited expansion of the war provided a stable government could be maintained in Saigon.

The day after Taylor's return, Huong announced that the United States was extending additional military and economic aid to South Vietnam to "strengthen its air defenses," increase the number of men under arms by 100,000 more than the existing force of 615,000 and "accelerate economic and rural development." Huong also announced joint U.S.–Vietnamese planning was under way "to achieve greater effectiveness against the infiltration threat." At this point, the United States had committed about 22,000 American military personnel.

Two weeks before Christmas, 300 miles north of Saigon, a Viet Cong regiment overwhelmed a government fortress and captured the strategic valley of An Lao, the main supply corridor between the Communist Do Xa headquarters in Annam's Quang Ngai Province and the populated coast. An American adviser who survived said the battle was "like the worst days of the Korean war. All the ingredients were there, the miserable rainy weather, the sticky mud, the awful oily stench of napalm and death, and the seemingly senseless assaults of Communist human waves to capture barren hills." Although it was not evident at the time, this was the beginning of Giap's "glorious counteroffensive," the shift from guerrilla warfare to the third and final phase of a war of movement.

Five days later, Ambassador Taylor was awakened by a telephone call at 5:30 A.M. A junior Vietnamese army officer was on the phone. He informed Taylor that during the night the army had dissolved the provisional legislature (the High National Council), had arrested Tran Van Van and four others, and had taken them to the remote mountain town of Pleiku. Fifteen other "political agitators" (most of them prominent Cochinchinese) had been arrested. He assured Taylor that Huong was still premier. The action had been carried out by General Nguyen Chanh Thi, the moustached military governor of Annam, and Nguyen Cao Ky, the air force commander. (Unlike Ky, Thi, as I was to learn later, was not a Dai Viet but was subject to their manipulation through his friend and adviser Colonel Lieu.)

In midafternoon, Thi, looking like Hollywood's idea of a fierce Asian pirate, said the arrested council had been dominated by Tran Van Van, who, according to Thi, had led the opposition to a scheme proposed by himself and Ky for compulsory retirement of all generals after twenty-five years of service. Though he did not say so, the target of the "Young Turk" generals, as the Thi-Ky military faction was inevitably dubbed by the press, was clearly the veteran General Dong (Huong's invaluable ally in maintaining law and order against the Buddhist rioters in Saigon), as well as other staunchly anti-Communist senior Cochinchinese generals. Thi accused the council of "frustrating conciliation with the Buddhists" by refusing to expand their membership to allow more of Tri Quang's supporters in. Thi claimed that both Huong and the elderly chief of state, Phan Khac Suu, had agreed to the dissolution of the council. This was a clear untruth; both had been informed of the generals' action after the event and had violently protested the arrest of their ally Van, who had been chiefly responsible for installing them in office. I called Huong, who said he had been notified of the arrests at one o'clock at night by General Khanh. When Khanh asked him if he would remain as premier, Huong told me he had said, "I'll think it over." Huong explained that morally he should resign in protest, but he feared that was just what Tri Quang intended him to do. Not surprisingly, Tri Quang called off a scheduled protest march against Huong and told his followers to "return home and await further orders."

Ambassador Taylor was furious. He advised Huong to defy the purge and summoned Khanh, Thi and Ky, and the fourth-highest ranking general, Nguyen Huu Co, to his office. As Taylor later described the meeting, "I talked in very blunt terms that, soldier to soldier, should have been understood. I said the United States was not going to throw good money after bad in Vietnam. We have a clear record of the meeting, and if it is ever needed it will be available. I did not ask Khanh to get out of Vietnam. At one point, Khanh said, 'Do you think it would be helpful if I ceased to be commander in chief?' I said, 'Yes.' Khanh put the whole thing together, whipping up the Young Turks. Only a few generals, five or six, were involved. Khanh was specifically responsible. Some of them, Thi and Ky especially, are dangerous to the point of being mentally unbalanced. Ky threatened to bomb Hanoi if the United States cut off aid. Khanh's just a queer fellow. He's capable and energetic but I think if you took him apart you couldn't find a principle in his entire makeup."

Taylor's deputy, Ambassador U. Alexis Johnson, described the meeting as carried on in "pidgin English and fractured French." No interpreter was present. General Thi, who spoke little English, claimed that Taylor had said, "The United States is not going to throw pearls to swine," a gross and calculated misrepresentation. Khanh told everybody that Taylor wanted him to pack up and leave the country.

The next day Khanh called Beverly Deepe, correspondent for the New York *Herald Tribune,* to his house and told her in an on-the-record interview that Taylor had engaged in "activities beyond imagination." He said, "If Taylor does not act more intelligently, the United States will lose Southeast Asia and we will lose our freedom." Vietnam could not be made over "in the image of the United States," he went on. "Taylor is not serving his country well."

Khanh went on the radio to attack the Americans officially in an order of the day to the Vietnamese armed forces: "We make sacrifices for the country's independence and the Vietnamese people's liberty, not to carry out the policy of any foreign country." He defended the purge of the High National Council on the grounds that it had been "exploited by counterrevolutionary elements who placed partisan considerations above the homeland's sacred interest." This was apparently a reference to Tran Van Van's aristocratic and wealthy background and his staunch defense of the Cochinchinese majority's right to choose its own government. As Taylor said, General Khanh was cornered now and utterly unscrupulous.

Khanh insisted that the Vietnamese army command retained the right of "acting as an intermediary to settle all disputes and differences if they create a situation favorable to the common enemies—Communism and colonialism. Better," he shouted, "to live poor but proud as free citizens of an independent country rather than in ease and shame as slaves of foreigners and Communists!" The Viet Cong's clandestine radio came right in on cue: "Khanh's speech is new proof of the fascist and dictatorial aspect of the American puppets in Saigon."

Taylor suspended discussions with the Saigon government on moves to expand the war and reduce mounting infiltration from North Vietnam. Instead the Embassy issued a statement: "A duly constituted government exercising power on the basis of national unity and without interference from any group is the essential condition for prosecuting the anti-Communist struggle and the basis of American support." The United States was belatedly standing for legality. In Washington, Secretary of State Rusk said that Taylor "speaks for the government of his country."

Two days after the purge, Taylor and U. Alexis Johnson met Khanh alone. "If I do step down as commander in chief," Khanh said, "are you prepared to defray my expenses abroad, including travel in the United States?" Taylor said yes. "Could this include some other generals, too?" Khanh wanted to know. Later in the day, Khanh telephoned Taylor to say, "I can't give you a definite answer yet."

The next day Taylor met a dozen American correspondents in the Embassy conference room. "The fighting is going on in four fronts," he said. "The government versus the generals, the Buddhists versus the government, the generals versus the ambassador, and, I hope, the generals versus the VC." As Taylor analyzed the situation, the young generals had thrown out the only thing resembling a legal repository of South Vietnamese sovereignty, leaving the United States no choice but to temporarily suspend further military and economic aid:

"The generals have the patriotic but childish attitude they can come in and break the crockery and then let someone else pick it up. If Huong accepts the generals' conditions, his position would be untenable, and he would have no other choice but to resign. We cannot continue very long on this patchwork basis. It is time for a showdown as to whether or not the government controls the armed forces in this country. . . .

"The day before yesterday the generals decided to launch an anti-Taylor campaign, and that's what they're doing. I'm not prepared to consider going home. I came back from Washington with an additional package of aid. But we can't use it until we see how much of this crockery can be put together. Hopefully, as time moves on and people stand back from the event, they will see Khanh's role is not in South Vietnam's interest. The important items, aircraft and additional helicopters, are not due to arrive for a month; until then we don't have to make any deliveries under the new program.

"Huong, if he's wise, would resign. Or he can bow down. He might try to temporize since he's afraid, physically afraid, of the Buddhists. Clearly, this is what keeps him awake at night. There's a tendency at home to keep going no matter what. Basically, Huong can do three things: First, he can sit and be the army's puppet. Second, he can resign and automatically bring in the military. That would get them right back in the chair where they have to assume responsibility. As opposed to having a civilian puppet government with the military in the rear, it's better to put the military out front where they can be counted. The best thing would be if Huong got up and said, 'It is my intention to maintain civilian government and carry out authority. The army will be under the government and fully supported by the government against the VC.' Then he'd be in the driver's seat."

I went directly from the Embassy that day in late December to Sir Robert Thompson's villa near the Presidential Palace. Until he left for England in mid-1965, I sought Sir Robert's views during every crisis; he was the wisest, most experienced Western observer in Vietnam, save possibly for his equally brilliant aide, Dennis Duncanson, and I was greatly indebted to them for giving me an early understanding of the political nature of the war. Both were forceful advocates of putting top priority not on the military aspect, as Taylor had done, but on the problem of subversion. Sir Robert was the first to say that it was irrelevant whether or not Tri Quang was a Communist, for he was certainly the enemy of everything the United States was trying to accomplish in Vietnam. To Sir Robert it was folly not to act accordingly.

Sir Robert interpreted the generals' dissolution of the High National Council as "a surface reflection of the army consolidating power in the countryside, particularly to destroy the growth of civilian power in the provinces."

"We are getting very close to the August–September situation again," he went on. "The military has chosen to demonstrate it is the real basis of political power. The Americans have only themselves to blame. It is American policy in Vietnam that has allowed people like Khanh to get where they are by creating such a big conventional army. One should have built up the civil government apace with the army, especially a civil-controlled police force as a counterbalance."

I told him about Taylor's scene with the generals.

"Ky had better not bomb Hanoi. God knows what would happen in Saigon. Of the four generals, Co is the most reliable, a solid citizen and the most highly qualified soldier. But these so-called Young Turks are practically all in their thirties and as military commanders have fought no significant battles. They want power and the VC are a very tough nut to crack, so they turn on their lesser enemies. When you get down to that age group, you are quite likely to run into people whose mentality is such they can be brought over to work for the VC and think they're being patriotic doing it. In young men like Ky and Thi, with a fascist mentality, it's fairly easy to switch to Communism. Hundreds of young officers did in China."

"Are we losing the war?" I asked.

"Damn close. It's going exactly the way the Communists planned it. It's a protracted struggle, but when you start going downhill you gather speed. Everything can end this way. Two things can happen. An erosion of the authority of government and a split in the armed forces. If these two things occur, the National Liberation Front is more or less in. The government is already badly eroded, especially Huong's authority. Huong says wait until I ring Thi and Thi says wait until I ring Ky and Co.

There's no decision-making power. I think we depend very much on the character and integrity of Huong, the one bright spot in all of this. If the army takes over, it gives Tri Quang the chance to take an antifascist line again. But it's a fallacy that a guerrilla war has to go into a war of movement to win. It only happened in China. It's quite possible the Embassy would be notified by telephone at five-thirty some morning, 'We've negotiated a ceasefire. Please withdraw all American military personnel within the next six months.'

"We've got to the stage in the war now where any peak of activity becomes the maximum peak. There's a steady deterioration, but when it hits the bottom, it's something that could sit on the bottom a long time. The Vietnamese Army may be powerless to save the country, but it's undefeated. The VC can't take over the cities until the army is split in some way. The only other thing besides Huong that we've really got working for us is the peasant, the peasant in the army, the village militia, holding on. He knows what the VC represent, and he's not going to give up so easily. The most conspicuous and consistent thread in American policy has been to pursue the course familiar in Korea, viewing Vietnam as a length of trench in the cold war front. One institution in Korea was that of a huge army. But once it's created, it challenges the civilian government. There's no corps-level fighting in this war; there's barely divisional fighting. There's nothing for most of the generals to do but get involved in politics. But it's really frightening to think young men like Thi or Ky might take over."

The terror campaign began three days later, on Christmas Eve. One moment the elegant shops and cafés along the Rue Catinat were crowded with shoppers, and people hurried by carrying papier-mâché manger scenes and poinsettia plants; the next moment downtown Saigon inexplicably flew apart.

The streets were showered with glass, and everywhere people fell to the pavement. Thick clouds of yellow smoke rose from a fiery mass in the center of the Brink Hotel, a downtown American officers' billet. Outside, in a parking lot, cars were exploding like mortar shells, and Vietnamese and Americans with blood running down their faces and arms poured out into the street. The screams were drowned out by sirens of police cars, the bells of ambulances and fire engines. Glass and debris were scattered across Lam Son Square in front of the opera house and the Continental. Mobs of people ran in all directions. A tall American soldier just in front of me suddenly lunged around and shouted at the Vietnamese, "There's your goddamn VC!"

A dazed blond navy nurse was standing by the hotel's gate, unaware her arm was bleeding. "I was just going out the door with my Christmas presents," she said. "My God, I was standing right in the door." Blood-soaked bodies were carried by on stretchers. Someone shouted to stand back; there might be another bomb inside. The hotel's entire ground floor had been blown out except for the steel girders, and the blast had torn a hole straight up three floors over the garage where a dynamite-packed car had been parked. One man with a bandaged head kept moaning, "I was in there." Two Vietnamese girls in waitress uniforms were crying hysterically at the gate as a young American soldier kept reassuring them that everyone was out of the building. The armed forces radio station, which had been playing Christmas carols all day, was a mass of wreckage. Toward the back of the crowd, I saw General Khanh, staring at the building with an impassive face.

The ceiling plaster in my room next door at the Continental had fallen, coating everything with white dust and rubble. The water pipes and electric wiring were severed, but a servant brought candles and I cleared the debris off my desk to file a cable. American military police with submachine guns were guarding the downstairs foyer, and the whole of Lam Son Square was cordoned off with concertina wire. I stood on the balcony and watched the body of a little girl who was still alive being dug out from the rubble of the servants' quarters. The bells of Saigon's Roman Catholic basilica were playing for the Christmas Eve Mass.

Huong managed to stay in power three more weeks. General Dong called on Saigon's people to "remain calm and not let yourselves be fooled by the insidious plots of the Communists." Dong said, "Dissatisfaction is a sign of democracy, but once again I wish to remind you that democracy is not anarchy."

It was Washington that first began to buckle. Secretary of State Rusk warned that there were "certain kinds of assistance that are simply not feasible" if instability persisted in Saigon.

But Rusk reaffirmed American support of the South Vietnamese war effort on the grounds that Southeast Asia would be lost to the Communists if the United States ceased its aid. In mid-January 1965, Taylor, at Washington's urging and against Huong's advice, invited Tri Quang to the Embassy in a futile attempt to reason with the monk.

Huong was clearly at bay now, appealing to the population to ignore "malevolent lies by extremist elements to serve their own interests." On January 18th, he was forced to reshuffle his government and take four young generals, including Ky, into his hitherto all-civilian Cabinet. Tri Quang kept up the pressure against Taylor. Rioters sacked the American library in Hue, burning 8,000 books. In Saigon, small crowds of monks and nuns stoned the American press center and screamed in front of the Embassy, "Taylor is killing Buddhists!" The self-immolations began again when the Buddhists claimed that a seventeen-year-old schoolgirl in Nha Trang burned herself to death to protest Taylor's policies.

Huong made one last desperate appeal over Saigon radio that all violence come to an end, warning that if South Vietnam were "taken over by hoodlums," they would "hand it over to the Viet Cong and their masters, the Chinese Communists." He concluded, "In this solemn hour, the life of the nation is in the people's hands." But most of the Vietnamese people were only dimly aware of what was happening at the political center in Saigon. They were more preoccupied by the sharp increase in Viet Cong attacks.

A young American lieutenant almost literally heralded the new phase of the war on New Year's Eve. Stationed near the Catholic refugee settlement of Binh Gia, southeast of Saigon, he first spotted some approaching Viet Cong through his binoculars 1,000 yards away. They advanced slowly and deliberately and announced their presence with bugles. They were dressed in khaki uniforms, field gear and steel helmets.

"Those aren't Viet Cong guerrillas, they're regular troops. Bring in more air!" the lieutenant shouted over his radio just before it was shot off his back. A Vietnamese Marine battalion, arriving to reinforce the settlement, was ambushed and almost completely wiped out.

As Giap moved into his counteroffensive to crush the South

Vietnamese Army and as Viet Cong terror and Buddhist hysteria generated an atmosphere of blood and tension in Saigon, it was becoming increasingly clear that the alternatives were either an outright victory for the Communists or the United States' own major involvement in the fighting.

Five

The Killing at Tan Buu

Since the Binh Gia battle, the puppet army suffered continued and extremely serious defeats . . . the most important thing is that we must continue to basically annihilate the puppet army.

—Le Duan, March 1966

Graham Greene once wrote that there is a point of no return unremarked at the time in most lives. I think few of us in Vietnam in early 1965 knew it when it came or that for ourselves and the United States everything had permanently changed.

Certainly I was quite unaware of anything fateful approaching that January evening as I stood with a laconic young American captain on the porch of a Delta farmhouse; we were watching Vietnamese peasants harvest their rice in fields golden under the late, flat sun. Little naked boys rode buffaloes through a water ditch, and a flock of skittish white ducks paddled in and out of fragile fishermen's cranes. At that period, in the ninth month of my stay in Vietnam, I still thought winning the war in the rural countryside was just a question of having the needed drive, determination and red corpuscles: just pour in enough fertilizer sacks, money and manpower, and you had it licked. I did not feel involved with the Vietnamese themselves, and had even written an article suggesting that if the United States intended to withdraw its advisers and support from South Vietnam it had better start paving the diplomatic ground for it. I looked forward to reassignment elsewhere in a few months' time.

"It looks peaceful, don't it?" the captain said. He was a tough Italian-American professional named Emacio from Coeur d'Alene, Idaho.

Behind us in the farmhouse Emacio had borrowed for a command center that afternoon, a courteous old Vietnamese padded back and forth, pouring tea into his best porcelain cups. The porch was fragrant with orange bougainvillea and burning joss sticks in memory of the family's dead ancestors. I thought Vietnam very beautiful in those days.

Emacio's eyes followed five men in pointed hats and black trousers walking north along the muddy country road. "They could be Communist guerrillas, perhaps massing for an attack on us tonight. Or just rice farmers going home from the fields. You never know. Some of the villagers do know, but they're afraid to tell us. Afraid we aren't here to stay and when we leave the Viet Cong will kill or torture them. First, we've got to win their loyalty by helping them teach their children and giving them medicine and making them feel they're always going to be protected from Communist reprisals. I think then we'll have it licked. But it's going to take a long time."

There had been intelligence reports that day that the Viet Cong might be massing in the countryside for an attack on the little Delta town of Thu Thua, where I was spending the night with Emacio's militia unit. The district chief had sent two patrols of local militiamen out to sweep the swampy mangrove jungle along the riverbank south of town. But now, after two hours, they came straggling back in their ragtag floppy hats and tattered peasant pajamas, two single files across the paddy dikes, some of them with chickens and fresh cabbages slung across their shoulders.

I had flown down by helicopter from Saigon that morning. The province, Long An, was perhaps the most strategic of all the country's forty-four provinces, reaching as it did from the wilderness of mangrove swamps along the Saigon River to the

South China Sea on the north and to the desolate Plain of Reeds on the Cambodian border to the west. From 2,000 feet the feeling of serenity and permanence of the vast expanse of Delta rice lands seemed to deny the existence of a war: endless vivid green and golden fields, the grey mirrors of flooded paddy, the pale green of sugar cane and darker green of banana and pineapple groves and the treelines along the canals where the houses were. Looking closer over the shoulders of the two American door gunners, helmeted like Martians, with their machine guns poised to return sniper fire, I could see entire abandoned settlements, their rooftops gaping holes, collapsed mud walls ripped apart by artillery fire, charred ruins of what had once been villages and homes.

These were the late President Ngo Dinh Diem's strategic hamlets. Beginning in March 1962, Diem, with the help of Malayan-experienced British advisers led by Sir Robert Thompson, had managed to regroup the thousand village communities in Long An into 220 fortified hamlets. (A "hamlet" in Vietnam is a community of around 2,000 people living in what Americans would call a village; a "village" in the Vietnamese context is an administrative unit comprising four or five hamlets.) In little more than a year Diem had isolated the Viet Cong into a remaining thirty-five. Although the Communist reaction had been negligible at first, the cracks in the hastily applied program began to show. An attempt was under way to rectify them in the summer of 1963 when the Buddhists in Hue began their campaign accusing Diem of religious persecution and the Viet Cong in the Delta launched an all-out campaign to smash the strategic hamlets. Roads were mined, bridges blown up, fences torn down. Diem's schools and clinics were destroyed and the peasants ordered to go back to their old homes. Hamlet militia posts were attacked and weapons lost to the Viet Cong. The final blow to the central government's attempt to put down civil insurrection in the Delta came with the murder of Diem himself in the *coup d'état* of November 1, 1963.

Throughout 1964, there had been a steady loss of population to the Viet Cong movement as the succession of weak and unstable post-Diem governments, lacking administrative wherewithal after a wholesale purge of government officials who had served Diem, were paralyzed into inaction. In early 1964, there were 219 strategic hamlets left in Long An Province; now, as 1965 began, only twenty-four were left. The villages were beginning to encircle the towns, in apparent validation of Mao Tse-tung's thesis of a people's revolutionary war.

A new pacification plan called "Hop Tac" (the Vietnamese phrase for "togetherness") had been under way since September 1964 to try to break the Communists' growing stranglehold on Saigon. It was to be carried out under a new orderly schedule of priorities for fortifying villages in the seven provinces ringing the capital city. The tactical principle was to arm all the hamlets in a fan-shaped fashion radiating from the capital city's suburbs to less secure rural areas, to provide mutual protection and easy reinforcement. In the "pacified zone" the Viet Cong military force, but not the political underground, had been theoretically eliminated; its people were being equipped with farm tools, medicines, schools and seeds to rebuild what were now officially called "New Life" hamlets.

The helicopter had spiraled down rapidly over Tan An that morning; too gradual descent would risk Viet Cong rifle fire from the outlying hamlets. A steady stream of civilian traffic flowed down the grey ribbon of Highway Four, the lifeline carrying 2,000,000 tons of rice into Saigon each year. Barges moved slowly up and down the coppery Occidental and Oriental rivers toward the capital. But for Americans, only in the air was there a real measure of security. Even so, the week before a helicopter had been shot down from 1,500 feet.

A swarthy American major who introduced himself as Connick was waiting with a jeep to drive me to Thu Thua. Tan An, the provincial capital, resembled an American county seat; the market was crowded with processions of cycle-rickshaws moving at their easy pace and a gang of children playing war games. Only a few villas in the town—the provincial headquarters and those occupied by American military advisers—were fortified with barbed wire and Vietnamese civil policemen in tight-fitting white uniforms. Connick called them "the white mice."

But out of town, every village became a fortress, although deceptively calm. Barefoot, copper-skinned farmers with patient, strained faces looked up as we drove by. Most were working in rolled-up black pajamas and pointed straw hats, sloshing knee-deep in mud behind huge, mud-caked black water buffaloes. Laughing naked children played along the muddy road, and hairy black pigs rooted in the ditches. Each village was encircled by a barbed-wire fence; some had moats around them filled with hundreds of sharply pointed bamboo spikes.

Connick said that while the hamlets looked safe by day, the Viet Cong made them hostile targets at night. Wires were clipped; loudspeakers blared forth propaganda and threats from the darkness of the fields. He said the peasants ignored the propaganda but were becoming terrified by a rapid rise in Viet Cong atrocities. He pointed out one hamlet, just beyond Tan An town, where the Viet Cong had crept in one night to behead the young village chief. His body was found in a paddy the next day, and a small boy brought the man's head, in a straw basket, face up, back to his family.

Farther on, our jeep passed the ruins of a small French fort, a crumbled whitewashed structure that looked as if it came out of "Beau Geste." Connick said that it had been overrun by the Viet Cong, who killed all seventeen defenders in less than ten minutes before reinforcements could arrive. The previous April, guerrillas had entered the town itself at night and kidnaped fourteen *"hoi chanhs."* These were defectors who had surrendered to the government side; their camps were a constant Viet Cong target.

We stopped briefly at a new defection center, this time built outside town. A score of peasant youths, most of them still teenagers, squatted in black pajamas under a thatched roofed shed. They described the Viet Cong as the "resistance" or as "liberators" who told them the Americans brought many weapons to their country and wanted Vietnamese to kill Vietnamese. One boy said he had been told that Americans raped Vietnamese women and ate infant children. I offered them cigarettes and each took one with a grin.

As we drove on, Connick explained that things were changing. His American advisory team was getting the local Vietnamese commander to tear down the old French outposts and form mobile patrols for night operations. They were trying to get more villagers into fortified hamlets, without affronting them or failing to give them real protection. He was worried, though, about the decline of morale in the police and local militia force. They were suffering heavier casualties and a loss of weapons lately; recruiting had fallen off and many units were under-strength. The local Viet Cong were now using terror tactics to reduce morale still further. In July 1964, they had attacked a civil guard post at Cai Be, just twenty-five miles to the south, while most of a company was out on patrol. Forty women and children had been killed, including the wife and all five young children of the company commander.

I told Connick I had flown down to Cai Be from Saigon right after the attack. The battle was over by then, and there was only a roar of rocket and machine-gun fire from a distant treeline. The scene of the slaughter was a field of rubble and smoldering ashes, with a few flames still burning palely in the sunshine and the stench of burned flesh. A constant buzzing of flies filled the air.

The company commander, bent like an old man, was barely coherent as he told how the bamboo huts and brick houses of his company's family quarters were demolished in sudden, surprise mortar bursts in the night. As he spoke to newsmen, he stood beside the crude wooden coffins of his wife and children in a kind of vigil. He had lost everything.

Four green-clad Vietnamese soldiers were scooping up the charred remains of unidentified bodies into a straw mat and carrying it across a dirt road to the village schoolhouse. Inside lay the bodies of a dozen naked little boys and girls. Except that their faces were encrusted with mud and ashes, they might have been sleeping.

Across the road, living children, barefoot and still wearing striped and flowered pajamas, dug into the ashes along with their parents, looking for valued household possessions: lamps, cooking stoves, mirrors and straw sleeping mats. Scattered around were blackened steel helmets, pans of rice and charred chopsticks, and what looked like unexploded mortars and grenades. Beyond a grove of coconut palms, lying sprawled among the young green rice shoots, was the anonymous corpse of a Viet Cong guerrilla. His face, spattered with blood and grime, was as young as a schoolboy's.

A few hundred yards away, the village of Cai Be was untouched. Sampans moved up a yellow canal; women washed clothes and children played. A crowd of silent and sullen people were boarding a rickety bus to Saigon with their arms full of baskets of clothes, cooking utensils, ducks and chickens. Their faces showed that the viciousness of the attack had not been lost on them.

I had not forgotten that day at Cai Be; it was the first time in Vietnam I had seen the war's real victims. No wonder the peasants in the Delta seemed so exhausted and wary, unconvinced that the government side was winning the war. Often they did not seem to care. "*Che do nao cung vay* [All regimes are the same]," my interpreter heard the people in Cai Be say.

But Major Connick seemed to have enough confidence for both of us. "To these villagers, power grows out of the mouth of a gun, just like Mao Tse-tung says," Connick went on as we drove along the country road. "When the VC walk into a village and say, 'Give me so much rice or your son or I'll kill you,' there's not much an unarmed farmer can do. That doesn't mean he's pro-VC."

Connick revved up the jeep as we crossed an open field and the wheels dug into the muddy, rutted road. "If it takes five years, we'll stay here and do the job; let's face it. It took the Viet Cong many years to get this entrenched, and it's going to take a lot more years to get them out. These people want peace, honest government, and they want promises to be carried out. It's going to take a lot of long, hard, dedicated work, but I think the war is being slowly and steadily won in Long An Province. I know bad news sells better for you guys in the newspaper business. But for the professional soldier, this is an excellent opportunity to do what you're interested in. Where else today can you get training to be a soldier-statesman? That's a fact of life. We may end up fighting this kind of war all our lives."

We passed a large billboard Connick had erected as a morale builder. It showed a pretty Vietnamese girl against a background of rice fields. Connick told me the legend in Vietnamese was "Welcome, Visitors, to Long An Province, Gateway to the Mekong Delta. We Encourage Rural Development." "I wanted them to say, 'A Province That Fights Communists,' but the local headman changed it. I felt sure it would be full of holes by now. But the local VC must like it, too."

"Sure, it's dangerous out here," Connick said as we drove along. "You get shot at. But unless you think about it and sit around getting shaky, it doesn't bother you. You're here for a week and it seems like Main Street, U.S.A."

After we arrived at Thu Thua and Connick returned to town, I spent the afternoon on patrol with Captain Emacio. When we returned to the small barbed-wire fortress that served as the militia headquarters in Thu Thua town, the soldiers were decorating it for Tet, the approaching Lunar New Year. Several youths in faded fatigues were pasting long strips of red paper on the walls of a small yellow-brick temple behind their barracks. They said the strips were brushed with the Chinese characters for happiness and riches. Inside, they placed firecrackers and symbols to keep demons away during the seven days of Tet, when all the gods were said to abandon earth for the palace of jade in heaven. Even the Viet Cong would celebrate Tet and for one week there would be no war. While the youths worked, an old man who was the company bugler harangued them in Vietnamese. One of them laughed and said that the old man was warning them there was going to be an attack that night and he was moving into the town surrounding our outpost.

Just before dusk a squad leader returned from patrol to report that one of his men had tripped off a booby-trapped grenade in a rice field. The steel fragments had burst in his chest. Emacio said it had never happened before so close to his outpost.

Three miles to the north, in the little hamlet of Tan Buu, two American advisers assigned to a Vietnamese infantry company had just been radioed orders to pull out the following morning; they were to report to their battalion headquarters five miles east at Go Binh village on the main highway between Saigon and Tan An.

When the order came, Lieutenant Bill Reach and Sergeant Antonio Solis had just finished sharing a meal of rice and fermented fish sauce with the Vietnamese company commander they advised. They had spent thirty days in Tan Buu, just ten miles south of Saigon's outskirts. Their Vietnamese company was supposed to provide security for government pacification workers as they identified and arrested whatever Communist political underground existed in the village. Solis, a handsome thirty-two-year-old of Mexican descent, had left his wife and three children in Corpus Christi, Texas, to come to Vietnam three months before. In their short time together, he had grown to admire Lieutenant Reach, a blond, soft-spoken West Pointer from New York City, who had a way with the local villagers. Walking through Tan Buu that afternoon, inspecting a newly built bridge and marketplace, a swarm of children had surrounded them, shouting "Okay, okay." They all wanted to hold the Americans' hands and touch the hair on their wrists. The older people in Tan Buu had seemed more reserved.

At night the entire company withdrew into a large French colonial villa on the edge of the village. With its red-slate roof and ornate, baroque architecture, the villa looked imposing and alien beside the low thatched-roof mud huts. Just before Christmas, while Reach and Solis were out on patrol with two platoons, some Viet Cong guerrillas had entered the village and torn down much of its defensive fences and barbed wire. The fortifications had been rebuilt, but Solis himself didn't like the setup. Still, Solis told himself, they only had one more night to go. What the hell.

After dinner, Lieutenant Reach wrote a letter to his wife, Rosemary, by kerosene lamp in the second-floor bedroom he shared with the sergeant. As Solis packed his gear, he could hear the drone of voices downstairs and the coughs and movements of a platoon of soldiers who slept in the hall outside their room. Outside on a balcony a sentry with binoculars paced back and forth. Cicadas snickered in the reeds along the banks of the Ben Luc River. Solis wondered if there were any patrols or ambushes out. "Man, I don't know about you, Lieutenant," he said, "But I'll be glad to see the last of this place."

At three o'clock in the morning, Solis was jolted awake by an explosion near his head. Plaster and chunks of brick were falling. What sounded like 60-mm. mortars were exploding against the roof. "Incoming mail," he shouted to Lieutenant Reach. They grabbed their steel helmets and pulled mattresses over their heads. Reach got on the radio to sector, "We've got to evacuate the building," he shouted. "Send in hueys!"

Solis discovered that the single door into the corridor wouldn't open. He pounded on it with his fists and tried to kick it in, but it wouldn't budge. "Maybe it's blocked with debris," Reach shouted. A shell burst against the outside wall, and smoke and fumes poured into the shattered windows. Mortars shrieked and exploded all around them for some minutes. Then a shell scored a direct hit on the door, splitting it down the middle and knocking both men flat on their backs. As they stumbled down the stairs in a daze, Solis saw that the house was deserted. The entire Vietnamese company had vanished. Blood was spattered on the landing ceiling. When they reached the open doorway, a machine gun opened up outside from very close range, forcing them to fall back inside for cover. A concussion rocked the house, and slabs of concrete and fragments spattered the walls. They were choking and coughing now and had to get out.

They dived through the door and crawled into an abandoned machine-gun emplacement waist-deep in water. A Vietnamese soldier was crouching there alone, a hand over his face, trembling violently. One of his arms, smashed and bloody, was hanging half off; he had apparently been left behind by the rest of the company. As they hesitated in the wet darkness, Solis saw five black-clad guerrillas creep by a few feet from his head and enter the villa. He was almost certain they were not carrying rifles. Perhaps suicide killers. By now the Americans had been spotted, and the Viet Cong across the road were trying to lob grenades into their hole.

"The river!" Solis shouted above the blasts. The Ben Luc River was only fifty yards away behind the villa. The lieutenant started up first and fell back as a spatter of machine-gun fire ripped across his chest, killing him instantly.

Alone, Solis managed to edge himself up and roll out of the bunker toward the villa's garden wall. Half crawling, as glass and fragments along the ground cut his chest, he could hear the terrified animal screams of the soldier left behind. Gaining the reeds, Solis lowered himself flat in shallow mud and slipped deeper and deeper into the reed bank and water until all but the top of his head was covered. He thought he saw several figures plunging in and trying to swim the river, which was peppered with machine-gun fire.

He heard the Viet Cong spraying the inside of the villa with machine guns, followed by the concussions of grenade blasts, and he could see the outlines of a guerrilla squad down the bank. The men climbed into a sampan and started moving toward him, combing the reeds. Once he heard a garbled outcry, followed by a gurgling human sound. After what seemed to him like half an hour, an American flareship appeared overhead, dropping orange parachute flares that lit up the whole countryside with the yellow glow of artificial daylight. He prayed it would go away. Then four armed helicopters flew low over Tan Buu, beaming searchlights into the village and around the villa.

The men in the sampan went away after that. Solis lay in the cold water and mud for what he thought was about two hours. Once he heard the voice of a Vietnamese speaking through a megaphone in the village, but most of the time the only sound was the slight rustle of reeds when he breathed. When the horizon began to be streaked with light, Solis crawled ashore. His ears were caked with dried blood from the concussion, and his bare chest was a mass of cuts and scratches. He stumbled in a dreamlike daze toward what was left of the villa, now a shell of rubble although the walls still stood. The air was heavy with the acrid smell of explosives.

At the gate, silhouetted in the misty grey light, a group of black-garbed figures stood over the body of the lieutenant. They were weeping. There was no sign of the vanished company. As the village chief bandaged his wounds, Solis saw the first of the relief force from his battalion at Go Binh come marching up the road. The bodies of eight dead men were lying along the road. The peasant boy who had shared their foxhole would never leave it.

Solis was vaguely conscious of other people around him, but he did not see or hear them clearly. He stood staring off at the villagers from Tan Buu, in their pointed hats and black pajamas, walking out to their fields to cut the new rice harvests, the peasants who had given them no warning.

Helicopters and cars from Saigon had reached Tan Buu by the time we got there from Thu Thua. Photographers were taking pictures; a little Vietnamese general with a swagger stick was being interviewed by newsmen; there were colonels from the American military command.

Sergeant Solis was in shock and unable to speak. For him the struggle for the loyalty of the Vietnamese villagers was over. I watched him staring out for a moment, oblivious to the stir around him, before they carried him onto a helicopter, a solitary and infinitesimally small figure swallowed up in the endless ocean of green and golden rice fields.

The next day newspaper readers in Moscow could learn of the night's attack at Tan Buu village:

> South Vietnamese patriotic armed forces continue to launch fruitful attacks against puppet forces. On 9 January a large full-scale operation was launched near Saigon. The guerrillas attacked a rebel unit and a U.S. officer was killed. Gunfire could be heard in Saigon because the fighting took place near by. A portion of seasoned troops who had been called to Saigon to oppress demonstrators were hurriedly sent back to the front. An atmosphere of confusion is prevailing at the U.S. military command in Saigon. The military authorities are demanding a quick restoration of the dictatorial and militarist puppet government.

Even this rated only a paragraph on an inside page. The major Vietnam story in *Pravda* that day was commentary on Soviet Foreign Minister Andrei Gromyko's statement five days earlier pledging renewed Soviet support for the Hanoi government in the event of an American attack. Gromyko had reiterated Soviet support for the "national liberation struggle of the South Vietnamese population."

In New York, the *Times* speculated that Gromyko's statement was motivated by Moscow's conviction that Viet Cong victories would soon compel a peace settlement. Said the *Times,* "The Kremlin evidently does not want to be left out of the negotiation of any such settlement."

In Peking, Foreign Minister Chen Yi declared, in apparent reply to Moscow, "The South Vietnamese question can be settled only through negotiations without outside interference." In Saigon, the U.S. Military Assistance Command announced that Lieutenant Reach's death brought the number of Americans killed in combat to 142. That same day, the government of the Cochinchinese civilian premier Tran Van Huong, and the Vietnamese armed forces commander, General Nguyen Khanh, issued a formal communiqué announcing that a current "political crisis" had ended, after nearly two months of street rioting.

But in Tan Buu village, where such news came late, if at all, the guerrillas had hidden their weapons and were again farming their fields, waiting for another night to fall in the Mekong Delta.

I found Sergeant Solis a few days later in the Saigon downtown navy hospital, where he told me the story of the attack. Antonio Solis was an uneducated man from the slums of Corpus Christi; he groped for words in an inarticulate way that made what he said totally believable. He was still scratched and bruised but otherwise unhurt.

What bothered Solis was why the entire Vietnamese company had abandoned him and the lieutenant. No one seemed to have made any attempt to contact them or help them get out of the room, if the door had indeed been blocked by falling debris. Solis had been told that the Vietnamese company commander was hit in the legs and knocked out of action from the first, which could have explained the complete collapse of discipline within the few minutes the two Americans were trapped in their room. Still, the company was heavily armed with 81-mm. mortars, 57-mm. recoilless rifles and heavy machine guns. Why hadn't they been fired? Solis had no idea what had happened to the missing company, but we assumed they eventually straggled back to the battalion.

Then there were the villagers. The province authorities had received persistent reports about local guerrillas massing for an attack; it had been expected that night against the outpost where I had been at Thu Thua. Yet not one of the villagers around Tan Buu had made any attempt to inform either the Americans or the Vietnamese company commander. U.S. intelligence afterward estimated that nearly 800 guerrillas had taken part. The local peasantry must have had at least an inkling of it.

"Sure, they always smiled and seemed friendly," Solis said. "The kids would run up and hold your hand. They liked us all right. But far as I know, nobody said a word. I don't understand it myself, after all we done for 'em."

The next day Solis was evacuated to the Philippines for recuperation and rest before returning to Vietnam, and I went back to Tan Buu again with an American major who had volunteered to take me in his jeep. It was a cloudy, windy afternoon, and long before we reached Tan Buu we could see the red roof of the villa. Now it was only a battered shell; life had deserted it. The Viet Cong had ripped huge holes in the walls with demolition charges and grenades but had left it standing, almost as if it were intended to be a grim reminder that the white man's day in Asia was ending.

We went inside and climbed the debris-covered staircase. The villa had been stripped of everything, but in the rubble on the floor of the bedroom, I found a single engraved pink check from the lieutenant's New York bank. The major was nervous and said, "Let's get the hell out of here."

Outside, the Tan Buu headman was waiting, a frail, anxious Vietnamese who wanted to know if a Vietnamese Marine battalion that had come to reinforce Tan Buu was going to stay permanently. He explained, "The Viet Cong say they will come back. They tell people they will attack us until the government troops go away from Tan Buu."

The headman told us that until a company from the Vietnamese Army's 25th Division came with the American lieutenant and sergeant, Tan Buu had not been bothered by either the government or the Viet Cong. He said the villagers had resented the government company because its soldiers were Annamites from the north who spoke an alien dialect and treated the Cochinchinese villagers with contempt. In turn, he said, the Annamite company commander had feared and distrusted the villagers and had barricaded his men at night inside the old French villa. The Viet Cong guerrillas, the headman explained, were local Cochinchinese like the villagers.

It was in early December, he said, that the company first came to Tan Buu with barbed wire and made the villagers erect a fence around the village. He was given 30,000 piastres to pay for improvements in the village but had been afraid to spend the money: "I feared displeasing the district chief. I did not know what to do."

Then he told us about the Viet Cong attack just before

Christmas while Reach and Solis were out on patrol. The guerrillas tore apart the new fence and warned they would come
back. When they returned to surround the villa that night, he ran
to hide in a sugar-cane field. He said the soldiers of the missing
company had scattered into the countryside. He estimated that
hundreds of guerrillas surrounded and entered Tan Buu, gather-
ing all its people in the marketplace. One man with a megaphone
told them that they had killed two Americans, one black and
one white. He said that the Americans, like the French, came
to conquer Vietnam with their traitorous Annamite mercenar-
ies. Then the attackers made the villagers give them rice and
money.

The headman thought the Viet Cong force had stayed about an
hour before dispersing when a flareship and three helicopters
with searchlights came. They took three boys from the village
with them. After a week the three boys were sent back to Tan
Buu. They said the guerrillas had ordered them to report how
many Americans came to the village each day and how many
soldiers were stationed there. The headman said that he told the
boys they must join the village militia to defend Tan Buu. All
three refused.

Before returning to Saigon, we stopped in the village to speak
to the two new American advisers stationed there. They were
drinking beer with some soldiers and local peasants. One, a
young captain, said, "It pays to stay in the village and get to
know these people," adding that he had picked up some of the
language.

Since it was nearing dark, we raced back to Saigon. The major,
who had been in Vietnam only nine days, drove as fast as he
dared to avoid any electrically detonated mines, slowing down
through the fortified villages, then speeding up to seventy on the
long open stretches.

We didn't talk much on the way back, but as we entered the
capital's outskirts, he blurted out, "Jesus God, what are we doing
here?"

A few weeks later I heard that government forces had
withdrawn from Tan Buu, leaving it under Viet Cong control.
The new American captain had been killed on patrol. The
headman was decapitated. For the next three years Tan Buu

remained in Communist hands, even though it was just ten miles from Saigon.

Less than three months before, in October 1964, Lieutenant Reach had been transferred south with the South Vietnamese 25th Division from Quang Ngai Province along the central coast. I decided to go to Quang Ngai.

I arrived in the middle of a monsoon downpour. When the rain let up, the pilot of our twin-engine Caribou walked with me across the muddy strip. "I'm sorry we can't stay until somebody comes," he said. "But we have to take off before that ceiling gets any lower." From a field telephone in a tin shack, the pilot called the American military compound in Quang Ngai to arrange transportation into town for me.

I stood in the rain and watched the Caribou gain speed along the mud strip. It rose faster than you might have expected, banked sharply, and headed toward the grey humps of enemy-held mountains, the Chaîne Annamitique, which ran like a spine down Vietnam's central coast. At the end of the airstrip was some kind of Vietnamese outpost. A formation of olive-clad troops was standing in the rain. Much closer, a dozen or so men in black pajamas crouched under a mahogany tree.

Without warning, a shot was fired. It had that cracking sound bullets make if they come close enough. Maybe it was only a farmer shooting rabbits. Or maybe it was a Viet Cong sniper. It was like that in Vietnam. Bob Hope had a gag for it: "They tell me the enemy is very close; imagine me not knowing which way to run." You never knew, and so you did as I did then and stayed put, just standing there in the rain and trusting to luck until a jeep arrived.

Quang Ngai City looked like any southern Delta town: one long street of wooden stalls, cut up every hundred yards or so by a canal, a church, a pagoda or a bridge. There was the usual cluster of French provincial administration buildings, and on one end, across a moat, a military ghost town of tent frames and abandoned barracks where the 25th Division had been head-quartered. In its center was a small sandbagged compound. The American provincial military advisory team still held out there. The team's intelligence adviser, a tense haggard captain, told me that almost the entire province had fallen to the Viet Cong once the 25th Division pulled out in late October. The captain grinned apologetically. "The possibilities are frightening in this province. But the actuality is livable. It's become livable because, well, because the VC haven't done anything. We're hanging by our thumbs."

The captain had been in Quang Ngai almost a year and was due for rotation home. This was how he said the province had been lost to the Communists:

The Viet Cong's parent political organization had first expanded its control over an estimated 80% of Quang Ngai Province's total population of 600,000. This had been relatively easy to do after the 25th Division was ordered south, because the five remaining government battalions were outnumbered by nine Viet Cong battalions. Moreover, hidden in the mountains not far from the province capital was the Do Xa, a notorious jungle bastion of caves and tunnels that served as the Communists' headquarters for South Vietnam's eight northernmost provinces.

Quang Ngai Province and its neighboring provinces of Binh Dinh, Phu Yen and Quang Nam had been solidly held and ruled by the Communists from 1926 to 1930 and again from 1945 to 1954. After the Geneva agreement, 80,000 soldiers from this region were ordered back to North Vietnam, leaving their wives and children behind. Most had since been re-infiltrated and formed the hard core of the Viet Cong political and military forces in the four provinces.

The Do Xa needed such articles as radio and printing equipment, armorers' tools, and medicines not available from village sources and too difficult to bring from Saigon. This appeared to guarantee the provincial capital's safety, since it served as a Communist marketplace. The only serious Communist attempt to seize the capital itself, a small market town of 15,000 people, officially known as Quang Ngai City, had been in 1962, prompting the Diem government to recruit and form a new division, the 25th. Two of its regiments had been stationed in Quang Ngai Province itself.

The Viet Cong's village political underground was essential for supplying recruits, food, arms and ammunition to the Viet Cong company and even battalion-sized units. But the local commanders of the government forces, supported by their American military advisers, had not made this political underground their primary target. Instead, following a pattern established throughout the country, they turned to large-scale operations mounted to seek out and destroy the Viet Cong companies and battalions in the field. The Viet Cong commanders were able to frustrate this tactic by seldom concentrating their forces, except for actions they initiated themselves where they had the advantage of surprise. In the rare event that a large Viet Cong unit was caught in the open and suffered heavy casualties, the political underground made good their losses within two or three months.

In Quang Ngai, a situation had developed that was similar to what was happening throughout South Vietnam except in the Mekong Delta. By early 1964, the Viet Cong controlled the mountains, the remoter valleys and the fringes of the jungles. During the spring and summer Tri Quang's quasi-religious Popular Salvation Movement appeared in the province demanding the replacement of all village and district chiefs who had served under the Diem government. This front agitated among the population, charging those who had served Diem with religious persecution. By early fall, they had managed to take over the administration of most hamlets and villages along the densely populated coastal plains.

By October 1964, the Viet Cong were ready to rapidly expand their hold over the entire province. Inexplicably, the Vietnamese Army's high command chose this moment to send the 25th Division south.

In Quang Ngai, as the last units of the 25th Division pulled out, district guerrilla platoons began moving into government-controlled areas, already softened up by the Buddhist Popular Salvation Movement, to give protection and support to the advancing political organization. Eventually regular units followed, billeting their troops in outlying hamlets. The number of attacks on small government outposts rose sharply, as did the number of ambushes, road mines and weapons lost. The provincial government commanders at this point faced an almost impossible task. If small patrols entered Viet Cong regions, they were ambushed. If major forces went in, they were harassed by sniper fire, mines and booby traps, without making any significant contact.

The American intelligence officer told me that when a large operation arrived at a village, the forces invariably found it vacated except for old men, women and children, none of whom would give any information. "Why should they?" he said. "They know we're going to withdraw in a few days and that anyone who talks gets his throat cut." As operations in Quang Ngai got bigger, he went on, the troops became progressively more frustrated. More and more chickens and vegetables got stolen from the villagers, more and more suspects were tortured to provide information. As the normal processes of law and order collapsed, the government began itself adopting Viet Cong terrorist methods. It shot and decapitated captured Viet Cong officials and copied the guerrilla practice of emasculating the dead and stuffing the genitals into the corpse's mouth. "I am not inhuman," the province chief had told the American adviser, "but with the Communists we have to do what they do with us." As soon as the smallest opposition was met on operations, the government forces called in artillery and planes; villages were bombed and shelled and innocent peasants killed. Refugees swarmed into the towns to further erode the already-weakened government administration. With Viet Cong propagandists waiting to exploit the government's lack of enough forces and its mistakes at every turn, the military war in Quang Ngai had produced far more Viet Cong recruits than it killed.

Asked about subversion, the province chief had said, "We must bring the Communists from dark to light. Capture them, arrest them. They have tried to take over the provincial capital several times, infiltrating their terrorists into Buddhist demonstrations. Their intention is to create as much civil disorder as possible while the Viet Cong mass a force to attack the city. But before they invade, they must have spies and guides within the town itself. They must have eyes. We must shut their eyes."

The intelligence officer ended his briefing by saying that the provincial capital was now considered too insecure to leave planes overnight at the airstrip and the last helicopter had just been moved out. Although roads were heavily mined right up to the town, Vietnamese officials and American advisers had to drive them; otherwise they might as well give up and evacuate the province, since they would not have been able to function. In theory, air support and reinforcements could reach the town in little more than an hour from the big American base at Danang, 100 miles north. But during the winter monsoon the ceiling was often too low even for helicopters to risk flying into the inland piedmont at night.

"So you see," he said, "ordinary things like a rainy night or a full moon mean a lot to us. The VC capability here compared with what they actually do leaves me perplexed. Of course, the VC are well aware of the wrath a spectacular massacre of Americans might incur with the States. Also, it's unlikely just yet they want to be burdened with administering the province. And they'd be open to air attacks."

As we talked, night fell and stars began to appear through the breaking clouds outside his tent. "If tonight's the night . . ." the intelligence officer said, breaking off with a shrug. "How about a martini? In Quang Ngai, you learn to take the terrible with the bad and the lousy with the awful. Do you prefer an onion or an olive?"

I didn't sleep much that night. Just before going to bed I was briefed on attack procedure. A siren would shriek and each man was designated a foxhole on the perimeter. Mine was near the command post. Most of the advisers in Quang Ngai slept in black Vietnamese pajamas they called their "running suits." Alert instructions were posted on the wall of the guesthouse, like hotel regulations.

The next morning I found two West Point classmates of Lieutenant Reach; they had volunteered with Reach for duty in Vietnam and had all been assigned to Quang Ngai Province until Reach was transferred to Long An Province along with the 25th Division three months before. I told them what I had heard from Sergeant Solis about the attack on Tan Buu and asked them what they knew about the 25th Division. At first they were reluctant to be critical but finally said that it had the worst reputation of the South Vietnamese Army's ten divisions. For a long time there had been rumor and suspicion that some of its battalions were heavily penetrated by the Viet Cong, especially in the past year, when a newly created Buddhist chaplain corps had become very active. (Some predominantly Catholic battalions, however, had fought well.)

According to his classmates, Lieutenant Reach had not been satisfied with the explanation given for moving the 25th Division south. Rather than providing security for the new pacification plan around Saigon (Operation Hop Tac), Reach had written, the deployment of the division in Long An suggested that it was being used primarily as an anti-coup blocking force against any potential movement of government troops into Saigon from the Delta.

Reach had said that the two regiments were supposed to give Long An a 3,000-man strike force to deal with hard-core Viet Cong units. This would have freed some 4,200 locally recruited regional and popular forces for the static defense and pacification role originally planned for them. Instead, the 25th's two regiments were stationed along main Highway Four into the Delta defending fixed positions, and other American advisers stationed in Long An complained of having to use regional and popular forces, originally intended as a local militia, in their "search and destroy" operations against the Viet Cong main force. The result was needlessly high casualties among the lightly armed and poorly trained irregular forces and a lack of real security anywhere in the country's most strategic province.

Moreover, by pulling the 25th Division out of Quang Ngai, the Vietnamese Army's high command had, in effect, handed the Viet Cong Quang Ngai Province on a silver platter. The Communist military forces had seized control of most of the villages on the densely populated plain in little more than three months. With this accomplished, the Viet Cong could easily cut South Vietnam in two at its narrow waist by launching an all-out drive across the bordering central-highlands province of Kontum. This, in turn, would effectively sever the southern half of the old imperial kingdom of Annam, with its capital in Hue, from South Vietnam proper, the former Cochinchina.

I was puzzled by Lieutenant Reach's accusation. Why would anyone suspect a coup by the predominantly Cochinchinese government troops in the Delta against the Cochinchinese civilian premier, Tran Van Huong? Huong was thought to have a popular following in the Mekong Delta. Putting Annamite troops south and west of Saigon and along the single highway to the Delta made no sense unless someone was trying to prevent the southern, Cochinchinese troops from coming to Huong's defense in the event of a *coup d'état* by someone else.

The two lieutenants didn't know much about the Vietnamese

general who commanded the 25th Division except that he was a North Vietnamese who had come south as a refugee in 1954. I was about to ask them more questions when a Vietnamese priest in a black cassock came running across the road toward the compound. He was very agitated and said he had just heard on Radio Saigon that a military coup had deposed Premier Tran Van Huong's civilian government. "Khanh has sold out to the Buddhists," the priest said. "God help us." It had happened.

I headed back to the airstrip at once, catching a ride with a Filipino pacification adviser. He cursed most of the way. "It is terrible. Even at the height of the Huk rebellion we had a stable government. Our people were militantly patriotic. They fought for their rights. But here . . ." He made a contemptuous face. "These people have no voice. They don't even know what's happening in their government in Saigon. How can we make any progress?"

On the cargo plane back to Saigon, an American corporal strapped into the bucket seat beside me was equally bitter. "I'll tell you something, mister. A lot of G.I.s coming over here don't know why they're fighting. If I get killed here I want my parents to know why. Who knows the big reason? You could have all the newspaper correspondents you want over here and nobody knows why. That's the truth. Sorry 'bout that."

In Saigon, Barry Zorthian, the American mission's information chief, said he had only a short official statement. "Until we can assess more clearly the nature and extent of the important events set in motion this morning, it would be premature for the American mission to comment or render judgment." But I noticed that Zorthian was referring to the premier as "Mr." Huong, whose whereabouts, he said, were unknown.

The consensus among a dozen American correspondents holding a post mortem in the Continental bar seemed to be that while General Khanh would try to give the military takeover some form of legality, real power now lay with the so-called "Young Turk" generals and their Buddhist ally, Thich Tri Quang. I filed a hurried, routine cable to my newspaper. In those days I was not aware of the existence of the Dai Viet brotherhood, much less that it had just seized power in South Vietnam.

In retrospect, it now seems that the fall of the last indigenous South Vietnamese, or Cochinchinese, government the country was to have was probably precipitated by President Johnson's decision to militarily involve the United States directly in the Vietnam war. There is considerable irony in this, since a major American war effort in Vietnam depended on a political base in Saigon.

It had happened this way: On January 23, 1965, in the little town of Washington, Missouri, William P. Bundy, the Assistant Secretary of State, had declared, "Thousands of highly trained men coming from the north, along with crucial items of equipment and munitions—these have from the start been the mainspring of the Viet Cong insurgency." Bundy went on to say that while the United States sought "no wider war . . . withdrawal is unthinkable." Regarding the "enlargement" of American involvement in Vietnam, Bundy said that for "such eventualities the aggressors themselves share the responsibility."

Bundy's speech, with its implication of military over political considerations was like a green light to Tri Quang and the Dai Viets. General Khanh, in the name of an "Armed Forces Council," dominated by Ky and Thi, ousted Tran Van Huong and his Cabinet the last week in January. They did it, they said, "to resolve the crisis created by the Huong government's inability to achieve national unity or even maintain law and order."

This time Ambassador Taylor, who was away in Bangkok at the time of the takeover, put up no fight at all; the President had accepted his proposal to bomb the north, apparently dropping his earlier precondition of a stable political situation in Saigon. Huong's fall received scant attention in the American press, since in Moscow that day Tass announced Soviet Premier Aleksei Kosygin would shortly visit Hanoi. In Washington, President Johnson announced that he was sending McGeorge Bundy, his special assistant for national security affairs, to Saigon. Johnson told a news conference that the United States was determined to continue to "help the people of South Vietnam to preserve their freedom."

In Saigon, convinced that with Tri Quang and the northern generals now coming to power the people had just lost it, I tried to find Huong. His last known statement was "I have not resigned. I have no intention of resigning." His housekeeper said that he had first been put under house arrest and then, with Ambassador Taylor's help, had fled to the Italian Embassy. I tried there and learned he had left. They would give no further destination.

The next few days were too busy to think about Huong. McGeorge Bundy arrived in Saigon to make a personal assessment for Johnson as to whether a political basis existed to support a big American ground and air military commitment, a mission almost immediately overtaken by events. At two o'clock in the morning of February 7th, the Viet Cong mortared Pleiku Airbase, killing eight Americans and wounding more than a hundred. I stood behind General Westmoreland and Bundy at a dying major's bedside. Westmoreland said, "Sorry it happened, boy." The major managed to whisper, "That's the breaks of the game, General." A doctor told Westmoreland, "I'm awfully glad you could see him. It meant a lot to him. He can't possibly pull through." We walked through ward after ward of badly wounded men that morning; Bundy was dressed in a grey suit for his jet flight back to Washington. Not all the wounded thought the United States should retaliate. Captain John Gray, a helicopter pilot from Seattle who suffered shrapnel wounds in his back and shoulders told me, "Hell, we could go for a year without another one like this. I don't think it's something we should get all excited about and take rash actions."

That same Sunday afternoon, February 7, 1965, forty-nine American carrier-based fighting planes bombed the North Vietnamese army barracks at Dong Hoi. In reaction, a million and a half Chinese marched in a mammoth anti-American demonstration in Peking; De Gaulle called once more for neutralization of Indochina; Pope Paul declared, "The hour is grave"; U Thant appealed to all parties in the war to move to a conference table; and Taylor stated that the northern air strikes aimed at a limited objective, "namely to oblige Hanoi, to persuade Hanoi, to desist in its efforts to maintain the insurgency."

Three days after the Pleiku attack, on February 11th, the Viet Cong blew up a hotel housing American servicemen in Qui Nhon, killing twenty-three, and attempted to land an assault force in sampans in the Qui Nhon harbor. The following day, the United States again attacked military depots and supply dumps in North Vietnam; South Vietnamese pilots, led by Ky, also joined in these raids.

Specialist Robert Marshall, a coal miner's son from Harrisburg, Pennsylvania, later told me the Qui Nhon explosion came without warning one evening as he was sprawled out on his bunk reading an Admiral Hornblower novel. At a few minutes after eight, he said, rifle fire cracked over his head and hit a wall. "I grabbed my rifle and ammo," he said, "and ran out on the balcony and started returning fire at two VC in the street. I didn't see the American machine gunner who'd been stationed there since they hit Pleiku. Maybe he'd been hit. Anyway, I lay down and started firing out the drainage port. Both VC were wearing black. People were running down the street. Then two more VC jumped out from behind a newsstand across the street and opened fire. I killed those two and then ran out of ammo. I went back inside and grabbed three magazines, and then the whole hotel just went up. At the moment of the blast, I had nothing on but my shorts and I grabbed a steel army cot and pulled it over my head. The building just sort of disintegrated right around me, slow like. When it finally quit settling, I looked around for loose pieces and was careful not to jar anything. It was pitch dark under all that rubble. I listened to hear voices and get my sense of direction. Finally, I felt a breeze and headed toward it. I kept telling myself, keep calm, keep moving out, and you'll be okay. I must have crawled across the whole building, but I finally reached a small crevice, but I couldn't get out. So I had to work my way all the way back again. Later some lights came on from the wreckage operation, and somebody outside slipped me a flashlight. Almost the whole time I was in contact with three of my buddies. I could hear their voices but couldn't see them. One guy hollered something was in his stomach and he couldn't breathe. Another had one of his legs caught under all the debris. All three were unable to move and injured and in pain. One thought he had broken his back and another his pelvis. I kept calling their names and trying to keep them calmed down. We must have kept talking the whole time we was in there. One of the guys had got his clearance papers to go home and he said, 'Well, it looks like you might beat me out of this damn country, anyhow.' Every once in a while they'd be quiet, and I'd start calling their names again. I guess it was the instinct for self-preservation that kept me going. My dad was a coal miner and I like to be out in the air."

In all the excitement, the premier of South Vietnam until just a few days before was forgotten. In Saigon, I learned from Sir Robert that British Ambassador Etherington-Smith had offered Huong the safety of the British residence, where he had gone on the eve of Bundy's visit. In London, a Whitehall spokesman told newsmen, "As far as I know he is still there. I understand no formal request has yet been made for asylum. It is more correct to say he is taking refuge in the ambassador's house." He quoted Huong as telling the ambassador, "I think my life may be in danger."

Interest faded quickly in the fate of the man who might have saved South Vietnam. General Khanh, having outlived his usefulness, was dumped by Thi and Ky and the younger generals two weeks later and sent into exile. His replacement as nominal head of the army, a General Tran Van Minh, lasted only eleven days. Minh was replaced by an even more obscure personality, General Nguyen Van Thieu. In Washington, the U.S. Marine Corps was ordered to ship 3,500 men to defend Danang Airbase, the first American combat troops to be sent to Vietnam.

In the harsh tropical sunlight at Saigon's Tan Son Nhut Airbase, departing American wives and children said tearful goodbyes to husbands and fathers. Down the tarmac, Air Vice-Marshal Nguyen Cao Ky and a score of Vietnamese pilots in orange flight suits were garlanded for their heroic first air strike against the north. Hardly noticeable were eight coffins being loaded onto a cargo plane not far beyond, the dead from Pleiku on their journey home.

Six

Near Defeat

We were determined to win and were confident that we could defeat the enemy in the special war, but we had not been able to anticipate that the U.S. imperialists and lackeys failed so rapidly.

—Le Duan, March 1966

While American troops were just starting to come ashore in Vietnam, the rest of the country slid rapidly downhill. In late March 1965, after nearly two months of bombing, the northern air strikes remained basically preparatory and probing, designed to interdict communications, bridges and radar installations. The next line of targets in this carefully planned offensive were important complexes near Hanoi and Haiphong. But Hanoi so far showed no sign of a change in policy. At the same time the arrival of more and more American combat units seemed to have given the North Vietnamese Politburo a powerful additional motive for destroying the South Vietnamese Army as rapidly as possible.

As events of the next few months were to indicate, almost as soon as they seized power from Huong's southern government, the northerners began maneuvering toward a compromise deal with Hanoi. With Huong in flight and General Khanh in exile, Tri

Quang seemed to have emerged as the most powerful man in the country. In what looked like a take-charge gesture, he had given lengthy front-page interviews to the publishers of Saigon's three English newspapers. It was assumed Tri Quang could name almost anyone he wanted to as premier.

And yet when the new premier was appointed, it turned out to be not a Buddhist supporter of Tri Quang but Dr. Phan Huy Quat, who had run the education and then defense ministries in Hanoi for the French-sponsored Bao Dai government from 1949 to 1954. Dr. Quat had also served as foreign minister in Khanh's 1964 government and was one of the few Dai Viets who openly declared his affiliation with the brotherhood. Within weeks, the American Embassy cabled Washington that Dr. Sung was the "grey eminence" of the Quat regime and ran things through Quat's new Secretary of State, Bui Diem.

At first I was mystified. Tri Quang and the younger generals led by Thi and Ky had ousted Huong and were in a position to name the premier. The Tri Quang-Dai Viet alliance now seemed to me to be established, but I did not yet understand why the young generals at this point faded from the political stage—not realizing then that most of them were Dai Viets themselves, and hence under discipline.

Tri Quang himself set the tone for the new government and explained much in an interview with the widely circulated *Far Eastern Economic Review* within two weeks of Huong's fall. Tri Quang declared, "Now is the time to negotiate. The Vietnamese nation wants a negotiated peace—a settlement that will guarantee the sovereignty of North and South Vietnam as two separate entities with no encroachment upon one another." Tri Quang was speaking to the Asian audience of a highly respected Hong Kong publication, but such an utterance would have been treasonable in Saigon itself in the minds of most Vietnamese, who regarded negotiations at that point as tantamount to ratifying Hanoi's victory.

When Quat also took a vaguely pro-neutralist stand, I began to see why Tri Quang had approved of him as premier. Their mutual sympathy and support became more apparent when Tri Quang sponsored a new "peace movement" in Saigon, nominally led by Thich Quang Lien, a bonze in Tri Quang's entourage who had done postgraduate work at Yale and spoke passable English. A number of Saigon professional men and academics, mostly refugees from North Vietnam, signed a petition demanding instant peace. Quat publicly called this a "nationalist movement." This provoked such a storm of public criticism that Quat hastily disavowed the movement and arrested two of its leaders. In a well-publicized ceremony (government press planes were provided), the two were forcibly pushed across a bridge at the Ben Hai River dividing North and South Vietnam. They were welcomed with open arms and a week later turned up in Paris with North Vietnamese passports, where they joined Quang Lien in opening an office to promote early peace talks.

The Quat government also sent Dr. Sung and a vice-premier, Tran Van Tuyen (a Tonkinese lawyer whose leftist reputation had led the Catholics to demand that he be excluded from the government), on a "good-will" tour to Paris and nine Afro-Asian capitals. Many Catholic and Cochinchinese leaders protested that the trip was secretly laying the groundwork for peace talks, which they felt would be disastrous at that moment.

A few days after Tri Quang's "Now is the time to negotiate" statement, I stopped over in Hong Kong en route to Washington on an annual visit to consult my editors. The Vietnamese-born Hong Kong journalist who had interviewed Tri Quang, Mrs. Tuyet Nguyet Markbreiter, told me there was no possibility she had been misunderstood. Mrs. Markbreiter was an unapologetic Viet Cong sympathizer. As I crossed the Pacific, I thought Washington must surely now see Tri Quang at least as an enemy of U.S. policy, as Sir Robert did, if not as the conscious Communist collaborator I was beginning to suspect he was.

I was wrong. On a wintry Washington evening, as we sat in his gold-carpeted office, Secretary Rusk told me he had cabled the Embassy in Saigon for clarification of Tri Quang's position as soon as the published interview was brought to his attention. "Tri Quang not only denied ever making an appeal for negotiations," Rusk told me, "he is even telling us privately that he endorses heavier bombing of North Vietnam." (Later, Sir Robert said in Saigon, "Tri Quang told General Taylor that he favored American bombing of the north, and then went straight to the French to explain that he was only lulling Taylor's suspicions so as to have a free hand to press on with his undercover campaign for peace at any price—or rather peace at the Communist price. A man who will do things like that will do anything.")

That evening Rusk said that he understood Tri Quang's position toward negotiations to be almost identical with the American one: that a withdrawal north of the 17th parallel of all North Vietnamese troops and political agents would have to be part of any peace settlement. "I don't anticipate any major Buddhist campaign to end the war and get the Americans out," Rusk said.

The Secretary described Hanoi's response to the air strikes as "so far mild—they haven't sent troops across the 17th parallel. We realize Hanoi cannot completely call off the war. There are men in the south who won't obey Hanoi. But if the North Vietnamese will stop what they are doing—and they know what they are doing—then the counterinsurgency in the south will end; there will be no need to continue it."

McGeorge Bundy at the White House ruled out the possibility that Tri Quang was consciously collaborating with the Communists. "We don't regard Tri Quang as flatly endorsing negotiations. We are willing to give the Buddhists the benefit of the doubt. Tri Quang is not an instrument of the National Liberation Front."

I was not able to see Secretary McNamara alone but attended one of his briefings at the Pentagon in which he sketched out his philosophy of limited war for limited objectives. "My God," he said, "we're trying to counter guerrilla raids, not Red Chinese en masse." He compared American policy in Vietnam with the Cuban blockade of 1962, saying, "It's the same thing, a question of delicate control, the queer relationship of applying military force for limited political objectives in a nuclear age, the close relationship of military pressures to political aims."

I returned to Saigon convinced that failure to tackle the problem of political subversion was undermining the entire American enterprise. The military problem remained paramount in the minds of the men in Washington because it was the easiest to cope with.

Since the fall of Huong, what little political spirit there was seemed to have gone out of South Vietnam. The military factor so predominant in the councils of Saigon and Washington had affected everyone's thinking. The United States seemed to be confronted with an almost impossible task. What could one do now? So much had been eaten away. If I was right in thinking that Tri Quang was a crypto-Communist, then any Vietnamese authority capable of opposing the Viet Cong had probably been disposed of or subverted by him. The amount of subversion in the country since mid-1963 would have been immense. With a sufficient military buildup, the United States could solve the military problem. But how, with Tri Quang and unrepresentative northerners in power, could it make the whole thing work and infuse the Cochinchinese civilian population with confidence that they had a chance to live under a non-Communist system? Washington hoped it would be politically possible. But it would mean that the United States would have to do a lot more than press the button for automatic solutions.

Maybe Mao Tse-tung was right when he said: "Man, not weapons, decides the issue of war." The decisive factor was what went on in a man's mind. Ironically, we in a free society were talking about the human values of freedom but relying on our economic and military power. Hanoi, while proclaiming Communist materialism as a doctrine, was using all the weapons of psychology to build enthusiasm and dedication which no amount of material things could replace. It was Ho Chi Minh who talked in Churchillian terms of blood, sweat and tears, and fighting on the beaches. Fighting for five, ten or twenty years, or however long it would take. Somehow the non-Communist side needed to recapture the nationalist cause and set the people marching again. But not with Tri Quang. Not with Dr. Sung. Not with the northern generals.

If the Viet Cong could be forced to suffer a series of military defeats in the coming rainy weather, there might be a chance. It would leave Quat and those favoring neutralism in embarrassed retreat in Saigon, and then perhaps it would be Hanoi's turn for an agonizing reappraisal. Of course, a third military possibility was that the monsoon season would bring no decisive victory to either side. In that case, the conflict might settle down to a prolonged war of attrition with the outcome dependent on morale, manpower, pacification and social reform in the south, and the ability of the United States to cut off the flow of arms and reinforcements from the north.

But time was rapidly running against us now. The advent of the Quat government with its peace maneuvers was quickly followed by a purge of the Vietnamese Army, a sharp rise in urban terrorism, and an end to specific Viet Cong propaganda appeals to overthrow the Saigon government. On the international stage, this was accompanied by increasingly bellicose statements from Moscow and Peking, and intensified pressure for peace talks in the non-Communist camp. In mid-March 1965, Peking announced that it would intervene with men and assistance if the Viet Cong requested them; Premier Chou En-lai warned that the "Russian and Chinese people will close ranks" if the United States sought to "provoke a wider conflict." Soviet Party Secretary Brezhnev declared in Red Square that many Russians were ready to volunteer to fight in Vietnam's struggle for "freedom and independence." The Viet Cong's own Liberation Radio threatened to call on "various countries to send youth and men to South Vietnam." In the West, Canadian Prime Minister Lester B. Pearson urged a bombing pause; seventeen nonaligned nations wanted immediate talks "without any preconditions"; U Thant sought to visit Moscow and Peking; France called for a new Geneva conference; British Foreign Minister Patrick Gordon Walker proposed a peace mission to Hanoi; and Moscow endorsed a Cambodia conference.

At the height of this activity, Hanoi declared a settlement was possible on the basis of the 1954 Geneva agreement. But North Vietnamese Premier Pham Van Dong (not to be confused with Saigon's General Dong) announced four preconditions for such a settlement: 1) the United States must withdraw its troops and cease "acts of war" against the north; 2) both Vietnams must agree to ban foreign bases from their territory; 3) the internal affairs of the south must be settled in "accordance with the program of the National Liberation Front" (which called for elections); and 4) reunification of Vietnam must be effected without foreign intervention. By insisting on *de facto* recognition of the NLF, Hanoi made clear that it was interested only in negotiations that would ratify its victory.

President Johnson's response came in his April 7, 1965 Johns

Hopkins speech. While the United States was prepared to begin "unconditional discussions," the fundamental issue of the war remained that the men in Hanoi wanted to impose their political control over the south and the United States intended to prevent them. In the same speech, Johnson offered Hanoi a way out. He declared that while attempts were made to end the war, a vast regional development program should be undertaken by all industrialized nations, including the Soviet Union, "to improve the life of man" in all of Southeast Asia, including North Vietnam. He pledged that he would ask Congress "to join in a billion-dollar American investment in this effort" and suggested that the Mekong River could be developed to "provide food and water and power on a scale that would dwarf even our own TVA." This appeared to checkmate the international Communist propaganda offensive for the time being.

The change in internal Communist propaganda in Vietnam was spotted by a number of American and British specialists in Saigon. From the formation of the National Liberation Front in 1960 until the Quat government in February 1965, Viet Cong propaganda had focused on inciting specific groups of South Vietnamese to rise up and overthrow the Saigon government. Students were urged to revolt against any government that drafted them into the army. Policemen and soldiers were told they were being involved by the Americans against the will of the Vietnamese people. Similar appeals were made to Buddhist women, the Chinese community, the rice-growing peasantry. As in China, there were constant emulation campaigns such as "The First City to Win the Flag," a contest to see which local Communist underground first dared to fly the Viet Cong flag over the government's provincial headquarters.

Now all specific appeals were dropped. Attacks on the Quat government were instead couched in careful generalizations, such as criticism of the "rebel administration." Some analysts linked the change to Hanoi's attempt to enhance the NLF's international image; it had opened offices in Hanoi, Peking, Jakarta, Moscow, Prague, Algiers, Cairo and Havana. The Viet Cong's clandestine Liberation Radio boasted that the Communists had widespread support from "patriotic elements within the South Vietnamese puppet administration, police and armed forces."

The rise in urban terrorism, the global peace campaign, and the northerners' seizure of power in Saigon had begun with the Christmas Eve explosion. Toward the end of March, the capital was rife with rumors that a Viet Cong suicide squad would try to blow up the American Embassy.

It happened on a clear, hot morning. Ambassador Taylor was in Washington. I was scheduled to interview Deputy Ambassador Johnson in his fifth-floor office at 11:15 A.M. but had returned to the Continental to change clothes. The Embassy was housed in an old Chinese hotel on Ham Nghi Street, just a few hundred yards from the Saigon River in the congested heart of the financial and market district. Traffic was heavy, and the streets and cafés crowded with people. Outside the Embassy, six policemen ambled along a roped-off sidewalk.

At 10:46 A.M. a Vietnamese youth on a Lambretta scooter drove up on the side street and parked across from the Embassy. Moments later, a Renault Fregate sedan entered the same lane and stalled about four yards from the Embassy building. The driver got out and told a policeman he was having motor trouble. The policemen blew their whistles and told him to move on. When they walked toward him, the driver opened fire with a pistol.

On the Embassy's ground floor, Vice-Consul Tom Wilson interrupted a telephone conversation, "Was that a backfire, Edie?" Edith Smith, a pretty honey-blond consular officer, was already at the window. She saw men shooting at the police. One fell, riddled with bullets; a policeman stumbled back clutching his stomach. The scooter driver buzzed off. Edie screamed, "There goes a man with a gun. They're shooting. There's a car out there. A bomb! Run, Tom!"

The two ran into the reception room, away from the street wall, shouting "Get down!" Wilson was dropping to the floor, his hands clasped behind his head, when 250 pounds of dynamite, crammed inside the car, exploded. Every window in the Embassy burst inward, a blizzard of jagged glass slivers. The ground floor was a mass of rubble. Parked cars spun in the air and landed in twisted heaps. A young Embassy stenographer, Barbara Robbins, who had come to Vietnam six months before, died at her desk. In the front entrance, Navy Storekeeper Manolito Castillo, who had stopped by the consular section to ask about his insurance, was instantly killed by the blast.

Besides these two Americans, twenty Vietnamese were killed outright in the blast. The number of wounded or those who died later was never fully known, since many were carried immediately to hospitals or homes; the wounded were estimated at more than 200, most of them Vietnamese pedestrians who happened to be in the street.

Within two days President Johnson asked Congress for a million dollars to build a new Embassy in Saigon and quickly got it. With grisly black humor, Radio Hanoi crowed: "There remains only one means which can enable Johnson to find a relatively secure site for his agents and henchmen in Saigon. It is to rapidly move the site of the new U.S. Embassy to Washington and place it on the White House lawn."

The Embassy bombing was ostensibly aimed at the United States; the consensus of world opinion seemed to see it as retaliation for the northern air strikes. Sir Robert, as always, saw it in terms of the Vietnamese internal political struggle. He thought Hanoi's real intention was to hurt as many Vietnamese civilians as possible. He told me that he believed Hanoi's aim was to drive a psychological wedge between the Americans and Vietnamese.

Hanoi had always used terror with logic as part of its psychological warfare. During the nine years of Ngo Dinh Diem's regime, terror had been directed against village and hamlet officials, labor foremen, schoolteachers, and other rural leaders in the Communist drive to force a breakdown of the government's countrywide administration. Well over 25,000 such Vietnamese civilians were murdered or abducted between 1956 and Diem's fall, according to official U.S. figures. In the first two years of insurgency against the Diem government that began in 1959, there had been 6,130 murders and 6,213 abductions. In early 1960, for instance, the Viet Cong sacked and burned a Buddhist temple in Tay Ninh Province, stabbing to death a teen-age boy who tried to stop them. In early 1962, guerrillas hacked to death with machetes an elderly Vietnamese labor leader who was visiting a rubber plantation near Saigon. In the fall of 1963, a young girl, a schoolteacher in the southern Delta province of

Kien Hoa, was tried as "an enemy of the people" and beheaded. It was a part of the struggle that went virtually unreported; few horror pictures of these crimes were ever published, unlike the Buddhist self-immolations or the government atrocities that shocked American television audiences.

After Diem's fall in November 1963, the Americans had discovered that their comparative immunity from Viet Cong terror no longer existed. The Viet Cong bombed an American stadium during a softball game and blew up a downtown movie theater patronized exclusively by Americans; Americans on the streets became the targets of grenades.

During the spring of 1965, the pattern changed again. As Sir Robert so astutely pointed out, the Communists wanted to demoralize the population to the point that they would not resist a compromise peace. What appeared to be American targets were hit, but most of the victims were Vietnamese. The Embassy bombing was followed by an attack on the fashionable My Canh floating restaurant, where the diners, fleeing a preliminary explosion, were ambushed with a Claymore antipersonnel mine set off from a crowded children's playground along the Saigon River. Twelve Americans and four other foreigners were killed, but twenty-seven Vietnamese died, and more than eighty, most of them children, were wounded. Once President Johnson formally committed U.S. troops to combat in Vietnam on July 28, 1965, this form of terrorism ended, not to reappear until 1968.

As the incidence of urban terror rose in Saigon that spring of 1965, I decided in April to do a series of articles on it. Someone suggested talking to General Dong, whom I knew only through his reputation as the Saigon military governor who had stood by Huong against Tri Quang's Buddhist hysteria until the end. Dong, although of northern origin, had been reared among the fiercely anti-Communist Nung tribals in the mountains south of China's frontier (where his father was a minor mandarin official sent there by the imperial court at Hue). As a colonel in the French Army during the Indochina war, he had commanded a division of mixed French and Vietnamese troops. Under Diem, Dong had earned the sobriquet "Tiger of the Delta" for his harsh antiguerrilla tactics.

The day of the interview, I found General Dong in a rage. He paced up and down the floor of his enormous office at the old French army headquarters on Le Van Duyet Street, denouncing Tri Quang. He said the bonze, allied with Generals Thi and Ky, was trying to pin corruption charges on him and other senior generals in the army. Dong explained that after the American Embassy blast he had been asked by some senior American officials to set up a counterterror intelligence net of his own, employing Nung tribals, and also to recruit and train two new battalions composed entirely of reliably anti-Communist Roman Catholic peasant youths to defend Saigon's vital Tan Son Nhut Airbase.

Dong said that the Communists had apparently learned of his new network, which was housed in several old tenements in Saigon's twin city of Cholon. He believed they had informed the newly appointed Saigon police chief, Colonel Pham Van Lieu, a northern refugee closely associated with Ky, Thi and Tri Quang. Lieu's police raided the houses and arrested Dong's Nung agents. A number of Saigon newspapers had then received anonymous telephone calls that a top Vietnamese general was trying to prevent the arrest of some gamblers because one of the houses involved belonged to his concubine. This story appeared in government-controlled newspapers. In one published version it was said that the house in question belonged to the general's sister. Dong, although unmistakably identified, had neither a concubine nor a sister. He said it was a clear frameup, as both General Westmoreland and the CIA in Saigon were aware.

Dong told me that a similar case had been rigged up against the Vietnamese navy commander, Rear Admiral Chung Tan Cang, a Roman Catholic and staunch anti-Communist. In the admiral's case, Dong said, a whispering campaign was under way to plant the patently untrue idea that Cang had been a close ally of the now-exiled General Khanh and should be purged as unreliable. Stories also appeared in the government's newspapers that Cang was using naval craft to smuggle goods along the coast. Dong knew of two instances where these stories were delivered to the newspapers by Buddhist bonzes close to Tri Quang.

"What I want to know," Dong summed up, "is what are the Americans going to do about it?"

That evening General Westmoreland met the press at a

previously scheduled military briefing. He defended both commanders. "The charges against both General Dong and Admiral Cang are libelous fabrications," Westmoreland told us with considerable heat. "Dong is the best tactician in the Vietnamese Army and Admiral Cang is the only Vietnamese who can run a navy." The next day Westmoreland threatened to withdraw all American advisers and support from the navy unless the admiral was immediately reinstated. The navy's junior officers rallied behind their commander, and four mutinous commanders fled down the Saigon River on a gunboat. General Dong also remained firmly in his job.

That evening, Takashi Oka, correspondent for the *Christian Science Monitor* and an old friend of mine, gave a dinner party for about a dozen foreign correspondents and Premier Phan Huy Quat. Quat's *chef de cabinet*, Bui Diem, also attended to serve as interpreter; Quat spoke only French. Dr. Quat, a slight, silver-haired physician, was a pipe smoker with the cultivated air of a Paris-educated Tonkinese mandarin. Bui Diem had been his personal aide since the late forties, when they had served in Bao Dai's government and then fled south together as refugees. The knowledgeable in Saigon said that Quat was a decorative figurehead for Dr. Sung and Bui Diem.

That night, while the new premier talked for hours in French about the virtues of democracy and the pluralistic system of society, Bui Diem drank heavily of the table wine. He was sitting next to me and once, toward the end of the evening, whispered with a tone of utter contempt toward Quat, "And we call that a prime minister." During the general conversation as we broke up, I asked Quat about the charges brought against General Dong and Admiral Cang. "We have evidence they have been indulging in graft and corruption," he said. The remark shattered any faith I might have had in Quat.

A few days later, on April 12th, the official government press agency announced that General Dong and Admiral Cang had been temporarily relieved of their posts pending an investigation of charges. At that time, General Dong commanded most of the troops around Saigon and Admiral Cang the gunboats along the Saigon River bordering the downtown quarter of the city. If the charges against them could not be proved, it was implied, they would be reinstated. Apparently this sounded reasonable enough to Westmoreland, who took no steps to intervene a second time.

The same day I learned that Quat, without any public notification or debate, had formally abolished the Vietnamese civil service which had existed since French colonial days. He used this action as the pretext for forcibly retiring a number of senior Cochinchinese administrative officials. One of the victims, the director of the national post and telegraph office, which then controlled all foreign cable traffic, at once publicly accused Quat of forcing his resignation as part of the second wholesale purge against senior anti-Communist civil and military officials since Diem's fall.

The purge of Dong and Cang was quickly followed by the ouster of three divisional commanders in the Mekong Delta, the commander of the armored unit in Saigon, and the chief of the internal security apparatus and secret police. All the purged officers were either Cochinchinese or Roman Catholic refugees from the north.

At a press briefing, a number of veteran American correspondents pressed Taylor for some explanation of this purge of anti-Communist elements in the Vietnamese Army. Taylor asked to have the names of those involved. Sol Sanders of *U.S. News & World Report* named half a dozen. "I've yet to hear Napoleon mentioned," was Taylor's memorable response. He seemed remarkably complacent.

"I don't see any pattern that justifies that complaint," he went on. "I know of no pro-Communist generals being assigned. Of course, I'm not privy to many of the things that go on. But Quat has adroitly brought the generals behind him. . . . Most of the opposition seems to be a strange alliance between northern Catholics and southerners. . . . But Quat has real but quiet strength in Tri Quang and the young generals. I think you have to take a certain amount of turbulence as a fact of life here. The war situation creates tensions, an atmosphere of anxiety tends to exaggerate political feelings."

Taylor refused to discuss the military war in detail. "Don't get me into a military field," he said. "I'm a civilian out here."

To many of us in Saigon, the world press seemed equally

complacent about the purge. The London *Times* noted that Admiral Cang had been a "close friend" of the exiled and discredited General Khanh (which, as Cang told me, was untrue.) The New York *Times* reasoned that General Dong had "antagonized" Buddhist leaders, "who wield strong political influence." There was little comment on the incredible folly of purging an army of its ablest commanders just as the enemy had launched his final offensive to destroy it. The purge would go on, until by the end of 1967 only two of the forty Vietnamese officers of the rank of general under the Diem government remained. Also in the spring of 1965, General Duong Van Minh (known as "Big Minh"), the popular Cochinchinese who led the first post-Diem government, was exiled to Bangkok. Within weeks, a former defense minister, General Tran Thien Khiem, and Tran Van Minh ("Little Minh") were effectively exiled as ambassadors abroad.

Few voices save Westmoreland's were raised in their defense. General Nguyen Huu Co, a onetime defense minister and deputy premier Sir Robert had said was "reliable, a solid citizen and the most highly qualified soldier in the Vietnamese Army," would be described on his ouster and exile by the Washington *Post* as "a strictly political general. . . . He and his wife are said to have become wealthy using his connections. Because Co was a southerner in a government dominated by northerners, he gained a certain amount of showcase value. Though not popular, Ky hesitated to move against him." Another of the more capable Catholic or Cochinchinese generals to be purged, Dan Van Quang, was described by the New York *Times* on his fall as "a military-political overlord who was almost universally considered corrupt" and "who opposed the introduction of American troops into his crucial sector of combat operations [the Mekong Delta]."

As he had done for Admiral Cang and General Dong, Westmoreland angrily tried in a press briefing to defend General Quang as "an able commander . . . his attitude was not at variance with any such plans." Few, if any, newspapers carried Westmoreland's defense. As so many times before, the American press and public found the Dai Viets' fabrications more convincing than the truth. But it is not surprising that when the Vietnamese Army began to deteriorate visibly during the next three years, "lack of leadership" was most often cited in Saigon as the reason.

One might ask why the South Vietnamese themselves did not do more to stop the purge of Cochinchinese and Catholics from the army and administration in that spring of near defeat in 1965. In retrospect, I think they felt that everything turned on the military situation. If the Viet Cong offensive could be stopped and enough of the army stayed intact, the Cochinchinese majority, stiffened by the anti-Communist Roman Catholic refugees from Tonkin, might rally to prevent a neutralist takeover. The way would then be open for a return to power of genuinely representative South Vietnamese.

I think many political leaders were simply waiting to see if the United States could and would turn the military tide before sticking their necks out. American troops were coming ashore as fast as possible, but the logistical problem was enormous. General Westmoreland was banking heavily on the air strikes against North Vietnam to plug the time gap. If the North Vietnamese could be jostled into reducing their supply of reinforcements and arms to the south, or if they simply could not get supplies through because of bridges down and railways destroyed, time might work on the side of the Americans and South Vietnamese.

In early May of 1965 as the air strikes, entering their fourth month, kept up pressure against the north and more American paratroopers and marines landed on the coast, General Giap's strategy to systematically defeat the South Vietnamese Army piecemeal became readily apparent. Desertions were running about 5,000 a month, and each day Saigon received news of fresh losses. On May 11th, the Viet Cong overran the provincial capital of Song Be, fifty-two miles north of Saigon, and held the town for seven hours before being driven out by American planes bombing the city; five Americans were killed in hand-to-hand fighting in their messhall. More than 200 Vietnamese casualties were reported, half of them civilians. A ranger battalion defending Song Be was decimated, another battalion fighting a second battle just north of Saigon wiped out. Although the 25th Division was supposed to be protecting the western flank of the capital, it was rarely engaged in combat, and there were reports of Viet Cong penetrating Saigon in large numbers.

The month of June brought heavy rains and over a thousand

government troops officially reported dead or wounded as heavy fighting erupted simultaneously near Quang Ngai City, where the 25th Division had been, around Hue and in the highlands provinces of Pleiku, Kontum and Darlac. There were 51,000 American military personnel in Vietnam, but only 20,000 could be described as combat troops and these were defending rear bases. In Saigon, General William DePuy, Westmoreland's chief of operations, told the press, "The important battle of the summer of 1965 is now joined." Pressed for an answer as to whether this meant large American units would be thrown into pitched battles with the Viet Cong, since the South Vietnamese Army had been losing one battalion per week, DePuy said, "The time will come when they will play their role." Bombing was stepped up in the north and American units grew rapidly. The rumored presence of North Vietnam's entire 325th Division in the highlands led most of us in Saigon to conclude that Hanoi was pressing for a final showdown and that American combat troops would be needed to stop them.

On June 10th, a thousand Viet Cong overran the district capital of Dong Xoai, sixty miles north of Saigon and not far from Song Be. In the twenty-four hours the Viet Cong held Dong Xoai, they looted everything in sight and then used flame throwers to burn down half the town's wooden houses. General Westmoreland estimated that more than 1,500 soldiers and civilians on both sides were killed in the fighting; it was the biggest battle of the war until Giap's offensive of 1968. A twenty-eight-year-old American Special Forces sergeant, one of the few survivors of Dong Xoai, told me the next day what it had been like repulsing Communist human-wave attacks for fourteen hours until his camp was overrun: "You just fire and fire until they're on top of you, and that's about all you can do. The attack began at midnight with a mortar barrage, followed by five human wave attacks. We fought these off, but the sixth wave managed to penetrate our camp. All we had was fifteen Americans in the Special Forces unit, nine Seabees who'd come to help build up our camp's defenses and two Cambodian companies. The VC would mass, come over the walls with grenades and flame throwers, then reassemble, mass and come at us again. For fourteen hours it was just assault after assault. They'd come in waves of about a hundred men dressed in black pajamas or our own Special Forces uniforms or just bare-chested and in skivvies. Just before each assault they'd start yelling and screaming like crazy people. Once they'd got inside there was a lot of confusion. Somebody'd yell, 'Watch out! They're coming up behind you!' Then there'd be moments of silence when you could hear a pin drop. The Cambodians got completely wiped out. But they fought wonderfully. They fought to the last man. At dawn, me and about a dozen of the Americans left fought our way back to the district chief's house in the compound but we had to abandon it by early afternoon. The air force and armed hueys lay down a wall of fire and bombs around our camp and the woodlands and a couple of times we had them strafe our compound when it was completely overrun by VC. By one o'clock the headquarters building shattered on two sides, and about thirty of us, including some women and children, made it to a big howitzer pit. The VC were about ninety feet away and moving in with mortars. You couldn't see good since we were trying to keep our heads down and stay alive. Then four F-100's dropped napalm all around us—must have been less than fifty yards away—and three choppers came in for us. If they'd come any earlier, it would have been suicide. One of our men bled to death. He died just as we got him on the chopper. A few of the Vietnamese got left behind. One of them, my interpreter, just kept yelling at me that if the Americans would get out the VC would stop attacking. He said it was the Americans they were after. I'll never forget that guy as long as I live."

Westmoreland was bitterly critical about the way the Vietnamese command had conducted the battle. "Reinforcements were committed piecemeal," he told us, "and this played into the hands of the Viet Cong. As at Binh Gia, the big mistake was piecemeal commitment. When they attack in mass in a fairly isolated area, there are not comparable government troops because there is nothing to defend. The Viet Cong work this plan to ambush reinforcements. They've done it along roads and now they're beginning to do it with helicopters."

If Westmoreland then suspected active subversion in the Vietnamese Army he did not show it, although eighteen months later I was to learn that the Vietnamese chief of operations and the chief of intelligence at the time were members of the brotherhood. But Westmoreland rationalized to us, "There are, of course, great hazards in war. And we were a party in selecting those landing zones where the reinforcements were ambushed. I can't blame the Vietnamese. We were sucked in, too."

As the Communists pressed their offensive around Saigon, General Giap's strategy to effectively cut South Vietnam in half also began to unfold clearly. By late June, Viet Cong had wiped out two government battalions at Ba Gia, just west of Quang Ngai City, seized the district capital of Toumorong in Kontum Province bordering Quang Ngai, and forced Westmoreland to secretly move most of the heavy artillery out of the little mountain town of Kontum that served as the provincial capital in expectation of imminent attack. Ten days later, Communist forces overran the district capital of Dak To and were close to controlling the two provinces along the 15th parallel separating most of Annam from Cochinchina.

Since June 17th, B-52 planes under the Strategic Air Command from the island of Guam, 2,500 miles off Vietnam, had begun bombing Viet Cong concentrations north of Saigon; there were favorable reports from Westmoreland's headquarters and critical press commentary.

After the effective fall of Kontum and Quang Ngai provinces, where the government held little more than the provincial capitals themselves, President Johnson declared that the United States would send even more troops to Vietnam than the planned 75,000. Johnson told a press conference that "new and serious decisions" might be taken to "increase . . . the present level of our efforts." It was now clear that the United States was gradually committing itself to fight a land war in Asia, and that the South Vietnamese Army was close to the point where it would be unable to carry on as the major fighting force.

Three days after Johnson's announcement, Defense Secretary McNamara arrived in Saigon. The near defeat in Vietnam had caused a breakdown in the usual organization and security precautions, and newsmen were able to stand fairly close to McNamara's side throughout his three-day tour of the country. From the questions he put to military men in the field, it was apparent that McNamara was studying not only how the United

States could turn the military tide, but also how the country could eventually be pacified and American troops be withdrawn.

Just before leaving for Washington, McNamara met the press. "The situation is critical," he said. "It is substantially worse today than a year ago. . . . The lines of communication are broken, many parts of the country are isolated, the Viet Cong have increased the pressure against province and district towns, and fatality rates are up." Noting a vast increase in the size of Viet Cong forces and their use of terror, he warned that "a major proportion" of the Communist troops had not yet been committed to battle. He said the expected American buildup, which he hinted might reach a third of a million by spring, would be used to occupy coastal enclaves and provide a strategic mobile reserve for the Vietnamese Army, which had lost its ten elite battalions in almost that many weeks. But he anticipated that the South Vietnamese could continue to carry out most of the ground fighting in large operations. He ruled out a joint command: "I think the present arrangements are satisfactory and see no reason for a change in the future. Each government commands its own troops."

"I don't think the Viet Cong can achieve victory in their terms during the monsoon," he went on. "If we bring in additional Americans and the Viet Cong decide to cut their losses and retreat, it would give us a chance to advance welfare programs and build a political infrastructure inhospitable to the Viet Cong which would resist the Viet Cong." He dismissed calls by General Khanh and General Ky for an invasion of the north as "so much Fourth of July oratory."

Someone asked, "Why are the VC winning?"

"I think it is the result of a very substantial increase in assets, support, matériel and strength which has not been countered by a corresponding increase among the South Vietnamese. Our buildup in 1962 was not expected by Hanoi. These people plan meticulously, plan in detail, and are quite content to carry out their plans over a long period of time."

Asked about the persistent political strife in Saigon, McNamara said, "Are the political crises caused by the war or the other way around? It's a chicken-and-egg situation."

The last few weeks in July were the ebb tide of the Vietnam

war until 1968. The Viet Cong effectively cut the country in half; they seized control of most of the national highways, including six out of ten leading into Saigon itself; they attacked Danang Airbase, setting 2,000,000 gallons of fuel on fire, and forced half a million refugees to flee into the towns.

It was not until mid-August that American marines scored a significant victory. On the Van Truong Peninsula south of Danang, they trapped an entire elite Viet Cong regiment between the Marine position and the sea; more than 800 VC were killed. It was the first big battle by American troops in Vietnam and was costly but successful. General Earl Wheeler, the chairman of the Joint Chiefs of Staff, had already declared, "The tide is turning in our favor."

Politically, Saigon was already responding to the deepening American involvement, as reaction set in against a compromise peace.

The purge of anti-Communists from the army and government had reached its height in mid-May when Premier Quat ordered the arrest of about fifty prominent Cochinchinese and Roman Catholics on trumped-up charges that they were plotting to overthrow his government. Among those arrested was the chief of military security. Roman Catholic leaders, perhaps stiffened by the arrival of 53,000 American and Korean troops in the country, immediately charged that Quat's accusations were fabricated. A few days later, Phan Khac Suu, the arthritic elderly chief of state, advised backstage by the Roman Catholic clergy and such Cochinchinese leaders as Tran Van Van, precipitated a show-down. Suu refused to approve two Cabinet changes by Quat on the grounds that he was replacing too many indigenous South Vietnamese with northern refugees.

A delegation of eminent Catholic priests promptly presented to Suu a list of charges against the Quat government. They accused Quat of discriminating against native-born Cochinchinese and Tonkinese of the Catholic faith for the purpose of selling out South Vietnam through a compromise peace settlement based on the formation of a coalition government with the National Liberation Front. Responsible men who, I felt, could stand on their anti-Communist records were, in effect, accusing the northern regime of treason. With the Cochinchinese leadership behind them, they could fairly claim to speak for the South Vietnamese people.

Rioting broke out in the Catholic sections of Saigon. Quat ignored the charges and held countrywide elections for municipal and provincial councils. He appeared anxious to give his émigré government some semblance of legitimacy and popular represen- tation. But a large proportion of the 471 councilmen elected out of 1,500 candidates were civil servants and military officers on the government's payroll or men identified with the Dai Viet brotherhood, Tri Quang's Buddhist organization, or Communist front groups. Less than 10% of the eligible voters went to the polls, and many Saigonese shrugged off the results as rigged.

Then, on June 8, 1965, the State Department announced that American military commanders in Vietnam could commit their troops to combat in support of South Vietnamese units if requested by the Saigon government. This decision represented a qualitative change in the war and the nature of the American commitment.

The day after the announcement, Quat called an extraordinary press conference in which he said that his government could not solve "the current political crisis" and that he was handing power back to the military. During Quat's five months in power the Tonkinese generals, in alliance with General Thi in Annam, had managed to purge and themselves replace most of the senior Cochinchinese and Roman Catholic commanders. Thus, as it appeared to me, Quat's move represented no real change in the power structure. The government remained under the control of men loyal to either Tri Quang or Dr. Sung. Quat was jettisoned as a premier too closely associated with what most Vietnamese regarded as a move toward capitulation.

Quat charged Suu with obstructing efforts for a political conciliation. "Up to this point," he said, "the good will of the government has been unable to keep the problem from deteriorating into a critical situation. This situation has harmed the war against the Communists, which should have top priority. . . . In the existing political climate, the government finds it impossible to carry out programs or implement plans."

Tran Van Tuyen, Quat's deputy premier, who had accompanied Dr. Sung on his mission to Paris and a number of Afro-Asian capitals, attempted to refute Catholic charges that Quat was plotting a compromise peace. The Paris trip had been a simple "good-will mission," he said. "If we are conniving with the French government to bring about a neutralized solution of the war," Tuyen told reporters, "there was no need for us to go to Paris; there is a French Embassy in Saigon. It is a groundless charge and a very comical story." Quat and his Cabinet ministers addressed the press for three hours in what amounted to a lengthy defense of the government against the Catholic charges of virtual treason. Quat's police chief, Colonel Lieu, whom Van would later name as the Dai Viet who recruited Ky and the others, accused Colonel Phan Ngoc Thao, an ex-Viet Minh Roman Catholic who had been a press attaché in Washington, of being a secret Communist agent. Thao had been tried and sentenced to death *in absentia* the previous March for his role in two abortive countercoups to prevent the North Vietnamese refugees from seizing power, first against the Khanh government and then against Quat's own regime. At the time of this press conference, Thao was still in hiding. He was to be shot the next month while seeking refuge in a Catholic monastery outside Saigon and subsequently tortured and strangled to death in a Saigon hospital. Saigon rumor had it that Lieu and Ky's men committed the murder after General Thieu put the finger on Thao and revealed his whereabouts to Lieu's police. This was another reason that General Thieu, although a Catholic, was opposed by much of the Roman Catholic hierarchy in Saigon. Before his capture and death, Thao had written American friends lengthy letters explaining why he sought to prevent a North Vietnamese seizure of power in Saigon.

Three days later, Suu and Quat formally resigned, handing over the government to the generals. The Washington *Post* commented, "Premier Quat apparently could not stand up to the combined opposition of the militant Catholics, who coveted more government posts than Quat was disposed to give them, and the 'southerners' who supported President Phan Khac Suu in trying to keep the premier from putting too many non-Communist northerners in his cabinet." Few commentators took any notice that the southern-Catholic majority had accused Quat of treason; it was another one of those mystifying communications breakdowns between Saigon and the United States that left the American people so uninformed.

The ten most powerful generals in the Vietnamese armed forces met at once to elect a new premier. General Nguyen Chanh Thi, the ex-paratroop sergeant in the French Army who had risen to be warlord of Annam, won on the first ballot. "I could have had it. I was elected first," Thi was to say in later years of bitter exile in Washington. But Thi was not cast in such a starring role in the script of the charade. The junta's chairman, Nguyen Van Thieu, a quiet, enigmatic figure who was little known then even among Vietnamese, opposed Thi on the grounds that he would be unacceptable to the Americans. Nguyen Cao Ky, the self-styled air vice-marshal of the Vietnamese Air Force, was then elected premier.

Such Vietnamese as Tran Van Van, former Premier Tran Van Huong and the Roman Catholic leaders were apprehensive; Quat was gone but the Quat regime remained. It was announced that Bui Diem, Dr. Sung's chief lieutenant, would stay on at Ky's side as his *chef de cabinet*. The situation disturbed Ambassador Taylor. Ky was the man he had once described as "dangerous to the point of being mentally unbalanced," the desperado who threatened to bomb Hanoi if the United States cut off aid. Ordinary Saigonese were also dismayed. Nguyen Cao Ky was known around town as a playboy; he and his fellow pilots ran up bills in bars and restaurants and refused to pay, twirling their pistols to discourage protest. Many knew Ky as a jaunty, reckless "cowboy" who sported a tailored black flying suit with a lavender ascot, a vaguely menacing figure of fun.

Ky made his acceptance speech in Saigon's riverside Dien Hong Palace before a vast green curtain hung with the Vietnamese eagle. He said that his government would be provisional, and he called for austerity. "I hope in a few months to be able to return power to a civilian government, at which time I will go back to the air force. I'm just a pilot. As a pilot I don't like politics. But the generals have picked me because they have confidence in me. They picked me more to risk my life than as an honor." Even his worst enemies had to admire Ky's sense of theatre.

Within a week, this self-effacing "pilot" severed diplomatic relations with France, flatly refused to take anti-inflationary measures urged by the Bank of Vietnam, fired its manager, and warned that anyone who opposed his rule would be harshly dealt with. "We are ready to sacrifice 10,000 traitors to save 14,000,000 [sic] free Vietnamese," he declared. When Saigon's newspapers protested, he ordered a press conference and announced that all Vietnamese-language newspapers would be closed for a month. When newsmen and editors in the hall roared their objections and started to mill toward the dais, Ky signaled the armed guards to move in and told the newsmen to sit down. They did. "I will shoot all corrupt officers, cowardly soldiers and speculators," Ky said, speaking with his curiously soft voice, his eyes hidden behind black harlequin sunglasses. "My government and I have accepted this responsibility before history. Opposition remains nothing to me."

In Hue, Tri Quang told his followers, "I will give this man a little time." He told a sympathetic Vietnamese interviewer, "Ky is nothing but a military fascist. The Vietnamese people cannot accept a government led by such a fascist. . . . I hope this war can be stopped as soon as possible either by a ceasefire or negotiation. A small country like Vietnam can rely only on itself. There is no outsider we can rely on. I see Hanoi practicing *kho nhuc ke,* the ancient dishonor stratagem. . . . The North Vietnamese are determined; although they suffer hardship, they are ready to endure to the end."

By the end of July that year, Marshal Ky was no longer a comic figure to the Saigonese. He had arbitrarily decreed that the death penalty would be extended to economic speculation, hoarding, "hooliganism," support of neutralism, and sabotage of the country's economic position by spreading rumors. He also warned that ties with the United States should not become "bonds of slavery" which would render "pointless the struggle for freedom against the Communists." He told a British correspondent that he admired Hitler, that Vietnam could "use five or ten Hitlers."

The curtain was rising on a new act in the long charade. But before it began, there was a visit I wanted to pay. My destination was a hospital in a residential section on the city's outskirts. As you stepped down the sun-dappled paths, past gracious, mildewed French architecture shaded by tamarind trees, the patients strolled by, like little boys in their flappy blue pajamas. The wards with their large open windows were rather like pavilions; and you could walk along the long quiet terraces and see all the wounded, lying in their beds. The wards were classified by injury; in a dozen or so, all the men had one or sometimes both eyes bandaged. Then came the lung patients, some of them healthy-looking and crouched on the floor, playing cards. Further on were abdominal wounds and the wards for the men awaiting plastic surgery.

Inside, the pale yellow walls smelled of antiseptic, urine and pain. The South Vietnamese Army had been defeated, and this was Cong Hao, the country's biggest military hospital, where they brought the maimed and wounded of a people who had fought bravely for their freedom for many years and now would have lost without foreign help. There were too many wounded; they lay in the halls, on the floors, waiting to be tended, many of them moaning, one man vomiting until a nurse came.

But the grounds were superbly tended; gardeners had cunningly clipped the hedges into a green menagerie of elephants and pelicans, kangaroos and rabbits, as humorous and reassuring as wallpaper in a children's nursery. Dusty, ancient ambulances rattled by, engines wheezing and flags flying, rather comically, like inadequate stage props in an amateur performance of *What Price Glory?* Planes droned overhead, but the sleepy gardens, young green after the just-ended monsoon season, were fragrant with newly cut grass.

In the emergency room, combat casualties lay on stretchers waiting for the doctor. An ambulance driver patted one on the shoulder and said goodbye with a grin. They had come from fifty miles south in the Delta, he said, just escaping a Viet Cong roadblock. Helicopters were available only at night when the highway was too dangerous. One of the wounded was a youth with handsome, delicate features and long black hair. One eye was bandaged. His name was Nguyen, he told my interpreter; he was twenty-two and from a small village on the central coast where his widowed mother owned orchards and twenty acres of rice land. Now she lived alone. His two older brothers had been killed in the fighting at Quang Ngai. A year before he had been a student in the coastal town of Phan Thiet, where he was drafted. After three months training, he was sent south to serve as a rifleman in the Mekong Delta.

The doctor arrived then, a frail Vietnamese with glasses and a sparse moustache. He had studied medicine in Toulouse and when he returned home from France was drafted into the army's medical corps. That had been eight years ago. He hoped to return to civilian practice—"Our country has only two hundred civilian doctors now, you know"—but . . . He smiled and made a hopeless gesture. Every day there had been more than a hundred new patients. Some days more than a hundred and fifty. Few of the wounded discussed the war or politics, the doctor told me. "They are just soldiers and go on fighting. They do not talk politics because they do not want to interfere."

As he read the young student's chart, the doctor's manner softened. He patted the boy gently on the shoulder and lifted up the cotton sheet from the foot of the stretcher.

"Foot blown off by a mine," he said, telling me in English so it would not be understood. He spoke to the boy in Vietnamese for a moment, then turned back to me. "After treatment here, the boy will go back to his unit in My Tho to wait for the local military council to meet. The council will decide whether he can go home or not, whether he must stay to work in some light job. He should go home. He wants to go home. When the wound is healed, we will send him to the rehabilitation department for an artificial limb. He says his wife has come south with him. She rents a house outside the camp for 300 piastres a month and they have a two-month-old son. It must be a very small house."

As a private with one son, the boy now received $18 a month; if he were totally disabled he would receive $35 a year. The doctor thought that there were around 50,000 partially disabled veterans in the country and perhaps 5,000 totally disabled.

The doctor spoke to the boy again. "He says he is an infantry rifleman and that he has killed no VC."

A wounded sergeant muttered from a nearby stretcher, "Who can know where the bullets go?"

The doctor lifted up the bandages from the boy's forehead. His right eye was shut but swollen and watery. Unclipping an X ray from the foot of the stretcher and holding it up to the window, the doctor motioned us over. The black film showed the boy's skull; in the black socket of his right eye was a jagged rectangular shape a quarter of an inch long. "Steel fragment. The eye will have to come out."

An orderly called the doctor and he turned away. Painfully and with great effort, the boy reached down, groped for the X ray on his legs, clutched it and held it up to the light. He stared at it. There was no outcry, just thought—the deep private thought of someone faced with the final, permanent collapse of so much of his life. After a moment he lowered the X ray carefully into place and stared upward.

I told my interpreter to ask if there was something we could do. At first the boy did not seem to hear and then he said, yes, he wanted to send telegrams to his wife and mother, who did not know where he was.

The words started pouring out, so fast it was hard to catch them. "The war must end . . . so there is no more killing . . . so I can go home to my village and live with my family. . . . I want to go home. . . . I want the Americans to stay and help us make a better life . . . to show us how to do things so farmers like my brothers will not have to work so hard, my brothers . . ."

He was crying hard now and in shame trying to dab his good eye with a pajama sleeve. I thrust some piastre notes into my interpreter's hand and went outside to stare at the hedges shaped like rabbits and elephants.

The interpreter brought out the two cables a few minutes later. The first was addressed to Mrs. Ho Thi Loi, Long Phu Village, Bai Dinh District, Binh Thuan Province.

> I was transferred to Cong Hoa Hospital this morning, the nineteenth of August, and am being treated at the eye section. My wife and baby are still in Go Cong Province; they do not know where I am. I will send them a cable through a foreigner who just came visiting the hospital. I was wounded on the left foot and it was amputated. My right eye is also wounded and might be operated on in the coming days. Come and see me if you have time and means.
>
> Your son

To his wife:

> I was transferred to the Cong Hoa Hospital in Saigon this morning and am being treated at the eye section. Come and see me if you have the money.
>
> Dearly yours,
> Nguyen Van Quy

Seven

The Search for a Counterinsurgency Doctrine

The "Special War" strategy has basically gone bankrupt, along with the dismissal of Taylor, the father of that strategy.

—Le Duan, March 1966

General Westmoreland used to say that by striking hard in the summer and fall of 1965, Ho Chi Minh could have finished the South Vietnamese Army. But Ho gambled on being able to pull down the political structure. And there his plan went wrong.

Westmoreland believed that the Communists fell short of victory because they were stronger militarily than politically. And yet, Le Duan, in his captured March 1966 letter, takes the reverse position. He admits quite candidly Hanoi's surprise at Saigon's political collapse in late 1964. He blames the Communists' inability to fully exploit this situation on the failure of their military forces to "annihilate the puppet army" before Westmoreland had built up enough troop strength to turn the tide.

One of the great puzzles to me was how much Westmoreland suspected about the charade as it unfolded over the years. He always described the war as "primarily a political struggle," but he seemed to define this in terms of American domestic support. In the nature of things, Westmoreland's contact with Vietnamese civilian leaders was almost nonexistent. He deferred to the Embassy's political judgment even though he outstayed two ambassadors and a whole succession of State Department political officers. Not all his commanders were this self-disciplined. Lieutenant General Stanley R. ("Swede") Larson once exploded to me in exasperation, "What's wrong with those Americans down in Saigon? Why can't they produce a decent civil government to match the military effort?"

I suspected that Westmoreland seriously questioned the behavior of certain Vietnamese, especially for purging some of his best commanders and committing troops to battle piecemeal to a series of battles in 1965, but he kept his own counsel. The nearest I ever came to broaching the subject of Dai Viet control of the government was to be in late 1967, when I asked, "Considering the political situation in Saigon, how do you envisage the war ending?" Westmoreland understood what I was getting at and gave a proper general's answer. "That's not my job, Dick; my job is to keep the military pressure on."

After the successful mid-August 1965 Marine action on Van Truong Peninsula, Westmoreland began to regain the initiative over Giap's forces, although maximum pressure on the Viet Cong ground forces did not begin until the following spring. That fall heliborne American paratroops broke a three-month-long Communist siege of strategic Duc Co outpost in the highlands and reopened the road between the two highlands strongpoints of Pleiku and Kontum. With 6,000 Vietnamese troops sweeping into a pincers movement, a ninety-mile highway linking the highlands town of Ban Me Thuot with the coast was regained. In mid-October, American forces joined Vietnamese troops in relieving the siege at Plei Me; on November 14th began the series of savage battles between the U.S. First Air Cavalry and an army of 2,000 North Vietnamese regulars from the 325th Division in the Ia Drang Valley, near Chu Pong Mountain. The Ia Drang campaign permanently broke Communist control of the central highlands. Not only did the high plateau dominate twelve provinces with a population of almost 3,000,000 people, it also had great symbolic value. Vietnamese with fresh memories of the Indochina war felt that if the army were defeated in the highlands, Ho Chi Minh would seize Saigon as he had Hanoi eleven years earlier.

By January 1966, Westmoreland was mounting sweeps into Viet Cong territory on a scale inconceivable the previous fall. The first main effort was to clear Route 19, running between the populated plain and the high inland plateau, and coastal Route 1 and the rice-growing areas of the central coast. South of Quang Ngai and north of Qui Nhon, a series of complicated operations (variously christened Masher, Double Eagle and White Wings, to our confusion) set out to trap a force of 2,000 to 3,000 North Vietnamese and Viet Cong troops. The trap, drawn around the An Lao Valley inland from the outpost of Bong Son, did not catch the whole force. But Giap's strategy to cut South Vietnam in two at the 15th parallel had been successfully countered. Failing to isolate the southern half of Annam, Giap began preparing for his direct invasion across the until-then demilitarized zone, with the aim of eventually seizing Hue and the two northernmost provinces, about half as much territory as in his earlier campaign.

South along the coast, other operations were engaged in similar tasks of clearing coastal areas of Viet Cong main-force units. Around Saigon, Westmoreland began to seek out and obliterate Viet Cong jungle sanctuaries with bulldozers, firebombs, defoliants and high explosives. In the far north, U.S. marines were averaging 300 patrols and 150 ambushes every twenty-four hours in their drive to pacify one of the most heavily Viet Cong regions in the countryside. They were also making limited progress in dismantling the Communist underground in the hamlets, but soon General Giap would succeed in diverting most of these marines to the northern frontier.

In most of the country, we were no longer reduced to holding isolated posts along highways, airfields and towns. In March 1966, the Viet Cong overran a garrison of Montagnard irregulars at A Shau on the Laotian border just south of the 17th parallel. This was to be the last tactical Communist military victory (in the sense of taking and holding the ground) until Giap launched his second "final" counteroffensive in late January 1968, almost two years later. The American forces, of course, still had a long way to go, but they had become skilled jungle fighters, demonstrating to Giap that a military victory was no longer in the cards.

Sometime during the winter of 1965–66, as it became obvious to the Vietnamese that the military situation had appreciably changed in the Saigon government's favor, a crucial psychological moment arrived. Opinion swung sharply against the Communists. But it was also clear that even if Westmoreland could continue to fix and clobber the Viet Cong main forces in successive battles, the war would not be won as other wars had been. In the best possible circumstances, all that could be expected was a Communist retreat from big pitched battles to smaller guerrilla operations. Then vigorous pacification would be required to clear the Viet Cong from the countryside, especially around Saigon and Danang and in the densely populated Mekong Delta. But no such large pacification was possible without a Saigon government politically acceptable to the Cochinchinese masses. It had to be capable of moving in quickly with policemen, administrators, intelligence teams and economic benefits for the disaffected peasantry.

Many Vietnamese and Americans in Saigon felt that President Johnson, having committed American troops to prevent military defeat, now had three choices. He could stick with General Ky's unrepresentative northern regime on the argument that, even though Ky was a Tonkinese surrounded by fellow northerners, he seemed to have the will to win against the Communists. Or the President could take over political direction of the country, as he had virtually done on the military side, under a disguised American neo-colonial rule. The third choice was to drop Ky in an effort to find a Cochinchinese partner capable of providing a viable political basis for the American war effort.

At first we incorrectly assumed Johnson had made this third choice. In July of 1965, when he had formally committed American troops to battle in Vietnam—although the marines and paratroopers had actually been involved in sporadic fighting since March—Johnson had shown his awareness of the weak political base in Saigon by recalling Maxwell Taylor and appointing Henry Cabot Lodge to a second tour as ambassador. Lodge arrived in August of 1965 declaring the need for radical social reform in Vietnam. He said he believed that the combined American-Vietnamese military campaign would "give us all the opportunity to bring about a true revolution which will make possible a new and better life for the Vietnamese people." Lodge brought with him the legendary American counterinsurgency expert, Edward Lansdale. Lansdale had been the mentor of the Philippine's great antiguerrilla fighter, Ramon Magsaysay, as well as Diem's first American political adviser in the mid-fifties.

General Taylor had completed a one-year tour as ambassador when he yielded to Lodge. The architect of America's counter-insurgency strategy and limited war doctrine who began as a hopeful politician had ended as a disappointed soldier.

In January 1965, midway through his tour, Taylor had said, "Our primary problem is political. Without stability of government, obviously we can't carry forward these programs that require leadership and continuity of effort." Such counterinsurgency experts as Sir Robert Thompson agreed and maintained that Taylor's immediate aim, once the bombing of North Vietnam had begun in February 1965 and the U.S. marines had landed in March, should have been to destroy the political subversive organization of Hanoi, initially in the Saigon government and the towns.

Taylor alone can explain why this did not happen, since he had the benefit of advice from Sir Robert Thompson and Premier Tran Van Huong, both of whom understood the situation. Sir Robert consistently advised Taylor to make countersubversion his top priority, rather than the military side of the war. So did Huong, whom Taylor saw frequently over a three-month period. Yet the shooting war remained Taylor's preoccupation. His critics said this was because Taylor regarded the irregular war in Vietnam as another aspect in the art of fighting, rather than a complex, primarily political struggle for political ends.

Taylor was also the principal advocate of bombing North Vietnam, on the grounds that it lifted South Vietnamese morale and "let Hanoi know they cannot wage war on the south with impunity." Sir Robert's position was that the northern bombing was largely "irrelevant" to the political struggle in the south. In late 1967, he was to say, "My view of the bombing is that I would do everything to de-escalate it and concentrate solely on infiltration into the south." My own feeling was that the pressure of the bombing served the purpose of making Hanoi move too quickly. In the charade, timing was almost as important as the event itself.

Taylor left Vietnam apparently unshaken in his 1961 counterinsurgency doctrine. In his resignation letter to President Johnson, he said, "I shall depart with the feeling that our policy is the right one and will lead to a successful conclusion if we persist with confidence and determination."

In retrospect, I believe that Taylor's mechanistic approach, adopted as the unquestioned U.S. counterinsurgency doctrine by the American military establishment in Vietnam, was the principal reason for the failure to solve the problem of subversion. The Pentagon's programs to deal with the war's nonmilitary aspects through "psychological warfare" and "civic action" were limited in concept and subordinated to military requirements in practice. An exception were the U.S. marines, who put primary emphasis on trying to root out the Communist political underground in the hamlets.

The Ky regime's own approach to pacification was to adopt many of Mao Tse-tung's techniques. Counterinsurgency experts such as Dennis Duncanson criticized these programs—many of them advised and supported by the Central Intelligence Agency—on the grounds that the government reduced itself to the level of the Viet Cong by employing Communist Chinese institutions. At the national training center for pacification workers, officially called "Revolutionary Development Cadre," ex-Communist instructors applied such Maoist thought-control methods as autocriticism, self-emulation campaigns and three-man political cells. Some 2,200 recruits every two weeks began a twelve-week training cycle at the Vung Tau center; by 1968 nearly 50,000 Vietnamese youths had undergone this process. In theory, these workers were sent to rural hamlets in fifty-nine-man teams after graduation to carry on propaganda, military security, economic projects and political indoctrination. The program was headed by General Nguyen Duc Thang, a Dai Viet, who was criticized for sending the teams into insecure areas, where they were often cut up by the Viet Cong. In 1966, they had a 17% casualty rate, and after the 1968 Tet offensive, 40% never returned to work. The fact that most were young village boys tended to affront older peasants; some villagers ridiculed them as *"bay qua den,"* or black crow gangs, the crow being the idiot bird in Vietnam. It was also said of this Vietnamese-CIA approach to pacification that teams of indoctrinated young peasant boys were no substitute for conventional government, as represented by trained administrators and policemen.

(Of the five Dai Viet generals named by Van, Thang probably ranked second in importance to Ky. Although most of his family had remained in the north—a brother was a senior military officer in Hanoi and a sister wrote for the Paris Communist journal *Humanité*—Thang gradually established a reputation as the Americans' favorite general. This was remarkable, since he had successively headed the Vietnamese Army's intelligence and operations branches in 1964 and 1965, when the army was being purged and committed to battle piecemeal, and under his leadership pacification showed a marked decline. A bluff and hearty man who often visited villages in black peasant pajamas, Thang seemed to overcome American doubts about his past and present record by the sheer force of a robust, gung-ho personality.)

Of all the schools of counterinsurgency, the British placed most importance on civil government. They maintained that top priority must be put on establishing law and order through a large, competent police force and the creation of an effective civil administration, rather than on simply waging a military war. "They call this a people's revolutionary war—but it is not such a war," Sir Robert once said. "The Communists' aim is not really to win a war by winning battles but to collapse a social structure."

Sir Robert's pragmatic approach, based on his experience as Defense Secretary during the Malayan insurgency and his four years in Vietnam as Diem's chief adviser on pacification, is outlined in detail in his masterful study *Defeating Counter-Insurgency.* Sir Robert lists five cardinal principles of counterinsurgency: the government 1) must have a clear political aim, 2) must function in accordance with law, 3) must have an overall plan not only for security measures and military operations but also including all political, social, economic, administrative, police and other measures bearing on the insurgency, 4) *must give priority to defeating the political subversion,* not the guerrillas, and 5) in the guerrilla phase must secure its base areas first.

Sir Robert's fundamental premise was that the Viet Cong represented an illegal armed civil-disobedience movement. Prisoners should be tried and treated by civil courts for breaking the law—the implication being that the issue of negotiations should not arise, since legally constituted governments do not bargain with gangsters. The Communists, in his view, would seek negotiations only to ratify their victory or to save their political underground.

Sir Robert also assumed that Communism in Vietnam did not feed primarily on ideas or peasant grievances, as Edward Lansdale was soon to contend, or on armed strength, as General Taylor saw it, but relied on intimidation and exploiting personal ambition. Sir Robert once told me, "Forget the Viet Cong are Communist. This is not a people's war but only a revolutionary type of warfare designed to enable a minority to gain control over the people. They are a very small group of absolutely ruthless, absolutely determined, intelligent men who are out to build a power structure and intend to let nothing or no one stand in their way." Dennis Duncanson told me months before I had ever heard of Le Duan that the key phrase on which the Communists based their strategy in Vietnam was "exploiting internal contradictions in the enemy camp." Sir Robert maintained that no matter how atrocious Communist terror became, the Saigon government must always assume a strong public posture of morality, decency and legality.

Everyone agreed that the problem was to defeat the technique of guerrilla war as applied by a small Communist minority in one small Asian country. General Taylor and the American military establishment saw the problem in military terms and Sir Robert and the British in political terms.

One politically oriented American was Douglas Pike, the U.S. Information Service officer whose *Viet Cong* is the authoritative work on their organizational techniques. Pike had a somewhat different approach. His view was that the Viet Cong's success lay in neither military force nor subversion of the government but in the development of what he called their "organizational weapon." Pike defined this as a gift for establishing a mass-based, countrywide organization employing both coercion and rational appeals to self-interest. We used to argue amiably for hours; I contended that he was missing what was happening right under his nose in the capital. Once Pike replied, "Their main thrust is to organize and arm the peasantry. That's how they win, Dick. They don't win by your little hanky-panky plots in Saigon."

Perhaps the most authoritative American counterinsurgency expert was Edward Lansdale. Some months before he returned to Vietnam with Lodge, Lansdale had written an article in *Foreign Affairs* in which his thinking sounded rather like that of Lawrence of Arabia. T. E. Lawrence described his enemy in the Arab world as "an idea, a thing intangible, without front or back, drifting like gas." Lansdale described Communism in the article as an idea that cannot be "bombed, smothered or ignored" out of existence, but must be "opposed by a better idea." This kind of thing captured the imagination of Asians; visiting Japanese correspondents often asked to see Lansdale first.

When Lansdale first arrived in Saigon, many of us expected him to ring down the curtain on the charade. Although he was then fifty-eight, he still had an air of youthful idealism; with his haggard good looks and brown hair only tinged with grey, he might have stepped out of the pages of an Eric Ambler spy thriller. One saw at once why he had inspired major characters in both *The Ugly American,* by William J. Lederer and Eugene Burdick, and Graham Greene's classic on the Indochina war, *The Quiet American.*

In *The Ugly American,* Lansdale was thinly disguised as Colonel Edwin D. Hillandale, a harmonica-playing good guy known in Manila as the "Ragtime Kid," who "enjoys eating and loves to be with people, any kind of people." In a frankly admiring sketch, Lederer and Burdick wrote, "In 1952 Colonel Hillandale was sent to Manila as liaison officer to something or other. In a short time the Philippines fascinated him. He ate his meals in little Filipino restaurants, washing down large quantities of *adobo* and *pancit* and rice with a brand of Filipino rum which cost two pesos a pint. He embraced everything Filipino—he even attended the University in his spare hours to study Tagalog. . . . The counsellor up at the American Embassy always spoke of him as 'that crazy bastard.' But within six months the crazy bastard was eating breakfast with Magsaysay and he soon became Magsaysay's unofficial adviser."

But there was another side to Lansdale's complex personality, and British author Graham Greene turned it into literature in his bitterly brilliant *The Quiet American*. The novel is a despairing portrayal of a young CIA operative who blunders tragically through the intrigue, treachery and confusion of Vietnamese politics. Innocent and well-meaning, but ignorant, the American leaves a trail of blood and suffering in his wake. Greene's young American has been sent to Indochina in the early fifties to help create an indigenous political force that can resist a Communist takeover when the French pull out. In May 1954, Secretary of State John Foster Dulles had dispatched Lansdale to Saigon with broad secret orders to see if anything could be salvaged following the fall of Dien Bien Phu. Lansdale moved into Diem's palace at the time that he was defying the Geneva agreement (which Diem and the United States had refused to sign), resettling the Catholic refugees from the north, and beginning to make South Vietnam a nation. How much credit, if indeed any, should have been given Lansdale for this was not known. In early 1961, Lansdale had been one of President Kennedy's top advisers on counterinsurgency, along with Taylor, Walt Rostow, the CIA's Richard Bissell and Secretary McNamara's deputy Roswell Gilpatric; by late 1961, Taylor had supplanted all of them in influence with President Kennedy.

Greene's bitter criticism of American diplomatic maneuvering in Vietnam is voiced in the novel by its narrator, a skeptical British war correspondent: "Innocence always calls mutely for protection when we would be so much wiser to guard against it; innocence is like a dumb leper who has lost his bell, wandering the world, meaning no harm."

In the novel, the Lansdale figure, after becoming involved in a terrorist explosion in central Saigon—an incident that actually took place—is murdered by the Communists. At one point, Greene's narrator declares, "You and your like are trying to make a war with the help of a people who just aren't interested." The

young American replies, "They don't want communism," and is
told by the Englishman, "They want enough rice . . . They don't
want to be shot at. They want one day to be much the same as
another. They don't want our white skins around telling them
what they want."

When Lansdale came back to Saigon in September 1965, it was
rather like Greene's quiet American coming to life again. No
wonder the Vietnamese, whose household gods included the
dragon, the unicorn, the turtle and the phoenix, called Lansdale
"the phoenix" among themselves. (Lodge was "the dragon.")
What would he do?

The correspondent of the *Economist* reported to London what
sounded like inside information: "Americans in the know here in
Saigon say that Mr. Cabot Lodge's new job is one of 'exchanging
smiles and handshakes.' General Lansdale, who operated subtly
here once before between 1954 and 1956, has a different task. It
is to maneuver behind the scenes and muster whatever support
and force is required to push through the new American policy.
This is to replace Marshal Ky's 'national leadership committee' by
a civilian government."

Ky told an American friend, "When I saw General Lansdale, I
told him, 'I understand you are a kingmaker. Fine, no problem. I
have no ambition to be king. So we can be friends.'"

Lansdale himself said, "What does a man do when he returns
to a country, ten years later, with great stress on its social and
political structure, great suffering, great pain. I have no great
plan. It's more subtle, more complex, far more human than that.
One's got to move in with tremendous gentleness; these people
have been divided and hurt and a lot of clumsiness could divide
and hurt them more. But there isn't much time. They need rule of
law, consent of the governed in how they are governed and a life
in which kids have some hope of tomorrow. I feel the Vietnamese
are in their last quarter; if they can't get something now for the
future they won't ever get another chance. This is the ninth
inning and we either do it now or not at all. Hopefully we can get
something going these people will have a voice in."

Lansdale had been "very surprised" when Lodge asked him to
accompany him to Vietnam but said that they had "a wonderful
working relationship. Lodge feels the Ambassador's position and

protocol limit his role: he can't talk with the No. 1 guy and then sit down with everybody else. I'll be sort of an alter ego in carrying out the buttoning-up process at the working level. Ky and the generals are deadly serious about getting closer to the peasantry and wanting to do a hell of a lot for the people. I think the top folks are serious; I have a tremendous feeling we can help them express themselves better in terms of concrete actions. Ky is eager to get out to the villages. He's seeing people and they're reacting to him. Suddenly here is the prime minister of the country face to face with the people; here he is talking with them. For a thirty-four-year-old gent, Ky's starting to get awfully mature. He's not hopping into a jet anymore to get away from it all."

I asked him what he and Lodge meant by "social revolution."

"A revolution of the spirit along with social change; breaking off with the way they've been doing things and doing them in a new way. If you applied a strict Confucian ethic that would be a social revolution. You see, the Viet Cong's chief political asset is their image of morality; Ho Chi Minh is a nice old guy patting kids on the head. Kindly Uncle Ho; lives simply, lives by a code of ethics. This same image carries down pretty well through the Viet Cong officer corps. The officers don't live better, they carry the same weapons into combat, live right beside their men. These are people with a set of ethics; they can say, 'We are of you, we are of the people.' They come in as familiar people, not as strange creatures from Cloud Seven or World Nine."

Lansdale was brimming with plans for sweeping land reform, rural electrification, bringing back all the able administrators purged for serving Diem, restoring Confucian ethics, getting American officials closer to their Vietnamese counterparts, and putting more restraints on the use of artillery and air strikes. But he said nothing about the problem of subversion. Soon Lansdale had an entourage of close Vietnamese friends: General Thang, Dr. Sung. Lansdale the phoenix. I remembered something else Greene had said in *The Quiet American:* ". . . but nothing nowadays is fabulous and nothing rises from its ashes."

Lansdale's initial effort received a setback in September when a civil airplane crashed near Quang Ngai City, killing the able Vietnamese pacification minister and Jerry Rose, a former

American correspondent who had been working as an adviser in Ky's office and knew a great deal about Vietnamese internal politics. Both engines had failed on takeoff, the minister and one aide had jumped from the plane, and millions of piastre notes were thrown out the door. One survivor was initially reported but on inquiry he seemed to have vanished. Shrouded in mystery, the crash soon faded from public interest. General Thang took over pacification along with the national training center for pacification workers at Vung Tau, which Ky succeeded in removing from direct CIA operational control. Lansdale said his work had been set back at least three months.

The Lansdale influence on Marshal Ky became apparent in Ky's speeches. Gone was the young Hitler image. Instead, the new Ky talked of land reform, rural electrification and low-cost housing. In his first state-of-the-nation message in mid-January 1966, Ky formally pledged a new constitution by the following October and national elections in early 1967, leading to the return of popularly elected civil government. Ky said he would appoint a group of citizens to draft a constitution that, subject to a national referendum, would become law in November 1967. He promised that the emphasis of his government would not be on merely waging war but on "pacification" and "reconstruction" of the countryside.

But Lansdale's influence was soon superseded. In October, the *Economist* had reported that to replace the generals with a civil government meant "using the resources at General Lansdale's disposal—a vast intelligence network, plenty of hard cash and the presence of American troops—to stop the generals from shoving their way back through a counter-coup." In actuality, Lodge put no resources at all at Lansdale's disposal.

Lodge had brought Lansdale with him on the recommendation of Vice President Humphrey and Robert Kennedy. But on his own he had assigned Philip Habib, the career State Department officer, to run his political section. Habib was credited with successfully operating behind the scenes to give South Korea's ruling military junta at least the appearance of a constitutional government. Now Lodge brought him to Saigon to do the same thing with Ky and the Tonkinese generals.

A rivalry developed between Lansdale and his supporters and

Habib, who was joined in a "dump Lansdale" movement by the mission's influential information chief, Barry Zorthian. Zorthian, an honors graduate from Yale of Armenian descent, ran Saigon's swollen "public-affairs office" in a high-powered, Madison Avenue fashion; he exerted a major persuasive influence on the Saigon press corps. In early 1966, Zorthian told a group of American correspondents gathered for a briefing in his office that Lansdale was a "straw man" who was "on his way out." When I protested, Zorthian said, "It's guys like you who built him up, Dick, and you're going to be stuck with him when he falls down." Soon an impression was generated that General Westmoreland also opposed Lansdale and that the rivalry somehow had become one of military versus civil camps. It was not until late 1967 that Robert Komer, who by then had become a deputy ambassador in Saigon, told me that Westmoreland had, in fact, sided with Lansdale's supporters from the start.

Lodge, however, increasingly leaned on Habib's political judgment and moved him to a suite adjoining his own offices. Lodge also bypassed Lansdale by vesting authority for nonmilitary programs in a new deputy ambassador, William Porter, who had experience in counterinsurgency as a former ambassador to Algeria. Porter, an able, popular diplomat, made the best of a bad situation.

On January 21, 1966, a week after Ky had promised elections for a new civil government in early 1967, Habib sent Lansdale an official memorandum, signed by Lodge. The memo explicitly forbade Lansdale any further contact with Vietnamese civilian and military leaders except for General Thang, his counterpart in the pacification setup. At the same time, Lodge asked Washington to give Lansdale the diplomatic rank of minister counselor. When I asked Lodge why he had promoted a man whom he had just, in effect, stripped of his power, the ambassador replied, "After all, Ed's fifty-eight-years old. I'm only sixty-four, you know." Earlier, when I asked Lodge what Lansdale's job really was, he had said, "You know how Vietnamese are; they like to talk eight hours straight. Ed's the only one who has the patience to listen to them." I wondered why Lansdale was never allowed to meet Tri Quang. "I know Tri Quang better than anyone else," Lodge huffed. "I ought to. He lived ten weeks out in that conference room." When it was suggested that Lansdale had a reputation as the leading American counterinsurgency theoretician, Lodge snapped, "Ed's just one of two. Porter's the other." It was in this conversation that Lodge ratified Habib's victory with the phrase: "There are no civilian politicians in South Vietnam, just survivors of conspiracies against Diem and the French." I recognized this as the line Dr. Sung had been putting out for years.

From then until Ellsworth Bunker succeeded Lodge as ambassador in the spring of 1967, Lansdale seemed to have no function in Saigon except as a glorified idea man who wrote position papers of obscure destination. (When Bunker arrived in Saigon, he asked Lansdale to stay on as a political adviser and told him that he could see any Vietnamese leaders he pleased. Later, Lansdale was reportedly instrumental in helping to establish Bunker's close rapport with a number of leaders.) Why Lodge went along with the Habib memorandum remains a mystery. More than most Americans in Vietnam, Lodge verbally endorsed Sir Robert Thompson's political approach to counterinsurgency. Lodge once told me that while he felt Diem had done much for South Vietnam, he was out of touch with reality toward the end. I remembered this when I asked Lodge in the fall of 1966 what the Americans intended to do about Dr. Sung's maneuvering to gain control of the National Assembly. "Who is Dr. Sung?" the ambassador asked. He had been in Vietnam more than twenty months at the time.

Eight

Judo

*The introduction of U.S. troops . . . into South Vietnam
boosts rather than lowers the possibility of rallying various
political forces . . . the cost of living is skyrocketing and the
urban dwellers' life turns out to be more and more unbearable.*

—Le Duan, March 1966

As the war got bigger, the exodus from the countryside
began. The flood of peasants seeking refuge in the towns
eventually grew to 5,000,000—almost a third of the nation—
straining the already-eroded administration.

It always seemed hotter in Tay Ninh Province, northwest of
Saigon, than anyplace else in the southern Delta; perhaps it was
the lack of a river or sea, or the closeness of the Communist-held
jungles that stretched beyond Black Virgin Mountain into
Cambodia. It seemed especially hot the day I talked with a
Filipino doctor in charge of Tay Ninh's small hospital. He told me
civilian casualties were pouring in every day by ambulance,
helicopter and oxcart.

Some of the wounded were Viet Cong. "The soldiers and police
bring them in chained and manacled, and we try to save their
lives," the doctor said. "Sometimes they've been badly beaten.

Afterwards, I don't know what happens. Maybe they take them out and shoot them. I don't ask anymore." The surgical ward was suffocating. The patients—men, women and children thrown together for lack of space—kept their eyes fixed on the doctor. Beads of sweat clung to their foreheads. There was no fan.

"Here's an eight-year-old boy cut by shrapnel," the doctor told me. "All his guts were hanging out when they brought him in—but he's all right now. We sometimes get very small children. We have to amputate legs, arms. Some with shrapnel wounds. It is difficult with the children since I cannot speak Vietnamese."

In one bed lay a tall man swathed in bandages. "This policeman was shot just a mile from here. The liver was lacerated, stomach had two holes. But there's one good thing—he's alive."

A boy grinned at the doctor. "Seventeen years old. Perforation in stomach. Gunshot wound."

A pale young girl lay flat against her pillow, her long black hair tousled against a white sheet. Her face was impassive as she watched the doctor; the sheet lay flat over the lower half of the bed. "Twenty-three years old. Both legs shot off by misdirected friendly artillery." The doctor shot me a quick look. "Yes, half the combat wounded we are getting now are civilians."

"Is there any reward to your assignment here in Vietnam, Doctor?"

"Yes. You become very versed in traumatic surgery of the abdomen and chest—gunshots, grenades, shrapnel—their effect on the inside of a man is much the same. And you learn to control your emotions. Sometimes VIPs come to visit and ask how the patients got hurt and what we need. They always say, 'You're doing a wonderful job, Doctor.' I have a standard answer by now. 'Bedsheets.' We never got any."

By September 1965, the Pentagon announced that 600,000 peasants had fled their homes the previous year—many of them flood victims—and that 20,000 civilians had been killed or kidnaped by the Viet Cong during the previous eighteen months. By then, nearly 8,000 refugees reached the towns each week. More than 200 camps were built to house them on the outskirts of the population centers, but the Viet Cong started to attack these regularly.

Westmoreland's command began reporting accidental bombings of friendly villages in 1965: forty-eight killed in De Duc hamlet in Binh Dinh Province, twenty-six killed in 1966 in a village just outside the Delta's largest city of Can Tho, thirty-one killed when a fleet of sampans was mistakenly strafed on the Bassac River, fourteen killed in 1967 when a hamlet housing Viet Cong defectors was hit just outside Saigon. Major General James W. Humphreys, the director of the U.S. aid mission's public health service was to estimate that 50,000 civilians were treated at hospitals for war-related injuries in 1966.

Just before Christmas 1965, General Westmoreland briefed us on the intensified war. "Until now," he said, "the war has been characterized by a substantial majority of the population remaining neutral; they bent with the wind, seeking the side of the stronger. . . . In the past year we have seen an escalation to a higher level of intensity in the war. This will bring about a moment of decision for the peasant farmer. He will have to choose if he stays alive. Until now the peasant farmer has had three alternatives: he could stay put and follow his natural instinct to stay close to the land, living beside the graves of his ancestors. He could move to an area under government control. Or he could join the VC. . . . Now if he stays put there are additional dangers. The VC can't patch up wounds. If the peasant becomes a refugee, he does get shelter, food, and security, job opportunities and is given a hope to possibly return to his land. The third alternative is life with the VC. The VC have not made good on their promises; they no longer have secure areas. There are B-52 bombings, the VC tax demands are increasing; they want more recruits at the point of a gun, forced labor to move supplies. The battle is being carried more and more to the enemy."

When Westmoreland was asked, "Doesn't that give the villager only the choice of becoming a refugee?" the general replied indirectly: "I expect a tremendous increase in the number of refugees." Obviously, Westmoreland was trying to balance common humanity against military necessity. But although this road was paved with good intentions, it was inherently impossible to cope with refugees and civilian casualties as long as the Saigon government was run by Vietnamese who would not cooperate. I remembered a remark of Lansdale's: "The VC use our military power, judo-like, against our political interests."

A journey I took through the coastal provinces of Annam in August 1965 suggested how Hanoi planned to do this. As long as the charade held the stage in Saigon, they could make the United States military forces their unwitting political accomplice against the primary enemy, the South Vietnamese people. In a strategical sense, of course, the United States was the primary enemy, but tactically it was the South Vietnamese. If Hanoi could destroy the social structure and the popular will to resist, it could get Saigon to sue for a compromise peace, pulling the political basis for the war out from under the United States.

It was no accident that the worst refugee problem in 1965 was in Quang Ngai and Binh Dinh provinces, where Hanoi had come close to cutting the country in half. I found Quang Ngai City in a state of siege. The newly appointed province chief was a Buddhist physician with no previous administrative experience. He had been recently appointed to the post at Tri Quang's insistence and was visibly terrified. He stood in his large office before a sand-table replica of the city, studying the innumerable opportunities for ambush and attack between the painted canals, toy buildings and green-felt paddy fields. "The VC aim to occupy the city," he told me in a trembling voice, "so what we must do now is make a bastion of Quang Ngai. Why don't the Americans come? Then we could sleep again at night."

Outside his office, the little town's streets, parks, sidewalks and schoolhouses were crowded with dirty, hungry peasants; Viet Cong had burned down their hamlets and driven 45,000 of them like cattle into Quang Ngai City a few days before, to fight for food, water and shelter. Sick and hungry people were everywhere; if this kept up the provincial chief would not need to worry about his bastion plan; the city would fall by itself.

From one refugee settlement on the town's outskirts, we could see a hamlet about half a mile away, its thatched huts half-hidden by a grove of mahogany trees. In front about 200 people were standing in the drizzling rain. With their black umbrellas and pointed hats they resembled a congregation of mourners at a

burial. An old woman said that a platoon of guerrillas had
entered the hamlet the night before and the people had fled to
the treeline for fear the province chief in Quang Ngai would shell
it with artillery or call in American airplanes as he had done with
other friendly hamlets in the vicinity. They had been standing in
the rain for eighteen hours, wet and hungry and afraid to go
home, but also afraid to go into town, where there was no food.
Jim May, an American civilian-aid official, told me that if Saigon
didn't send more rice within a few days, "the honeymoon is over;
Quang Ngai could starve to death before the rains lift."

The refugees along the streets were in an ugly mood. One
woman cried, "The government cadres keep the money and rice
for themselves and let us starve." A youth shouted, "If you don't
give us rice we will join the Viet Cong." Some of these may have
been agitators. Many farmers told how the Viet Cong had killed
their cattle and burned down their hamlets. Some people
complained that the government gave them propaganda instead
of food. One official handout read: "The Viet Cong have followed
the Communist Chinese and Russians to divide Vietnam into two
parts. That is why Vietnamese are fighting Vietnamese." The
refugees were using the paper to start fires.

Just south along the coast in Qui Nhon, Sister Karen, an
American nun from Kentucky, who had been running the town's
Catholic hospital for five years, told me, "The Communists are
awfully close to winning. Frankly, I feel the war is rapidly
approaching a climax. It couldn't be much worse and have the
country survive. You see, the trouble with the refugees is that you
have to face the problem first. That it exists. This has to be done
by people who can do something about it." Sister Karen led me
through the biggest refugee camp in Qui Nhon. It was grim;
15,000 people had been jammed into a single city block with one
water well. For two months a steady stream of peasants had
poured through the gates of Qui Nhon cathedral. Most of them
were Catholic and had managed to bring along a few cherished
possessions—a lamp, some mats, a holy picture, a rosary, a
mirror, blankets. They told similar stories of having been beaten
and tortured by the Viet Cong, of seeing friends and relatives
murdered, of having their homes burned to the ground.

"These people are hungry," Sister Karen said, "but they've been suffering hardship and living in hell for twenty years. They accept things more easily than we would. They were mostly poor, but farmers and fishermen, and they lived respectably in their villages. They had plenty to eat and a clean life. A decent life. They had self-respect. It's not only that there are so many children among them but that even the old people have such a childlike faith. They're really teaching us what faith is. I keep thinking of 'Blessed are they which are persecuted for righteousness' sake: for theirs is the kingdom of heaven.' "

So these were the inheritors of the kingdom: hungry, dirty Asian peasants, some scarred by war wounds, others ravaged by disease. One family had lost five children to typhoid in fourteen days. But nothing seemed to shake their faith; they sat in their hovels, fingering rosaries, their lips moving silently.

In Danang, Vietnamese troops were holding back refugees from the city's gates at gunpoint. One shattered young American official told me he had just visited a hamlet after it had been mistakenly bombed and napalmed by American aircraft: "The village dispensary was full of people with napalm burns all over their bodies. One man had just lost his wife and four children and his house had been burned down. He just sat there, waiting for the rice dole we were handing out. How he must have hated us." A Vietnamese civilian official I spoke to in Danang said, "If the VC come into a village, the people flee to avoid American bombing, because the government then declares it a target." A senior American official there felt that "the Viet Cong has torn off its mask and shown its real self through indiscriminate terror and burning down these villages. But so have we. If the American military had its way, we'd go through this country and burn down the villages one by one. But then, what's the alternative?" A U.S. marine in one of the bars told me, "Quite a few of the guys say we ought to start at the bottom and work our way right up. Like in Korea. In Korea, we destroyed everything and it's all built up now. That's the only way we're ever going to win here." A drunken Vietnamese air force pilot said, "Intelligence say many, many VC in village. We drop bombs. Destroy many, many villages. Sometimes VC run, run; too much VC, shoot with gun when finish with bomb."

In August, Westmoreland ordered major new restrictions on in-country bombing and shelling. That same month, the American Embassy, which had been reluctant to take over the refugee problem itself, launched its first emergency relief program. James S. Killen, Taylor's civilian-aid director, initially resisted the program, arguing that the Vietnamese administrative system could not be made viable unless the Saigon government controlled the purse strings of American-financed budgetary support. In Washington, General Taylor came to Killen's defense and told a Senate hearing that only if aid was handled by "responsible Vietnamese ministries" could the United States "leave behind a class of social-minded, trained administrators." While defensible in theory, the total administrative collapse made the argument academic. Killen was sent home and Taylor's advice ignored.

The refugee problem was never to be solved. In late 1967, the American aid director for the northern provinces sent a secret report to the U.S. Marine commander urging "a crash program" to feed and house refugees. The official called the existing program "a highly visible failure" and warned that the "psychological loss to the allied cause is incalculable, not only among refugees but on the Viet Cong claim that the Vietnamese government is not interested in the rural people." (By the spring of 1968, nearly 5,000,000 South Vietnamese at one time or another had been uprooted from their homes since the fall of Diem.) This was exactly the effect Le Duan and his colleagues in the Hanoi Politburo were trying to produce; it was a skillful, calculated, logical exploitation of human suffering.

In the fall of 1965, it seemed very late for South Vietnam—almost the midnight hour—and yet the country went on. The Vietnamese people had an extraordinary ability to adapt to any situation. This was a liability, in that they adapted to problems rather than tackling and getting rid of them. But it was also an asset; without this ability to adapt, their day-to-day life would have disintegrated completely.

United States opinion tended to see Vietnam as one vast, boiling battleground; a marine once told me, "My folks thought I had to start fighting for my life the minute I got off the plane." In reality, until the DMZ opened in 1967 as a fixed battlefront, the battles and terror struck like unexpected summer lightning, and in most of the country ordinary life went on. Markets were open, buses came and went; admittedly there were a lot of shady deals, but life went on.

One thing, however, affected everybody: food. The pivotal urban population had to buy rice.

Starting with the fall of Diem and throughout 1964, South Vietnam slipped rapidly into an artificial war economy. By January 1965, after nine years of American investment totaling $2.2 billion in economic aid and $1.2 billion in military aid, the country's crippled economic machinery had to be heavily fueled with American dollars just to keep running. The United States was paying 80% of the country's trade deficit, or, equally divided among all the South Vietnamese people, $30 of the average man's $100 yearly wage.

Hanoi seemed aware that a massive depression would follow a Communist victory and that generous Soviet aid would be required to reconstruct the economy. Thus Hanoi's economic strategy during the war was to disrupt and damage the economy as much as possible without destroying its industrial or agricultural base. Development projects such as the An Hao-Nong Son industrial complex inland from Danang, were rarely attacked; the Communists simply tried to keep them from operating by hitting transportation and communication links around them—roads, canals, and telephone lines. Rather than tear up the French-owned rubber plantations and Saigon's large textile mills, the Viet Cong tried keeping them shut for months on end through labor strikes by Communist-controlled unions.

But until the Dai Viet brotherhood seized power in February 1965, there had been little inflation despite the gradual intensification of the war. The September 1964 price index was exactly the same as a year earlier for home and export goods, although there was a small increase in prices of imported goods. Wholesale prices had understandably risen 15% since 1960 for three reasons: a devaluation of the Vietnamese piastre under Diem, the rise in world prices, and a rise in the government rice price as a production incentive. But, apart from seasonal price fluctuations, the year-to-year situation had remained remarkably stable. Then, in the summer of 1965, South Vietnam's economy experienced radical change. An almost-classic wartime inflationary situation was created, with monetary expenditures expanding fast at a time when real production was not only declining but was being subjected to severe distribution difficulties by the Viet Cong.

Four main elements lay behind this: 1) General Giap's 1965 monsoon offensive and the mass exodus of peasants into the towns, which led to a dislocation in production and a large-scale breakdown in communications and distribution; 2) the Saigon government's mounting expenditures in order to pay the salaries of 700,000 men under arms, plus 100,000 civilian workers, at a time of declining revenue; 3) rapidly expanding expenditures by the burgeoning American armed forces, coupled with a crash military-construction program of $1 billion; 4) growing internal subversion of the economy.

The chief economic mechanism used by the United States to fight inflation was to pour in more consumer goods and food, rather than try to increase South Vietnam's domestic production in wartime. In 1966, the U.S.-financed Community Import Program amounted to $350,000,000. These CIP funds went to buy American oil, cement, fertilizers, medicine, chemicals, machinery and other goods. They were shipped to Vietnam and sold to local businessmen for Vietnamese piastres. The buyers were mostly rich Chinese importers who belonged to a kind of club; its membership was controlled through the issuance of import licenses. (South Vietnam's Chinese community was thought to control about 65% of the economy and virtually all of the import trade. The Vietnamese throughout their history had shown little entrepreneurial skill.) In turn, officials in Ky's government got a payoff for issuing these licenses.

The purchasers of the American-financed goods, then, were men who could afford to pay for them. The proceeds of the sale of these goods were turned over to Ky's government to pay the salaries of soldiers and civil servants, buy rice for buffer stocks and contract services. An additional $75,000,000 worth of food was supplied in 1966, most of it intended for refugee relief although some turned up in Saigon markets.

In short, this was the system: The United States gave goods, goods were sold to people with money to pay for them, and the money went to support the war. The effect was to nourish an urban economy in which the middle and upper classes benefited. The policy did almost nothing to improve the lives of slum dwellers or the peasants, who comprised 80% of the population. A Vietnamese peasant spent cash only on kerosene, cheap cloth and beer, and bartered for most other things. What did affect the peasant in 1966 was $150,000,000 in direct U.S. aid which went for pigs, corn seed, barbed wire for local defenses, and the building of schools, bridges, roads, markets and hospitals. Some of this was siphoned off into the pockets of officials out in the provinces. And the net effect of U.S. economic policy was to make the rich richer and the poor poorer.

Once inflation became serious, as it did by late 1965, corruption was almost a necessity for soldiers and civil servants on fixed government salaries, whose real income began to be swallowed up at a rate of 11% per month in early 1966. A Saigon taxi driver, for instance, made about $125 a month, while a Vietnamese army captain with a family made around $90. For low-salaried enlisted men, thievery from the peasants became endemic as the only way to keep themselves and their families fed.

The Ky government, from the moment it took power in June 1965 until the presidential elections of September 1967, took one step after another that in effect worsened the inflation and fed the growth of corruption and social decay.

Premier Quat had formally abolished the Vietnamese civil service. One of Ky's first acts in office was to ban further free transport and housing for government employees and to reduce the salaries of senior officials 50%, forcing many highly qualified men into private business. Under Ky, Saigon's city bus system almost stopped functioning. Tens of thousands of cheap Japanese motor scooters were imported, and as free-spending American soldiers turned Saigon's taxi fleet into more of a procurement than a transportation system, ownership of a scooter became almost imperative for middle-class Vietnamese. Hundreds of military officers and civil servants began moonlighting by offering the services of their scooters as a kind of impromptu taxi. Some of them took to pimping and their daughters turned to prostitution, although probably on a much smaller scale than was claimed in Communist propaganda.

Ky and the brotherhood generals opened two large Saigon

nightclubs, Maxim's and La Siren; a table was always held for
Ky, and the minimum charge for a drink was $3.25—what most
Vietnamese soldiers lived on for at least a week. There was
nothing surreptitious about this; Ky and his wife attended a red-
carpet opening of Maxim's, as gaudy with white-gloved troops
and kleig lights as any Hollywood première. Part of the Maxim
establishment, which included two restaurants and several bars,
was a massage parlor called "The Golden Hands" catering to
Americans. Ky also received 25% of the weekly profits from
Cholon's big Phu Tho racetrack, according to a CBS exposé. One
sometimes heard street vendors and taxi drivers describe Ky as a
man who surrounded himself with "war profiteers and gangsters."

Starting in late 1965, Hanoi made rising food prices its major
propaganda issue. A typical Liberation Radio appeal: "Compatriots, your money is only an inflated banknote which cannot cope
with the increasingly grave shortage of foodstuffs and constantly
rising cost of living. Compatriots! Do not stand idly by deploring
your lot. Rise up! Hold meetings, stage demonstrations with
thousands, tens of thousands, to compel the American aggressors
and their puppet rulers to solve the price problem."

Such appeals were coupled with calls to protest the requisi-
tioning of land for U.S. military installations, food shortages, and
the hardships of economic life in the cities. There were also
contradictory boasts that the Viet Cong had severed supply
routes. Hanoi broadcast almost daily: "We are holding the
lifelines of the enemy's economy in the towns and cities and
controlling their communication links. Get ready to rise up!" On
October 15, 1965, the Viet Cong called for an hour-long
nationwide general strike. It was universally ignored. But on
October 16th there were large antiwar demonstrations in many
American cities and European capitals. This phenomenon
happened again in late March 1966. One day 20,000 persons
marched in an antigovernment demonstration in the old imperial
capital of Hue; the next day there were simultaneous antiwar
demonstrations in New York, Chicago, Washington, Detroit,
London, Stockholm, Tokyo, Oslo, Toronto and Buenos Aires. In
early 1967, when I mentioned this before an executive session of
the Senate Foreign Relations Committee, Senator Fulbright
asked if I meant to imply that these events were all part of a

"worldwide Communist conspiracy." I told Fulbright my guess was that Hanoi learned of prescheduled foreign demonstrations and then announced some agitational movement of its own for the preceding day so that it would look to the Vietnamese people as if the global demonstrations were intended as a gesture of sympathy and support for the Viet Cong rather than simply antiwar protest.

Viet Cong propaganda unaccompanied by terror, intimidation or deception was almost never effective in Vietnam. A typical reaction was that of a Saigon schoolteacher who had listened to the Liberation Radio broadcasts and told me, "Anybody would be crazy to want the VC to take over. My house, my wife, money, everything would be the government's. Before, when I was a boy, they came to the Delta and took my father's land. Then they took my bicycle. Even my bicycle. I was too rich for them. But there is still the feeling here that the United States might someday decide to pull out and anybody who sticks his neck out now will lose it then. Most people seem to feel it's better not to commit yourself too far on either side."

The cost-of-living index, if one used January 1965 as a mean of 100%, rose to 270% by late 1967. (This was before the massive dislocation of the economy in Giap's 1968 Tet offensive, which forced prices up an immediate 80%, although within two weeks this dropped to only 14%.) The money supply went up about the same amount. Much of the rise came from the price of rice, which jumped 200%. By late 1967, the United States was dumping $500,000,000 worth of goods a year into Vietnam, and the economic officials in Saigon began urging Washington to put greater reliance on domestic production. Oddly enough, per-capita real income rose statistically from $15 a head in 1964 to $40 a head in late 1967, suggesting that a few profiteers were making vast fortunes from the war.

I first began questioning the economic performance of Ky's regime just a few days after Ky assumed office in June 1965, when he refused to take the anti-inflationary steps recommended by the Bank of Vietnam and the American economic officials. His refusal seemed so illogical. Ky took the line that firm anti-inflationary measures were politically unacceptable and fired the bank's manager. His first economics minister, Truong Thai Ton, was notoriously incompetent and later was named in U.S. Senate hearings as one of several of Ky's Cabinet ministers who had demanded kickbacks from American exporters.

At the Honolulu conference of February 1966, President Johnson asked Ky to sign a number of economic agreements pledging immediate anti-inflationary steps on behalf of his government. As soon as Ky returned to Saigon, he replaced Ton with a new economics minister, Au Truong Thanh, a half-Chinese professor at Saigon University. Thanh promptly repudiated the Honolulu economic agreements on the grounds that they were politically infeasible. The American economics mission in Saigon did' not reveal this to the press until almost two full years later.

The day Thanh's appointment was announced, a Vietnamese friend asked if Ky and Johnson had made some kind of deal in Hawaii to arrange a peace on compromise terms with Hanoi. When I asked why he put such a question, he told me that Thanh was a notorious pro-Communist, who had been allied with Nguyen Huu Tho and Huyen Tan Phat, the National Liberation Front's president and deputy, in a 1954 movement to protest the partition of Vietnam, and again, in 1956, to advocate reunification elections. He remembered that Dr. Sung had also played a behind-the-scenes role in this movement (which I was later to confirm in official U.S. files). The record showed that in 1960 Thanh had been arrested by the Diem government as a suspected Communist sympathizer. He was also known to be a close associate of Tri Quang. Students in Thanh's Saigon University classes told me that their professor had Marxist views.

Thanh's performance did nothing to allay my suspicions. By early June 1966, inflation threatened to go completely out of control, especially after several weeks during which Thanh withheld American imported rice from the market until Ambassador Lodge personally protested to Ky. In mid-June, Thanh bowed to American pressure and agreed to act on International Monetary Fund recommendations that the South Vietnamese piastre be devaluated by 50%. The devaluation, which pushed the cost-of-living index up 31% in July over May, was expected by American officials to buy at least eight months of relative price stability.

To make the devaluation work, Roy Wehrlie, the head of the American economics mission, received Thanh's written pledge that he would keep the price of rice artificially low by selling imported American rice at about half its cost and by keeping the price paid to Vietnamese producers steady. Since the average city dweller spent 15% to 20% of his total income on rice, this was the key mechanism to make the devaluation succeed. Severe restraint was also put on the supply of money. In particular, banks were asked to limit their loans and advances to the private sector.

The immediate effect of this was to keep money comparatively short. The rapid increase in prices came temporarily to an end in August. The cost-of-living index stabilized over the period August to October 1966 at a level slightly lower than July. Encouraged by the result, the White House invited Thanh to visit Washington in early October. Thanh was briefed on future American plans and policy and spent long hours with Robert Komer, President Johnson's special aide on the nonmilitary aspects of the Vietnam war.

During Thanh's stay in Washington, the political struggle of the Cochinchinese and Roman Catholic coalition, led by Tran Van Van, against the Ky regime resulted in the resignation of all native-born southerners from Ky's predominantly Tonkinese government. Using this as a pretext, although Tran Van Van flatly regarded Thanh as a pro-Communist, Thanh announced his resignation and flew back to Saigon on the eve of the Manila summit conference. Before resigning, however, Thanh broke his pledge to Wehrlie and substantially raised the price of American imported rice. This sent market prices soaring again and wrecked all the stabilizing effect of the June devaluation. (In late November, Nguyen Van Hiep, a Chinese deputy in the Assembly and a member of the Saigon municipal council, publicly accused Thanh of having "deliberately sabotaged the economy." Hiep presented Lodge with a documented dossier of charges. The Viet Cong attempted to assassinate Hiep the following year.)

Thanh retired to the wings and did not again have a role in the charade until the 1967 presidential election, when he was officially disqualified as a candidate on the grounds that he held "pro-Communist" sympathies. It seemed that the National

Assembly, which took the action, shared my friend's opinion.

The Ky regime defended Thanh's destructive parting shot as a political move that would put money into the hands of the peasantry and raise revenue to offset the massive budget deficit. But the real effect of Thanh's action was to shorten the breathing space afforded by devaluation from eight months to barely five. The cost of living and the money supply once again began to rise. The Ky regime also reneged on its promised tight-money policy. Commercial bank claims on the private sector rose 45% between the end of September and the end of November alone, compared with a slight fall in the same two months in 1965.

With Thanh's resignation, Ky broke up the Economics Ministry into two parts, then three, then reunited it and put it under the incompetent Ton again. After a few weeks, the U.S. economics mission was informed that Ton, who had never put in a single appearance at his office, was ill with hepatitis. According to William Sharp, an able young economics officer in the U.S. mission, the Economics Ministry became so paralyzed that it did not take any steps to combat inflation until March 1967. By then it was too late for the Ky government to announce the annual official rice price in time for the spring sowing. This price in previous years had been the key determinant of rural income in South Vietnam. For five months there was no economics minister or functioning ministry.

In early March, the Ky regime provoked still another price crisis by letting their stocks of U.S. imported rice dwindle to almost nothing. The American mission was not informed and had no way of checking the warehouses, since the rice supplies in some apparently full ones turned out to be already allocated to Vietnamese army units. Saigon's rice retailers, who normally put in applications and got deliveries of rice five days later, were put off for several weeks. Then, on a single day, rice retailers all over the city were simultaneously informed that the government had completely run out of rice. Predictably, in the panic and speculation that followed, the price of rice shot up nearly 20% in ten days.

Saigon newspapers owned or influenced by the Dai Viets immediately published stories quoting unidentified government officials who blamed the crisis on inadequate American rice deliveries, a patent falsehood. The United States quickly rushed 20,000 tons of rice from Taiwan and diverted another 20,000 tons from ships en route elsewhere. A Ky government delegation, after ignoring American recommendations to do so for four months, finally went to Bangkok to buy emergency rice.

The victims of this economic subversion were, as always, the ordinary Vietnamese.

"Oh God, the price is too high," I heard a shabbily dressed civil servant say in one shop. "How can I live?" A dock worker told me, "People are unsatisfied with the government. General Ky used to promise he would help the people have a better life, but now everyone is frightened about the price of rice and corruption is worse." A priest in the slums said, "As a Catholic I know that if we recognize the National Liberation Front, our life will get much worse. But the situation is getting delicate. Many people don't care who wins; their lives are so miserable. They just think about peace so there will be plenty of rice, they can return to their villages and their children can come back home and live."

In late 1967, the United States agreed to "scrape together" 750,000 tons of American rice while hoping for another 200,000 tons from the southern Delta to meet an overall deficit of 900,000 tons in Saigon and the northern coastal towns. After the 1968 Tet offensive it was doubtful this much would reach Saigon from the Delta. The year Ngo Dinh Diem fell, in 1963, South Vietnam had *exported* 322,500 tons of rice.

Nine

Land to the Tiller

> *In a colonial country where the majority of laboring people were peasants, the problem of democracy basically was land. Without solving the problem of land, it would be impossible to attract all agricultural laborers to enthusiastically rise up and oppose the imperialists and achieve national independence.*

—Le Duan, December 1966

"This earth which formed their house and fed their bodies and made their gods . . ." So wrote Pearl Buck in *The Good Earth*. It was this deep attachment of the Asian peasant to the soil he tilled, to the earth in which his ancestors were buried, that told the real story of the Mekong Delta.

When I returned to Long An Province in 1966, a year after the killing at Tan Buu, it was again harvest time. The golden fields on the great fertile plain between the Saigon, Bassac and Mekong rivers were dotted with men and women winnowing the precious rice against tall curved shelters of plaited bamboo. Hardly a grain was lost. In black pajamas and pointed straw hats, barefoot and bronzed by the January sun, these peasants had the sturdy look of men and women who could endure disease, natural disaster and war so long as they had some land to till and call their own. The problem was, of course, that very few did own land.

Someday, one felt, historians would say that everything was done but the obvious in Vietnam. Vietnam was an Asian rice culture. The country's entire social and economic fabric was woven around the growing of rice. More than any ideology, it was the southward push for rice lands from the crowded, hungry north that provided the real impetus for the war.

Since my first visit in the spring of 1964, the heaviest fighting had raged in the jungles and rubber-plantation country north of Saigon, the rain forests and grasslands of the high plateau, and the swamps and coastal rice flats of Annam's narrow coastal plain. But the rice-rich heartland around Saigon and the upper Delta remained the prize for which the war was being fought.

In 1964, Long An was being held up as the showplace of how a combined Vietnamese-American military and economic pacification effort could defeat a Communist-led insurgency. Visitors went there if they wanted to see how the protracted guerrilla war was going in the countryside. For the next few years almost nothing would change. From 1964 through early 1968, there was no dramatic turn in the fighting in Long An; the government won some villages and, as with Tan Buu, lost some. There were few signs of serious deterioration once the Viet Cong advance that followed Ngo Dinh Diem's fall was arrested. But there was no improvement, either; since it was primarily a war of subversion in the Delta, the creeping Communist political initiative simply crept farther. Other peasants replaced the thousands of Viet Cong and government troops slain in battle. Every time a loyal village chief or a Communist commissar was killed, another man stepped from the ranks to fill his place. But American military and civilian advisers agreed there were more Viet Cong sympathizers in the countryside and towns each year.

Most important, in Long An in early 1966, the government and the mass of peasantry still seemed to be on opposing sides of the fight. Although in areas of South Vietnam where there was a non-Communist political base and the peasants knew what Communism was they opposed it, in Long An most prosperous landlords had fled to the government-held towns, and the bulk of the Viet Cong officers were sons of landless tenants (as were the rank-and-file troops on both sides). The political commissars told the peasant youths they faced three enemies: bloodsucking landlords,

American imperialists and the fascist puppet government in Saigon. Since the peasants had no experience with either Saigon or Americans, except as symbols of what they thought to be a foreign invasion, the focus was on the landlord's exploitation of their labor, which they understood. Unlike the Tonkinese refugees and Annamites who had experienced Communist rule, or the sophisticated Saigonese, the bulk of the Mekong Delta peasantry thought the National Liberation Front genuinely represented a Cochinchinese movement for land and independence. Hanoi wisely sent few Annamite or Tonkinese officers and commissars into the Delta; as General Westmoreland put it, "Northerners are not welcomed by the Viet Cong in the Mekong Delta." Only landless or very poor farmers in the Delta were put in command of guerrilla units or qualified as Communist party members. The government's social order was the exact reverse. Most of the military officers, civil servants and community leaders came either from the old mandarin and landowning gentry class or from the new urban middle class (as indeed did most of the Politburo members in Hanoi).

In September 1966, Le Duan said that the "two main slogans" used in Communist propaganda and the principal justification to its rank-and-file soldiers were "national independence" and "land to the tiller." Ambassador Lodge once told me he regarded the Communist promise of land reform as "perhaps the greatest appeal the Viet Cong have." The Mekong Delta was the world's richest rice-growing area. Eighty per cent of the South Vietnamese people were rice-cultivating peasantry. Yet in the southern Delta half the peasants owned no land and 77% were sharecropping tenants—80% in strategic Long An Province. This land-ownership pattern explained better than anything else why, despite a huge cost in lives and matériel, the war in the Delta was no closer to being won.

The history of land reform in Vietnam is a story of deception, half steps and unfulfilled promises.

In the early fifties, the last Indochinese emperor, Bao Dai, became sufficiently alarmed by Communist promises of "land to the tiller" to institute the country's first land-reform measures. He tried gradually to reduce land rents from 50% of the crop to 15% and to ensure tenure. As the youthful imperial ruler himself superciliously described it, "Numerous humble little Vietnamese, little preoccupied with politics, have gained possession of the soil." But, in practice, most of Bao Dai's reform laws were rendered inoperative by generous safeguards to the landlords. The young emperor's wife herself, who had vast land holdings, used these very safeguards to evict her tenants when they demanded lower rents in accordance with her husband's law. Bao Dai became the laughing stock of Saigon; what had been a well-intentioned effort ended as a fiasco.

Ho Chi Minh had come to power claiming to be the leader of an authentic national movement for land and independence. But behind the Communist seizure of North Vietnam in 1954 and its attempt to conquer the south lay a powerful historical under-current. The whole history of Vietnam had been the story of a search for secure land by a teeming peasant population who managed to retain their ethnic distinction despite more than a thousand years of domination by Chinese dynasties.

This was the relentless push down the coastal deltas along the South China Sea that destroyed the more civilized Cham and Khmer kingdoms in its wake and finally spilled out over the Mekong Delta in the eighteenth century. In a sense the southern Delta, or Cochinchina, as the French named it, was Vietnam's Wild West and was settled much the same time as American pioneers were first reaching California and Oregon. The historical drive continues to this day. It lies behind the dreams of many Vietnamese—not only the Communists—to seize control of Laos, Cambodia and beyond.

Ho Chi Minh used land reform as a justification for destroying the north's Confucian social structure and substituting a totalitarian Communist one. But it was always a cruel deception; collectivization was not land distribution. After Ho's guerrillas seized power in Hanoi in 1954, Truong Chinh, the extreme Maoist of the Hanoi Politburo, was put in charge of land reform. Truong Chinh carried out the program with Chinese cadres and used every available bit of force and propaganda devices to stuff it down the throats of the Vietnamese peasantry.

His program resulted in one of the most brutal and bloody peasant oppressions of modern times, shocking the Vietnamese peasants and battle-hardened soldiers even more than the methods used in the war against the French. Truong Chinh first redistributed land into small holdings, then went on to collectivize it through forced "cooperatives." It is authoritatively estimated by such observers as the late Bernard Fall that more than 50,000 Tonkinese peasants died in the process; another 100,000 were imprisoned or deported to the mountains. A climax was reached on November 2, 1956, when the world's attention was turned to Hungary and the Suez crisis. To crush the rebellious peasants, Hanoi sent in its 325th Division, which later would be the first to infiltrate south in 1965. The division reportedly killed more than 6,000 peasants in three days. According to P. J. Honey, the British authority on North Vietnam, tens of thousands of innocent people were killed in the most heinous tortures to set an example for the others. The Communist regime itself was threatened, and Ho hurriedly held a "correction of errors" campaign and forced Truong Chinh to resign as party secretary-general and make a public "autocriticism." Had not Truong Chinh had the personal support of Mao Tse-tung, his career would have been ended; instead, he remained a powerful behind-the-scenes figure in the Politburo.

Neither Ho Chi Minh nor the Viet Cong were agrarian reformers in any sense of the word; rather, they exploited the land issue as another internal contradiction to weaken and divide the enemy. This, in turn, created an extremely important internal contradiction in the Communist camp itself. A vast majority of the Cochinchinese guerrillas had been deceived into fighting for Cochinchinese independence from northern as well as foreign domination and for the right to own the land they tilled. These were the two things the Hanoi Politburo, if victorious, would have to deny them.

In late 1967, Adam Malik, the able foreign minister of post-Sukarno Indonesia and one of the most perceptive Asian leaders I ever met, told me that he believed Ho could not possibly win in South Vietnam, because the Communists could not take their final step into power without dropping their masks. Malik predicted this would trigger another spontaneous bloodbath as had happened in Indonesia. Malik believed that at that moment the Viet Cong rank and file would themselves join the anti-Communists and non-Communists in rising against both Hanoi's political structure in the south and the secret Mandarin Dai Viet brotherhood in Saigon. He was confident the uprising would take place, providing an American president like Johnson remained in office and was willing to persevere long enough.

Certainly, as the war wore on, it became increasingly apparent that Hanoi saw itself as waging two distinct though closely related conflicts: the ideological war between Communists and anti-Communists for the loyalty of the non-Communist majority and the civil war between Tonkinese and Cochinchinese, which was an extension of Vietnam's historical past. For this reason, I think, it was imperative that Hanoi seize control of the rest of the country, including Saigon, with Tonkinese-dominated forces before the moment of victory, when the Cochinchinese insurgents would no longer be deceived. Why Barry Zorthian, the American information chief in Saigon, did not exploit this internal contradiction in the enemy camp with the vast propaganda apparatus at his command remained a puzzle.

Both the Americans and the Saigon governments chronically failed to expose the Communist deception on land reform. Moreover, the only real advances in land reform itself were made under Ngo Dinh Diem. Between 1955 and 1957, Diem pushed through laws legally limiting rent to 25% on the first rice crop. He also put a ceiling of 247 acres on individual holdings, plus another 75 acres if the owner farmed the land himself. This was obviously too conservative and limited an approach as compared with similar reforms in Taiwan and Japan, where a 10-acre to 15-acre ceiling was enacted and enforced. The Japanese reform was rammed through by General MacArthur during the American occupation. In Taiwan, Generalissimo Chiang Kai-shek was determined to avoid the mistake that had helped defeat him on the mainland. In both Taiwan and Japan, this dramatic change in the pattern of rural land ownership laid the basis for rapid economic advance by creating the purchasing power of a broad-based class of small owner-operators in the countryside.

But limited as they were, Diem's legal rents were never enforced. In 1967, most landlords were still collecting 30% to 50% of the crop from their tenants, often with help from local army commanders in return for a bribe. Other landlords were allowed to follow soldiers reoccupying Viet Cong-controlled countryside to collect their back rents.

An example of this took place in early 1967, when Vietnamese and American forces reoccupied Long Huu island in southern Long An Province without firing a shot. During the one year they had administered the island, the Viet Cong had redistributed land, giving everyone, including the former landlords, 2.5 acres apiece. They also collected 1,100 piastres, or about $100 in taxes from the new owners. This was a much higher amount than the tenants had been paying in rent to the previous owners.

When Long Huu was retaken, the peasants were allowed to keep the 2.5 acres to farm, while land titles were restored to their former owners. Vietnamese government officials on the scene managed to sell Colonel Sam Wilson, the able counterinsurgency expert running the project as special aide to Ambassador Lodge, on the notion that the Long Huu peasants preferred renting their fields, since this was cheaper—at 25% of the crop—than the Viet Cong taxes. Wilson told me, "Ownership itself is not an issue. The peasant really wants the right to squat on a piece of land at reasonable terms." This sounded like sophistry to me, and my interpreter and I hunted down the Vietnamese research team who had produced this finding and grilled them until one broke down and confessed that he had been ordered to lie to Wilson. "Of course all the peasants want to own their land. What do you think?" he said. "They told us they were afraid to say so for fear the Americans and government officials would accuse them of being pro-VC."

Despite its shortcomings, the Diem government did achieve the expropriation of about one-third of the Delta's arable rice land. Yet by 1967, only half of this had been redistributed to 116,000 families. The Ky government, once it came to power, held on to the rest. More than half a million acres of prime Delta rice land, including at least 160,000 acres in relatively secure areas, were rented out by Ky's regime. The proceeds were shared by local officials, most of them Vietnamese army officers and Ky's men in Saigon.

On July 4, 1964, *Pravda* published an article by a Soviet correspondent who claimed to have been in South Vietnam with the Viet Cong forces. He asserted that the National Liberation Front had confiscated more than 5,000,000 acres of land from "traitors and collaborators" and redistributed it to landless tenants. Three-fourths of this land, he said, was in the

Cochinchinese Saigon region and Mekong Delta. The Soviet journalist claimed that this redistribution had produced decisive changes in the south's social structure and had raised two-thirds of the landless to the category of "medium peasant." That same year, the NLF, in a Liberation Radio broadcast, declared that peasants under its control were "masters of more than 3.2 million acres of South Vietnam's total 8.6 million acres of cultivated land."

The *Pravda* article, not surprisingly, was largely propaganda. The American mission had several land-reform experts on its staff—detached agricultural technicians with no political axe to grind—who spent years studying the land issue. They were never able to learn of a single instance where the Viet Cong had distributed permanent land titles. Instead, peasants, as in Diem's program, were given provisional titles with the implication that this was "people's land," which was presumably destined for eventual collectivization. Most peasants chose to ignore this; they seemed to regard Viet Cong tax receipts as bona-fide land titles.

The record of Nguyen Cao Ky on land reform is a remarkable study in unkept promises. In Honolulu in February 1966, Ky pledged, along with President Johnson, his support for "social revolution, including land reform." In the Manila communiqué of October 1966, Ky promised that "land reform and tenure provisions will be given top priority." In the Guam communiqué of March 1967, Ky promised "reform of land policies and tenure provisions." At Guam, Ky also told a press conference attended by the White House press corps accompanying Johnson that he had distributed 2,000,000 acres of land to the South Vietnamese peasantry. This was an outright falsehood but was widely reported. At no time, from June 1965, when he assumed office, until President Thieu was sworn in on October 31, 1967, did Ky ever transfer title of a single acre of land from a landowner to a poor tenant. Not one. Ever.

What Ky did do, under intense pressure from Ambassador Lodge, a strong advocate of land reform, was to distribute 63,000 permanent titles to substitute for provisional ones handed out by Diem in 1957 to 116,000 farm operators. In other words, at all his well-publicized "land distribution" ceremonies, Ky substituted one piece of paper for another to farmers who had already owned and tilled the land for a decade. It was a step forward but a very superficial one. Ky also gave title to some squatters who had cleared new land, but on a negligible scale.

Thus the pattern of land ownership in the southern Delta remained a social and economic cancer, isolating the Saigon government from the bulk of the South Vietnamese peasantry.

What needed to be done?

The basic problem: As of mid-1967, according to official Embassy statistics, South Vietnam had 2,400,000 farm families with an average membership of five persons in a country of 8,600,000 acres of cultivated land, of which nearly 6,000,000 acres was rice land, the bulk of it in the Mekong Delta. Of these families, 700,000 shared in varying degrees in the ownership of land and 1,700,000 families were completely landless. Tenants comprised between 65% and 70% of the total rural population, which in turn accounted for eight out of every ten South Vietnamese.

In the twenty-two provinces of Cochinchina proper, only 23% of the farms were owner-operated as compared with roughly 80% in Japan, Thailand and Taiwan. Nearly 50% of the Delta's population had no land at all, and 77% had either none or less than 2 acres, which was not enough to make a living. U.S. farm experts estimated that a Vietnamese farm family of five needed at least 5 acres of rice land to support itself. Along the populated coast of Annam, only 11% of the peasantry were totally landless; the more equitable pattern of ownership under the old imperial kingdom at Hue had made the problem less acute.

The biggest need was to increase the basis of ownership, to achieve the kind of transformation of the social and economic structure that had occurred when Japan and Taiwan became economies based on a broad pattern of rural owner-operators. Such division of land also depended on sound government policies regarding the availability of credit, fertilizer and marketing facilities to ensure that smaller holdings became economically viable.

It was estimated that a 7- to 10-acre holding would be ideal for the average Cochinchinese farm family. If a 10-acre retention rate could be pushed through, as MacArthur had done in Japan, the basis of permanent political stability and economic prosperity would be established. This would eliminate the rootless, landless tenants as a social majority in South Vietnam instead of leaving them to form a ready pool of Viet Cong recruits.

Some experts felt it was also imperative to enforce 25% legal maximum rents by expropriating the lands of violators. They believed that Saigon should immediately ban military commanders from using their troops to collect rent from the peasantry. Responsibility for rent collection, land payments, earnings from government land, taxation and power to settle land disputes—all these should be given to locally elected village councils.

The price of the Ky regime's inaction was not only enormous in terms of American and Vietnamese lives but also in the demoralization that infected the political attitudes of those involved. What seemed to be absent in the Delta was the kind of political code Theodore H. White has described as President Johnson's "grass-roots liberalism": "You get yours and he gets his and we all share what there is to share." In Long An Province this got no farther than "you get yours," and he, the peasant, had no recourse but to try to get his by joining the Viet Cong.

But as the war intensified and Viet Cong taxes soared, especially during 1967, many peasants began to suspect that under Viet Cong rule nobody kept his. This created the kind of political vacuum that led thoughtful Vietnamese to regard the war as a pointless slaughter. They felt they stood to be the losers no matter who won. Caught between the landlords, many of whom charged double the legal rents, and the Viet Cong tax collectors, who shot first and talked later, the peasants in Long An were ready to call a plague on both houses.

Yet to the uninformed, who still appeared to be in the majority, Le Duan's "slogans" had great appeal. "Land to the tiller," "national independence," and "the government exists for the people" were novel and explosive ideas to a man who worked knee-deep in mud fourteen hours a day, growing half his rice for somebody else, and whose idea of government might be a venal tax collector or a soldier who carried away his ducks or chickens. Such a man, if his home was destroyed or his relatives were killed by misdirected bombs and shells, might make a Viet Cong convert without knowing anything about Communism or that Hanoi was directing the war.

One American captain who was going home after a year in Long An told me, "These people have a country that doesn't need a government. They could go back 2,000 years and they'd be happy. Fish in every pond, crabs in every paddy, bananas, coconut and ducks. All they need is a little land of their own. Of the Vietnamese in this province, 5% are honestly pro-government by their own personal beliefs and ideology, 5% are with the VC for the same reason, and the other 90% are right."

Although many of the farm boys defected from the Viet Cong in large numbers whenever American troops came into a Delta area, they remained politically committed to the Viet Cong's announced aims. Of some three dozen interviewed at an "Open Arms" camp in Long An, almost all came from families with "one-half hectare of land and no buffalo" or nothing at all. Most of them wore brand-new shirts and trousers bought by their families for them to defect in. Almost none of them had ever heard of Communism. They thought the name "Viet Cong" or "VC" hilarious, and referred themselves to the insurgent forces as the "Liberation Army."

Most had defected out of self-interest and fear of American firepower. One told me, "I figured sooner or later the government would win. The Front had nothing. They took the land from the big owners but gave the people nothing." Another said, "Everybody wants to know if the Americans will give us jobs in Saigon. They say they're giving out jobs. Do you think I could get work in the harbor as a navigator?" A seventeen-year-old with an unruly shock of black hair explained, "I was afraid of being killed by all the bombs and shells. During a big operation some foreign soldiers came and burned down a hundred houses. It depends on the group of soldiers. Some are good and some are bad. The first group came and did nothing. The second arrested my father and I hid so the house was empty. A third group came and set our house on fire so I came here."

A Vietnamese district chief I talked to sympathized with the young peasant-guerrillas. "In the four years I've been in this district," he said, "Saigon has done nothing about land reform. Saigon should start talking less and doing more. Eighty per cent of the people in this district are landless, and while they hate the VC, they don't like us any better."

In Saigon, I asked Ky at a palace reception why his

198 The Long Charade

government did nothing about land reform. "The great difficulty is in surveying the land," he said. "I have asked the Agriculture Ministry to ease restrictions to give peasants title to their lands more speedily."

One met such evasions from most of the top officials in the Ky regime. When I submitted fifteen written questions on land reform in late 1966 to General Nguyen Duc Thang, Ky's pacification chief, Thang replied with an eight-page, typewritten memorandum, the gist of which was that land ownership was no longer a burning issue with the peasantry. In a typical passage, Thang wrote, "In the past, land reform constituted one of the major causes of the Viet Cong. However, after so many years of living in Communist-controlled areas, the rural people have fully learned Viet Cong deeds do not reflect their words. Therefore the slogan 'Land to the tiller' has become less and less effective and less attractive to the rural population." In answer to a question citing evidence that many villagers were forced to pay double the legal rent, Thang not only denied that this practice was widespread but added, "Actually, there are now a certain number of farmers who, taking advantage of the insecure situation in the countryside and of the complicated procedures governing lawsuits, refuse to pay land rent to landowners."

Ky's provincial officials often parroted the line of the Saigon generals. The Long An province chief, a colonel, told me, "All the land we can distribute in secure areas, we have already given out." The chief of the province's only almost-secure district flatly contradicted his own boss. He said that 85% of the district's people were landless and that a fourth of the land was owned by absentee landlords who lived in the provincial capital or Saigon. "If a free election in Thu Thua district were held tomorrow," he said, "I believe the 85% who are landless would vote for the Viet Cong. We also have 8,000 refugees living here who have fled Viet Cong-controlled hamlets. I think they would all vote for the government."

There was no great mystery about what the peasantry wanted. A U.S.-financed survey taken by rural schoolteachers in early 1966 asked a large sampling of peasants how they would spend a sudden windfall of money. Sixty-two per cent said they would buy land. This was followed by 19% who would build a house,

13% who would buy hogs, chickens or a buffalo, and smaller percentages who wanted to go into business, or buy fishing and farm implements, jewelry, transistor radios, bicycles, sewing machines, food and clothing. Another survey concluded that the peasants first of all wanted physical security, then good land tenure and ownership arrangements, reasonable rents, market facilities, schools for their children and medical care, in that order.

In late January 1966, I went to see General Dong, the top Vietnamese military tactician who had been purged after staunchly defending Premier Huong the year before. Dong had been ill for some months but had survived massive antibiotics prescribed by an American navy doctor, glucose injections by a French physician, and rare herbs from an elderly Chinese healer. I found him curled up on a sofa reading a Georges Simenon mystery. He apologized for his blue peasant pajamas and ordered a decanter of scotch.

Dong's large stucco villa was fortified with a high wall and barbed wire; several Nung bodyguards always stood watch by the jade-green gate, and others, their shy grins belying their reputations as warriors, trimmed hedges or weeded beds in the general's luxuriant garden, ablaze with frangipani, bougainvillea and jasmine. Beyond the wall, traffic hummed faintly in the teeming old Chinese quarter of Cholon and children's laughter echoed within one of the villa's inner gardens. The general's wife of thirty years, a Nung tribal woman, rarely appeared. The general himself spent his days in the small, crowded rooms toward the back of the villa where the household lived, but he always received visitors in a dim elegant hall paneled in teak and furnished in traditional Chinese style, with heavily ornamented lamps, bamboo scroll paintings and vases of jade and cloisonné.

That day I asked him about land reform. "Pacification and especially the human equation in pacification is the key to victory," the general said. "Let me tell you the story of the major failure of my career. It was in 1953 and I was a colonel commanding twenty-two light Vietnamese battalions assigned to pacify part of the Red River Delta in Tonkin. We had a good technique and plan. First, we held clearing operations, then followed with a light battalion to hold. We had mobile groups with security and administrative cadres and medical and social teams just as they do now. But I fail. Why? After five months I fail. Our political asset was to have been land reform."

His assignment was in Bui Chu Province in the northern Delta, Dong said, which had almost a million people, a fourth of whom were Catholic. Ho Chi Minh had just signed a land-reform decree, he said; the Communists had confiscated all land from the French, the Catholic church and landlords, and distributed it free to landless tenants. In return, the new owners had to pay 25% of the crop in taxes to the Viet Minh. To counter this, Emperor Bao Dai had issued a land-reform decree giving land to tenants with only a 15% rental, 10% less than the Viet Minh offered.

"I am the first man who must apply," the general continued. "I reported to the emperor after five months his plan cannot work. Why? Most of our cadres are landowners, big and small. They never apply Bao Dai's decree strictly like the Viet Minh do. It is not in their interest. We cannot apply. It is not a realistic plan. In Bui Chu Province there were also two very big landowners, the Catholic bishop and the minister of the interior. The bishop told me, 'No, we cannot apply land reform.' 'It is signed by His Majesty,' I told the bishop. 'If you do not apply we cannot win. The situation is deteriorating rapidly. Most of the people who till your land are not VC but can be exploited by VC even though they are Catholic. If you don't sacrifice this material interest of yours, you will lose your Catholic people, you will lose your land and perhaps you will lose your head.' The bishop was a dignified man, a kindly man, and he looked me straight in the eye. 'Do you really think I want these lands for my own personal wealth?' he asked. 'You are wrong, Colonel. I have more than two thousand people to feed—my nuns, priests and seminarians. This land supports our schools, hospitals and orphanages. If I get only 15% and must pay taxes to the Emperor, I get nothing.'"

General Dong paused as if he were remembering the fat, elderly bishop in his black soutane against the flat green landscape of the Red River Delta. "The bishop shook my hand and said farewell, declaring, 'I cannot accept your land-reform program.' The bishop enlisted the support of the interior minister. I handed in my report and was relieved of duty by the emperor. I thought my career as a military officer was finished. Some months later the Viet Minh captured the province. It was the big failure of my life."

Land reform was important; local land problems in the Delta had to be solved. But simply going to the source of peasant grievances and remedying them did not solve the problem of subversion posed by Le Duan. Americans like Lansdale felt that the growth of Communist power in the Delta fed primarily on land grievances and nationalism. But I agreed with Sir Robert: Le Duan's organization relied primarily on intimidation and exploiting personal ambition. Le Duan's key phrase was "exploiting the internal contradictions of bourgeois society." With that tactic, you could support landowner against tenant if he had more to offer you than the landless man. We kept making the mistake of seeing the propaganda as the reality, the justification as the reason. The real basis of the Viet Cong's "popular support" lay in the statistics of terror victims.

It was cool and quiet that night in early 1966 in the provincial river town of Tan An; most of its 50,000 people slept undisturbed until dawn. An American infantry brigade had recently been garrisoned in the town and it was well protected.

Except for white searchlights around the American barbed-wire encampment, the streets were black, with only the faint yellow half-light of candles and oil lamps showing from the houses. The shadows up the narrow lane from the policeman's house were full of life: children laughed and played games; old women in black pajamas squatted in the doorways; young men and soldiers drank iced beer at little wooden stalls where rice and pork soup boiled on sooty hearths.

The policeman sat in his living room talking with his father, holding his five-year-old son. Tran Van Co, a thin, grave farmer in his late thirties, had become a policeman along with his three brothers just two years before. Their father, a white-bearded Confucian schoolmaster who owned fifty acres of rich rice land across the Oriental River, had fled with his family into the town after Viet Cong political commissars had seized his two oldest sons and executed them as "enemies of the people."

From the back of the house came the voices of women and the

policeman's six children. Shortly after eight o'clock the house trembled with the burst of howitzers from an American artillery position a few hundred yards down the river. Each night, at hourly intervals, the big guns at Tan An pounded the nearby paddy fields with harassment and interdiction fire. A few minutes later, a squad of Vietnamese soldiers passed the house on one of the nightly patrols they made from a nearby river outpost. All the available town policemen were on duty guarding the official Vietnamese and American compounds within an inner ring of the town.

Silently, four young men came out of the shadows of the river and tied their sampan to the quay in the dark behind a rice warehouse. They walked along the land toward Co's house, passing the men eating and drinking, the old women in the doorways, and the playing children. Two carried Thompson submachine guns, one a carbine, and the fourth a paper-wrapped package. All wore green army fatigues and rubber sandals.

No one cried out or gave an alarm. Perhaps the four men were not noticed or were thought to be soldiers patrolling from the outpost. But it grew quieter as they approached the policeman's house, until the only sound was the sound of their footsteps. One stepped inside Co's door. There was one long burst of fire that ripped across Co's chest, the old man's back, and tore apart the skull of the little boy resting in his father's arms.

Screams shattered the quiet, and the fourth man tore open his package and thrust printed broadsheets and little paper flags of the National Liberation Front into the hands of terrified people along the lane, including Co's own children. The broadsheets said, "This execution is to avenge crimes against the people by dirty landlords, the puppet government and American imperialists."

The three murders brought the number of South Vietnamese civilians killed or kidnaped by Viet Cong terrorists to 2,780 in under three months. They took place less than half a mile from the heavily fortified villas of the province chief and his American military and civilian advisers and less than a mile from the big American brigade headquarters across town. They occurred in a province twice the size of Rhode Island, inhabited by more than 400,000 people, protected by a military force of more than 15,000 men but fewer than a thousand policemen, 90% of them recruited and trained during the previous eighteen months. There were five full American combat battalions in the province, a hundred more American military advisers, but only three American civilian police advisers.

I had heard the burst of fire from a friend's villa not far away where I was spending the night. In the morning I took an interpreter and went to the policeman's house. It was blistering hot in Tan An that day, typical pre-monsoon weather, and the little house under its corrugated tin roof was steamy and enervating. White-garbed family mourners went to and fro, and the air was heavy with a cloying smell of incense and death. On the porch, old men beat drums, gongs and clappers, and played high-pitched flutes in a wailing cacophony of Oriental grief. The family members had wrapped white bandages of bereavement around their heads; they sobbed and fell to their knees near two large carved red wooden coffins and one tiny one.

The place was swarming with policemen, some in grey-and-white uniforms and others in mufti. Most of them were crying, and one by one they prostrated themselves full length on the floor in front of the coffins. A tall man whose eyes kept watering as he spoke introduced himself as the oldest living brother. He said he had just returned from digging graves in the family's native village. The next day, he told me, he would take the three bodies by oxcart to be interred in the family's ancestral burying ground even though the Viet Cong controlled the village.

"Six of my family have now died at the hands of the Front," he said. "I hate it with all my heart. But I wish the American President and American government can win over the Viet Cong very soon either politically or militarily so that we can go home and cultivate our land and feed our families. All this killing must stop. There is too much hate, with brother against brother, cousin against cousin." An old lady with a shriveled, defeated face told me as tears poured down her cheeks, "My son was killed doing his citizen's duty."

Outside, the policemen stood discussing the crime. "The army does not provide enough protection at night," said one. "The Viet Cong fire too much across the river."

"Co was killed because he was too loyal to the government side. He was an educated man."

"It is too dangerous for a policeman to live so far out on the edge of town. But Co had no money and had to have a poor house."

"Now the Viet Cong cannot face American soldiers, so they must kill policemen in the town to show people they are still here."

I retraced the path of the assassination squad down the lane to the quay. Even in sunlight it felt insecure. Coolies down by the warehouse were lifting heavy rice sacks onto carts. The people along the lane, even the children, were silent and incurious. They looked once and averted their eyes. The coolies had impassive, almost contemptuous faces. "We are poor men. We get only a hundred piastres a day. We know nothing. No one saw the killers. We only go about our business and try to feed our families."

Security was the key to the situation. And yet the town had been rimmed with American forces and artillery. Security could not be created by superior American firepower. The Viet Cong were the ants in the cracks. The assassination team that had slipped down the river in a sampan was not part of the Communist main force; such men could not be eliminated by military sweeps or any number of helicopters. As soon as they put their Thompsons and carbines back in their plastic covers and hid them, the four killers could walk back into town, indistinguishable from other soldiers and peasants. They could be eliminated only when security forces had established themselves on a permanent footing and the people were convinced they were going to stay—always. Until then, people were naturally afraid to give information, no matter how much they hated the Viet Cong. You could see it in their faces.

From 1957 to 1967, the Viet Cong assassinated at least 11,000 civilians and kidnaped 40,000 more. These were the school-teachers, the policemen and the hamlet chiefs, the natural leaders of the community. Almost 3,000 members of the Vietnamese civil service had been killed. In 1959, the known murders were 200, rising to more than 2,000 during 1963, the year Diem fell. In 1965, the year of the American troop commitment, they were 1,800, and about the same number in 1966 and 1967. In 1966, for instance, despite the presence of over a million Vietnamese and allied soldiers (one for every fifteen or sixteen civilians), terrorism had gone on unabated. Firepower and more and more troops were obviously not the antidote to terror.

The Communists were extremely clever. The more the military predominated, the more elusive the terrorists became. Logically, those who disturbed the peace, disobeyed the laws of the land, should have been treated as outlaws, brought to court and tried. But as enemy soldiers in a big military war they were untouchable under the Geneva conventions on treatment of prisoners of war. The political underground and terrorists had to be put in the category of civil disobedients, armed gangsters, to be pitted against a civil authority rather than people engaged in a quasi-conventional military war. There stood the only chance of carrying through pacification.

Permanent security in the towns and villages had to mean a large and competent police force. Both Taylor and Lodge had been converted to this need. It had been the main burden of Sir Robert Thompson's advice since 1963. The increasingly bitter frustration of Thompson and his fellow British police and civil advisers was understandable; their advice was consistently disregarded.

In late 1964, under Huong's government, Taylor had initiated a program to expand the existing civilian police force of 43,000 to 72,000 by the end of 1966. Yet once the Ky government took power, the force got stuck at just a little over 50,000. Lodge, who was concerned because the American military buildup had no effect on the level of terrorism, brought pressure on Ky; by the end of 1967, there were about 64,000 police. But Ky would not allow the police to recruit anyone between the ages of twenty and thirty-three, thereby starving the police of the kind of recruits they needed. The military draft was given an overriding priority. Moreover, as the economy went from unemployment in 1964 to a severe shortage of manpower in 1967, partly caused by the billion-dollar U.S. military-construction program, the police were unable to get more recruits, even among the unsuitable middle-aged men.

By mid-1966, all but 1,500 of the police force were engaged in duties in Saigon and the other towns. The Ky regime in three years never allocated more than a thousand men to village police work, although the country had 2,560 villages and nearly 14,000 individual hamlets and the charts in the Saigon office called for 20,000 such rural police. Everywhere I went in Vietnam, Vietnamese province and district chiefs and American military men, especially the more politically oriented U.S. marines, complained about the shortage of civil police, who were often their best source of intelligence because they were closer to the people.

The basic strategy of antiguerrilla operations was to cut off the enemy from vital supplies. Throughout my three and a half years in Vietnam, this remained so far from achieved that the Viet Cong were still able to cut highways at will, while it was the Americans and the government forces who hopped from airbase to airbase. A police-run "resources control" program launched in October 1964 did spectacularly well until it slowly went downhill after the Huong government was overthrown in late January 1965. Under this program, at mobile and fixed checkpoints encircling Saigon, police arrested nearly 5,000 suspects, confiscated more than a million tons of rice, 93,000 medical supply units, 225 items of signal equipment and fuel supplies, engines, Communist bloc goods, and 32,000 grenades, ammunition bandoliers and explosive charges. This was far more than all the multimillion-dollar B-52 raids and massive American-Vietnamese military ground actions collected in the same period, and the police carried it out at an infinitely smaller cost in lives and money. Also arrested were nearly 2,000 army deserters, 29,000 draft dodgers and nearly 60,000 other lawbreakers. The original intent was to expand the resources-control program to all the country's major towns and cities. But under the Ky regime, the whole police-expansion effort ground to a standstill.

The security situation around Saigon itself became the ultimate absurdity. For all the concern about traffic on the Ho Chi Minh trail through Laos, it was freely admitted that the Viet Cong got a large part of their supplies, including ammunition and medicine, from Saigon. La Thanh Nghe, the country's leading pharmaceutical manufacturer and a member of Ky's Cabinet, was named in U.S. Senate hearings in early 1967 as the recipient of more than $900,000 in kickbacks from American drug companies. Nghe was also accused of being the Viet Cong's chief medical supplier, but the Ky regime never opened an investigation into the charge. Instead, it backed Nghe as a candidate in the 1967 Vietnamese Senate race, where he was defeated by a narrow margin.

Why did the United States allow the Tonkinese in power to block police expansion over a three-year period, when it was so obviously the answer to rural terrorism? It seems to me that this can be explained, if not excused, by the constant search for a military answer to what would remain a civil question.

For pacification to succeed, it was essential that the government in power take a strong stand in upholding rule of law, so that people could respond to a legal authority. Conversely, Le Duan would obviously try to reduce the moral posture of the government in power to the level of the Communist forces, so the population would come to see the opposing sides not as a legal established government and illegal insurgents but as two rival terrorist organizations.

As the conflict wore on, it became increasingly hard to explain the deliberate publicity given the Saigon regime's torture and maltreatment of prisoners. Public military tribunals meted out seemingly arbitrary sentences of death and life imprisonment even while high officials watched and brass bands played. Public executions came to resemble Roman circuses. Ky's police chief, Nguyen Ngoc Loan, appeared almost deliberately to be cultivating a public image as an alcoholic sadist, flaunting a bottle of beer or a pistol at affairs of state. Once I discovered that his beer bottle had actually contained tea. Another time, four foreign correspondents, including myself, were invited up to interview Loan in a downtown apartment and found him sprawled face down in bed, dead drunk. The corridor leading inside was spattered with vomit and broken gin bottles. Standing around were a dozen or so drunk or doped secret police with sweat-beaded foreheads, glassy eyes, and unholstered pistols shoved into their pants pockets. Some of them had marcelled hair and long carefully manicured fingernails. They looked feverish and maniacal.

It should have been apparent to everybody, as I am sure it was to Le Duan, that no government that met Communist terror with official terror of its own could win popular support or respect. Clearly, the outrages practiced by Diem's police force and petty officials in his last year played directly into Hanoi's hands. But it was Ky's own people who spread the story, true or not, that Loan's men had murdered one wounded military opponent by strangling him to death in his hospital room, slowly tightening a leather thong tied to the man's neck and testicles. I myself knew many Saigonese who told me they were aware of Communist sympathizers and activists within their own circles but would never inform the police for fear of being arrested and accused of being Viet Cong themselves.

Once the police and internal security apparatus became so feared and distrusted by the population, the government was left with little defense against subversion. And the United States, as the responsible foreign supporter of this government, could expect to suffer a consequent loss of popular respect and trust. The expressions on the faces of Co's neighbors that morning in Tan An said plainly they wished the Americans would go away if they could not protect them.

Without permanent security in the towns and villages, there was no law and order. Without law and order, the government administration could not function. Without functioning administrative machinery, it was all but impossible to create a genuine non-Communist political base.

And without such a base, as I was now convinced, the struggle against organized Communism here in the countryside was doomed and what Le Duan stood for would someday win, even if North Vietnam were bombed off the face of the earth.

Ten

To Honolulu and Back

Here in the mid-Pacific, halfway between Asia and North America, we take the opportunity to state again the aims of our government . . . a government—indeed a generation—of revolutionary transformation. . . .

—*The Declaration of Honolulu*

Of all the Americans directly involved in Vietnam during my years there, only Lyndon Johnson came to seem as down to earth as the Vietnamese peasants themselves. I never interviewed the rank-and-file Viet Cong in the southern Delta without thinking how close their aims of land and independence were to those of the President. The powerful American leader and the enemy's cannon fodder, who died by the tens of thousands, were fighting for the same thing. That was what made the long charade so monstrous.

President Johnson was badly advised on the political background in Vietnam, not only by his own commanders and officials but by liberal critics of the war, who rarely went to Vietnam. Only a few Western scholars, such as Bernard Fall, Dennis Duncanson and Douglas Pike, had made much point of Vietnamese regionalism. Yet regional differences were crucial.

In Cochinchina—Saigon and the Mekong Delta—pioneering and agricultural expansion had eliminated many relics of feudalism. The French colonial system had been considerably democratic. It had produced well-informed and cosmopolitan nationalist leaders like Tran Van Van and Tran Van Huong who channeled their political activities along conventional lines. In Tonkin—Hanoi and the Red River Delta—a tremendous problem of excessive rural population had added a touch of desperation to a people with a tradition of anarchism, warlord armies and secret societies. Nationalism took extreme forms—i.e., the Communists and the reactionary Dai Viets—producing such leaders as Ho Chi Minh and Dr. Sung.

I could never understand why such overwhelmingly important facts were so rarely placed before the American public. Such an eminent historian as Arthur M. Schlesinger, in his book *The Bitter Heritage: Vietnam and American Democracy, 1941–1966*, was to argue that the Viet Cong, representing a strongly held nationalist and Communist viewpoint, should have the right to participate fully in peacetime political life. That is, if the Viet Cong could then command a natural majority for their Communist policies, so be it. But Schlesinger did not explain the Tonkinese-Cochinchinese division or seem aware how this "natural majority" might be reached with Tonkinese forcibly controlling both the Saigon and Hanoi governments. Had the American public and its President been aware of such realities, there might well have been intense pressure to install a Cochinchinese government in Saigon.

I felt it was unfair to criticize President Johnson alone for not taking Vietnamese political realities more into account, when the entire American nation remained in ignorance. The relevant information was not hidden away in secret State Department files; it was available in any encyclopedia.

Until early 1966, lacking a clear political policy, Johnson seemed to be playing poker, matching the Communist military escalation with a counterescalation. This game seemed relatively straightforward: a prolonged war of attrition with the outcome dependent on morale, perseverance, money and manpower. It was a limited war for limited political objectives. As Defense Secretary McNamara defined it: "Our political objective is an independent South Vietnam. It is not to destroy Hanoi or Red China. We must make it clear that we don't want to destroy anyone. We must control application of power to fully support our political objectives." With the war so delimited, military odds seemed to clearly favor the United States. Nobody wanted Vietnam enough to wage nuclear war for it.

Johnson's decision to commit American troops to the fight in 1965 grew out of the thinking of a single-minded man who had come out of the hard frontier of Texas and risen to political power during the American depression and the early days of the New Deal; he was an old-fashioned populist whom James Reston once described as "a believer in an unbelieving and cynical world." But when it came to Vietnam, Reston was wrong to romanticize Lyndon Johnson. John F. Kennedy and the New Frontier's galaxy of intellectuals were believers. They believed in social revolution, dramatic and rapid social change, just as Lansdale had from his experiences in the Philippines and Vietnam in the fifties. They thought the wave of the future in Afro-Asian countries lay with the emerging revolutionary leadership. Missing in this approach was the harsh practicality of the man from the Pedernales. Johnson had been one of the few Americans to grasp that the Asian millions were not seeking revolution but the gradual evolvement of a better, more secure material life. Moreover, he felt they would accept mutual regional security backed by American power as an alternative to the hegemony of an awakened and Marxist China. He seemed to have a sure sense that Asian peasants would prefer the spirit of the Pedernales River Electric Cooperative to that of the Caves of Yenan. And I believed he was right.

The American aim, as defined by General Taylor during a Senate hearing, was also "to give the people of South Vietnam their choice of government." The danger by early 1966, when it was becoming increasingly obvious that the northerners in Saigon ruled by force rather than popular consent, was that many Americans might conclude that no anti-Communist government in South Vietnam could muster enough support to survive without using repressive measures. Such a notion would be repugnant to the normal American, who would further question the commitment of American troops to a government and people who no longer seemed worth fighting for. If Le Duan could achieve this, he would destroy the political basis of the war.

In early 1966, Johnson apparently reached the decision that it was not enough for the United States to fight for South Vietnam's choice of government, it must also sponsor elections and a program of rapid social reform. He caught everybody by surprise, including presumably Le Duan, by calling the Honolulu conference the first week of February on only twenty-four hours' notice. I do not believe Johnson was fully conscious of the favorable impact in Vietnam of his Hawaii meeting with Ky. He seemed rather to act from an instinct that something was politically and socially wrong in South Vietnam. Also, he acted in response to domestic political considerations. The war by then, as one American senator described it, had become "as popular as a rattlesnake" in the United States. At Christmastime, Johnson had begun his thirty-seven-day bombing pause over North Vietnam. In January, he sent a dozen top American officials and diplomats all over the world to clarify his policy and allow Ho Chi Minh and the Hanoi leadership to show themselves as the intransigents. On the first of February, Johnson announced resumption of the bombing and appealed for a United Nations Security Council meeting "in our continuing pursuit of peace."

While General Westmoreland's military buildup had arrested the Communist military advance and South Vietnam had, in McNamara's phrase, "stopped losing the war," there was at least a year to go before the United States could maintain and employ a sufficient force to start the long haul toward militarily defeating the Viet Cong main forces. The Pentagon's dynamic doctrine of extending the American enclaves bit by bit to cover the whole country promised a reasonable way out of the military stalemate. But it would take a long time.

Military and diplomatic problems could be solved, but the political problem remained, both in Vietnam and the United States. It was essential for Johnson to find a partner in Saigon capable of providing a political basis for the war effort. This meant finding leadership with enough popular support to justify Johnson's decision to commit American troops. Johnson had gone into Vietnam because he believed a majority of the South

Vietnamese people wanted the help of the United States in preventing a Communist takeover; also, he thought it was in the long-term interest of the United States to provide that assistance. It is hard to imagine any Western leader who had the resources and the will doing otherwise.

I, too, had become convinced that most politically aware Vietnamese did not want the Communists to win. In the United States, one often encountered the belief that while the Saigon government supported us, the mass of the peasantry were with the Viet Cong, or were at least neutrals caught up in the struggle. This was misleading. Certainly, a large minority of the South Vietnamese peasantry supported what they regarded as a peasant movement for land and independence: the National Liberation Front. But this in no way meant that they supported a Communist takeover in Saigon; most of them had never heard of Communism, nor did they know Hanoi was running the war with Russian and Chinese backing. Sir Robert once classified the Communists into three broad types: the naturals, ranging from idealist to criminal; the converted, or those who joined because of government excesses and abuses of power; and the deceived. Most of the Viet Cong's peasant supporters belonged to the converted or deceived; had they known what was involved in a Communist victory, I am confident they would have opposed it. Those Vietnamese who *were* politically conscious—the educated southern middle class and even poor Saigonese—no more wanted the naturals (men like Le Duan) taking over Saigon than the average American would like to see such men take over Washington, and for exactly the same reasons. But it was also growing apparent by early 1966 that this had to be made clear and convincing to the American people.

An increasing loss of nerve, brooding indifference and cynicism did, however, exist even among the educated anti-Communist element. As the war grew in scale and intensity, freedom and democracy—what the United States said it was fighting for— became empty words in Saigon. With wholesale corruption, inflation and social decay, Nguyen Cao Ky's promises depreciated in value faster than Vietnamese currency. The Tonkinese were telling the people they could not afford the luxury of an open system as long as the war lasted. American officials like Habib, trying to repeat the South Korean experience, nodded approval. Ky promised a return to constitutional civil government, but few Saigonese believed he would give up power without a fight. Some articulate Vietnamese felt they were being deliberately deceived by the Americans. They had an almost mystical faith in the power of the United States and would have experienced a traumatic shock had they realized how little Washington knew about the Mandarin Dai Viets. When I told one purged general that I doubted President Johnson had ever heard of Dr. Sung, he wouldn't believe me. "It's high politics," he said. "If they're really that naïve in Washington, we are lost." It was a common and incorrect assumption among Vietnamese that Washington knew more than it let on, and that it was consciously collaborating in what many regarded as a tyrannical and ineffectual rule in Saigon. To some despairing Roman Catholic and Cochinchinese leaders, the problem looked well-nigh insoluble. If the Communists won, Saigon would be enslaved by Hanoi. But under the northern generals, the alternative—national independence and freedom, as symbolized by a decent Cochinchinese civil government—was nowhere in sight. By early 1966, in the streets and cafés of Saigon, the question was beginning to be asked, even by soldiers whose daily lot was fighting and dying: For what and for whom? After twenty years of war, suffering and waiting, the South Vietnamese people were still far from getting a government of their choice. Understandably, they watched the Honolulu conference begin with brooding suspicion and apprehension.

Johnson met the plane carrying Ky and General Nguyen Van Thieu, the ruling junta's shadowy chairman, at Honolulu airport. The President declared, "We meet in a time of testing and trial, but we will talk also of hope and harvest." Johnson appeared anxious to reassure the Vietnamese leadership about America's will to persevere. In his opening speech Johnson told them, looking Ky right in the eye, "Gentlemen, let me make clear our resolve and determination. . . . We, South Vietnam and the United States, are brothers-in-arms. We will not tire. We will not flag. We intend to work with you. We intend to help you. We intend to fight with you in defeating the Communist aggressors."

Ky's reply, delivered with apparent emotion and sincerity, seemed to burnish a young soldier's staunchly anti-Communist image. You didn't have to like him, Ky said, but at least he had the will to fight the Communists: "We pledge our determination to continue to fight against Communist aggression as long as it is necessary, to accept sacrifice and death as long as the war requires it. . . . And we pledge not to betray those valiant sons of America who have given their lives in this sacred cause." Ky spoke with just the right tone and Johnson appeared visibly moved and impressed.

In private, Johnson ticked off a number of social, economic and political reforms, and got Ky's written signature affixed to a pledge to deliver the goods as fast as possible. Besides the anti-inflationary measures already discussed, these included land reform, police expansion, better medical facilities for refugees and civilian war casualties, greater restrictions on the use of air and artillery, a more attractive amnesty program for Viet Cong defectors, more secondary education and a wide-ranging program of agricultural help for the peasantry. The President was not trying to bring the Great Society to Vietnam, as some commentators suggested; he was trying to do the right things needed to win the war.

In this sense, the Declaration of Honolulu was the most important non-Communist social document to come out of the Vietnam war. The American statement of purposes represented an historic change: "The United States pledges to give full support to measures of social revolution, including land reform, based on the principle of building upward from the hopes and purposes of all the people of Vietnam." Together, South Vietnam and the United States committed themselves to the "defense against aggression," the "work of social revolution," the "goal of free self-government," the "attack on hunger, ignorance and disease" and the "unending quest of peace." They accepted the philosophy that Jeffersonian democracy could be adapted to Asian needs as the answer to Leninist mobilization of the masses through force, terror and deception. Land would go to the tiller; the people would choose their own government; police and courts would be created to re-establish rule of law; insurgents who dropped their arms would be given amnesty and welcomed back into the national family; all peasants would be given security, seed, schools and hospitals.

William Bundy and the State Department drafters who hastily

wrote the Declaration of Honolulu borrowed many of Lansdale's phrases. But the parts that counted, the concrete programs to be carried out under an orderly timetable, were Johnson's. As the President told Nguyen Cao Ky in Hawaii, "I want to see those coonskins hanging on the wall."

It was the operative phrase. Hanoi, as subsequent events showed, got the point all right. But for many, Johnson's crude, corny façade obscured his serious ideas about America's responsibilities in the world. Walter Lippmann, for instance, had quarreled with other presidents before, but he had never opposed one with quite the same bitterness and tenacity he brought to his attacks on Johnson and the Vietnam war. Lippmann interpreted the Honolulu Declaration as "a web of ringing generalities about the hopes, the good intentions, the high-minded purposes of the Johnson administration. . . . I read it as a refusal by the President to put limits on our war aims."

Even the New York *Times* looked for some ulterior motive. "The President was seeking to take away headlines—and possibly witnesses—from the televised inquiry of the Senate Foreign Relations Committee into his policies in Vietnam and his conduct of the war." Three days later the *Times* had more charitable second thoughts: "The heavy emphasis . . . on the need for social, economic and political reform in South Vietnam as an integral part of winning the war apparently was the primary achievement of the Honolulu Conference."

In contrast to American liberal reaction, the Vietnamese man in the street seemed to sense instinctively what Johnson was trying to do. A Saigon taxi driver was typical: "I am not an educated man, but from what I saw on television in the market, General Ky promised a social revolution and the American President promised a better life for us. So I appreciate what they try to do if they make good their promises."

Hanoi took the Honolulu Declaration very seriously. With unprecedented hysteria, Hanoi's official party newspaper, *Nhan Dan,* ranted, "Noisy advertising, poppycock, a trick to deceive the people . . . while the U.S. imperialists burn all, destroy all, kill all." "Cunning and extremely repugnant," echoed the Viet Cong's Liberation Radio. This denunciation of the Honolulu plan kept up for weeks. Hanoi's propagandists noted that the "Lodge-

Lansdale group is considering the rural pacification program as a vital program" and that "pacification is now directly carried out by the U.S. imperialists instead of its local South Vietnamese lackeys." "The military war has failed," they went on, "and the Johnson clique must now trumpet pacification. As soon as Honolulu was over, the U.S. Congress passed an additional $275,-000,000 for the pacification program. . . . But does the Johnson clique construct the countryside or devastate it? . . . The U.S. ruling circles have threatened once again, but the South Vietnamese people have replied to them, 'Don't forget the lessons of the Taylor-McNamara pacification plan.' "

The test facing Le Duan was critical; President Johnson had unexpectedly seized the political initiative. There was no question this time of skillfully turning the enemy's physical strength against him, like a weak judo expert against a bigger, stronger opponent. That had worked with American military and economic power, but this new challenge was different. Toward the end of the Honolulu conference, Johnson had used every bit of persuasion and pressure at his command to commit Ky in writing to social reform and holding national elections for a new civil government by early 1967, possibly by February. Johnson also invited Ky to a second Pacific conference, tentatively scheduled for June, to report progress made. Le Duan needed to ensure that this meeting would never be held and that no real progress would be made in the Honolulu program. The Vietnamese themselves understood this. General Dong told me, "The Communists conceive of the Honolulu plan as the last card to be played by the Americans in our country; they will try to destroy it."

The challenge was political. As I have earlier observed, Johnson in his military conduct of the war seemed to be playing poker. But his sudden decision to push nonmilitary programs at Honolulu came more like a gambit in chess. To combat it, as we shall soon see, Le Duan also turned to the principles of chess: he would aim consistently for the initiative and sacrifice some of his key players as a means of regaining it. Le Duan's immediate goal, I believe, was to gain time.

Time seemed on everyone's mind in the days just after Honolulu. At a Saigon dinner party for visiting White House aide

McGeorge Bundy, I asked Lansdale, "Is it too late for Vietnam?" "It is very, very late," he said. Lansdale seemed discouraged. He said he had never met the President: "Oh, we shook hands and I sat across the table from him in Honolulu, but that's all." Lansdale said he had penciled the phrase "including land reform" into the Honolulu Declaration, since the State Department drafters had forgotten to put it in. Secretary of Agriculture Orville Freeman, who was also at the party, was enthusiastic about Ky's interest in rapidly pushing land redistribution. "Ky brought up land reform before I did," Freeman said. "He asked how we could get it moving faster."

Bundy told me the Honolulu Declaration was intended in part to create a more positive moral imperative for the American war effort than just anti-Communism. "Anti-Communism alone has never been much of a cause anywhere," Bundy said. I asked how Saigon looked since his last visit, a year before, at the time of the first air strike against North Vietnam and the northerners' seizure of power in Saigon. Bundy replied, "Last year Saigon was despairing, a city doomed. Now I find everybody's still arguing, but over how to win it this time."

Colonel Wilson later explained to me the nature of Bundy's post-Honolulu Saigon mission. In Honolulu, Johnson had told Lodge in private he was concerned that the American military seemed to have free rein in deciding both military and political questions in Vietnam. The President told Lodge that he, as ambassador, was to exercise supreme authority over the entire U.S. war effort. Bundy had written instructions for everyone to that effect. Johnson planned that William Porter, as Lodge's civilian deputy, would take over the civil effort as General Westmoreland's opposite number. Lodge was to function as a kind of super-ambassador over both.

At first Lodge balked, preferring the status quo. He wanted Porter to remain in the function of a deputy chief of mission, much as U. Alexis Johnson had been for Ambassador Taylor. The President overrode Lodge's objections. He said he wanted a civilian political judgment on the scene that could make the key tactical decisions between civil and military action, the kind of decision that had to be made quickly in the field and which Johnson himself could not make back in Washington. But, as

Wilson later told me, "Somehow what was supposed to happen never did happen."

The British in Saigon, as usual, diagnosed the trouble in the American mission with cool detachment. Dennis Duncanson, the last of Sir Robert's group still left in Saigon at the time of the Hawaii conference, told me, "The Honolulu Declaration registers the fact that the two governments are broadly in agreement in what they intend to do: to resist the Communist threat and to put added emphasis on the nonmilitary side. In theory, all these things are fine; one just hopes they apply them. But the basic reason the Communist threat has advanced so far is inefficient government and an extraordinary weakness on the part of the rural administration; it is very corrupt and there's a lot of highhandedness and pettiness. The defects of the Diem regime were such that it could not succeed in repelling the Communist threat. If the Diem government could have been persuaded to change, to improve, perhaps things would have gone differently. But even Diem was never able to tackle the problem of subversion."

Duncanson said he had heard rumors Lansdale might resign: "It would be a great loss. Lansdale has experience and understanding in pacification problems. But I don't see how his cure of remedying peasant grievances can solve the problem of subversion. Then, even if it could, it's very difficult for Lansdale to impose his own concepts if there is not a broad consensus at the top. There are limits to what any one man can do. What is needed is a coordinated body at the top. The American mission doesn't always coordinate as it should. Lodge presides over this body. But he presides, not commands."

President Johnson's intent at Honolulu became even more clear when Vice President Humphrey arrived on his first visit to Saigon and declared his mission was to show that the "United States is prepared to back hopes with deeds." Humphrey told newsmen, "The President wants to make it crystal clear to the world and to the Communists that we have a common commitment to help the South Vietnamese people build a society of economic progress, of hope and justice."

Humphrey said after a two-hour conversation with Ky that he found the young premier "on fire" over Washington's effort to "export what the United States is best known for—a concern about humanity and our knowledge in building a decent progressive society." Ky replied in front of newsmen, "I am sure prior to your visit you were not convinced of the ability of the young generals, call us the Young Turks if you will, to rule our nation. I am sure now you must recognize we are more civilized than the civilians, that we desire freedom more than free men and love democracy more than you do."

During the next three days, in visits to Saigon's slums and villages, hospitals, farms and American bases, Humphrey expanded on a single, simple theme: There were two wars in Vietnam, the war on the battlefield and the war against poverty, hunger, illiteracy and disease, and the second one was the more important. It could be won through a Vietnamese "social revolution, an upheaval for a better life" and would be accomplished "from the bottom up," originating with the peasantry. It would take a long time and require sustained American support, support, Humphrey implied, that was contingent on the Vietnamese demonstrating the "will and determination" to help themselves. Humphrey did not mention Communism during his speeches.

The Vietnamese crowds loved Humphrey; he waded into throngs of children, ignored the language barrier and talked to everybody, patted heads, pumped hands and even engaged in a hog-calling exhibition. After his departure the Viet Cong mortared two of the hamlets he visited.

The Vice President seemed equally affected by the Vietnamese. "The single most important thing I've seen," he told a group of newsmen as we walked through a village, "is the people. They're magnificent; their children are beautiful. When I see those teachers and students, they're not crying, they're not holding their hands out, they're building. They have faith. I think that's what I've learned in Vietnam."

Humphrey went to the villages and slums to demonstrate to the Saigonese that while the generals in power might seem only interested in waging war, an American vice president wanted to know how the poorest Vietnamese lived. As his motorcade sped toward the airport, it passed under an odd pink banner strung among the standard government farewell slogans; it said, "Thank you, Mr. Humphrey."

But the political visions of Honolulu seemed to fade even as the motorcade passed through streets glutted with the new cars of war profiteers and the military elite, past rows of gaudy cabarets where homeless children slept on the pavement and garbage rotted in the gutters.

Almost invisible on one of these streets were ten cement culverts abandoned in a vacant lot. Thousands of people passed by them every day, but few noticed the ragged, emaciated figures slipping in and out of them. Nearly fifty men, women and children had been eating, sleeping, breeding and dying in these culverts ever since they had lost all proof of their identity in a big fire in the slums just before the fall of the Diem government. Most of the 3,000 or so other fire victims salvaged their personal possessions and documents, and found homes elsewhere.

Among those not so fortunate were a ragpicker, an old lady who lived by rummaging through garbage cans and an ex-paratrooper who had survived the battle of Dien Bien Phu. Illiterate, inarticulate and desperately poor, they had been without identity papers since the fire. At first, they tried to get new ones but were turned away during the administrative collapse that followed the Diem *coup d'état*. As months and even years went by, they grew afraid to try. Officially, they ceased to exist.

In the beginning it had not mattered much. The post-Diem governments came and went in rapid succession. The creaky old French colonial administrative machinery all but stopped functioning, and most procedures were waived. But the longer the Ky regime stayed in power, the more the police began tightening up. Papers proving one's identity again became essential. No one could travel outside the city, obtain licenses, hold certain jobs, qualify for refugee relief, enroll children in free public schools, own property, or risk any dealings with the police or civil authorities without identification papers.

My interpreter first noticed the culvert dwellers one day as he passed on his bicycle. We went to see them early one afternoon and found about a dozen sitting behind the culverts out of sight on the banks of a canal. It appeared to be lunchtime and they were wolfing down their noon rice, surrounded by piles of junk, ash pans, rusted car fenders, bedsteads and old pipe, like so much human debris. There was no shade. In the noonday sun and dust, the culverts were suffocating. From inside one of them came the hideous rattle of tubercular coughing, amplified as in an echo chamber by the concrete cylinder. A rat scuttled by, flies buzzed, and the air was sour with rotting garbage and human decay. Filthy, cramped and squalid as a culvert was, its inhabitants seemed to think it was better than nothing. They were anxious lest my presence attract a policeman. Now, at least, they had somewhere to sleep and store their possessions.

"We have each other," said the ragpicker. He had a face pockmarked like a walnut shell and wore a black felt hat with a broad uneven rim. "My wife died last year. I am alone now. If we cannot cure a sickness ourselves, one of the men who pedals rickshaws will take the sick man to the government dispensary."

The ragpicker, whose patched black garment was filthy, said he lived by scavenging junk at the city's garbage dump. "We took one lady to the hospital to have her baby, but the baby died and she came back to live in the culvert and died, too. Her husband was a soldier who left her here one day and never came back. Maybe he got killed. Nobody ever knew. We had to take her to the hospital just before she died. She had no identification card. If she died in the culvert there would be a lot of trouble for the rest of us. The police would come to investigate. Now they only come two or three times a year and tell us to move on."

"Nobody ever stops here. Never, never," said the old lady. She had a dirty towel wrapped around her head, her gnarled hands were black with grime, and her mouth oozed betel-nut juice. But she had bright little eyes very deep in their sockets and a strange melodious voice. "Nobody sees us," the old lady chuckled. "How can they talk to us?"

A gaunt younger man wearing only striped undershorts was apprehensive. "If you tell about us in an American newspaper, the police will come to know and make us leave the culverts. My wife is ill now, what will become of us?"

He said he had been a paratrooper at Dien Bien Phu the day it fell in May 1954. He had volunteered to parachute in six weeks before the end. He looked fifty but said he was thirty-eight. Dien Bien Phu was such an historic symbol one forgot how recent it was.

"During the fighting after General de Castries ordered

everyone to surrender, thousands and thousands of Viet Minh came. I was a prisoner for four months. We had to walk to Thanh Hoa on the coast. It took us one month and twelve days, moving only from six in the evening until midnight. The Viet Minh still feared French planes. I never heard of Americans in those days. Many of the French soldiers died along the way. They could not live on rice as we could. The second of September we were exchanged on Samson Beach and came south by ship. I was Tonkinese but a parachutist and so must follow my unit. A year later I left the army and earned my living as a mason and house painter. But I lost everything in the fire and had to become a rickshaw man. My wife is also a refugee from the north. She got very sick after we moved here to the culverts. It is her heart and lungs. That is she you hear coughing. My two children are dead. The first died in the fire. Afterward I had no house and we slept under a veranda on the street. My baby was only three months old. It caught cold one rainy night and died a week later. I do not think about war and politics any more. I am too poor. I work too hard to make my life."

He recited his story with an impassive face and monotonous voice, as if nothing could touch him now. I asked what he thought the government should do for him, especially as an ex-paratrooper who fought at Dien Bien Phu.

"First of all, I am only a poor man and it is not for me to ask the government to do anything. But since you ask, we need most of all an identity card and a family census card, then a small and poor house in which to live. And, if possible, a job. Now I have to share my rickshaw with another man, since without papers I cannot get a license myself. I lost everything in the fire. The authorities demand three witnesses who know me and will take responsibility for my actions and swear I am not a Viet Cong. They must go several times to the police station and always wait a long time. We are only poor men who must work every day to feed our families. We cannot spare the time and I have no money to pay my friends so they go with me. Once I was ashamed to live in a culvert and tried to built a hut of straw and bamboo here on the canal bank. The police came and destroyed it and took the materials away with them. They said, 'You cannot build a hut without permission from the mayor.' I told them I was a poor man and lost my house in the fire and had no identity papers to be able to ask permission. The policeman said flatly, 'No, it's illegal.' What kind of a law is that? Now prices are so costly I have only enough piastres to buy food. Even when a baby is born here the hospital authorities will not give a birth certificate, since no one has a family census card."

After I gave them repeated assurances no harm would come to the people in the culvert, the ragpicker and ex-paratrooper went off to work. But the old lady stayed on, her rheumy eyes twinkling with curiosity and interest. Another culvert woman said the old lady had once been very beautiful.

"That was a long time ago," the old lady said, explaining that she was now fifty-eight. "My parents owned a sampan and we used to go up and down the Saigon River buying fruit and vegetables in the countryside. It was like paradise. When I was twenty-one, I was sent to be the maidservant of a fortune teller. He had been blind from birth and at first I pitied him. Later we fell in love and married but had no children. He was a very fine man and had a miraculous way of knowing someone's character and past by touching the bones of his fingers. Until the fire we had a small house of our own. I was gone that day and he was all alone. After he died, I never went across the canal to Saigon again. I would dearly love to go to the theatre once more. But, as you see, I have no clothes."

The old lady showed me her basket and hook and a grimy cloth bag full of garbage, which, she said, she collected to sell to a Chinese merchant for a few pennies each day.

"I just go through the garbage piles along the street and try to find wood, paper, plastic, aluminum or bits of cloth. You would be surprised what people throw away nowadays. I buy some rice and save the rest for days when it rains or I get ill. Then I go to Cau Cong dispensary, where the government gives injections and free pills—good pills."

She smiled; there was no petulance or despair on her wrinkled face, just a kind of wonder.

"In my present life, I suppose I should rather die. But I cannot die. I just follow my neighbors here in the culverts and if they can resist, so can I."

Two street urchins were also among the culvert dwellers; a

nine-year-old and an eleven-year-old whose fathers had been Vietnamese army privates killed in the war. The mother of one was a bar girl in Danang; the other one's mother had died of tuberculosis. Both had once gone to village schools, studying "geography, history, reading and arithmetic," but since losing their parents had joined the horde of war orphans on Saigon's streets, shining shoes, running errands, begging, swimming in the river, and, before they discovered the culverts, sleeping in cars parked along the streets. "A different one every night," said the smallest, with some pride in their daring.

It turned out they had taken part in Tri Quang's antigovernment riots and had once helped to stone the American library on Le Loi Boulevard. "Some students told us to come," the oldest said. Did they want the Americans to go home? "No, no," they protested. "They make jokes all the time." "Like the French." "Red face, long nose, belly too big. Some good and some bad. The bad ones tell us to go away. 'Dee dee, kid.' " It was a perfect mimicry of a G.I. The boys said they went to movies two or three times a week; they liked war pictures best but not war itself. "I don't like to see the dead ones." Did they know the Viet Cong? "They kill people." Who governed the country? "The Thieu-Ky clique." What did they want to be when they grew up? Both had the same ready answer: "A soldier like my dad."

I suppose you could find people living in such destitution anywhere in the world. But they were people, not automatons. Not yet. If President Johnson and the American people kept faith with them, there was still a chance to defeat what Le Duan stood for.

Eleven

Revolt in Annam

Deceive, tempt and confuse the enemy.

—Sun Tzu

In the weeks after Honolulu, Saigon was filled with speculation over how the Communists would respond. Almost a month passed and then, in the second week of March 1966, the next act in the charade began. One morning the Ky regime startled the capital by announcing the dismissal of Nguyen Chanh Thi, the tempestuous military governor of Annam, whom many considered the most popular and powerful general in the country.

Of all the Vietnamese generals, Thi was the one I knew best. He was from Annamite peasant stock and had grown up in a nearby village, although he was fond of saying he was a "citizen of Hue." While he had a peasant's shrewdness and was well liked by his American advisers, Thi was believed subject to Tri Quang's manipulation. Thi had been a paratroop sergeant in the French Army who had caught the eye of Colonel Pham Van Lieu, the veteran Dai Viet who recruited Ky in 1949, and Lieu had made Thi his personal protégé, helping him rise to the position of Diem's palace guard. Thi and Lieu had taken part in an abortive coup against Diem in 1960, and had fled together to Cambodia where they lived in exile for three years. After Diem's murder, Thi returned and was made commander of the northernmost sector of First Corps. Along with Ky, Thi had been a prime mover in the purge of anti-Communist Catholic and Cochinchinese generals from the army in 1965 and had come close to becoming premier instead of Ky.

The first touch of fantasy in this episode was supplied by, of all people, Philip Habib. Habib held a press briefing at the home of Barry Zorthian, the information chief, a few hours after Thi's ouster. Zorthian hastened to emphasize that the political officer's appearance had been scheduled two weeks before by "coincidence." Habib told us, "The decision to dismiss Thi has been coming for some time and we regard it as a favorable step in the direction of greater stability . . . the beginning of the end of fiefdom; Ky is going to show the authority of the central government's power."

Someone asked, "Was Thi about to make a power grab?"

Habib said no.

"Can Ky make it stick?"

"I think so," Habib answered. "Thi went along with it today. Thi has been urged for some time to mend his ways. It's never quite reached the crisis stage, but we've been aware of it for some time. However, it was the Vietnamese government's own decision, their own sense of confidence, their own sense of what they ought to have." I assumed he meant that, after Honolulu, Ky was confident enough of his own position to go after his chief rival.

The press was baffled; didn't Habib expect Annam to go up in arms? After all, most of the top military officers and civil officials in Annam owed Thi their jobs.

"As far as Hue goes," Habib said, "we find the great myth of authority Thi had in the central provinces will be severely shaken. The government did its homework vis à vis Tri Quang and he goes along with it. What they've done is taken the hardest nut and knocked him off. It was Thi's obstreperousness, his unwillingness to bow to central authority. I don't think Tri Quang will do anything. I don't think Tri Quang is a neutralist or has a soft attitude toward the war."

I was incredulous. Here was a senior American official, who had come to dominate the political thinking of the American Embassy in Saigon, seemingly ringing up the curtain on the next act in the charade. I immediately cabled my newspaper that Tri Quang was moving into his long-awaited showdown with the United States. I never doubted he would exploit Thi's dismissal to the hilt.

I then went to see Thi in his small Saigon villa. Soldiers blocked the gate. One said Thi had gone away, a second that he was ill. Fortunately I could see him standing just inside the door, and he waved to me to come in. Thi offered me tea and sat down on a sofa under a large framed photograph of himself with Ky. Colonel Lieu, the national police chief, was also in the room, still playing the role of Thi's best friend.

Thi acted very secretive and pleased. "I cannot explain my project to you, but you will know very soon." He denied rumors he had resigned but said he might go abroad for medical treatment. "But I will be back in a short time." Lieu was also coy. "For the moment," he grinned, "Saigon is calm."

I said that South Vietnam would be losing a good fighter.

"Thank you very much," Thi said. "I will not be gone long. Too many generals get into politics. But when I have free time from military operations, I go to the villages and outposts to tell people what is Communism. During my twenty-three years in the army, I have always fought the Communists. The Americans who live in Danang know my anti-Communist actions. Either the Communists die or I die."

Thi walked me back to the gate. As soon as we were out of earshot of the house, he gripped my arm and said in a low voice, "Tell General Lansdale just these words for me. 'They are trying to drive my people into the arms of the Viet Cong.' He will understand." (Nearly two years later, I learned in Washington that Lansdale had been close to Thi and had twice talked him out of attempting *coup d'états* against Ky.) At the time, the contradiction between this message for Lansdale and Thi's apparent collusion in what was going on puzzled me; I think now that he must have suspected he was being betrayed by Tri Quang and the brotherhood but hoped he could outwit them, much as General Khanh had tried and failed to do in late 1964. Neither Thi, Khanh nor Van, I believe, ever really understood what formidable opponents they were up against.

The day after Thi's dismissal was announced, Habib's analysis of its effect fell apart. Far from "going along with it," Tri Quang's Buddhist organization issued a press communiqué demanding that all generals "who have done meritorious service for the revolution" be "restored to their position so they can take part in the reconstruction of the country." The communiqué also demanded that Ky call a national congress, that he renew his government's dedication to social revolution, and that "all generals serving abroad or at home should return to purely military duties." A general strike in favor of Thi was announced in Danang. Several thousand people gathered at a rally where a speaker shouted, "Many of our people are poor and hopeless. We need somebody to help us. Bring back General Thi!" Agitators in the crowd demanded Thi's return as "a revolutionary hero."

Back in Saigon, Thi was jubilant. He told me, "If I have succeeded in realizing popular aspirations at all, it is shown by these students and soldiers." I asked Thi about the Honolulu plan. "All countries seek social revolution," he said. "It was not invented at the Honolulu conference." Asked about rumors he might accept a diplomatic post abroad, Thi growled, "Only a thief becomes an ambassador." My impression that day was that Thi felt he could pull it off, that he was popular enough in Annam to challenge Ky's power in Saigon.

Thi's first attempt to fly back to Danang was blocked by General Nguyen Huu Co, the Cochinchinese defense minister who himself was to be purged within a year. Co stood in Thi's path at the airfield with a squad of soldiers and shoved a machine gun into Thi's stomach. "Shoot if you dare, cowards," Thi snarled, but he returned to his Saigon villa. The next day Ky invited Thi to lunch and inexplicably arranged air transportation for him to return to Danang, but without reinstating him. When Thi grinningly told me, I didn't like the looks of it. It was almost as if Ky were deliberately trying to stir up trouble in Annam. Thi arrived back in Danang on March 15th, just five days after his ouster. A crowd of 7,000 people gathered to welcome him. Thi leaped up on a table and appealed to the crowd, "I promise the population and I promise the soldiers I will always be on your side to continue the revolution." But then he sounded the responsible note that was soon to be his downfall. "Think about our country and not about me. Don't let the enemies of the nation exploit your troubles. Don't let yourselves be exploited by the Communists."

Which was exactly what Tri Quang seemed to want them to do. In Saigon the same day, he told Charles Mohr of the New York *Times* that the Ky government was "rotten" and that Ky himself "got more hated" since his meeting with President Johnson in Honolulu. Tri Quang said his Buddhist group was opposed to the Ky regime because "power struggles and purges have been going on right from its birth." He said he hoped Thieu and Ky would give up power "as soon as possible." Radio Hanoi at once began describing Tri Quang's "struggle movement" as a righteous cause. The president of the National Liberation Front made an unprecedented personal appeal over Liberation Radio calling for nationwide demonstrations during what he termed "Anti-American Day." Westmoreland's headquarters reported that Viet Cong were infiltrating Saigon.

Thi's dismissal, however, remained a regional issue. Despite stirrings of a civil revolt in Annam, Saigon and the rest of Cochinchina remained uninterested and unaffected. But while the spotlight stayed on Thi, a related horror show, which did affect Saigon, was being acted out on another portion of the stage.

This began with the arrest of Ta Vinh, one of the country's richest Chinese importers, on charges of "economic sabotage." Despite threats of a business boycott from the economically powerful Chinese colony, Ky, his Cabinet ministers and several other generals attended a Kafkaesque show trial. Ta Vinh was refused permission to produce witnesses in his defense, including American officials. Two military bands played the national anthem, and Ta Vinh's wife and eight small children sobbed and shrieked in the courtroom as the death sentence was announced.

Up until midnight before execution day, Chinese bookmakers in Cholon still gave 5 to 1 odds General Thieu would grant clemency. Secretary of State Rusk sent Thieu and Ky a cable, personally delivered by Lodge, protesting the severity of the sentence. Ta Vinh's wife, a practicing Buddhist, went to Tri Quang and begged him on her knees to intervene. The bonze did nothing.

It was still dark when I walked down Le Loi Boulevard from the Continental Hotel to the execution site, five blocks away. It was rather like going to the theatre. White-gloved paratroopers ushered reporters into a small ringside park in the center of a traffic circle. In front of the yellow baroque railway building, a sandbagged bunker had been erected with five wooden stakes. Crowds of people had been pushed back into side streets by the police. Coils of concertina wire and a ring of paratroopers with steel flak vests, helmets and fixed bayonets guarded the inner circle near the firing pit. A few of Ky's officers stood in clusters, smoking, chatting and joking. Ta Vinh's wife and children and three other Chinese women in pajamas were allowed to come inside the traffic circle. Then, as a crowd of television cameramen and press photographers gathered around them, a phalanx of police began brutally pushing back the women and children with rifle butts. The screams grew more intense, flashbulbs popped and cameras whirred. Ta Vinh's wife clutched a tiny baby in her arms, her face dead white and beaded with sweat despite the predawn coolness. She swayed and sobbed, tears pouring down her cheeks. An unidentified fat Chinese woman by her side cried in perfect English into the television cameras, "No law on earth would punish a businessman this way. No civilized country in the world would do this."

An agitated American soldier next to me said, "It's too drastic. Can't we stop it?"

A Vietnamese student I once had interviewed slipped up to my side. "It's pitiful," he said. "They are very clever. It's very cleverly staged, isn't it." With that, he vanished into the crowd. What did he mean? Did Ky *want* his regime to have a fascist image— or what? I didn't understand.

Sirens screaming, a motorcycle escort roared up ahead of a motorcade of trucks and military jeeps. With paratroops at his side, Ta Vinh was dragged from a closed van. He looked dignified and wore a black well-tailored suit. A stout Catholic priest was by his side; the Ky regime had announced Ta Vinh's conversion to Catholicism in his death cell. The Chinese importer was tied to the stake and blindfolded. Military trucks focused blinding headlights on our eyes that obscured the firing pit. Within seconds, a volley of shots rang out like a string of firecrackers exploding. The firing-squad commander leaped forward and administered the *coup de grâce*.

Ta Vinh's head and body rocked forward as if he were making a polite bow. I could see blood spurting from his stomach. His wife started to howl, a long unearthly animal cry that echoed round and round the silent marketplace.

"Vietnamese justice," an American voice said. "With American bullets," said another. "Ky should shoot three or four Chinese to bring down prices," said an old Vietnamese man. A woman in black pajamas shouted back at him, "Ta Vinh's wife is a very good woman! I know her!" The two began haggling about rising food prices. A wild-eyed Vietnamese boy grabbed me by the arm and hissed like a maniac, "Vietnamese people want more Chinese must die." Other youths surged forward into the firing pit to meticulously examine the stake for bits of blood and flesh; they said it was lucky to touch a millionaire's remains.

And the anti-Chinese pogrom did not end there. A few days later, the press was invited to the inauguration ceremony of Premier Ky's newly formed "Anti-Fraud Group" in the gilded central gallery of the Saigon Prefecture. Curious, I arrived to find some 400 men in black shirts sitting at rigid attention. Many of them had the slack-jawed, brutal faces of hardened criminals—cheeks scarred with knife slashes, long moustaches, and shaved heads or very long coarse black hair. They did not look like any Vietnamese I had ever seen.

A student in steel-rimmed glasses in the same black uniform led reporters to the press section. He explained that the men were all paroled criminals Ky was trying to rehabilitate. All 400 had been either killers, rapists, burglars or professional thieves. In return for a pledge of allegiance to him, Ky had pardoned them and given each a new Renault taxi or a Lambretta mini-bus to earn their livelihoods. The student said that the Anti-Fraud Group was supposed to inform the government about Chinese merchants who sold above legal price ceilings or kept black-market goods in their warehouses. The men would receive thirteen weeks of part-time military training, he said, but he did not offer to explain how this would help in uncovering fraud. The Ky regime set official prices so low that Saigon's entire business community had to operate illegally in order to make the economy function. Black-market goods from the American post exchange were sold openly on Saigon's downtown streets.

Finally, flanked by a cordon of helmeted bodyguards and paratroopers, Ky strode into the gallery. The men leaped to their feet in rigid attention. At a signal from Ky, who also wore the black uniform but topped off by harlequin sunglasses, they sat down again. Ky himself sat in a tall gilded chair and stared impassively at the assembly. "Reptilian," an American reporter behind me murmured. Several students spoke, and twice the men shouted allegiance to Ky with upraised fists and a thunderous roar. Ky said a few words about the desire of his government to give ex-convicts a chance to reform themselves. The ceremony ended when a tall moustached man with tattooed wrists and one gold earring formally presented Ky with a large knife. Ky unsheathed it and slowly ran his finger along the blade as a hush fell over the audience. Then it was all over with a clump of jackboots, barked paratroop commands and the slam of black limousine doors. (If Ky's experiment in criminal reform was serious, it never succeeded; in early 1968, the officers of the Anti-Fraud Group were charged with embezzling millions of government piastres.)

In the days that followed Ta Vinh's execution, I was not surprised to learn that the Anti-Fraud Group was carrying out a terror campaign against the Chinese business community. Many Chinese shut down their shops for some weeks, causing a run on food and a sharp inflationary upsurge. Within two weeks of General Thi's ouster, soaring food prices and the mounting civil revolt in Annam threatened to reach serious proportions. In an interview on March 23rd at his office in the American Embassy, I found Ambassador Lodge deeply worried.

Lodge took me to a wall map to point out a spot on the Ben Hai River which divided the two Vietnams and said that a North Vietnamese divisional headquarters had moved across the river "within the last twenty-four hours." Lodge told me that

Westmoreland had flown up to the demilitarized zone that morning. A few days earlier, the Communists had overrun an outpost just ten miles outside of Quang Tri City. Survivors of a 100-man garrison had had to be evacuated by helicopter, leaving behind at least thirty dead. Lodge believed that the attack was by advance units of the 324B Division, which had now been joined by its headquarters. At that time, only one other full northern division was known to be in the south, the 325th in the highlands. Although we didn't know it then, this was the beginning of the northern invasion across the DMZ.

Lodge also told me that, according to the CIA, known Communist agents had taken over the struggle movements in both Hue and Danang that had originally been formed to protest Thi's ouster. Lodge said he was now convinced that Tri Quang was consciously collaborating with Hanoi. There was a marked parallelism in timing between the Buddhist struggle and troop movements across the formerly demilitarized zone. Lodge estimated that there were 20,000 Viet Cong and North Vietnamese troops in the northern sector of the country, most of them concentrated around Hue and Danang. Westmoreland by then had moved several American Marine battalions to Phu Bai Airbase, just outside Hue.

The ambassador said he had urged Ky to warn the people of the two northernmost provinces and the cities of Hue and Danang about both the military and subversive threat posed by the Communists. "If Ky makes the population aware of the really dangerous situation that exists," Lodge said, "what are now viewed as patriotic demonstrations opposing military government would be unmasked as Communist agitation against the state in time of war." Lodge said that at his urging, Ky had agreed to send a delegation north to study the situation and prepare for the declaration of a state of emergency. The ambassador was visibly disturbed.

"It won't work," I was told afterward by Professor Tran Quang Thuan, Tri Quang's chief press spokesman in Saigon. Thuan, although a convinced Marxist, was the most candid and articulate man in Tri Quang's organization. Throughout the Buddhist revolt, he appeared remarkably well briefed on both Ky's conversations with Lodge and the military situation in the northern sector. That day he said, "We have already instructed our cadres to denounce as false any government declaration that Communist troops are massing around Hue and Danang. If Ky declares an emergency and imposes martial law, it will be politically disastrous. Nobody will believe him." (The Buddhists could have been getting their information from Ky himself; at a palace breakfast Ky told me and several other American newsmen that he had been meeting regularly with Tri Quang or his intermediaries; other, more secret, meetings between Ky and Tri Quang had also been reported since the start of the crisis.)

By now the character of the revolt in Annam had radically changed. Thi had been unable to control popular sentiment as he had hoped. His apparent hope to create a base from which to challenge Ky had failed. Instead, speeches and banners by late March began demanding an immediate introduction of constitutional government. A strong anti-American tone was creeping in, and the United States was accused of "interfering" in Vietnamese internal affairs. The original demonstrators—peasants, civil servants and soldiers loyal to Thi—were replaced by Tri Quang's shock force of student agitators, street toughs, rickshaw men and presumably some Viet Cong guerrillas. The slogans became more extreme: "Down with all governments that don't respect Vietnam's sovereignty" and "Yellow-skinned people in Vietnam should not be oppressed by foreigners."

Agitprop committees in both Hue and Danang seized control of the radio stations to broadcast xenophobic and racist propaganda against the United States. In both towns, demoralized officials meekly handed over the stations, partly from official sympathy for Thi, but mostly because they were too frightened to do anything else. Organized government in Annam collapsed and was replaced by Tri Quang's struggle committees, which at once began purging, abducting and jailing anti-Communist elements. Thi himself fled to a villa in Hue, remaining there in isolation. One afternoon I flew up to Hue briefly to visit him and found Thi's confidence shattered; he was in a state of nervous tension and stuttered badly. Tri Quang flew to Hue and personally took command of the revolt. In Saigon, questions were raised as to why Ky had allowed the bonze government transport to fly to Hue. Ky did not answer them.

Among most Saigonese, however, there seemed to be little

public interest in the agitation in distant Annam. Yet both Thieu and Ky kept using alarmist language to describe a situation that was not visibly critical. Hue and Danang were both held by Buddhist struggle committees, but life in Saigon had not been disrupted and the country's survival had certainly not been threatened. Yet when several hundred students marching on the Saigon radio station were quickly routed by the police, government bulletins played up the episode and declared that some of the students had shouted, "Long live Ho Chi Minh!" No newsmen present heard anything of the kind, but the officially generated tension rose, especially as Ky's Skyraiders buzzed downtown Saigon.

One day a battalion of riot police, with green-painted wicker shields and steel helmets were rushed out to disperse a ragtag band of youths parading up and down with banners on a quiet suburban street. Before the police could move in, a surge of homeward-bound evening traffic swept over the demonstration, toppling banners and scattering would-be rioters in a mass of bicycles, scooters and cars. Around eight o'clock that evening, the same band, still less than a hundred strong, was allowed to march to the steps of the opera house outside the Continental. At a given signal, police fired shots in the air and threw tear-gas canisters for blocks around. I was having dinner on the hotel terrace when suddenly wine glasses spilled, chairs toppled, and waiters and diners fled inside to escape the fumes. The ultimate absurdity came when both Ky's police and Tri Quang's agitators started stoning the American press, who usually outnumbered everybody else at these "demonstrations."

Finally, on Sunday, April 3rd, Ky held a press conference. He first read a reasonable-sounding statement promising firm measures to restore law and order, and announced he would appoint a national political congress as the first step toward civil government. When I began to wonder why Ky had called the conference, one of his hacks in the Vietnamese press asked if Dr. Nguyen Van Manh, the Catholic mayor of Danang, had been misusing public funds to pay antigovernment demonstrators. With seeming spontaneity, Ky angrily replied, "Either this government will fall or the mayor of Danang will be shot. Danang is in control of the Viet Cong and we must liberate it. We will liberate Danang—the Communists control it." An American reporter pointed out that Danang was well protected by five battalions of U.S. marines. Ky retorted, "This is purely a Vietnamese question and has nothing to do with U.S. marines."

The next day General Le Nguyen Khang, one of the seven men Tran Van Van was to name as the hard core of the Dai Viet brotherhood, flew 1,500 Vietnamese marines and two companies of riot police to Danang. None of them even left the airbase. But the local army and police commanders of units providing security for the U.S. marines' pacification area around Danang began ordering their men into the town, on the grounds that they were needed to protect it from Ky's threatened invasion. Hundreds of pacification workers and village chiefs were abandoned to the Viet Cong. Roadblocks and gun positions were set up across all roads into town. Local Buddhists who opposed arming the pagodas on religious grounds were overruled in an atmosphere of frenzied agitation against Ky.

In Saigon, Tri Quang's man, Professor Thuan, called me to meet him at a Buddhist pagoda. When I arrived, Thuan said Tri Quang had secretly returned to Saigon and gone into hiding because he feared assassination. Thuan said Tri Quang had met with an American undercover man that morning. Since Robert Komer, President Johnson's Vietnam aide, was in town, I thought it might be either he or one of his party.

Thuan told me, "Tri Quang said he would give the order to halt the rebellion in Danang and Hue and the demonstrations in Saigon if Ky publicly agrees to Buddhist-supervised elections within three months. Tri Quang wants an elected single-chamber parliament. It would not only strengthen whatever government holds office in Saigon but also the United States position in Southeast Asia. Tri Quang proposed that after elections and the formation of such a parliament, the question of whether a continued American military presence was desirable would be put to a vote. You know as well as I do that the people hate the Viet Cong and such a vote would pass. Tri Quang said, 'The American troops now have come here without the consent of the Vietnamese people. We would put the question of American military and economic support to a vote by a newly elected assembly. If the assembly approved of the American conduct of the war and its policies, it would provide a legal foundation for the U.S. military presence in Vietnam.' Tri Quang also pledged his conditional support for the war effort if the United States agreed to his demands. He said, 'We will try our best with all our efforts and the help of the United States to successfully prosecute the war. Without the American presence, we would lose our country. Therefore American troops here are an actual necessity.'"

"But that's blackmail."

Thuan smiled. "Tri Quang also wants Ky and the present government to remain in office during the next three months as a provisional government until elections are held. Ky has privately agreed to the demand for early elections, but has still not fulfilled our condition of proclaiming a date and electoral laws publicly. Without elected government, we feel we can't effectively prosecute the war—for this reason there is an urgency to our efforts. Once the government announces publicly an acceptable election day and the procedures of the election, then normal life will return. We will just telephone the demonstrators in Hue and Danang and say, 'Stop all this nonsense.'"

So this was the meaning of the Annam revolt. General Thi had never really mattered. A few days after this interview, Tri Quang announced that Ky had privately promised to establish a constituent assembly in six months. Ky denied this and said he was rejecting the Buddhist demands on the grounds that they constituted outright surrender. A day later, on April 8th, the Buddhists announced the formation of a new "struggle movement committee" against the Ky regime. They charged that Ky had "brutally betrayed" the Buddhists and warned that "a civil war that will take tens of thousands of lives and cause the total collapse of national unity may well take place because of the shortsightedness, irascibility and irresponsibility of this government."

Washington fell for this bluff, appearing to believe that if they gave in to Tri Quang's demands he would stop there. A message was privately conveyed to Ky and Tri Quang that the United States would accept a three- to six-month timetable for elections but would not support elections run by Tri Quang's Buddhists, whom it now regarded as a small and unrepresentative minority. Washington's response alarmed some of the Roman Catholic clergy in Saigon. Father Tran Du, the prominent Tonkinese refugee priest, told me he felt Ky and Tri Quang were in collusion to get early rigged elections nobody else wanted. A conference of Catholic leaders from all forty-four provinces issued a statement calling on Ky to "react strongly" against "troublemakers."

On April 12th, Ky appointed a 170-man National Political Congress, which met in Saigon. Only ninety-two of those invited came, and twenty of these walked out when they saw that it was dominated by Tri Quang's men and Dai Viets. General Thieu addressed the congress and said the junta was eager to surrender power to a civil government "as soon as possible." When the conference ended two days later, Thieu signed a decree providing for the election of a constituent assembly by September.

Twenty thousand Buddhists—many of them the by-now familiar old Tonkinese refugee women and street urchins—marched in a victory celebration in Saigon. In Hue, Tri Quang appealed for an end to the civil revolt, which, he said, would just "create anarchy" and prevent elections. General Thi, now positive he had been betrayed, made one last desperate speech in Danang declaring that Ky had lost the confidence of the people and that the struggle must continue until Ky resigned.

In Saigon, the alarmed reaction of one rickshaw driver typified the fear of the man in the street that elections might be premature: "Elections are a very good idea. But first, all parties and all religions must unite in a single front against the Viet Cong and try to pacify the countryside. After that, we can carry out an election successfully. I am only a citizen and not a soldier or a politician. I wish to live in peace. But an election in five months is too soon."

By this time, almost unremarked, the hopeful spirit of Honolulu had faded away. President Johnson spoke of "a period of testing ahead." Senator Richard Russell spoke for many when he declared, "We can't possibly win if we are fighting an enemy in front of us while the people we are supposed to be helping are against us and want us out of the country."

Ky's April 3rd threat to "liberate" Danang and Thieu's mid-April promise of elections in September were followed by a month of surface calm. The semblance of normalcy in Saigon made one forget that much of Annam was still in rebel hands. I was busy covering the military war in the highlands and jungle, and did not learn until later that during this time, Buddhist and Dai Viet "people's courts" in the towns and countryside had arbitrarily taken over much of the rural administration in Annam, abducting, arresting and, in some cases, executing local government officials. The main political target of these Buddhist–Dai Viet rebels, who had won over most of the local Vietnamese army units to their side, was the regionally strong, staunchly anti-Communist Viet Nam Quoc Dang Dan party (VNQDD), which under Thi had controlled most of the administration in the five northernmost provinces. The VNQDD, founded in Tonkin in 1927 as a Vietnamese offshoot of Chiang Kai-shek's Kuomintang, provided Annam with a relatively powerful non-Communist political base. Dennis Duncanson, in *Government and Revolution in Vietnam,* describes how during this period Dai Viet gangs attacked and arrested VNQDD members and murdered their leader in Danang. Duncanson goes so far as to imply that the Dai Viets' successful attempt to get control of the key military commands and civil offices in both Hue and Danang may have been the main purpose of the Buddhist revolt. This would, of course, fit the pattern established in 1964 in Saigon, where the Buddhists were the main force in toppling governments but the Dai Viets were the ones who then stepped into power, their domination growing with each successive regime.

Thus from mid-April to mid-May, the civil revolt in Annam did not end; it just remained in a state of suspension. During this pause, Le Duan visited both Moscow and Peking, perhaps to reconcile the Chinese to the Russian view that final political victory could be achieved through political subversion and not a costly protracted guerrilla war. In January, Liberation Radio had called for "an intensified political struggle to end the war and force the American troops to withdraw through revolutionary violence, street demonstrations and general strikes." That phase seemed to be over by April.

In Danang, Ky's troops remained on the U.S. Marine airbase, and in Saigon the premier seemed eager to improve his relations with the American press. One evening he invited about ten of us to dinner at his house at Tan Son Nhut Airbase. Unlike the traditionally furnished homes of most Vietnamese leaders, Ky's house resembled an expensive nightclub: bright yellow-and-blue Chinese rugs, a red bar and stools, gaudy paper flowers and a big television set; Mai said her husband's favorite show was "Batman."

We ate at a long table set up on Ky's helicopter pad in a grassless front yard. Mai was stunningly beautiful that evening, and she sat by Ky's side. I remembered her description of Ky to a friend of mine as "an extremely honest man." She had said, "I am proud of him. I am sure that if his people love him it is because they know he is honest and that he puts his country above everything else, seeking only what is best for his people. He is not ambitious and his desire is only to save his country from Communism."

Mai was interesting in her own right. Although she protested she had no interest in politics, and a hard-eyed Vietnamese army major was always present when the American press interviewed her, Mai had been linked with the brotherhood long before she met Ky. Mai's father, according to Vietnamese living in Hanoi at the time, was a Communist agent infiltrated by Ho Chi Minh into the Tonkin capital as the deputy police chief. When the father later leaked some information to the Sûreté, he was assassinated and Mai was adopted by Le Van Thai, one of Dr. Sung's closest lieutenants and a Dai Viet since at least 1954. Thai had brought Mai and her mother to Saigon in 1954, financed Mai's education at a good Catholic convent in Dalat, and, after she had become an airline stewardess and won a Saigon beauty contest in 1964, introduced her to Ky. They were married a few months later.

That evening, as she sat gazing with apparent adoration at Ky, I wondered what role Mai was really playing. I was sitting just across from Ky as he droned on, sipping spicy Vietnamese wine. Although he wore a white sport shirt with "Aloha Hawaii" on it, a souvenir of the Honolulu conference, an anti-American tone began creeping into his remarks. He dismissed the idea that President Johnson had swollen his ego in Honolulu: "In the first place, he did not embrace me. Second, I'm not a woman. Third, he's too tall for me." He sneered at Saigon's civilian nationalist leaders: "It doesn't matter to me what they do. I don't care." He said that no one could overthrow him: "I defy my critics and enemies to oust me. I tell them, 'I am waiting for you at the street corner.'" Throughout the dinner, members of Ky's Anti-Fraud Group loitered in the shadows around the house; Ky would not be waiting for his political opponents alone. Toward the end of the evening, Ky slipped into Vietnamese and began regaling a few Vietnamese reporters there with what one later told me was a mimicry of President Johnson.

Emmet John Hughes of *Newsweek*, one of the Americans present, pressed Ky for his serious views on negotiations but got nowhere. "I'm anti-Communist and I'll stay that way even if I'm the only one left in Vietnam," said Ky. When Hughes asked, "Are there, then, absolutely no conceivable circumstances under which you could find negotiations tolerable?" Ky replied, "Absolutely not. I am perfectly willing one day to stand alone before Ho Chi Minh and tell him, 'I'll never give in to you,' even if I then have nothing left to do but go and shoot myself. Of course it doesn't matter what you Americans choose to do."

During this calm before the storm, I spent several weeks talking with a broad range of Vietnamese whose views were not so well known to the world audience as those of such men as Ky and Tri Quang. A series of twenty or so articles resulted. Perhaps the most representative among the well-educated Vietnamese was a professor of Oriental philosophy at Saigon University whom I shall call Le Van Tan, since he requested that a pseudonym be used. A Sorbonne-educated Confucian scholar, Tan took the long view. Governments might fall, bombs explode, and pitched battles rage on the city's outskirts, but since the start of the war in 1959, he had completed an introduction to Indian thought, a bibliography of classical Vietnamese Buddhist literature, and was then cataloguing systems of Hindu philosophy. Like most of Saigon's educated middle class, Tan had a thirst for contemporary Western culture. He had read all the James Bond books and never missed a Gregory Peck film. But in spite of the American presence, the war, and social disintegration under Ky's rule, he still saw Vietnam as fundamentally Confucian.

"Though we probably have twice as many practicing Buddhists

as we had a decade ago—maybe 2,000,000 now," he told me,
"Vietnam is still most deeply influenced by Confucian ethics. We
still worship three generations of ancestors in our homes. We
burn joss sticks, bow before a family altar, offer fruit, and make
an invocation to the dead spirits to join us. My mother still firmly
believes the spirit of my father returns to earth. Tet, or the Lunar
New Year, is another Confucian custom, and so is the right of the
elder brother over his mother and younger brothers as head of
the family. My two older brothers are in North Vietnam, so I
must take their place. But we keep in touch. All you need is a
friend in Paris to send on mail. Sometimes we send money, food,
once even a bicycle."

The walls of the professor's villa were lined with books. Most
of them were on Vietnamese philosophy, but I also saw Freud,
Jung, a Bible, a Modern Library Shakespeare, Jean Paul Sartre's
works, Romain Rolland and Will Durant's *Our Oriental Heritage.*
His lighter reading was on another shelf: Françoise Sagan, Pearl
Buck, Agatha Christie, and Ian Fleming. In a glassed-in cabinet
were mementoes of the professor's travels: an ivory Taj Mahal, a
Japanese doll, a photograph of himself in a gondola in Venice,
and pictures of a visit to India to meet the Dalai Lama. In one
corner of the room were stacks of *Time* and *Newsweek.* In
another was his wife's Singer sewing machine.

"Marxism is something quite foreign, quite strange to the
Vietnamese people," Professor Tan said. "The Asian version
especially is very bad because we are such poor people in this
part of the world. They tell us we must build for the future; that
the present generation must be sacrificed. I'm very doubtful
about this future. Also, in a Confucian society the two pillars are
the family system and respect for private property. The
Communists want to destroy both."

Tan said he was very disturbed about South Vietnam's coming
election. "Oh, I accept the election in principle. But I don't
believe it will take place peacefully, smoothly or in an orderly
way. I hope so. Sometimes I wonder how it can take place at all.
I agree with Tri Quang that Vietnam should have an elected
assembly and civilian government. But I disagree on how to
organize an election. I am afraid others can profit by the
Buddhist actions. I know Tri Quang only by his writings, which I

have studied carefully. I have the impression he is an extreme nationalist and is passionately committed to Buddhism, and that he believes he can live at peace with the Communists and convert them."

Tan mentioned that sixty professors at Saigon University had formed a group to discuss the election and warn the government about the dangers of infiltration. "I have the impression there are a few pacifists, even Communists, among us. I myself don't like war, but I think it is necessary for the time being. We are not warmongers, but we are being attacked. I must tell you all this publicity about anti-Americanism is giving a very false picture. The Vietnamese are a very hospitable people. Perhaps Americans could learn more about our culture, customs and ways of living. In traditional Confucian Vietnam, there have always been four classes: the *si*, or intellectuals; the *nong*, or peasants; the *cong*, or workers; and the *thuong*, or merchants. Soldiers were regarded as 'outcastes.' A general could be respected, but only because he was first an intellectual. We have an old Vietnamese saying, 'Intellectuals first and peasants second, but in bad times peasants first and intellectuals second.' Generals like Ky and Thieu qualify as neither; they have no education or breeding, which is very important in an Asian society. This distresses some of our people more than it might in a Western society."

I asked Tan what he would like to do after the war. He smiled. His benign, handsome face seemed already permanently etched with a certain sadness. "I'd like to be a professor, a thinker. I'd like to have much more time to write and get more of my work published. And, of course, to watch my children grow up happily." He paused for a moment uncertainly. "But, you understand, it is men like myself the Communists will execute first. When Ho Chi Minh took over the north, he killed practically the entire faculty of Hanoi University. He liquidated the educated middle class of Tonkin and created a new one out of the peasantry. I think most of us in Saigon understand this."

It was my experience that most Saigonese, forced like Professor Tan to live day after day in a waking nightmare, pursued normality above all else. A young university student once told me all he wanted after the war was "to be a normal citizen. I just want to live a peaceful normal life in an independent and reunified Vietnam. How many children I have, how big my house is, doesn't matter. Just to have a normal life."

This desperate pursuit of normality, which often looked like aloofness and indifference to outsiders, was shared by the poor. A dock worker told me, "I work for the Americans and make a lot of money from them. Business is business. I don't bother about war and peace or who is VC. Oh, sometimes I hear on the radio about trouble in Saigon, but I steer clear of those Buddhist demonstrations. They are as wind that passes in the street."

Another laborer told me, "I was walking down Le Loi Boulevard last week when my eyes watered from tear gas. The wind blew it right at me. I saw about thirty monks in yellow robes and a lot of screaming children. I turned around and went the other way. They just make trouble for everybody."

To most Vietnamese, deeply influenced by Confucian tradition, the key word was "harmony"; to Le Duan and his new young breed of brainwashed intellectuals it was "struggle." The mentality of such young men, the intelligentsia of a potential Communist Asia challenging the West, could be studied in Saigon in talks with Tri Quang's shock force of student agitators. In the spring of 1966, during those few weeks of calm, about fifty of them were living on Hien Vuong Street, in a pleasant, leafy residential neighborhood not far from the Buddhist Institute.

This house had the neglected, institutional air of a Y.M.C.A. in a small American town. There was little furniture except a few dusty desks and chairs. The walls were hung with inspirational mottoes and what resembled Boy Scout organizational charts, with colored reproductions of rank and insignia, even merit badges. There was a large framed photograph of a misty-eyed Vietnamese girl who looked like somebody's high school sweetheart until one learned that she had been one of the Buddhist fiery suicides. Some young monks lived upstairs; they were birdlike young men, with shaven, bony heads and brown robes, who usually greeted me in twittering singsong voices and then disappeared.

Behind the house was a garage and large jerry-built shed with a concrete floor and corrugated tin roof where the shock troops lived. I usually visited during the afternoon siesta hour, when twenty or thirty youths would be sleeping on straw mats spread out on the floor. Others would be playing chess, ping pong or volleyball in the alley outside. In one corner, behind a partition of flattened American beer cans, I listened one day to several boys, one of whom played a guitar. Like American folksingers, they softly sang:

> *Men are not our enemy,*
> *If we kill men, with whom shall we live?*
> *Our enemy's name is Cruelty,*
> *Anger, Immorality and Corruption.*

Despite the summer-camp atmosphere, this was the headquarters of what Tri Quang called his "Committee of Youth and Students to Safeguard the Nation." Most of the faces were familiar as those of ringleaders in anti-American, antigovernment riots since the summer of 1963. Since early March of 1966, they had been battling police and paratroopers, demanding an immediate end to the war and American troop withdrawal, and had burned American jeeps, attacked American soldiers and stoned the American press. I had seen one chalking the slogans "If Tri Quang Dies, All Americans Must Die" and "President Johnson Is a Communist." Yet, when you visited them, they were gracious and polite and usually offered you tea or a Coca-Cola. The leader was a pale tense youth in his early twenties with an unruly shock of black hair. He usually wore a grimy undershirt, and I often found him playing chess. By mutual agreement I knew him by an alias, Phan Lac Giang Dong, which he said meant "Happy River of the East." His father was an itinerant carpenter in Hue who went from door to door making repairs for housewives. He had three brothers: a teacher, a soldier and a student. Phan claimed that the student had had to have his right leg amputated after a police beating. Phan told me he had come to Saigon in the spring of 1963 to study public administration under a Buddhist scholarship but had spent most of his time organizing antigovernment agitation. He refused to discuss this, preferring to talk about literature and culture.

These boys thirsted for knowledge of the outside world. Once, I brought them a box of old books: they snatched them up and almost fought over them. Phan voiced contempt for American writers but said he liked Genet, Sartre, Gide and Camus.

Steinbeck was an exception to his American phobia, although I could never convince him that the migrant workers in *Of Mice and Men* were white, not black. Phan once told me that his favorite novel was André Malraux's *La Condition Humaine*. It was easy to see how he could identify with Malraux's hero, Kyo, the young Communist Chinese revolutionary eventually executed by Chiang Kai-shek's troops who were backed by "foreign" financial interests in the Shanghai of the twenties. Since the novel was based on Malraux's experience as a French teacher in Saigon during the rise of the Vietnamese Communist party, Phan in many ways was Kyo's real-life heir.

"I liked it," Phan told me, "because it describes the fate of human beings, that is, the lower classes of people, especially Asians." He read me his favorite passage: "No doubt the value of men lay only in what they transformed. The Revolution had just passed through a terrible malady, but it was not dead. And it was Kyo and his men, living or not, vanquished or not, who brought it into the world. . . ."

When I asked Phan his occupation, he replied, "A revolutionary, of course. But it is illegal in Saigon to read or possess the works of Marx, Engels, Lenin or Mao Tse-tung."

"What are you struggling for?"

"Our first aim is to bring peace to Vietnam. You will see. When the Vietnamese people can speak freely and have full sovereignty, they will decide to end the war. The election will provide this sovereignty. All of Vietnam's people should be allowed to vote, whether living on the government side or not. But elections are only one way to get peace. We Vietnamese, we want elections. But it depends on the Americans. I feel the United States will try and stop the election. Then we will struggle again."

"Why do you think the United States is fighting in Vietnam?"

"To test your modern weapons and to solve American economic troubles. You bring your surplus farm products to sell in our markets. But the French stayed here a hundred years and never understood Vietnam. Now the Americans stay only twelve years. With 250,000 G.I.s, they make a lot of trouble with our social life and cause inflation. Within one year, the cost of living has gone up 500 per cent in Hue and 300 per cent in Saigon. Saigon's thousands of bar girls are only war victims who have lost their

families in the countryside and must come to the city to do that
dirty kind of business. The Declaration of Honolulu was an
American trick. The Ky government is only an American puppet
government. The only Vietnamese who do not want to end the
war and unify North and South Vietnam are American puppets
and war profiteers."

With Phan it was at least possible to talk. This was not true of
some of the more fanatic youths in Tri Quang's shock force. One
of these had appeared on the cover of *Newsweek* carrying a
megaphone and looking about fifteen. In reality, he was in his
twenties, usually sported a paratrooper's beret and dark glasses,
and told me that both his parents had been killed by the French.
I remember during one conversation I asked if he liked
movies.

"I hate movies. I only go to Vietnamese movies."

"Do you like Vietnamese opera?"

"No. I hate love stories."

"What authors do you like?"

"Fidel Castro, Sukarno, Ben Bella."

Once, I told Phan I thought the Vietnamese countryside was
very pastoral, with peasants harvesting rice and little children
riding water buffalo. The *Newsweek* boy interrupted. "That scene
is gone now because of American bombing."

The lull continued until mid-May. And then at dawn on May
15th, Ky's troops invaded Danang. The battle lasted nine days,
killing 103 Vietnamese and wounding 400 more, most of them
innocent civilians. The initial assault was led by two Vietnamese
Marine battalions commanded by General Khang, whom Van
was to name as a Dai Viet and a high school classmate of Ky. The
marines immediately occupied half of Danang, after allowing the
Buddhist "rebel" forces—mostly composed of local Vietnamese
army units—to fortify themselves in Danang's main pagodas. Ky's
troops sprayed the downtown streets with machine-gun and rifle
fire and mortared Danang's American civilian hospital, although
no rebel troops were in the vicinity. The Defense Ministry in Saigon announced that the action was taken to "reinforce a number"
of local army units which had risen up "against the illegal struggle committee in Central Vietnam." General Thieu said in a

radio broadcast that the action was necessary not only to "maintain security and order, but to prevent Communist infiltration into urban centers." The invasion's aim, Thieu went on, was "to ensure necessary conditions for defeating the Communists, for carrying out the election of a constituent assembly and advancing toward a popularly elected government."

By now, four successive generals had been sent to Danang to replace Thi as commander of the northern sector. One of them, General Huynh Van Cao, a respected Roman Catholic purged in 1964 and just reinstated in the army, was ordered to attack the Buddhist pagodas by Nguyen Ngoc Loan, the brotherhood member Ky had just made police chief. Cao refused on the grounds that it would precipitate religious warfare, and fled for safety to the headquarters of General Lewis W. Walt, the American Marine commander. Thi had faded from the picture altogether, although he was still in Hue.

In Saigon, Tri Quang's Buddhist Institute charged Ky with "an act of treachery" that could lead to civil war, and appealed to President Johnson to "intervene." In Washington, Secretary of State Rusk warned that these disturbances were causing restiveness among the American people. Rusk said the United States was using all its influence to bring the Ky and Tri Quang factions together. I arrived in Danang on May 20th, five days after the street fighting had started. (A Vietnamese colonel at Saigon's Tan Son Nhut Airbase had tried to stop a group of newsmen, including myself, from reaching an American cargo plane. He pulled a gun on Sean Flynn, a free-lance photographer and son of the late Hollywood star Errol Flynn.)

Danang was badly scarred. Mutinous troops from the Danang area who had sided with the Buddhists had fallen back from their forward positions and were occupying the area around Danang's three main pagodas. As we walked through the deserted streets, there were several violent outbursts of firing from Danang's big public market. Rebel snipers hidden on the rooftops fired at pedestrians but did not seem to shoot at Americans, especially if they carried cameras and notebooks. Some of the streets were completely blocked off by fallen rubble and strewn with torn-off branches. At several points, trucks and buses had been turned on their sides, and monks, Buddhist Boy Scouts and rebel soldiers crouched behind them. We saw few civilians on the streets, and the shops were all shuttered. Some families were peering out of cracks in the doors and windows. Those I spoke with said they supported neither side, didn't understand what the shooting was all about, and prayed it would soon be over.

At Danang hospital, an American construction engineer told me he was in charge of building a new hospital wing. He said, "I get a feeling from my workers that the people here don't like either side, Ky's troops or the rebels." He said his men tried to come to work, but some had been beaten up by Buddhist youths. He showed me where Ky's troops had mortared the hospital for no apparent reason.

Another American, Kenneth Harbridge, said he had been in Danang about six months, running a Hong Kong mail-order tailoring business for the U.S. marines. Harbridge said his house was not far from Tinh Hoi Pagoda, scene of the heaviest fighting. He had seen Buddhist youths place pressure mines in the street, one of which killed his night watchman. A mortar fired from the pagoda had exploded in his garden, wounding a maidservant. Harbridge said the Buddhist rebels were inflicting most of the casualties themselves on innocent civilians and then dragging the dead and wounded back inside the pagoda. He and his Vietnamese staff, and other people in his neighborhood, were against both the Buddhists and Ky's troops. "They're ashamed of what's happening but are afraid to say or do anything," he said. "This is a real reign of terror up here."

Firing stopped at noon for the midday siesta. With the help of a left-wing Vietnamese journalist, I managed to reach the rebel military command post in Danang, which was located at Tan Ninh Pagoda, a beautiful old temple inside a grove of fig and tamarind trees. Oddly enough, Ky's marines and the rebel sentries were talking and joking across barbed-wire fortifications. When we expressed surprise, one said, "We are all brothers here."

Inside the pagoda garden, bonzes in yellow robes were strolling around while rebel troops, stripped to the waist and bareheaded, sat around talking or cleaning their weapons. They stared at us curiously. Near the back of the pagoda itself was an open pavilion; a long table and chairs had been placed inside in the shade. A young major sat there alone. Despite his haggard face, he still looked crisp and clean in his army engineer's uniform. He rose, shook hands politely, and in near-perfect English invited us to sit down. A small boy in a grey robe, his head shaven except for a long pigtail, served green tea.

The major spoke rapidly with my Vietnamese companion for some time. A crowd of curious soldiers gathered around; it struck me that most of them had crew cuts, uncommon in the Vietnamese Army. There were also several intellectual-looking men in civilian clothes. Somehow I felt almost as if I were visiting a Communist headquarters in the jungle. The major seemed to have read my thoughts; he turned abruptly to me and said in English, "Have no fear, my friend. General Ky says we are Viet Cong. But we are not Viet Cong. You can be assured of your safety here." He poured the tea. "We already have an agreement with Ky's troops on either side of us not to fire." He introduced a young Vietnamese Marine lieutenant as a liaison officer from Ky's troops. "The marines, as you have seen, have assumed positions at either end of the tamarind grove around the pagoda. But they are under orders to hold their fire. Is that not correct, Lieutenant?" The lieutenant nodded. "We are here to protect this pagoda and the others in the city. We will stay months if we have to and the local people will give us food. I have brought my troops from the battlefield to protect the people of Danang from being killed by Ky's soldiers and to prove there is no disunity or division among the troops in central Vietnam. It is my own personal desire that General Ky step down in favor of an interim government pending elections." After tea we shook hands with the major. He smiled pleasantly and told me to return the following morning at eleven. "I will see you again," he said.

That was on a Friday afternoon. Friday evening the American press camp was hit by three mortars, presumably fired from rebel positions across the Danang River. Three also hit the airbase. The next morning four South Vietnamese air force planes woke us by strafing and rocketing what we assumed were rebel positions. After the attacks had gone on for nearly an hour, hitting an American position and wounding some U.S. marines, General Walt ordered two U.S. Marine fighter jets into the air with instructions to shoot down the Vietnamese Skyraiders unless they returned to base.

During this diversion we could hear heavy ground fire coming from the direction of Tan Ninh Pagoda. When we were able to reach it, a little after nine o'clock, a sentry told us the pagoda had been bombed and strafed. This was impossible, since all the planes had been flying across the river. The trees around the pagoda had been shot up and branches were scattered about. The entire rebel battalion had vanished—except one, a dead man, with his hand shot off, lying astride a machine-gun position. I recognized him as one of the sentries we had seen joking with Ky's marines the previous afternoon. A French correspondent with us who lived just across the street said he had been forced to flee his house before dawn when it was stormed and ransacked by some Vietnamese soldiers.

The pagoda's façade was pocked with shell holes from what seemed to be heavy automatic fire and grenades. In the entrance lay two Vietnamese male bodies with shaven heads. They wore monks' robes. One had been cut across the chest with machine-gun fire. Strewn about in the dust were a dozen or so trampled and torn Boy Scout hats. The pagoda's interior was spattered with blood. Newsmen were encouraged to photograph the dead bonzes and a group of weeping women and children behind them. Half an hour later the pagoda was sealed off and newsmen were not allowed to enter. When I went to Danang's military headquarters to inquire about the missing battalion, I was told most of it had been captured or had surrendered. I was shown a group of prisoners but was unable to recognize any of them.

The atmosphere was equally strange at Tinh Hoi, Danang's biggest pagoda and the political command center of the Buddhists. Tinh Hoi was an impressive structure with a great curved roof, red lacquer doors, and a broad stone staircase facing a mossy tree-shaded courtyard. The monks claimed that the pagoda had been almost constantly shelled by Ky's invaders, but none of the buildings or trees showed any sign of being hit.

That day at Tinh Hoi there was a carnival air; several hundred soldiers, women and children milled about, and young men shouted harangues over a whining loudspeaker. In the midst of this confusion, I saw five large Vietnamese army trucks drive in flying Red Cross flags. Most of the boxes were emblazoned with the American aid handclasp emblem. As I stood watching, teenagers ripped open boxes of grenades and stuffed them inside their shirts. Mortar rounds, rifles and ammunition were distributed. During the unloading, a small boy in a Scout uniform slipped up to me and said in English, "We are sick and discouraged. All our friends are shooting and killing each other. But everyone is afraid of the bonzes." When I asked a monk how the Red Cross trucks carrying arms reached the pagoda, since it was supposedly surrounded by Ky's troops, the monk said, "Oh, they've gone back to the airbase." Yet when we came out sometime later, we found Vietnamese marines still manning barricades in all the nearby streets. Someone on the government side had let the trucks through.

Ky's marines had also driven a tank to the main pagoda gate; its guns were pointed at the pagoda's façade, where a score of pretty high school girls with long black hair and blue silk gowns sat chatting and giggling, seemingly oblivious to the danger. When I joined them on the steps, they crowded around, wanting to practice their English.

Another gruesome touch was a pavilion where ten corpses were laid out. They were covered with Buddhist flags and swarming with flies. Two yellow-robed monks were chanting and beating on gongs. Weeping men and women knelt by the bodies, some of them wailing to the bonzes. Later, the American consul in Danang told me that the Buddhists were accused of stealing some bodies from the Danang morgue for this exhibit of "martyrs" and that these were their relatives begging to be allowed to take their dead away for proper burial. Most of the dead, of course, had obviously been killed in the fighting. Despite burning joss sticks, the sweet, sickening stench of rotting corpses in the steamy tropical heat was almost overpowering; some had been there for three or four days.

One of the monks declared, "We will fight back until Prime Minister Ky withdraws his troops. We have orders not to negotiate. The people and soldiers have made heavy sacrifices." When a sympathetic Vietnamese newsman asked if the rebels could beat Ky, the bonze said, "I thought so up to three days ago when heavy tanks arrived. There were twelve altogether transported to Danang in American planes. The Americans are not neutral. They back Ky all the way." Which I knew was not true.

On the morning of Sunday, May 23rd, I committed a blunder that inadvertently helped to demoralize the rebels and bring about the collapse of the Danang revolt. A Vietnamese propaganda helicopter flew over Danang with a message that I misunderstood to be an appeal to the rebel leaders to attend peace talks with General Do Quoc Dong, the nominal commander of Ky's task force (which was actually run by Loan, Ky's police chief.) When I went to Tinh Hoi to ask the rebel leaders how they would respond to what I thought was an amnesty offer, they seemed startled and confused, and finally dictated a message I was to carry to General Walt. The message said: "We will accept the invitation to meet at First Corps headquarters this afternoon if General Walt supplies a car and security coming and going." Walt telephoned Ambassador Lodge, who told him to go ahead. In the meantime, I learned that the propaganda helicopter had actually been broadcasting an ultimatum to the rebels to give themselves up. But Associated Press had already flashed a bulletin to Saigon that appeared in most American newspapers that Sunday morning: "Rebel Buddhist leaders at Danang today offered to negotiate if the United States would guarantee their safety . . . There was no immediate indication whether the Buddhist offer would be accepted or whether it was aimed at finding a compromise or surrender."

Both the leaders of the rebels and Ky's troops were furious at the way I had confused things. A bearded rebel, who appeared to be the top political officer inside Tinh Hoi, shrieked at me, "You must tell General Walt the rebels intend to protect our pagoda and our religion to the death. The United States must intervene immediately. How can we negotiate? They will kill us if we leave here."

By afternoon it was apparent that Ky was pressing ahead with plans for a bloody assault against Tinh Hoi. A Vietnamese paratroop battalion arrived by landing craft from Saigon. They carried eleven armored personnel carriers mounted with heavy machine guns. The unit's American advisers had not been informed of the nature of the operation and were ordered to leave the battalion at Danang. Vietnamese marines were using tanks to block all the streets encircling the pagoda, except for a forest behind. The paratroop commander, however, a colonel from Danang, denied any intention of storming the pagoda, saying he planned only "a show of force."

In late afternoon, the big armored cars, followed by paratroops and the press corps on foot, moved into the forest. Like all military operations it was confusing, with shouting soldiers, villagers rushing away with their possessions, and scattered small-arms fire. Then, as if at a given signal, all the machine guns seemed to open up at once in a deafening burst of firepower. Lead pelted the trees over our heads. Some of the most experienced combat reporters said it was the heaviest fire they had ever seen. During a letup in the shooting, most of the press made their way back to the press camp and waited for the rebels to surrender.

After dinner, as we sat out on the riverside terrace, a jeep with a Red Cross blazon roared up. The young Vietnamese driver, his head swathed in bloody bandages, carried a Buddhist bonze and a girl with a bandaged arm. Their message was that the press was invited to Tinh Hoi for an urgent and important announcement. We assumed the surrender had come. About forty of us— Americans, Vietnamese, Japanese, British and French—grabbed our cameras and notepads and headed up the street. Someone put a white bedsheet on a broomstick and quipped, "At last, American intervention."

Tinh Hoi was five blocks away. Some of our straggling band had already entered the gate when orange tracer bullets were fired directly over our heads, followed by high nervous laughter from the pagoda's bunkers. Two Americans in the rear turned back. Those near me were too close, just across the road from the gate. We moved hesitantly forward, keeping near the houses. It seemed safer to go ahead than retreat. One trigger-happy soldier could have all three battalions firing at us.

It got dark just about the time we reached the entrance. My first impression was a weird cacophony of sounds: wailing wounded calling for water, bonzes beating gongs and screaming at the top of their lungs, crying children, a propaganda harangue over a microphone. There were fewer than 200 people left inside:

bonzes, Boy Scouts, women, children and not many troops. Just ahead was a series of grisly tableaux. A wounded woman lay with a tiny baby, just old enough to sit, screaming beside her. Another stretcher held a young woman with two bullet holes in her back. Torches illuminated a horror chamber where thirty or forty corpses lay rotting under Buddhist flags and great clouds of flies. The stench was sickening. Shadows flickered around the torches.

Tim Page, an English free-lancer and one of the bravest combat photographers, sounded almost hysterical: "I'm getting out of here. Who's going with me?" *Time* correspondent Karsten Prager, Page and eight others headed for the gate. They moved slowly across the street, hands in the air, chanting, "*Bao chi, bao chi,* press, press, no shoot."

Those who remained asked one of the rebel political leaders, a man of thirty in a Boy Scout uniform, when an announcement would come. He said to wait another five minutes. "What is the news from Saigon?" he asked me. He was trembling with fear. "Can you take me out with you? Can you take all these people out? But what will they do? Will they kill us?" He pulled me toward the stretcher with the woman and baby on it, but I turned away quickly. A man in a green uniform was blandly assuring some of the other newsmen that an announcement would soon be issued dealing with the reasons for the rebel fight against the Ky government. "You mean you got us up here just for that?" somebody said. "It's a trap," a voice called. "Shut up," said somebody else. "Whatever you do, don't get them excited."

All of a sudden a few shots cracked in the street outside and then a tremendous crash of heavy automatic fire broke all around us. It was set off when two sniper bullets were fired at the ten men trying to walk away from the pagoda. As Prager later described it: "We took cover on the edge of the road, then moved out again. Then all hell broke loose, triggered by which side it was impossible to tell. Up and down the dark street, from both sides, intense automatic fire raged. Five of us dived for cover into one courtyard, the others into an adjoining one. Outside in the street a tremendous explosion resounded—either an M-79 grenade or a 60-mm. mortar shell. Three of the other newsmen, peering out the door, were wounded by blast fragments." Photographer Page was wounded in the face and bleeding badly.

As the other correspondents wrapped mosquito netting around his head, Page kept repeating, "Don't take me back to the pagoda. Don't take me back to the pagoda."

(Our fears of joining the Buddhists' gruesome exhibition of "martyrs" proved well founded. One of Ky's commanders later said that toward morning Viet Cong guerrillas set up a machine gun on the pagoda terrace and started shooting any rebels who tried to escape or surrender.)

As the heavy fire burst around us, I dived under a truck. A Boy Scout was already there. He whispered to me, "You must go quick. Many, many VC here." I crawled over to a pit underneath a concrete statue of Buddha's mother, where Ronald Nessen of NBC and William Stout of CBS were crouched. Nessen felt the firefight had been provoked to trap us. He decided to round up his camera crew and make a break for it. We saw one Vietnamese hand a camera to an American and say, "Here, you take it. I quit. I'm getting out of here." During a break in the fire, we tried to find everybody scattered in the darkness. Nessen shouted, "Don't leave anybody behind. I'm not leaving until I've got all my men."

The interior of the pagoda was lit by only three candles. Schoolgirls and Boy Scouts huddled sniffling and sobbing with terror against the walls. Monks furiously beat gongs and screamed frantic appeals for American intervention. Outside, fire continued to rake the trees and pagoda walls. No one had moved the wounded who lay exposed and unprotected in the open. In a candlelit cell the pagoda's bonze superior was talking with some of the press. "I fear," he said, his face pallid and impassive, "that the paratroopers will attack us tonight or at dawn. I want the press to be here to see it."

Outside, Nessen had gathered his men. He took off his undershirt to use for a white flag and the cameramen trained their television lights on it. About twenty of us headed for the gate shouting, "*Bao chi, bao chi!*" One of the civilian rebel leaders pulled at my arm near the gate. "You cannot leave tonight; it is too dangerous." I just kept walking.

The first hundred yards were the worst. Nessen's undershirt drooping on its stick above us seemed a far from adequate protection. The rebel machine guns were trained at our backs for the first two blocks. We reached a jeep, and Stout and I jumped in the back. Nessen had trouble getting the engine started and then we had to turn around, backing and edging forward in the narrow lane. We had to drive at a crawl because some of the newsmen were walking alongside. Our faces trickled with sweat. The street was black, but one door was open showing light inside. We heard Prager shout, "Americans wounded! Get help!"

As soon as we reached the press camp, the American marines sent an armed jeep back to rescue the wounded men. A third and last group of newsmen got out of the pagoda when Thich Minh Chieu spoke over a loudspeaker and told both the rebels and Ky's troops to hold their fire so the American press could leave. No similar effort was made to get the women and children out. During the night there were sporadic bursts of heavy fire from the pagoda. In the morning a heavy rain set in, and around noon a rebel captain came out of the gate, laid his carbine at the foot of a Vietnamese Marine colonel, and saluted in a formal gesture of surrender. Many of the rebel troops and civilians were arrested, but some, including all the leaders and important monks, had escaped in the night.

The Danang civil war was over. In the afternoon the rain cleared, the sun burst out, and Danang's people swarmed into the streets. Shutters and boards hastily nailed across the front of shops were removed. The markets, closed for eight days, reopened, and the hungry populace swarmed to them. Everywhere, there were people walking, riding bicycles, or just standing on the sidewalk smiling. Danang was glad to be alive again. If anyone was disappointed that the Buddhist rebellion was crushed, their happy, relieved faces showed no signs of it.

As soon as I reached Saigon, I began writing a story that was picked up by Associated Press and appeared on front pages all over the world:

> Saigon—The collapse of the myth that the Buddhists represented a just but repressed popular cause probably began Sunday night in Danang when Associated Press reporter Robert Poos staggered into the American press camp livid with anger and bleeding from a chest wound.
> "The Buddhists trapped us in the pagoda and then opened fire when we tried to get out," Poos shouted with rage.

During the previous hour the scales had fallen from the eyes of some forty American and foreign newsmen who spent some of the most frightening moments of their lives within Danang's besieged Tinh Hoi Pagoda. In a kind of shock treatment that stripped bare the almost incredible cynicism toward human life of the Buddhist monks and rebel political commissars, newsmen were enticed inside for a fictitious urgent announcement, then were told it was too dangerous to leave for the remainder of the night after Buddhist forces provoked a heavy firefight with surrounding paratroopers and tanks. . . . In the early darkness, Tinh Hoi was a place of unutterable terror. . . . Perhaps the most cynical and outrageous touch was a wailing baby someone had propped against the body of a dead woman for the photographers' benefit. . . .

I made one mistake. The woman with the baby was not dead but wounded, as a series of photographs published by the Washington *Post* soon revealed. A congressional flap broke out when a congressman demanded an investigation, charging either the Associated Press, United Press International or myself with "inaccurate and irresponsible reporting." Everyone issued statements. The Washington *Star* managed to end the confusion by pointing out that I had not said the photographers themselves staged the picture. "But," said the *Star*, "he does contend that the Buddhists summoned newsmen to the pagoda after staging a scene to elicit sympathy—and support—for their position." In a reply to Congressman Harris B. McDowell, Jr., who first raised the issue in the House of Representatives, I tried to make the point a fundamental issue in the Vietnam war, perhaps *the* fundamental issue: How were newsmen on the scene to distinguish between reality and stage-managed appearance? "The issue is a profoundly important one in Vietnam and should not be lost sight of in the secondary matter of whether the picture was faked. Of course it was not, and this reporter never meant to imply it was. The stage-managing was done on a much vaster scale, and this propaganda apparatus is what should be investigated."

The Chicago *Tribune* called the pagoda report "one of the most significant news stories of the war," and *Time* quoted me as saying, "I don't think Tri Quang would have really existed without the American press." On May 21st, Ky went on public record with a charge that Tri Quang was a conscious collaborator of the Communists. Asked in an interview if he were willing to talk to Tri Quang, Ky said, "I am always willing to talk to anyone who wants a compromise, but I will never talk to either a Communist or a Communist sympathizer."

In the days immediately following, Tri Quang became recklessly extreme. His movement burned and sacked the American consulate and library in Hue, where American officials photographed Tri Quang smiling as he watched the flames. A wave of Buddhist fiery suicides followed. In June, Tri Quang further debased Vietnamese Buddhism by forcing the people of Hue and Danang to put their family altars on the roads to impede American troop movements. This more than anything aroused world Buddhism; the clerical hierarchies of Thailand, Burma, and Ceylon issued formal protests over the use of altars and recommended that Vietnamese Buddhism purge its ranks of Communists and refrain from further involvement in "purely political issues." Tri Quang's supporters in Saigon tried to save the situation by issuing a blistering open letter condemning the use of altars in the streets. Tri Quang was placed under arrest by Ky's police and flown to Saigon, where he was installed under police guard in a private clinic. In a brief interview, cut short by his doctor, Tri Quang, his face hollow and ravaged by a hunger strike, vowed to me he would continue his campaign to topple any American-supported government. Most Vietnamese held Tri Quang responsible for the three months of riot, rebellion and bloodshed, a travesty of the religion that teaches hatred ceases by love.

The United States, no longer clinging to the old illusion that Tri Quang was the leader of a nationalist "third force," took steps to exile the monk to Japan for the war's duration. Taylor's former deputy in Saigon, U. Alexis Johnson, who had been designated as the new ambassador to Tokyo, arranged with the Japanese government to send a delegation of Japanese Buddhists to Saigon to invite Tri Quang to Tokyo. But, offering no explanation, Ky refused to allow either the monks or the Japanese ambassador to see Tri Quang. My Japanese intelligence friend, "Mr. Moto," who had been sent to Saigon to explore re-establishing Japanese links with the Dai Viets, told me the episode had thoroughly disillusioned him with Ky; he even raised the possibility that Ky and Tri Quang had secretly colluded together throughout the Annam revolt, possibly as agents of Hanoi intent on wrecking the Honolulu plan.

General Thieu announced that national elections for a constituent assembly would be held September 11th and that the assembly would have six months in which to write a new constitution. To celebrate the government's victory, roman candles showered red and gold sparks over the Saigon skyline and Vietnamese troops marched down Le Loi Boulevard with flaming torches and brass military bands. It was a stirring spectacle. But while I sat watching in a sidewalk café, I wondered if my Japanese friend could be right. The same suspicion had first entered my mind in the spring of near defeat in 1965 when, after Tri Quang helped overthrow the southern Huong government and bring the northern-dominated regime of Premier Phan Huy Quat to power, Ky and Thi had inexplicably purged the army of its best commanders. At that time, I only knew of the Mandarin Dai Viet organization as a vaguely sinister and now-defunct old nationalist faction identified with Quat and his chief adviser, Dr. Sung. But my suspicion grew so strong that Tri Quang, the young generals and the old politicians were somehow linked in an effort to subvert the war, that I cabled my newspaper a full-page article warning of a fifth column in the Saigon government. It was published Sunday, May 2, 1965, and began:

> Saigon—A struggle between "win-the-war" and "end-the-war" forces in South Vietnam's power structure is complicating U.S. efforts to bring the war to a successful conclusion. . . .
>
> The prospect of a broad-based "end-the-war" government composed of Buddhist neutralist and pro-Communist forces is no longer remote. Many responsible Vietnamese contend such a coalition is already in control, although it dares not try to force out the Americans and negotiate directly with Hanoi as long as the mass of people feel there is still a reasonable hope of an early military victory. It is felt everthing now turns on the military situation during the next few weeks and months as Vietnam enters the rainy season. . . .
>
> The unquestioned leader of the end-the-war party is a fairly obscure religious figure, the Buddhist bonze, Thich Tri Quang. Senior American officials concede Tri Quang is the

most powerful political leader in South Vietnam. . . . The real power behind Quat personally, however, is not Tri Quang but a mysterious Mandarin physician, Dr. Dang Van Sung, who is the acknowledged leader of the militaristic Dai Viet party. Catholic leaders are uncertain whether Dr. Sung exercises a neutralist, pro-Communist or anti-Communist influence on the premier. Some suspect he is financed by the CIA. . . . Dr. Sung's principal ally in the military is General Nguyen Van Thieu, the defense minister. Tri Quang has formed alliances with two strongmen, General Nguyen Chanh Thi, the governor of Central Vietnam, and Air Commodore Nguyen Cao Ky, who last week urged an invasion of North Vietnam. These two, who both sport moustaches and daredevil mannerisms, are the desperadoes of the piece. Ky, who is 32, plays only a supporting role. General Thi is something else again. As one of his closest friends describes him, "Thi dreams of becoming the Fidel Castro or Nasser of South Vietnam." As another associate put it, "Thi personally feels he has adopted the French view on Vietnam but actually he is an unconscious instrument of Tri Quang." . . .

For the moment this strange and shifting alliance of visionary general, mysterious Mandarin, Marxist monk and pliable prime minister seems to be consolidating its position. The military purge has temporarily halted. The Catholics are convinced this maneuvering is to insure that the results of proposed National Assembly elections this summer are favorable to Tri Quang's plans. They maintain he hopes to engineer the election of an assembly loaded with either neutralists or pro-Communists who will vote for an American military withdrawal and direct negotiations with Hanoi.

In the meantime, the win-the-war party [which I described as the Catholic-southern coalition] intends to try to frustrate Tri Quang's bid for absolute power and themselves purge General Thi and his collaborators from the armed forces. Their success, they believe, will hang on the coming monsoon military campaign. . . .

The publication of this story in Washington naturally drew a storm of criticism from American officials in Saigon. Jerry Rose, the former *Saturday Evening Post* correspondent who was then working as a special adviser to the Quat government, was furious and told me I was dead wrong. Some months later I received a cryptic message from Rose that he wanted to see me, but before I did he was killed in the Quang Ngai plane crash. In the meantime, the Catholic-Cochinchinese coalition forced the Quat government to resign in June 1965, and, as the American forces began to turn back the Viet Cong's counteroffensive, Ky became premier. Gradually, as Ky seemed to be earnestly trying to do the right things, especially during the Honolulu period of early 1966, I stifled my suspicions, hoping that whatever fifth column had existed had gone out with Quat.

Now, a year later, my earlier suspicions revived. I realized I had been wrong about Thi and perhaps had been just as wrong in assuming that Ky had somehow joined the "win-the-war" forces this past year. Three months of riot and rebellion had effectively sabotaged the Honolulu plan, had actually delayed a return to civil government by at least six months and, under cover of the hysteria in Hue and Danang, allowed the first regular North Vietnamese division to move across the hitherto demilitarized zone in a direct invasion of South Vietnam. The U.S. marines' pacification effort had been set back six months to a year.

There had been an unmistakable stage-managed quality about the Danang fighting. Ky's declaration that Danang was a Communist-occupied area and that he would "liberate" it and shoot the mayor had sufficiently aroused popular feeling to enable Tri Quang to arm the pagodas. Ky did not invade immediately but waited almost a month, while the arming of the pagodas went on. An entire rebel battalion, which I first saw fraternizing with Ky's troops and then was supposedly attacked by them, had vanished without a trace except for one dead sentry and two monks. Everything about the nightmarish episode in Tinh Hoi Pagoda convinced me that at least some of the foreign press were to be killed or wounded in an attack to draw sympathy for Tri Quang's rebels against Ky. It had all seemed like a mock battle. The dead and wounded, the rebels and government troops, the terrified civilians caught in the middle were all real enough in themselves, but I couldn't help thinking of them as pawns in a chess game.

Then, too, as Dennis Duncanson was to point out, the revolt had weakened the only real non-Communist political base in Annam, the peasant-oriented VNQDD party, which together with Thi had run the provinces. As Duncanson wrote, "Thi . . . adopted an equivocal attitude at Hue while a 'Civilian and Military Revolutionary Force' intimidated government departments, the police, and the armed forces, ravaged Danang, and for weeks on end denounced the Government from Radio Hue. . . . The VNQDD suffered casualties in gang fights at Hue . . . and its leader was murdered at Danang." But why would the predominantly Tonkinese government in Saigon have its supporters in Annam join in a revolt against Ky?

I kept asking myself why. Was Ky working with Tri Quang? Had they simply been posing as antagonists while actually secretly collaborating all along? Were both working for the Communists? Even if they were not, was it in their mutual interest to wreck the Honolulu plan? Advance in pacification and land reform had a good chance of creating a rival political base among the Cochinchinese peasantry. Ky, as the leader of a militaristic North Vietnamese-dominated war government, had no genuine political base in the south. Neither, for that matter, did Tri Quang, also a refugee from North Vietnam. They wouldn't necessarily have to be consciously collaborating with Hanoi to see their own positions threatened by President Johnson's demands.

But if Ky and Tri Quang were working for Hanoi, how did the others I had suspected in 1965 fit in? Thi was now plainly innocent and had been discarded. Quat had faded away altogether and was living quietly in retirement. Dr. Sung had played no visible role in recent developments, and I couldn't remember his newspaper taking much of a stand one way or another. Yet the local Dai Viet faction in Danang, which Sung influenced, had sided with Tri Quang's Buddhist rebels against the Ky regime. Dennis Duncanson maintained that the actual net effect of the revolt was to weaken the only real non-Communist political base in Annam, the peasant-oriented VNQDD party, which under Thi had run the five northernmost provinces.

Much later, Duncanson was to write in his book that at the height of the revolt, "Dai Viet elements organized upwards of 20,000 people to march around the outskirts of [Danang] defended by their own 'Revolutionary Armed Forces,' sporting machine guns borrowed from the army." At the end of the revolt, Duncanson wrote, "quiet was bought at the price of ceding both civil and military commands to nominees of the Dai Viet." In other words, as in the Saigon coups, Dr. Sung's Dai Viets were the principal beneficiaries of Tri Quang's antigovernment, anti-American agitation.

But if Ky and Tri Quang were working together and Tri Quang's Buddhists were allied with Sung's Dai Viets in Annam, there had to be an important link between Ky and Dr. Sung to complete the triangle. But what was it? That I did not know yet.

Also, it seemed logical to me that if any one of the three was working for Hanoi, all three must be. And in that event the Communists had planned and orchestrated much of what had happened since March. Hanoi's political strategists, instead of responding with a mixture of planned action and unplanned reaction to unforeseen developments, would have actually projected a series of events over a long period. Some counter insurgency experts such as Sir Robert Thompson kept stressing that Hanoi's game was chess, not checkers or poker. Responsible and intelligent Vietnamese with forty years' experience with the Vietnamese Communists, contended that Hanoi's leaders planned their course of action years in advance and held as many as eight or nine alternative courses in mind to cover every foreseeable eventuality. President Johnson had held the Honolulu conference with less than a week's advance warning. More than a month passed until Thi's dismissal. Had the Politburo in Hanoi used that time to draw up the scenario we had just seen Tri Quang, Ky and the Dai Viets act out?

In retrospect, one can see that Le Duan himself was to provide some of the answer. In March 1966, a month after Honolulu, he had written to his field commander a lengthy analysis of the war in the south in which he explained how the incredible could be made not only credible but "scientific."

We must have a correct thinking method: the materialist dialectical thinking method. To understand the sociological reasoning method, we must do our best to distinguish it from the mechanical reasoning methods. To speak of revolution and war is to speak of politics. Politics is a science and *l'art du possible*. In a definite historical epoch, social facts may develop according to this possibility or another, within the scope of the definite conditions of this epoch. In the face of a changing environment, we Marxists-Leninists cannot but base ourselves upon the development of this environment's internal contradictions and upon the subjective and objective conditions it generates to anticipate its development possibilities, and, on that basis, to set forth the lines and policies which are appropriate to our requirements and goals. In the actual process of this development, we must always grasp firmly and in time the new development and the sudden changes in the situation in order to apply our revolutionary lines, policies, mottoes, and methods in a lively manner and in conformity to our goals. . . .

Social sciences are different from natural sciences, and social rules are not the same as natural rules. Each social phenomenon always has many causes which interact, contradict, and influence one another. These causes themselves also evolve and develop. Man cannot fully grasp these causes. . . . While studying social sciences if we reason in a simple and mechanical manner we can by no means find out the rules governing the dialectical development of things, and, of course, cannot manipulate this development so that it is consistent with our purposes and requirements. As shown by the revolutionary realities, mechanical and inflexible reasoning will lead to errors that are detrimental to the revolution. . . .

Le Duan believed human behavior could be reduced to a science and then controlled through massive collusive action. That was what made him such a formidable opponent. But to defeat such a man, it would first be necessary to understand him, to try to think like him. Americans, of course, thought with what Le Duan called "mechanical reasoning methods." When the post-Honolulu strife erupted in mid-March, just after Le Duan had written the above, Embassy sources told me that President Johnson had fired off a series of extremely angry cables to Lodge. He demanded to know who the Buddhists were and what they wanted and how this anti-American volcano could have erupted so soon after, and apparently in reaction to, his meeting with Ky in Hawaii. Without understanding Le Duan, it was impossible to give a reasonable explanation. To someone of Le Duan's mentality, it would seem quite logical and scientific when faced with a gambit (Johnson's Honolulu plan) to sacrifice material advantage or a bishop (Tri Quang) to regain time and the initiative.

In the days that followed the Annam revolt, I confided my suspicions to some friends in the American press corps and found that at least three shared them. But they took the attitude of one veteran correspondent in Vietnam, who said, "Better stick to the top of the iceberg. Nothing could ever be proved. Besides, you'll kill yourself professionally with all this political stuff. Better go out and cover the war."

The skeptical attitude of much of the press is fairly put by Ward Just, my colleague from the Washington *Post,* in *Toward What End* (Houghton Mifflin, 1968):

> There were marvelous theories about the true nature of the Saigon government, and most of them sprang from the fact that its most powerful members were natives of North Vietnam. . . . This odd state of affairs, the government in the South being run by refugees from the North, demanded some explanation, and in Vietnam the more intricate the explanation the more likely it was to be believed. Some theories were vastly entertaining. One was that a faction of the Dai Viet party (a political/commercial/religious sect in Central Vietnam) controlled the generals, from Thieu and Ky on down. . . . The objective was to discredit the American effort, particularly the effort to secure land reform and bring social justice to the countryside. The Americans had to be taught that what was required of them was men and money, not woolly theories about Western democracy and programs drawn from Jeffersonian political tracts. The specific instance which supported the conspiracy theory was the action of the Ky government to suppress the Buddhists [i.e., the Annam revolt]. Ky undertook this enterprise, according to the theory, to demonstrate that the Americans were supporting a reactionary government (i.e., his own) and thus bring censure from foreign liberals. The Buddhists, controlled by the Viet Cong (or, perhaps, vice versa), of course cooperated in their own demise. It was a magnificent conspiracy in which everybody was in league with everybody else. The American Embassy knew all about it, but was (in the words of the most hot-eyed advocate) "not yet prepared to move." The fact was that the Americans did not know what the Ky government's links were. . . . One thoughtful American political officer was convinced that the junta's machinations would never be known until the Vietnamese themselves talked.

In midsummer of 1966, of course, I did not know that one Vietnamese soon would, and that he would provide the missing link between Ky and Dr. Sung.

Twelve

To Pacify a Countryside

The more U.S. troops that are introduced into South Vietnam, the more military bases are set up throughout the country, the more they use barbarous means to kill our people, the sharper the contradictions between the U.S. imperialists . . . and the South Vietnamese population.

—Le Duan, March 1966

For all his political genius, Le Duan had a limited repertoire of tactics. As I hope I have indicated, the key to his success lay in his mastery of Lenin's principle of exploiting internal contradictions in the enemy camp. That was how he aimed to weaken and divide the Vietnamese and American people. He recognized that Communist insurgents could rarely win subversive wars, but that governments and their foreign supporters could be induced to lose them.

Among the important tactics first tried out in Danang and used two years later on a much bigger scale in the attacks on the cities were: breaking down rural pacification efforts by inducing local government commanders to withdraw their security forces to the towns, and sacrificing the more expendable members of the political underground to draw suspicion away from more important penetration agents. I became familiar with both these related tactics in mid-August 1966, two months after the episode at Tinh Hoi Pagoda, when I was able to visit Danang again.

By then the city seemed to have receded once more to a drowsy, sunbaked coastal town. The Chinese were back in business, their shops once more hung with gaudily painted signs: "Cheap Charlie's Laundry," "Reno Bar," "Wong Kim Chee, No VC, No VD." Only hectic activity around the harbor and airbase indicated that Danang was a major military center. But before the sprawling old Grand Hôtel de Tourane along the quay, a new billboard warned, "U.S. Personnel: Do Not Buy from Vietnamese in This Area. Do Not Fraternize with Vietnamese in This Area." There had been some ugly incidents, and below the surface one discovered the fear, intimidation and sense of isolation that still gripped Danang's people. The Ky regime had arrested and put in prison hundreds of students and intellectuals after the rebellion's collapse. But the American consul in Danang told me that local Vietnamese considered those arrested as the naïve, deceived elements in the rebellion. Almost all the hard-core leadership, the men politically conscious local people suspected were Communists, had escaped arrest and were now working underground.

In early August, Danang's new mayor, Lieutenant Colonel Le Chi Cuong, made a startling announcement. Colonel Cuong, an ex-paratrooper, had been chief in Phuoc Long Province when its capital of Song Be was overrun the year before as part of Giap's unsuccessful 1965 offensive. Since then Cuong had run Saigon's Tan Son Nhut Airbase and was a close friend of Premier Ky. Cuong announced that the leader of Danang's key spy ring was none other than Mrs. Le Thi Quach. This shocked Danang. Mrs. Quach was known for her leftist sympathies, but she seemed an unlikely figure to be controlling the subversive apparatus of South Vietnam's second largest city. The daughter of one of Danang's most respected families, Mrs. Quach worked in the American library. I remembered her as the pleasant and friendly guardian of Willa Cather and Booth Tarkington down on sleepy Doc Lap Street. Her family was probably the closest thing Danang had to aristocracy; her father had been one of the region's richest landlords until the Viet Cong confiscated his holdings. One of the city's main boulevards, its biggest high school and a pagoda were named after her grandfather, a celebrated Vietnamese nationalist who led the early struggle against French colonial rule in 1910.

But the mayor had charged Mrs. Quach and others with persuading military and police commanders to order their forces into the city during the rebellion, abandoning several hundred pacification workers and local chiefs to the Viet Cong. The mayor invited 2,000 of Danang's most prominent citizens to the town's biggest theatre one morning to hear Mrs. Quach and twelve other intellectuals publicly confess and beg for clemency. The theatre was jammed. On stage, incongruously strung between large photos of Robert Mitchum and Gregory Peck, was the usual government slogan: "Right Policy Triumphs Over Brutality!"

Mrs. Quach stood to one side, blinking into flashbulbs. She was a slight dignified woman in white silk trousers and a long flowered gown. Her fellow prisoners, except for one powerfully built youth accused of being a suicide terrorist and another woman, were all prosperous-looking, middle-aged men. Their dossiers were read out over a loudspeaker. They were almost all professional men: accountant, architect, army officer, civil servant, shopkeeper, and several professors and teachers. Two were university students. The other woman was an elderly cloth vendor charged with being a courier who rode buses to nearby towns carrying messages in invisible ink. Nearly half of the group were northerners who had come south as refugees in 1954; one was a confessed North Vietnamese army lieutenant. He said he had infiltrated down the Ho Chi Minh trail five years before with the assignment of proselytizing for the Communist cause among Vietnamese army officers. Two years before, he said, he had been sent to Danang to help the newly recruited Mrs. Quach in organizing an agitprop network among the city's intellectuals.

Mrs. Quach, speaking in a dull monotone, said she had been recruited in 1964 by an agent she knew only by the alias "the Sixth Child." He had been in Danang at the time of the Buddhist revolt, she said, but had escaped arrest. Others in the ring said they had played an active role in the rebellion led by Tri Quang. They had published newspapers, made radio broadcasts or helped organize antigovernment women's organizations, labor unions and student groups. At the end of this bizarre presentation, which itself seemed to be patterned on the Communist Chinese model of public confessions, the mayor announced that Mrs. Quach and the others would be given amnesty if they rallied to the nationalist cause.

As we left the theatre, two local leaders expressed their suspicion and disgust with the morning's performance. Do Ai, a local Kuomintang party leader, told me, "This is hardly a great victory for the police. Most of these people worked openly for the VC and everybody in town knew them. They are all minor figures. Any leading politician here can name you fifty more Viet Cong agents still at large, all of them middle-class intellectuals. In principle, a Viet Cong agent should be a poor man—a dock worker or rickshaw puller. In reality, the hard core here are all disgruntled intellectuals." The other man, Bui Van Giai, a Roman Catholic schoolteacher, said, "The Danang government, by revealing Viet Cong agents who worked in its own offices and for the Americans, has admitted itself to be Communist-infiltrated; this has hurt its prestige and standing with the people. To parade people accused of being Viet Cong before the public this way without a fair trial is distasteful and objectionable." (A month later Do Ai and Bui Van Giai were elected to the new Constituent Assembly as Danang's two deputies.)

I went to see the mayor at Danang's white gingerbread prefecture down by the river and asked if I could interview Mrs. Quach. At first he refused. But by threatening him with exposure of his spy ring as a farce, I was finally allowed to see Mrs. Quach in jail. The interview, limited to ten minutes, took place in a hot dreary little office in back of a small police substation during the afternoon siesta time. Three nervous police guards stood at attention, sweat trickling down their foreheads. A secret policeman in civilian clothes sat beside Mrs. Quach, across the table from me and my interpreter. Only Mrs. Quach, in the same flowered silk gown, looked cool and serene; she was a handsome woman with finely chiseled features and deep black eyes. Mrs. Quach told me her parents were looking after her four teen-age children. Her husband was employed as a mechanical engineer in Hanoi.

She smiled as she talked, seemingly oblivious to the flies, the policemen, and the crude, ink-stained table top on which she folded and unfolded her hands. She said she doubted that a significant number of Danang's people sympathized with the Communists. "They know nothing about Communism. Those who would understand Marxism-Leninism are very few."

The secret policeman, who apparently could not follow what she was saying, ordered Mrs. Quach to speak in Vietnamese. An interpreter from the mayor's office volunteered his services, but I insisted on using my own. Mrs. Quach evaded questions on Viet Cong policies, saying, "I knew only the small part that was my duty. But I do believe the number of nationalists among the Viet Cong is much greater than the number who understand they are fighting under Hanoi's leadership on behalf of the world Communist movement."

I asked about the formal charge against her. "That depends on the criminal tribunal," she replied. "But I believe and hope that having confessed my previous work, the government will forgive my mistakes. I am not a member of the party." This confession, if true, made the mayor's charge that she had been leading the spy network in Danang even more strange. The policeman interrupted to say that Mrs. Quach had been accused of engaging in Communist activities only for the past two years.

Asked her opinion of the American policy in Vietnam, she said, "The Americans have good intentions, good will. But it is what one does that matters."

"How can the war be ended?"

"The most powerful and wise men in your country and mine cannot answer that question. How can I? But I feel it must end as soon as possible—with a nationalist victory."

I went to talk with Mrs. Quach's elderly parents, who vehemently insisted on their daughter's innocence. Both were extremely old, with snowy hair, wrinkled cheeks and bright intelligent eyes. They received me in their home graciously but were distraught about their daughter's arrest. "My father-in-law was a great revolutionary," the father said. "He fought against the French colonialists. The people know, and history recognizes, his patriotism. None of my daughters could ever be a Communist." The old lady interrupted. "We were allowed to see her briefly yesterday and asked if she wanted a lawyer. A police officer said,

'No, it will not be necessary.' Le Thi Quach is well-educated and has always lived a happy life. When her youngest daughter was twelve years old, her husband slipped across the Ben Hai River and came here and tried to get her to go back with him to Hanoi. She said, 'How can I bring my children up under that kind of regime?' The director of the Vietnamese-American Association and other American friends used to come by and see her and take dinner with her here. I prepared the finest Vietnamese delicacies. She has always been so friendly with the Americans. Many Vietnamese army officers—colonels and majors—were her friends and former classmates and used to visit her." The old lady's eyes welled up with tears. "She is not guilty and no one who knows her believes it."

If her parents were stunned, Mrs. Quach's fellow staffers at the American library were visibly frightened. Only the janitor would admit knowing her at all. "She smiled at everybody," he said. When I asked if he thought she had been working for the Communists, he shrugged. "That depends on the government security office."

A plump Vietnamese librarian giggled hysterically at questions about Mrs. Quach. "How can I know anything," she stuttered, close to tears. "I work in the morning and she came in the afternoon. I didn't know her. Even parents cannot know the character of their children. I was only her officemate. How can I know? I work in the morning. I work in the morning."

Al Ball, the newly arrived American director of the library, said that Mrs. Quach had already been arrested when he came to Danang but that naturally he had asked around. "The Vietnamese have a strange attitude sometimes," Ball said. "One of the most eminent city councilmen told me, 'Many people knew about this woman.' When I asked why no one had told the Americans, he said, 'We felt it was not our business.'"

Only a teen-age Vietnamese boy coming out of the library with an armful of books would admit knowing Mrs. Quach well. "I was very surprised to hear of her arrest," he said. "Mrs. Quach was very popular. I met her many times here, and once at an American Christmas party, and at Mr. Murphy's goodbye party. He used to be director here. Mrs. Quach was always very talkative and spoke fluent English, of course, with an excellent

French basis. Very cultured. She was a little sharp-tongued. She always wanted to convince anyone in a conversation she was right. Once, just after the Americans started bombing the north, I came to borrow a book and she showed me some magazine pictures of American bombers. I said, 'They're beautiful,' because, you see, my hobby is collecting airplane pictures. She got very excited and said, 'Do you know these planes have bombed throughout both North and South Vietnam? The papers just put it that the planes bombed strategic points, but do you know they are bombing villages?' "

"Do you think Mrs. Quach was just saying that, or was she really working for the Viet Cong?" I asked.

The boy grinned. "The problem in Vietnam is that the Vietnamese and Viet Cong are never distinguishable. We all look alike, don't we?"

In Saigon some weeks later, I ran into an American official who had been associated with the Danang library during Mrs. Quach's days there. He, too, denied knowing her. "Mrs. who? I can't remember. She must have been one of those little old ladies in tennis shoes."

Mrs. Quach was released from prison some months later. About a year after her arrest, I went to her house for tea one afternoon. We talked for more than an hour, mostly about family life and her problems in raising four children during the twelve years she had been separated from her husband. Mrs. Quach was another of the war's tragic figures, Le Duan's pawns and his victims. She had been used and then discarded. But her story was instructive both as part of a tactic and that tactic's success in creating a climate of fear and intimidation in Danang. Nobody but her parents dared speak out in Mrs. Quach's defense.

Le Duan's interdependent tactic—to dislocate and break down pacification by inducing the withdrawal of local security troops in order to defend the towns—could be seen in the virtual collapse of the U.S. Marine year-long pacification program around the northern cities. A few people like Mrs. Quach—or, rather, the real leaders of the spy ring—could undo the work of battalions. That was why countersubversion was so important; the military war depended on it.

This was especially true around Danang. When the first U.S.

Marine Expeditionary Force had stormed ashore the year before, in early March 1965, its commander, Brigadier General Frederick Karch, had declared, "Our mission is to kill." Karch at once mounted day and night patrol operations to widen Danang's defense perimeter to a distance of 12,000 yards in each direction from the city's strategic airstrip. Within a short time, deeper reconnaissance patrolling gave the marines control of the main approaches into the hills and mountains rimming the flat Danang coastal plain. But it soon became apparent that this was no ordinary war. Most of the nearly 200,000 Vietnamese living within rocket and mortar range of the airbase had lived under some degree of Communist control for nearly twenty years; after the fall of Diem in late 1963, the Viet Cong had taken over the administration of many hamlets. The marines concluded that they could not secure Danang Airbase through the conventional tactic of defeating Viet Cong forces in pitched battles; they had to win the hearts and minds of these 200,000 Vietnamese villagers. Otherwise, small mortar squads could simply infiltrate back through the marines' forward positions and, with local support, attack the airbase.

Because of Danang's strategic importance—it was the major American base for the northern half of the country—the hamlets around it became the site of one of the most important American battles of the war, although it would never appear as such in the headlines of any newspaper. This was the struggle to win the loyalty of the local peasantry, a struggle that of all the American military forces in Vietnam only the marines would ever come close to fully understanding.

This battle was fought in a strange yet compelling setting—one of the most beautiful landscapes in Southeast Asia. South, near the white beach, was the airstrip with its fleets of jet fighter-bombers and a battery of Hawk missiles. Just beyond was Danang City, obscured by a haze of dust and treetops by day but at night an expanse of shimmering lights. A peak across the airstrip was crowned with a ring of tiny white missiles, and a long-eared Mickey Mouse radar turned back and forth slowly on the crest. To the east, the deep blue surface of the Bay of Tourante was broken by hundreds of orange-sailed fishing sampans. Over the jungled ridges of the Presqu'île de Son Tra and American-held Monkey Mountain with its domed radar installation, you could see warships from the Seventh Fleet on a clear day. To the north stretched the sandflats of the Son Cau Do River delta; twenty-five miles upstream in the mountain gorge called Elephant Valley were hidden the deep caves and tunnels of the Viet Cong headquarters for this northern region. Near the beach, the Son Cau Do River was crossed by Highway One to Hue; the French called it "the Street Without Joy." They fought and died for nine years trying to keep open its tortuous route along the coastal cliffs and through the mountains at Hai Van Pass. A ruined French fortress, bleached white as bones, stood abandoned near the long Nam O Bridge and the little hamlet of Kim Lien. Inland, to the west, curved two sloping green ridges along which two battalions of American marines were initially strung in an outer perimeter of defense. Clustered at the foot of the hills, as if for safety, were little hamlets. Their long narrow streets were broken here and there by a canal, a pagoda or a bridge. By day the hamlets were crowded and noisy; but as night fell the bells chimed, the gongs clanged in the pagodas, and the hamlets vanished into darkness and silence. Just past them lay what the marines called "Indian country," stretching into rolling green foothills with thickets of bamboo and stretches of elephant grass big enough to conceal a regiment. Beyond were the forest and mountains where the Viet Cong main forces were.

The area seemed to have every possible feature of terrain: ocean, rivers, canals, forest, fields, plain, mountains, villages and a city. "A perfect place to hold a map class," one of the marines described it. You could see it all from the high ridges the marines first occupied just after they landed in early 1965. From that height, the sporadic fighting below as the marines pushed inland was as scenic and decorative as an old panorama of the Civil War. Even the helicopters, droning in and out with reinforcements and fresh water and evacuating casualties, looked less like machines of war than giant green dragonflies.

In those first months, you could stand and watch the tiny figures of marines patrolling inland, moving in dispersed files along the canals, toy houses, ribbonlike roads, and across the tidy patchwork of pale green paddy fields and the darker green of the grassy hillsides. From the plain the clatter of gunfire rose and died. Artillery bursts exploded like Iowa thunder against the seaward slopes of the enemy-held mountains, sending up thick grey plumes of dust and smoke. Jets bound for North Vietnam streaked up from the airstrip. Spread out under the tropical blue sky, the landscape around Danang seemed a lovely green land of paddy fields and lumpy hills, across which little black figures moved, cycling and walking, digging and hoeing, and sailing in their little ragged junks. Out on patrol I used to look at the husky, open-faced young marines and think, At least the charade can't touch them here. I was wrong. It would be a long journey for the marines at Danang, and many would die along the way. And they would never reach their destination so long as the charade went on.

The marines soon discovered that the war in Vietnam became what they could see on either side of them as they moved out on patrol, that there was no way to tell friendly peasants from Viet Cong guerrillas; that distant drums could signal temple prayers or their own approach. They learned to tell the difference between the noise a man or a monkey makes in the brush, how to keep a squad from getting lost in eight-foot-high elephant grass, how to burn off leeches with a cigarette, and how to patrol ten miles a day in 105-degree heat without passing out.

They discovered that to sweep a Viet Cong village was to spread out through the thatched mud huts and search each one for caves, tunnels, weapon caches and documents. Most of the time they found only old men, women and children in the villages, hiding in pits dug under their beds. In a Viet Cong village, people just stared and averted their eyes. In a friendly one, the children would cry "Hello, hello" and "You number one." They started passing out candy, cigarettes and extra C-rations to the kids and going into friendly villages with a grin and the Vietnamese greeting "*Chou ong.*" In the fields and brushy hillsides they learned to move in widely dispersed files. They drew almost constant sniper fire. After the first few days, they no longer chased snipers. It took too much time.

They also learned that the Viet Cong were not their only enemies in Vietnam: there was the heat, the wild boar, leeches, scorpions, poisoned panji stakes with barbed steel tips, steel bear traps and water buffalo. The buffalo didn't like a white man's smell. The Vietnamese said it was because we ate butter.

In the summer of 1965, the marines had moved off the ridges

and down into the little hamlets on the coastal plain. At first the peasantry was terrified; the local political commissars had told them that the marines would kill everybody after raping the women, and that Americans were "giants with big stomachs who will eat all your food." Their first showpiece success was a community of several hamlets that the marines called Le My, after the crumbled old French fortress along the coast. When the initial firefighting was over and the Viet Cong guerrillas fled to the hills, the Marine battalion commander, Lieutenant Colonel David Clement, assigned each of his company commanders a hamlet to befriend. (These villagers had the most meager possessions. On one patrol the marine in command had some suspected Viet Cong spread out their belongings in the road before he sent them back to the rear for questioning. One old woman's display was like the history of Vietnam itself: a moth-eaten French legionnaire's uniform, a faded lithograph of Ngo Dinh Diem, a crucifix and altar candles, a Viet Cong flag and a rusted but treasured can of American dried milk.) Clothes and food, some sent by the marines' wives and mothers at home, some scrounged from relief centers in Danang, were given out to the villagers. Local Vietnamese officials who had fled to Danang returned, and a special Vietnamese "civic action" team was brought in to re-establish local government.

Within weeks, local boys began drifting back from the jungles, peasant women set up a market (where they did a brisk business selling the marines goods from Danang), a navy dispensary was established, and the villagers began bringing intelligence on the local Viet Cong underground to the marines. In midsummer of 1965, Defense Secretary McNamara visited Le My to shake hands with a beaming village chief as a Marine band played "The Colonel Bogie March" to the happy peasants. Colonel Clement quoted Julius Caesar's maxim on the Gallic wars to McNamara; the marines' "best defenses," he said, were their "generosity and compassion." (Caesar had written a subordinate outlining his strategy of combining military force with the demonstration of a superior way of life through technology and the establishment of rule of law. He had said, "Let us see if in this way we can win all hearts and secure a lasting victory. It is a new way of conquering, to use compassion and generosity as our defenses." The problem the marines faced was that, unlike Caesar's legions, they eventually moved out and left local security and administration to government-appointed Vietnamese. Almost every time they did, pacification collapsed.) Back in Washington, McNamara cited the success at Le My as evidence that Vietnam was not "a bottomless pit."

Le My reverted to Viet Cong political control as soon as the marines left it in Vietnamese hands and pushed on into the hills to expand their perimeter. Soon anyone driving the once safe little country road ran a gamut of mines and sniper fire. Necessity forced the marines to come up with a new approach. After seven months of sporadic fighting, one of the five Marine battalions around Danang had pushed local Viet Cong main forces twelve miles south of the airstrip. The Vietnamese government agreed to feed into the vacuum left by the U.S. marines some 800 Vietnamese security and pacification personnel in an effort to regain the loyalty of five villages held by the Communists since Diem's fall. A small battalion of 300 locally recruited militiamen were to provide security for 180 civilian police and technicians attempting to restore law and order and re-establish a civil administration, and there would be 200 CIA-trained pacification workers whose job was to identify and arrest the Communist political underground. The project, started in October 1965 and located south of Danang, or on the other side of the city from Le My, was given the Chinese name *Ngu Hanh Son*, which roughly translated means "the Battle for Five Mountains." One Marine general told me, "It would be far easier to seize the high ground on five actual mountains than win over the people in these villages. This is a people's war. Terrain here doesn't mean a goddamn thing. If you have the people, you don't need the terrain. And the only ones who can win back the people are the Vietnamese."

The five villages were set in a rich alluvial plain bordered by three rivers flowing into the South China Sea. Once it had been a thriving rural community. But when Diem fell, the local Viet Cong rose up. Most of the local officials, policeman and schoolteachers were converted, killed, or fled to Danang. The existing government collapsed.

During the day, the thatched villages, pelted with monsoon

rains or steaming dry under the sun, looked as calm and pastoral as ever. The Annamite peasants pulled their primitive ploughs behind black buffalo or turned the red sticky mud with their long-handled spades, planting and reaping their rice as they had done for a thousand years. After dark the war began. The peasants closest to the city took up carbines and shotguns to defend their villages. Those further south and still loyal to the Viet Cong met together under cover of darkness and formed guerrilla raiding parties. They might try to kidnap or assassinate a government worker, snipe at the militia outposts, or lay mines and booby traps. Some served as guides, couriers and spies for the army of 5,000 Viet Cong regulars encamped in caves and tunnels in the nearby mountains. Without these peasant-guerrillas on the plain to keep them fed, supplied and reinforced, the big army in the mountains could not survive. To ensure loyalty, the Viet Cong had taken away at least one son from each family in the five villages.

Sometimes the main forces came down to attack a forward Marine position. These were carefully planned in advance. An attack would begin with a barrage of accurate mortar fire, followed by an initial human wave of sappers armed with grenades and meat hooks to drag back the dead and wounded. A second wave of riflemen followed, with a third assault force of unarmed guerrillas coming behind to pick up the weapons of the fallen. To succeed, it was essential the Viet Cong attackers take the marines by surprise in the initial assault, before they had time to call in artillery and air support. And this required some degree of political control over the local peasantry.

The dead were often local boys, the sons of the peasants who were the bivouacked marines' neighbors. I remember once in-specting an ambush site at dawn with a young marine captain. Although one of his platoons was certain it had killed more than a dozen men during the night, only one body remained. Trussed to a bamboo pole at the edge of a green, mossy field, the dead Viet Cong looked very young: a boy wearing black shorts and a kind of raincape crudely fashioned out of parachute silk in a semblance of military uniform. Around his waist was strapped an old cartridge belt, two magazines of ammunition, homemade grenades and a packet of letters. The captain figured he must have been the local Viet Cong mailman. As he reached down and closed the dead boy's eyes, he said, "What makes these little guys keep fighting?" A corporal stripped the body of ammunition, grenades and documents. Well, what do we do with him now?" he asked the captain. Somebody said, "If it was you, they'd just leave you there." The captain's answer thundered back, "Put him back in that foxhole, take an entrenching tool and put some goddamn dirt over him. He died for something he believed in."

During battles, the peasants themselves sought safety in the deep earthen holes under their heavy wooden bedsteads. Existing in a kind of no man's land, most of the peasants carried identification cards issued by both sides. If they had sons or brothers fighting with the Viet Cong, some would beat bamboo drums to signal the activities of the marines. These drums had a weird, unearthly sound at night, especially as an accompaniment to marine foxhole dialogue. One night I was sitting in a machine-gun pit some miles south of Danang, staring into the darkness and listening to the marines talk. We could hear a radio in a nearby Vietnamese hamlet playing "Love Letters in the Sand." "Damn, I never thought I'd hear that over here," somebody said.

"Hey, did you guys hear Hicks stepped on a mine this afternoon? Forty pounds of TNT and a 155 shell. It didn't go off."

"That'd be enough to make your arches fall."

"Yeah, it could ruin your whole day."

"Did you guys see that big Buddhist shrine down by the river? We passed it today on patrol. The idol was ten feet tall. Some gook inside praying and chanting."

"Did you rub its belly for luck?"

"Don't touch the belly button. The floor falls in."

"Yeah, a crocodile pit."

"A mantrap lined with panji stakes."

"But don't worry, men. Tarzan will save you."

One of the marines started to read a poem one of their dead buddies had written about student antiwar protests at home: "You lucky guys, you laugh and sneer,/ He walks all day, stands watch all night . . ." That was when I heard the sound of drumming, and I asked about it. "It's the VC," said one marine.

"They're always beating on drums or tapping on bamboo when a squad leaves the lines. It's some kind of signal. A week ago, over in Ha Dam—that's a VC ville south of here—they started drumming, yelling and screaming to beat hell. We figured it was gonna be a Banzai attack, but the lieutenant said they was just getting drunk and raising hell." The boy reading the poem went on, "Where men are dying in the sand . . ." but I remember how we all stiffened up in the darkness, listening to the drums.

A hope to pacify the Five Mountains in three months was dropped the first week. The marines were able to push south as much as five miles a day, but in back of them the void would get bigger and bigger and the Viet Cong would seep back behind Marine lines to terrorize the people again. By February and March of 1966, village and hamlet chiefs were still being murdered at the rate of one or two a week in the Five Mountains area. But the peasantry, encouraged by the marines' presence, had once more started informing on the Communist political underground. As schools and markets reopened, the countryside sprang to life again. The crucial question, the marines felt, was whether the local Danang government could now restore an efficient administration while they provided the military muscle.

I remembered all this when I talked later at a party that spring to Dennis Duncanson, the last remaining counterinsurgency expert from Sir Robert Thompson's British advisory mission. Some months earlier, Duncanson had correctly predicted that as the American troop buildup progressed, there would be an appreciable change in the military situation in favor of the Saigon government. "In the best possible circumstances," Duncanson had maintained, "all that can be expected is that the Viet Cong will retreat from pitched battles to smaller guerrilla operations. When this happens, a brief psychological moment will arrive when there is a distinct swing of opinion away from the Communists." Duncanson felt that with the Honolulu conference that moment had arrived, but the United States was in danger of letting the opportunity slip through its fingers.

"Oh, there is a lot of moving, planning, marching to and fro," he snapped testily, "but nothing has reversed the massive collapse of government that followed the coup against Diem. Nor will it, until top priority is put on eliminating political subversion and the military campaign is made secondary to re-establishing law and order in the civil administration in the countryside."

Duncanson gestured with his martini glass toward Ambassador Lodge in a black dinner jacket and General Westmoreland in his white dress uniform. "All the king's horses and all the king's men aren't going to put Humpty together again. Humpty has got to do that himself. The only way this thing will ever be solved is for the Vietnamese government to start governing."

The marines' Five Mountains project collapsed almost overnight in early April after Ky declared in Saigon at the height of the revolt in Annam, "We will liberate Danang—the Communists control it." The local militia battalion assigned to provide security was ordered by its Buddhist commander into Danang to help defend it against Ky's invading forces. This left the 180 policemen and civilian technicians and the 200 pacification workers with little protection. As the Viet Cong guerrillas came swarming back, most of the workers fled to Danang. Far from governing, the government in the region simply moved out.

The U.S. Marine command did the only thing it could do and still provide some measure of security for Danang Airbase. It applied the Le My experiment on a broad scale, putting squads of young American marines out in the hamlets, to stiffen the will of what little militia and local government remained. This was done on an *ad hoc* basis at first at Phu Bai Airbase near Hue in August 1965, but eventually was formalized into what the Marine Corps called their "Combined Action Platoon" program, with forty-nine such units fielded in a state of high military proficiency by January 1967. These squads were eventually assigned to nearly ninety hamlets in the northern sector. The Marine commanders recognized that putting squads of young Americans out to live in Asian villages was a stopgap measure; they consistently stressed that only efficient and attractive local government could permanently win back the loyalty of the disaffected peasantry.

Yet, in making the best of a bad situation, it was remarkable how well the CAP teams—mostly composed of nineteen- and twenty-year-olds—succeeded in winning the villagers' respect and affection. Lieutenant Colonel William Corson, the able veteran counterinsurgency expert and author of *The Betrayal* (Norton, 1968), who first ran the program, told me, "Pacification was too important to leave to our professionals. You take some kid who didn't finish high school and has nothing to look forward to except to be a truck driver or filling-station attendant and plunk him down in Vietnam and make him responsible for the lives of 4,000 people and the result is spectacular. It's a manifestation of American populism in the twentieth century."

Unlike many of the American army units, the marines were encouraged to fraternize with the peasants. In Danang, I listened in on an orientation briefing for replacements being sent out to the villagers. It was delivered by a Marine captain who had been in Vietnam almost a year. "Now you guys," he began, "the VC say the marines are a vicious, savage, rapacious crew. It's up to you to show them differently. First, a warning. Don't buy consumables from the Vietnamese. We found a bottle of coke with glass slivers in it. Return what you borrow. Avoid unnecessary liberation of local items for your personal or unit's use. Wave to people as you pass. As long as they're waving, they can't throw grenades. Respect authority and your elders. If you're walking along a paddy dike and an old Vietnamese woman with a stick and two baskets over her shoulders comes along, move to the side. They're used to traditional deference to males and this goes over big. Remain patient. Part of the local custom is repetition of facts and questions. Respect tombs and graveyards. We end up in graveyards a lot because often it's the only high dry ground available in the area. But be careful where you dig your foxholes and bunkers. The arch in all homes is dedicated to ancestors; if their houses get destroyed, it goes where they go. Treat women and children with respect. Children are just the same the world over. You can tell them 'dee dee'—that's 'go away'—all you want, but they'll come back with their hands out. Shake hands when you say hello and when you say goodbye to a Vietnamese. And most of all, just be yourselves, men."

It wasn't always easy, though. I remember once standing at Danang Airbase with a group of young Marine replacements who had just arrived from California. As we waited for transportation, we watched military police lead a blindfolded and bound Vietnamese child down the ramp of a C-123 cargo plane. "What's he done?" someone asked. "Killed three marines with a Thompson," the guard said.

The guard's arm rested on the little boy's shoulder; the child barely came up to his cartridge belt. He looked too small to handle a submachine gun. The boy was barefoot and wore faded green pajamas and a man's wide-brimmed jungle hat with "Taylor" embroidered across the front. A piece of cloth, a Walt Disney print of flying elephants, had been tied across his eyes. The boy's forehead was beaded with sweat and his mouth twitched in little jerking spasms.

A sergeant said, "Six kids like that charged us a couple of days ago. One had a grenade, the rest rocks; anything they could get their hands on."

"What made him do it, Sarge?"

'What makes any of them do it. They told him we're invading his country." The sergeant spat. "They'll send him up to rehabilitation after they interrogate him. But they won't rehabilitate this kid. He's a killer now and will go on killing. Best thing they could do is take him out and shoot him." Later, I asked one of the marine replacements what he thought. "It's like something out of the movies," he said. "I don't know, I guess you never expect to see it in real life."

One of the first hamlets where a squad of U.S. marines was assigned to live was Kim Lien, just north of Danang along the seacoast. Before the Buddhist revolt, it had been the marines' most promising hamlet. As an official brochure described it: "The warmth of the individual young Marine, his open friendly nature, his initiative, his willingness to work long hours and his natural tendency to treat human beings as human beings are the reasons why Kim Lien is no longer a Viet Cong-controlled hamlet." A visit there, soon after my interview in jail with Mrs. Quach, suggested that the inability of the United States to face and tackle the problem of political subversion was the reason Kim Lien was reverting to Viet Cong control.

The small Buddhist settlement had been hard hit by the war. Its 1,633 inhabitants made their livelihood fishing and woodcutting, activities hindered by a night curfew and harassing artillery fire into the forested mountains. Though the brochure did not mention it, when the American marines occupied Kim Lien in early 1966, just three weeks after the Honolulu conference, its people had been subject to Communist political influence and indoctrination for nearly twenty years. A Marine company was garrisoned nearby to protect an oil refinery and three bridges along Highway One to Hue, including the strategic Nam O Bridge just north of Kim Lien hamlet. The Marine squad, fluctuating between eight and fourteen men, was to provide Kim Lien with "security," reinforce the image of the Saigon government, and, according to the brochure, "instill the residents with a feeling of friendship for the U.S. Marines." The marines were backed up by a squad of regular Vietnamese soldiers and some seventy village militiamen who were recruited by the local chief and trained by the Marine squad. A color guard of Vietnamese and Americans raised and lowered the red-and-yellow national flag in the hamlet square each day.

An economic boost was provided by hiring ten villagers as grass cutters and seven for construction work; $700 was spent in the hamlet for labor to build a beach where the marines took the village children swimming every afternoon. The marines were encouraged to buy such items as candles, mirrors, mattresses, cigarette lighters and film in the local bazaar.

A playground was built and volleyball games between the marines and the local village youths became a popular event every evening; sometimes a Marine band or drum-and-bugle corps gave concerts. Two navy medical corpsmen opened a dispensary. The marines chipped in to buy traditional Vietnamese funeral banners, went to weddings, and were encouraged to accept invitations to take meals with the villagers. The sergeant in charge of the squad personally visited all 352 huts in the hamlet to explain why the marines had come. Food and clothing from CARE and individual American donors were distributed.

The marines built the hamlet's first outdoor latrines and brought barbed wire to rebuild a fence to keep the Viet Cong out. Twelve-foot cement pillars were erected to form an attractive new entrance gate and more cement provided for new wells. A portable sawmill was set up, and some of the marines were working on a plan to harness the nearby mountain streams for irrigation.

Was this enough?

The last of ten items in the Marine Daily Log for Kim Lien the day before I visited it, August 12, 1966, supplied the answer:

1. Made roving sick call through woodcutter ville.
2. Two marines ate chow in woodcutter's ville with two ARVNs [Vietnamese soldiers].
3. Two marines ate *boi beo* [noodle soup] at local home.
4. Held language class in English.
5. One marine bought haircuts for four boys.
6. Arranged to complete two more wells.
7. Distributed modeling clay to five children.
8. Organized children's games.
9. Swim call for boys.
10. Found anti-Viet Cong posters torn down in the center of the ville.

Staff Sergeant Steve Turchik had just been assigned to lead Kim Lien's civil-action team a few weeks before. He told me, as he finished reading out the log, "This village is full of VC. Anything we put up that concerns the central government, like election posters, they rip down at night. We keep putting them up and they keep tearing them down. An old man told me, 'We don't want the marines helping us to build a well because we don't understand what they're saying and they don't understand what we're saying. Besides, my brother-in-law might kill them. He's a VC.'"

The team's interpreter, twenty-one-year-old Corporal Lyttleton T. Ward, Jr., whom the villagers called Tom, was one of the few Americans who had ever lived any length of time in a Vietnamese hamlet and spoke the language. Tom told me, "I don't think the VC have ever left this village. We're all just sort of living together here. Oh, we like to think if we got clobbered one night some people would come and tell us. We've been probed a few times. Whenever that happens old Mr. Thi moves his cows over to the other side of the railroad tracks beforehand. We could tell battalion intelligence, but they wouldn't believe us. But the morning after some action, sure enough, Mr. Thi's cows are over there. Mr. Thi is a very old man. He gets around and has his finger in every pie. He stays away from us and we stay away from him."

Ward, a lanky, crew-cut blond Virginian, smiled. "I suppose

people at home would like to think we're over there interrogating him all the time, but it's just not possible. He's not a VC; he's just trying to save his cows. It's like when we play volleyball every night. A former VC officer is captain of the villagers' team, probably still is a VC. But he's a real go-getter. Gives us a heck of a lot of help on putting the wells in even though he may be a Charlie. They probably come over to play volleyball to see where our grenades are. Some guy accidentally hits the ball under the grenade bunker and goes crawling in after it. Down in Chu Lai I heard they shot a VC squad and it turned out to be the whole village volleyball team. They caught a VC in the fishing 'ville' last week. He used to play volleyball with us a lot. He was a good athlete.

"The VC propaganda teams come in here and stay a month or so, trying to throw some little wrench into our gears. The day they put out their biggest load of pamphlets, some people came and showed them to us. The ones in English were all about the American Nazi party and the Ku Klux Klan. The ones in Vietnamese said, 'Don't go into the army. Don't cooperate with the Americans.' We figured a 'don't fight' campaign meant they were weaker than a 'fight' campaign.

"Our biggest problem is the village chief. Oh, he smiles a lot, a yes man, but he's never given us real cooperation. He'll come up here and beg stuff for his own house but won't do anything for the village. The most helpful man in the 'ville,' like I told you, is the VC officer. He gets everything organized. He wanted cement for some wells. The sarge told him to get the rock and sand and the holes dug, and he'd furnish cement. And he did."

I asked Corporal Ward if he thought the marines were making any progress.

He replied, "Our perimeter is expanding. We're about a mile out from six months ago. But there's a lotta miles in South Vietnam. That canopy on the hills over there is 100 feet high, and you can't bomb or shell it all. They're free to run all over out there in the boonies. The woodcutters here bring them up food. The VC live here all the time, but we don't know who they are."

While I talked with the marines, I sent my Vietnamese interpreter off separately to interview the Vietnamese village chief. The chief spoke freely with his fellow Vietnamese, but my interpreter came back feeling that he was not telling the marines all he knew. The chief was twenty-nine, a Roman Catholic, and he stayed across Nam O Bridge in a larger village at night. He said the Communist political underground in Kim Lien kept telling the people to tear down every poster the marines put up. It was kind of a test of the underground's control. According to my interpreter's notes, the village chief had said, "I know who they are, but I can't arrest them. I would be killed or kidnaped and tortured. They supply food for a hard-core VC company living over there on Hon Quang Mountain. The commander is Vi, Nguyen is his deputy, and the chief political cadre is Thanh. I know them. Sometimes I've seen them in the hamlet. Before the G.I.s came, I used to set out ambuscades and kill many VC. Now my men are afraid to go out at night, because if we shoot at the VC maybe the G.I.s will shoot at us. When the G.I.s first came, seven of my twelve policemen had been killed and I was contemplating suicide."

The chief said that his relationship with the marines had deteriorated since the Buddhist revolt in Danang: "During the struggle, Nguyen Bao Tri, a man in the next village, accused me of being a VC. The rebels captured me and shot at me when I escaped. I asked the marines to help me, but they said they cannot interfere in Vietnam's internal affairs. So I fled to Saigon. Then last week I arrest one VC political agent. He has good information to discover the VC in the mountains, but the G.I.s gave me no compensation. I think they don't treat me well. They know nothing about Vietnamese customs and look down upon the village chief. Roughly, there is no discrimination between the G.I.s and the people in the village. But once the people complained about the attitude of the marines when they gave candy to children. I told the G.I.s they should hand it nicely to the children, not throw it on the ground. They followed my advice."

The marines' only Vietnamese interpreter in Kim Lien also seemed to have a chip on his shoulder. He said he had been a bureau chief in the Health Ministry in Saigon before he was drafted into the army. "I am very proud to be here," he said. "The Americans come to cooperate, not like the French who wanted to colonize. But the G.I.s should not treat Vietnamese as inferiors. Without Vietnamese, how can the Americans work in a village? Even if they can speak Vietnamese fluently, like Tom, Americans cannot make the people understand their ways. People here in Kim Lien are quiet with the marines, okay on the surface, but in their hearts they don't want Americans in their village."

That was August 13, 1966. On September 10th, the Viet Cong struck.

The Kim Lien schoolteacher told me about the attack when I returned to the hamlet in the spring of 1967 and found the marines were gone.

"It happened the night before the national elections," he said. "The VC came from the seaside at night and overran the marines' outpost down by the river behind the schoolhouse. Three marines and one VC were killed and the marines lost a machine gun. It all happened in about fifteen minutes. They pulled the marines out of Kim Lien after that. Tom was all right and I heard he's gone home to America now."

The schoolteacher, a frail little Vietnamese in a threadbare blue shirt, had run out to our jeep to meet us, when I had driven in with two Marine sergeants from the press camp in Danang. He was all excited and told us a platoon of VC were living in the houses just across the road and were going around with a paper megaphone telling the people, "A new revolutionary situation is nearing, so the population must join the side of the Liberation Front."

"What does it mean?" he asked. "Are the Americans going away?"

The little teacher said the VC had entered Kim Lien at least twenty or thirty times, sometimes a full platoon of them, since the marines left. They gave everyone "safe conduct" passes, embossed with the Liberation Front flag, which indicated they were "valid for any puppet civil servant or soldiers who secretly want to serve the front."

An old man, standing in front of a big pink house with teak pillars and a red altar festooned with Buddhist flags, invited us inside for tea. "People here liked Tom and a Negro sergeant who was here when the marines first came," he said. "They used to pass by from house to house every day and gave us medicine, and they played and gave gifts to the children. They always made jokes and helped the poor people. One day a house caught fire by accident and Tom and the Negro sergeant gave the man all the wood and roofing he needed to rebuild his house. Tom used to say, politically speaking, that the woodcutters inland were pro-VC and the fishermen along the beach were pro-government. That was wrong. The marines lived on the fishermen's side of the village and so it was safe at night and they were not so afraid. We miss Tom and the others and wish they were back living in our village. Now the VC are everywhere."

We discovered that after the marines left, the local district chief had withdrawn all seventy local militiamen from Kim Lien to guard Nam O Bridge. Some had quit and a few had joined the Viet Cong guerrillas in the hills. The former Viet Cong officer had joined the government forces and was serving in the Vietnamese Army's 51st Regiment—possibly, if Ward had been right about him, as a penetration agent. The village chief rarely put in an appearance. "Only in the daytime to sign papers," the teacher said.

The two Marine sergeants and I walked around the village, growing steadily more uneasy. The entrance gate built by the marines still stood, but their dispensary had been torn down, the playground was overgrown with grass, and it was evident nobody played volleyball anymore. The barbed-wire fence had been dismantled, and we saw some of the villagers weaving baskets from the metal strands. There were no children shouting "Okay, okay" and running to meet us; in fact, we saw few children at all. There was no sign of the marines' electric sawmill; instead, women in black pajamas were sawing logs by hand.

That night the Viet Cong blew up Nam O Bridge, cutting off traffic from Danang north to the DMZ for some days. The Marine command said it required detailed preparation and that the Viet Cong demolition team must have been living in Kim Lien for some time.

Thirteen

The Voice of the People

The Southern people's revolutionary struggle will be long drawn out and arduous. It is not a simple process but a complicated one, combining many varied forms of struggle—from elementary to advanced, legal and illegal.

—Le Duan, December 1966

When I first met Dr. Phan Quang Dan, I thought of him as a sort of latter-day Vietnamese Candide. In the cause of democracy, Dr. Dan had browbeaten the last emperor of Indochina, had verbally fenced with great-power diplomats over green felt tables at Paris, Cannes, Geneva and Shanghai, made pilgrimages to appeal for support from Jawaharlal Nehru, Chiang Kai-shek and the Sultan of Morocco, suffered two years' imprisonment under Diem, deluged his fellow classmates at Harvard and the Sorbonne with correspondence, rejected a Cabinet post offered by Ho Chi Minh, founded a political party, published two newspapers, had written three books and mailed a dozen firmly worded letters to the New York *Times*.

At forty-eight, a pediatrician with a children's clinic in the Saigon slums of Gia Dinh, Dr. Dan seemed as bubbly and enthusiastic as a recent political-science graduate. In a country where politicians ran to conspiratorial mandarins, demagogic monks, medieval warlords and grim commissars, it was startling to find a man who looked and acted like a Western-style liberal. It went without saying that Dr. Dan would run in the September 1966 Constituent Assembly election. He could hardly wait.

Dr. Dan had been something of a legend in the Western press ever since he had won a seat in the 1959 National Assembly elections, outpolling the Diem government's candidate ten to one. Diem promptly jailed Dr. Dan. He once told me he had endured water torture at the hands of Ngo Dinh Nhu's secret police, been kept in solitary confinement in a pitch-dark cage in the Saigon zoo, and had lost his teeth from scurvy. "They poured water in your nose until you almost suffocated. Agonizing, but you got used to it. The hardest thing was solitary confinement. No sun rays for two years. They blindfolded me when they took me out for interrogations. Not a book. Nothing." Dr. Dan liked to muse over the past. "Diem had quality," he would say, "but he was a madman at the end." Dr. Dan was such a sympathetic figure I wanted to believe him. But Sir Robert had described Diem as a man with his faculties very much intact at the end. One of them had to be wrong.

To interview Dr. Dan in his shabby clinic, as I did just before the September 1966 election, was to be engulfed by wailing babies. I have a vision of little wet pink hands, enervating heat, the din of anxious, gossiping Vietnamese motherhood, and a steady parade of shrieking children marching toward the horror chamber for inoculations. The office was so threadbare and worn even the paper tulips looked wilted. Dr. Dan lived upstairs with his wife and a three-year-old son.

In mid-April, at the height of the Buddhist crisis, Ky had appointed Dr. Dan to chair the three-day national political conference that produced a formal demand for general elections by mid-September. Dan felt it was a short-lived personal triumph for him, since the world press treated the election decree as a victory for Tri Quang.

"Tri Quang on the cover of *Time!*" Dan sputtered indignantly. "He's just a witch doctor people go to until modern medicine comes along." Waving a sheaf of papers, Dr. Dan said that credit really belonged to forty-eight provincial council chairmen who had first met the previous October to sign a petition demanding an elected civil government. "Politically and religiously we are much divided," Dan said. "So in order to have national unity, you have to create a national organ which has been approved by everybody and can be contested by nobody. It is badly needed, especially in wartime." Dr. Dan seemed to envisage an assembly with more powers than simply writing a constitution. He pooh-poohed my suggestion that Tri Quang might win enough Assembly seats to demand an American withdrawal. Tri Quang, he said, had only been able to swing the votes of Danang and Hue and the two northernmost provinces in Annam during the previous year's election.

Dr. Dan treated Tri Quang's attempted civil insurrection in Annam as an unseemly nuisance. "There is no danger the Buddhists will control the elections," he said flatly. "It is just impossible. Far from being neutralist or pro-Communist, I'm afraid the Assembly will be too reactionary and rightist. I predict at least 70 per cent of the deputies will be middle-class people who may resist needed social reform. I personally favor a very strong executive. Not the American system, which requires stronger political organization, but something much more in accordance with our own traditions. The right to form a legal opposition should be constitutionally guaranteed. Land in Vietnam should go to every peasant who is now farming it, without owner compensation. So many resources, human and military, have been spent to keep land in the hands of a few men who should have been lucky just to keep their heads."

Oddly, many knowledgeable Vietnamese whose judgment I trusted did not share my enthusiasm about Dr. Dan. "He cried at his trial when Diem arrested him," they would say. "He cried at his trial." That was as far as most people would go. One of Dr. Dan's closest lifelong friends said a little more. Dr. Dinh Xuan Quang, like Dan, was a physician practicing in the Gia Dinh suburbs. Both had been ministers in the last government of Emperor Bao Dai. Quang was a kind elderly man who always seemed to talk in riddles. Just before the election, he told me, "If the Americans will really support Dr. Dan they can save him, but if they only give him half support they will destroy him."

Aside from Dr. Dan, only a few candidates of some national

standing were in the Constituent Assembly race: Tran Van Van, whom I knew then only as a Cochinchinese landowner and one of the richest men in South Vietnam; and Phan Khac Suu, the frail, snowy-haired Cochinchinese ex-president, who, on Van's counsel and advice, helped to install the Huong government and later forced the Quat government's resignation. Since the Ky regime's electoral law called for a peculiar multiple-candidate list system, Van and Suu were running on a joint ticket.

The other major figure in the race was Dr. Dang Van Sung. For the first time in thirty years, Dr. Sung was coming out of the backrooms of persuasion and was standing in an open election. Sophisticated Saigonese began revising their opinion of the election's importance. Now that Dr. Sung was a public personality, I had a legitimate reason for interviewing him and paid the first of many visits to the offices of his newspaper. *Chinh Luan* was on a narrow street of shabby, tightly packed shops near the central marketplace. Editorial offices occupied the second floor, and Dr. Sung's private office overlooked the busy street. With the noise of traffic outside and the whirr of an air conditioner, I always had to strain to hear what he said. To reach his office, you had to pass a row of underfed-looking clerks behind a counter and climb a dingy stairwell just before the press, an old-fashioned flatbed machine operated by five or six small boys. None of them looked more than eleven or twelve, grimy, ink-smeared, sickly little creatures with listless expressions who seemed to live permanently in the dank backroom housing the press. One day my interpreter and I interviewed them and learned they were orphans who earned a few pennies for rice each day and slept on the press at night. There was a distinct air of tension about *Chinh Luan's* offices; perhaps it emanated from the eyes of the murdered assistant editor, who stared down at you from the wall above Dr. Sung's chair.

As I have said, Dr. Sung was known as the most knowledgeable and well-informed source in the capital—the man who knew the inside story. Dr. Sung seemed indifferent to the squalor and shabbiness of his office. His telephone rang frequently during interviews. Often it was Bui Diem, Ky's *chef de cabinet,* calling from the premier's office.

At fifty-one, Dr. Sung was a pale man with black slicked-down hair, handsome, slightly flabby features and supercilious eyes. He was the sort of man who made luncheon appointments and then failed to apologize for missing them or even to acknowledge he had done so. Yet he was also extremely courteous during interviews, constantly offering cigarettes or proffering a lighter, much in the manner of a slick salesman who wanted to clinch a deal. Some American officials disliked him personally but respected his political judgment, even appropriating it as their own. I often heard Dr. Sung's analysis of current events parroted by influential Americans who assumed they had the inside story; many of Sung's rumors found their way into the editorials of the world's great newspapers and, I suppose, will live on when the histories of the Vietnam war are written. More than anyone else, Sung orchestrated the Dai Viet propaganda campaign to convince the Americans that no victory was possible with Diem, that Diem was incapable of providing leadership or carrying out necessary reforms. Before anti-Communist generals in the Vietnamese Army were purged, Dr. Sung spread the impression that either they or their wives were notoriously corrupt. When he related the scandal that a Madame Quang was smuggling goods to Cambodia with Viet Cong connivance, I knew that her husband, the commander of the Mekong Delta, would have a short official life. This pattern of character assassination before a purge was repeated with no fewer than half a dozen major military leaders.

That Dr. Sung operated subtly and masterfully in this kind of persuasion and character assassination was well understood by Diem just before his murder. Without naming anyone, Diem had said that such a man "refuses actual combat but seeks instead the moral attrition of the opponent." But until the gap between his words and deeds grew increasingly apparent as time wore on, Dr. Sung's Western liberalism was extremely plausible and convincing to me.

Dr. Sung was cordial and polite during our first interview in late July 1966. As the interview began, he first spoke in Vietnamese through my interpreter, apologizing that his English was poor. But when the interpreter stumbled over a phrase, he impatiently interrupted in English and never returned to Vietnamese again. Although it was heavily accented, his English was almost perfect.

The first question I asked was whether he was the leader of the secret Mandarin Dai Viet brotherhood. I told him I was doing an article on South Vietnam's political groupings for the election. Sung replied, "Vietnam is not similar to other countries. Almost all the politicians are concentrated in the cities. The rural candidates are not important. In my life I have failed many times in trying to build a mass-based political party. The Dai Viets had a good background in fighting the French but are now old and out of date. Once we were a big family, united against the French, but now the Dai Viets are divided into small factions, almost all the members are now in North Vietnam." Apparently he assumed I had not read the short biographical profile of him that the American Embassy had prepared for the press on all the candidates. Sung's stated that he had been the Dai Viets' leader since being elected secretary-general fifteen years earlier.

"Weren't you elected as leader of the Mandarin Dai Viet organization in 1951?" I asked.

"No, I turned it down."

Either he was lying or the Embassy's information was wrong. I asked about his campaign plans.

"I am running in the election as just a citizen," he said. "I don't care about being elected. I just want to help create a legal opposition in this country. Too many people look to the past. A party is like a living body; there are a lot of death cells that must be eliminated. The old men prevent the younger generation from emerging. Now I am trying to build up an independent minority, a loyal opposition. There is no hate in me; I want to destroy nobody. But there must be some dialogue between this government—that is, the soldiers in power—and the Vietnamese people.

"I am campaigning on an antimilitary plank. We want peace. We want peace more than anyone else in the world. Ky is too erratic, talking about marching to the north, fighting to the last drop of blood. I am not specifically against this government, but I am against rotten generals."

"If you are elected will you oppose the generals in the Assembly?" I asked.

"Of course. They will try to imitate Diem to control the Assembly, but they will be less efficient. Nhu was more subtle, he had more power and was more conspiratorial. But what can these soldiers do? They are united by nothing, only their uniforms." He smiled. Sung had a peculiar habit of cupping his hand over his mouth while he talked.

"The most powerful party in the elections will be the Americans. You want to say you are outside, but you are always in. You support the government. So there will be a lot of military officers elected. I would bank on it."

I asked if he thought the Communists would covertly back candidates and try to get their men into the Assembly.

"No, the time is too short,' he said. "Besides, what good would it do? Even if a minority of pro-VC got in, what weapon would they use? The VC cannot get many into the Assembly. There's no evidence of VC planning. Besides they are caught by an internal contradiction, caught by their own propaganda. Any VC cadre who suggested they could win by infiltrating the election would be attacked as yellow. They dare not." I gathered he meant that the Communist leadership could not admit to their rank and file how heavily they depended on subversion.

"Who is running the war in Hanoi?"

"Le Duan is the political director. Giap is only in charge of the military."

"Why have the Buddhists and so many other religions and parties threatened to boycott the election?"

"No party says officially they will participate. But all parties have men running. They are afraid of losing. It would be very awkward for a party to say it was running and not get enough seats. Then, the generals are too unpopular. No party wants to be accused of supporting the government or of getting in any way involved with the government openly."

"Do you think it is a good idea to hold elections in wartime at all?"

"We need elections for two reasons. The government must have a popular and legal basis and it is urgent to show this to international opinion. Thus it is important these elections are as free as possible. The generals are more interested in controlling the future Assembly than holding good elections. Ky is in the way of becoming a dictator. They are trying to rig the election, adopting exactly the same methods as Diem. But Nhu would have made a more thorough preparation. It is very awkward the way they keep changing the election laws. In Saigon they will be discreet, but out at the village level the rigging will be more open. There are no leaders in this country. Those in power are not trained in their jobs."

"How do you think the war could end?"

"Our information policy, this 'hush hush' policy of refusing to talk with the Viet Cong is very unwise. You cannot kill all the VC. This is not Korea. The army here has no moral prestige. If you were to weaken North Vietnam sufficiently to force negotiations on a basis similar to the Korean settlement, you would have to fight another ten years. However, the peasants are not with the Viet Cong any longer. The bombing has had that effect; it has forced the VC to get tough with the population."

Sung said he felt that it was imperative to have an elected government prior to negotiations. When I replied that many leaders opposed elections on the grounds that the Communists might be able to covertly elect their operatives, he scoffed, "Those opposed to elections so soon have internal politics too much in mind. They forget international needs. We are like frogs in a well in this country. You see, Vietnamese politics have been like a cinema movie for the last twenty-five years. Very complex, much intrigue. It is not as in your country. Here everybody wants to talk on behalf of workers and peasants, but workers and peasants don't run in elections. If a worker has the 300,000 piastres it takes to be a candidate, he wouldn't run, he'd buy something; he wouldn't waste his money. But since Vietnam is an underdeveloped country, the appeal must be made to peasants and city laborers."

With all my suspicions of Ky—and of Dr. Sung as the force behind Ky—I found Sung extremely convincing at this first interview, despite the persuasive role he had played the year before in Quat's "neutralist" regime. Like most of the Saigon press corps, I tended to regard the elderly Cochinchinese leaders such as Phan Khac Suu and Tran Van Van as ineffectual and reactionary feudal remnants who mattered little to the country's political future. I cabled my newspaper that Sung's was "a refreshingly candid and realistic voice":

> While the generals talk of impossible panaceas like marching north or devastating China, he seems to be searching for real

answers. Sung is acutely aware that a major obstacle to peace is the obvious weakness of the Saigon military regime. . . . Now, for the first time in a long political career, Sung is a candidate in the September 11th elections, running on a worker-peasant platform. He is the likeliest man to emerge as leader of some kind of democratic opposition.

But there was a shadow of the old doubt; my cable also said:

American officials define Sung's "Mandarin" faction of the Dai Viet party as a mostly North Vietnamese remnant of a much larger revolutionary party which fought against the French, was allied with Japanese militarists, later collaborated with the French, and now is said to comprise a secret elite brotherhood of about 200 members in Saigon. It is also acknowledged that Sung was former Premier Quat's chief political adviser. . . . He feels the generals in power have lost the vital popular mandate. . . .

As the election approached, both Ky and General Thieu assumed more hawklike postures. Thieu appealed for American bombing to destroy "all military, economic and manufacturing zones without distinction throughout North Vietnam," and also called for "the movement of troops into the hostile territory of North Vietnam if we have to." Ho Chi Minh obliged by ordering a well-publicized mobilization.

Ky, apparently to strengthen his anti-Communist image abroad, declared in an interview with *U.S. News & World Report* that "sooner or later, we as free men have to face the Chinese Communists. I think it is better to face them right now than in five or ten years." In Saigon he repeated this theme at a press conference, saying that if the United States was not prepared to keep fighting another fifteen years, "then we have to destroy the Communists in their lair."

Less publicized abroad than Ky's appeal for preventive war with China, but fully noted by the Saigonese, was Washington's gift to Ky of a four-engine American DC6B aircraft complete with TV, stereo, bar, and a big gold stripe down the side, estimated to cost $500,000. Ky also ordered the renovation of Ngo Dinh Diem's Independence (Doc Lap) Palace, which had been damaged in a bombing attack during the unsuccessful 1960 coup. According to a subsequent U.S. congressional investigation, Ky spent $3,000,000 in American aid funds on such elegant furnishings as heavy Chinese rugs for many of the palace's 200 rooms, imported French St. Gobain glass windows, and 3,400 lights to put around the twenty-one-acre lawn.

Two weeks before the campaign, in counterpoint to the Thieu-Ky appeals for massive escalation, President Charles de Gaulle arrived in Cambodia to declare there could be "no military solution." De Gaulle demanded that the United States withdraw its troops. Dr. Sung sneered at De Gaulle. "He is trying desperately to have a role in Vietnam; it is kind of a luxury for him."

The formal election campaign, arbitrarily limited by Thieu to fifteen days, began August 27th. Bitter attacks against the Thieu-Ky regime exploded in radio speeches and from rally platforms around the country. Dr. Sung led the denunciation of the generals. In a radio speech written by Sung but delivered by a *Chinh Luan* reporter, Sung told South Vietnamese to go to the polls to "wipe out all dictators and political puppets." It was startling enough so that I went to *Chinh Luan* to get a copy of the speech. After all, Dr. Sung was described as Ky's top policy adviser by such political officers at the American Embassy as John Burke and Lansdale. Yet the speech was unequivocal. "Up until now, many times, the population has voted," wrote Sung, "but each time, the result was only a puppet congress to legalize a government of dictators and puppets. We have decided to struggle to achieve a social revolution to eliminate all injustices in any form and wipe out all dictators and political puppets."

Out in the suburbs of Gia Dinh, Dr. Dan called for a constitutional bill of rights guaranteeing land to the tiller without owner compensation, the right of each village to elect its own council, the right of a legal opposition and the rights of speech, assembly and due process of law.

The most often repeated theme of the other candidates, including Suu and Van, was that Thieu and Ky and the northern generals had compromised South Vietnamese independence and sovereignty and had needlessly prolonged the war, causing casualties by ineffectual rule and personal enrichment.

The candidates said they did not want to be enslaved by Hanoi and Peking. But neither, in the name of prosecuting war, did they want to put up any longer with erratic and inefficient military rule, arbitrary arrest and imprisonment, rampant corruption, and state offices staffed by indifferent and unqualified military officers, in a society where the press was repressed, radio reduced to martial music and rigged news, and a badly paid army reduced to wholesale thievery in the countryside.

"After twenty years of war and suffering" was the common phrase, as speaker after speaker denounced the Ky regime for "betraying the revolution for freedom and democracy." The government allowed each candidate three minutes on the radio, three minutes on television, ten-minute daily speeches, question-and-answer periods on platforms with their opponents, 2,000 posters and a quarter of a million leaflets apiece.

On a typical day during the two-week campaign, I listened to twenty-five or thirty of these speeches. The people of Vietnam for a brief moment had a voice, and the message was emphatic and almost universal: they were not merely indifferent to the Ky regime, they despised it and everything it stood for. Most of the 530 candidates were young men of the professional middle class from small towns in the provinces who were entering politics for the first time. The simple, single message of nearly all was the promise to "work for the victory of the nation and the happiness of the people." But there unanimity ended except in the bitter denunciations of Ky and his government.

A Vietnamese army captain said, "Since 1954 we have had only leaders who exploited the war to become multimillionaires. With such dirty money they have lived happily beside the poverty of the nation. After twenty years of war we must bring justice to the people but through rule of law not violence." Another captain shouted to a cheering audience, "Only performances, not promises have value!" A Chinese merchant attacked the Ky regime for its terror trial and execution of Ta Vinh, the rich Chinese importer. He demanded constitutional guarantees for "free trading and protection of life and property." A former deputy minister appeared to single out both the generals and Dr. Sung. "After twenty years of war this country should not be handed over to corrupt mandarins and military dictators." It was a clear cry for help from the Vietnamese people, and it fell on almost deaf ears throughout the world.

At first, the Ky government, financed by Zorthian's huge information agency, seemed to be doing a creditable job in making the elections known to the people through radio, television, newspapers, variety shows, dragon dances, torchlight processions and even comic books. But it soon became evident that the Americans and the Saigon government were publicizing the electoral process itself, not the candidates or issues. A promised lifting of press censorship did not materialize, and some of the bitterest denunciations of Ky, prerecorded in the radio studios, were never broadcast.

Tran Van Van, who campaigned on behalf of both himself and the elderly Suu, was mercilessly heckled at the public rallies by Ky's toughs, often familiar faces from the Anti-Fraud Group. They accused him of evicting squatters (whom Van suspected Ky had sent) from his property and applying "old French laws against the poor." Another might yell, "You were the adviser of Tran Van Huong when he persecuted Buddhists!" Van would bristle with anger: "Huong was a tough premier. His policy was right because he was trying to protect South Vietnamese sovereignty against northern domination. He was against street demonstrations and a breakdown in law and order. There was nothing wrong with Huong." Van's courage and toughness, and a saving sense of humor, helped him weather the storm of the campaign, eventually winning sympathy as the target of what was obviously stage-managed heckling. But to some degree, he was tarnished with the image of a rich, reactionary and slightly comic figure. His eyes blazing beneath bushy-black eyebrows and his bony arms flailing the air as he shouted down hecklers, Van seemed the very prototype of the aristocratic capitalist landlord.

The campaign seemed to rouse little visible interest in the countryside. In a village across the Bassac River from Can Tho, I interviewed a fisherman. He kept mending his net as we talked, his callused fingers grasping a primitive wooden needle to stitch and replace the rotted braid. There was a certain timelessness in the precise way he worked with his hands, as if both he and the art were as ancient and enduring as the sluggish yellow Bassac River.

"I do not care who is premier," the fisherman said with some inner enjoyment, his sun-bronzed face wrinkling around the eyes.

"I have no mind about Saigon. If the premier wants me to go voting, okay, I will do my duty and go voting. One hears those who do not vote will be menaced by the police. But after voting I will live here, go on fishing, and my life will be the same."

It was the same kind of shrewd peasant amusement I got wherever I went in the countryside to canvass village voters. The fisherman said his only contact with the Saigon government had been more than a year before. "They came once to sell some cheap cloth and give out pills. But I was out fishing and got nothing."

While it was impossible to read the heart of a Vietnamese mending a fishnet or planting rice or selling tea in a village market, one got a strong impression of neither hostility nor enthusiasm. Just natural indifference over something they felt was unlikely to make any real difference in their lives.

In Can Tho City, the walls were plastered with posters, the trees hung with pink and blue banners, and loudspeakers blared forth patriotic music and election pep talks in the market all day. Unlike disillusioned and cynical Saigon, where only a few hundred people showed up at most rallies, the people of Can Tho turned out by the thousands for torchlight parades and to hear the candidates speak along the Bassac riverbank. But there was a strong undercurrent of war weariness throughout the country. One evening in Can Tho, as townspeople drank beer and promenaded along the river, a small group gathered around a handsome army private who sang the lament of a dying soldier to his sweetheart: "When we said farewell, we did not know it was forever. Call my name tonight when you see the swallows fly across the horizon."

My interpreter said he thought the private was a Viet Cong propagandist. After the song the youth told his audience, "We must have peace. If you try to kill all the VC their families will hate you and try to kill you."

"Peace," echoed an elderly millionaire landowner as he poured me a cocktail. "The people want food and jobs, that's all they care about. Next year the rice crop will be disastrous, all this bombing and defoliation. The generals see the war through a telescope. Ky is a pilot flying over our heads. From his height the trees look like grass. He cannot see what is happening in the Delta. We must begin a dialogue with moderates among the Viet Cong."

But war or peace, it all seemed much the same to the fisherman back in his village, mending his net on the odd heap of bamboo poles, split bamboo matting and planks on stilts he called home. The inner walls had been plastered with whatever scraps of paper had come his way: lottery tickets, yellowed Indian movie bills, illustrations from a cheap biography of Buddha, a glossy poster of President Johnson declaring, "We are in Vietnam because the American people have promised to help the people of South Vietnam preserve their independence and build their nation." The fisherman said the paper was of good quality and helped keep out the chill night breezes from the Bassac.

On the eve of the election, Dr. Sung made his final speech in the gilded upstairs gallery of the Saigon prefecture, his last performance as the champion of the people against the hated military despots. "I am the editor of a newspaper," he declared. "We struggled for the people before the election, and we will struggle for the people after the election. If the generals abuse the Assembly by trying to turn it into a puppet parliament and become dictators, we will denounce them. I do not fear to be jailed or exiled."

I went to see Tri Quang, who was then in the ninety-eighth day of his hunger strike and still under house arrest in Saigon's Duy Tan clinic. He was propped up in bed with a yellow angora comforter wrapped around his knees. The room was frigidly air-conditioned and fragrant with bouquets of roses and tiger lilies. A bottle of McKesson & Robbins 5% dextrose water was on a table, along with a powerful short-wave radio. Ill-concealed under a tablecloth was an expensive American television set. But Tri Quang was playing Gandhi. In case anybody missed the point, there were four photographs of Gandhi in the room and a large one of Tri Quang, naked save for a Gandhi-type loincloth. Tri Quang gave me a postcard-sized copy. He was thin, but hardly emaciated to the point of death as advertised.

I told him about Dr. Sung's final campaign statement: "If elected, I will create an opposition to protest any attempt to turn the Assembly into a puppet parliament. At first I may be only one voice, then there will be two, then three, and finally we will get the majority needed to overrule the ruling junta."

"He will stay one voice," sniffed Tri Quang. "What can Dr.

Sung do? Mind you, I do not say I am for or against Dr. Sung. But what he proposes is impossible. What can he achieve by himself?" He said he had no comment to make about the election and referred me to a Buddhist Institute communiqué of the day before which had declared that Ky and Thieu were "only dictators . . . who pay Vietnamese to kill as many other Vietnamese as possible."

"My paper in Washington won't print that," I told my interpreter, aware that Tri Quang understood English. "That's the same old stuff. Tell him to come up with something new."

Tri Quang smiled again, and this time it was genuine. "All right," he said, "I would like to pose President Johnson three questions: How can the government of generals like Thieu and Ky, who are popularly disliked and run a criminal regime, organize anything other than a rubber-stamp assembly to suit their own purposes? How can the people in the rural provinces be conceived as participating in a democratic election, since those under government control refuse to be enthusiastic and those under the Viet Cong are not taking part? And, finally, how can the United States achieve its policy of victory over the Viet Cong with this government and a puppet parliament?"

The most curious thing about Election Day in Saigon was not the festival air as whole families went to the polls together in their best clothes, but the fact that the overwhelming majority of the voters seemed to be middle-aged and elderly ladies in black pajamas and pointed hats. You forgot how many men must have been killed in the war or were out with the Viet Cong.

One woman told me, "I heard the candidates talk on the radio, but when I went to vote I forgot the name of the one I liked. So I just picked the handsomest picture." Another said, "I listened to each man on the radio and voted for a man who said he cared about poor people." But many of the soldiers and peasant elders knew the candidates. They declined to say whom they had voted for but discussed the issues.

One farmer said, "People who want the VC to win have no experience with the VC. We don't care if the deputies are rich or poor, soldiers or civilians, they must do something for the poor. We would be very proud to own land. Seed and fertilizer would be no problem if the government had credit banks like it did in Diem's time."

A second: "People fear the VC because when the VC say they will do something, they will do it for sure. They act behind your back and you don't know when or how."

A third: "All candidates must oppose the government to be elected. During Diem's time we heard the same thing, but afterwards they just sat idly in the congress house. The poor have a very miserable life in Saigon. Every day the government menaces us to move our huts, and at night the VC cadre come and make propaganda."

A fourth: "The VC fight with the nationalist soldiers, so they make the lives of me and my friends miserable. I am a poor man and live in an insecure area so I must come to Saigon to make my living. I think the VC cannot win. Nobody ever asked me what I thought before."

Most of the soldiers were also peasant boys from the countryside. The first I interviewed said, "To end the war we must apply reforms to have the support of the people in the villages. They are poor and must stay with their land, so many live with the VC. It is better to help the people than force them." Another told me, "Only a few bad elements in the army rape and steal. But since prices are so costly our money is not enough. Sometimes on operations we get very hungry. With or without money the villagers won't sell food to us, so sometimes we just take their chickens and eggs. What are we to do?"

On Election Day, about thirty correspondents from the Saigon press corps fanned out over the countryside, turning in reports at the end of the day to a pool run by Barry Zorthian's shop, an effective spot check that was oddly not repeated the following year. Don Oberdorfer of the Knight newspapers reported from Binh Duong Province: "There was no discernible pressure from any government source for or against any candidate." Charles Mohr of the New York *Times* had gone to Long An, and he wrote, "At no time did we witness or hear of any undue or special pressure tactics by government officials to force them to vote." Ward Just of the Washington *Post* wrote from Bien Hoa, "Apparently it didn't occur to anybody not to vote." Father Patrick Burke, a Catholic journalist, reported from the same province, "In this area all voters seemed to take their responsibility very seriously." The American press seemed to view the election as both reasonably good and unexpectedly serene and dignified. An unsigned pool report from the seaside resort of Vung Tau contained one jarring note: "Former Premier Tran Van Huong, who is under house arrest, voted before noon. . . . Huong was accompanied by a squad of military police who escorted him to and from the polling place . . ." I had not known that Huong was living under guard.

Nearly 81% of the registered voters (4,274,812 people) went to the polls, something just under 60% of the entire South Vietnamese population over the age of eighteen. The 117 Assembly seats were contested by 530 candidates; 735 had originally been nominated, but 59 were refused permission on the grounds of being "pro-Communist or pro-neutralist." Some 140 others were either eliminated on technical grounds or withdrew their nominations.

World press reaction focused on the voter turnout. "A victory for the Saigon junta," said the Manchester *Guardian*, adding, "This does not necessarily mean the same as a victory for democracy." The *Economist* in London concluded that the election "punctures the claim that the government's authority has virtually collapsed outside Saigon and a few other large towns. And it deflates the argument that the South Vietnamese are so war-weary that they have lost the wish to preserve a non-Communist system."

In Saigon, Nguyen Cao Ky called the election "the beginning of the end." General Thieu predicted that "Hanoi and the international Communists may now be having second thoughts." The American Embassy's comment was restrained but pleased: "A large proportion of the population voted, making a judgment on behalf of the Saigon government, whatever the motive."

Liberation Radio prophesied, "The Assembly will be controlled by the Americans and corrupt puppets." Tri Quang echoed the Viet Cong line and called the Assembly "a puppet parliament" and "rubber-stamp assembly."

Press reaction to the election suggested to me that the world audience had had a wholly inflated notion of Viet Cong strength in South Vietnam. The non-Communist and anti-Communists were not a spent force by any means. It was just that the peasant population at large had been so battered by the war that they were remaining noncommittal until they saw who was winning, and then they would back the winner. The non-Communist majority in Vietnam was weak and divided. The Communists' apparent strength was a measure of the weakness of others. If you took away the propaganda, the terror and intimidation, the deception and subversion, what would the Communist strength be? Douglas Pike told me there might be as many as 700,000 what he called "true believers." Most Vietnamese put the number at half of that.

The September 1966 election convinced me that neither the Viet Cong nor the northern regime in power could win a free election in South Vietnam. Ky had publicly backed nearly a hundred favored candidates; only four were elected.

But I was uneasy about the possibility that Dr. Sung and his men might have deceived the voters with their antimilitary campaigning and that, once elected, they might switch to supporting the generals and try to take over the Assembly. These fears were soon to be confirmed, but before this happened, South Vietnam had a brief, memorable moment of democracy. It happened during the Assembly's inaugural session in the shabby baroque grandeur of Saigon's old French opera house. At times the ceremony was straight out of Gilbert and Sullivan. But when the comic opera ended, there were a few breathtaking minutes when it seemed that an era of political repression had ended in South Vietnam.

Tamarind-fringed Lam Son Square below my balcony at the Continental was transformed that day with hundreds of yellow-and-red national flags, bunting and pink banners hailing the new Assembly. A brass band played stirring marches as rows of crisply uniformed presidential guards in red berets and white gloves stood at ramrod attention.

Many of the arriving deputies, mostly poor young men from the rural provinces in badly tailored suits, appeared overwhelmed by all the pomp and flourish as they edged their way up red-carpeted stairs and past potted palms. One delegation from Quang Ngai Province turned up in matching white Palm Beach suits that all looked as though they had been cut from the same bolt of cloth and probably were. They were mortified to see that the rest of the deputies wore dark suits.

Inside, the theatre's orchestra seats had been removed to make room for desks and chairs. Over the deputies' heads rose three tiers of ringed boxes filled with the familiar faces of the diplomatic corps, elderly mandarins, lesser warlords and ministers, Catholic priests and Buddhist bonzes—almost the entire *dramatis personae* of the long charade. In a well-placed box on one side of the stage itself sat the junta generals, resplendent in white dress uniforms, their chests glittering with medals and ribbons. Opposite was a chorale of Vietnamese singers, who burst into a rousing patriotic hymn as a kind of overture. Then, preceded by offstage ruffles and flourishes, Premier Ky and General Thieu strode in, both in white uniforms with dozens of medals and flashing sabres.

The oldest deputy, an elderly schoolmaster who automatically became the Assembly's acting chairman, declared that the new constitution would have to "assure the Vietnamese people their basic rights through a strong government entrusted with the prestige that can only come from the people in a government elected by the people." Then the silver-haired schoolmaster looked over his glasses at Ky and Thieu sitting in gilded chairs in the orchestra pit and said, "We are ready to receive constructive ideas but are determined to withstand all pressure."

Reading from a short prepared text, Ky appeared restrained and gracious, praising the election as the "most honest, most equitable and most impartial ever held in this country." There was only the hint of a warning note: "While the constitution must be responsive to people's feelings and aspirations, it must at the same time be suitable to the present condition of this country."

General Thieu called for a constitution that could be the "foundation for a lasting social revolution. . . . Through understanding and cooperation with you," he said, "putting the common interest above your private interests and those of your party and realizing your responsibility before the nation and history, I believe every difference will be solved." With this, the chorale burst into a chorus of "Vietnam Wants to Live!" the generals marched out, and with them followed the entire entourage of diplomats, soldiers, monks, priests, mandarins, warlords and ministers. *Exeunt lords and attendants.*

Within minutes the opera house was empty save for the

deputies, who kept their seats. Only a handful of reporters lingered on in the press galleries. Nobody seemed to know what came next. There was almost a tangible air of astonishment that free elections had come and gone, the pomp and pageantry were over, and now it was up to the deputies to decide what kind of government South Vietnam should have.

After some moments of whispering and confusion, Tran Van Van gestured from the back of the hall to the elderly chairman to ring his bell. When the bell rang, bringing the deputies to hushed attention, Dr. Dan went to the platform to formally introduce the acting chairman. Following Dr. Dan's lead, a young countrified-looking deputy came forward next and said excitedly over the microphone, "I should like to propose that the Assembly immediately cable all the parliaments in the world telling them how strongly the Vietnamese people oppose the Viet Cong." There were cheers and applause. A second young man leaped to the speaker's dais. "I wish to second that proposal. The world must know our true feelings." A third declared, "We must elect our permanent chairman here and now."

But Dr. Sung was already nudging the deputy sitting beside him, a heavyset, moonfaced man who ran a bicycle repair shop in the slums. This deputy lumbered to the dais and shouted that he was opposed to any precipitous action. As if at a signal, some twenty deputies rose and moved into the aisle. Although there were some confused shouts of protest, the session broke up a few minutes later.

It had been an oddly moving scene. If I had harbored any doubts that the election had not been reasonably free, they were erased. South Vietnam had experienced a fleeting moment of genuine democracy that had not been in the script for the long charade. I would never forget the fervor of those young deputies from the country trying to tell a skeptical world that the South Vietnamese people did not want Communism.

But Dr. Sung's complex maneuvering to seize control of the Assembly began at once. Most of the deputies wanted a constitution which would ensure that any Saigon government would have to perform reasonably well or face being replaced through an orderly legal process. Sung wanted to legitimatize the existing Thieu-Ky dictatorship. He was helped by Philip Habib, the American Embassy's political chief, who favored a constitution on the South Korean model, where an elected military president appoints his own civil premier as the working executive. The Cochinchinese and Catholics, led by Tran Van Van, sought a directly elected civil president and a runoff election in the event of many candidates. They tried to limit the presidential minimum age to forty. Ky was thirty-six. Habib told me this was "playing politics" with the constitution and said that Van was a "southern separatist." Habib sent a young foreign-service officer to interview each deputy shortly after the Assembly opened, to solicit their views on a constitution. For most of the 117 deputies, this was their last personal contact with the American Embassy for the next six months.

What had not been evident during the election campaign was that many brotherhood members had posed as bitter critics of Ky just to get seats. Once elected, these Dai Viets formed the hard core of a pro-Ky bloc. When I asked Dr. Sung directly to confirm that twenty-three Dai Viets were elected, he declined to give a number but said, "There are now enough former Dai Viet deputies to go from a clandestine to an open, broad-based party with moderates among the Catholics, Buddhists, Kuomintang, soldiers and independents. People are tired of extremism and division." As a candidate Sung had declared, "We will denounce the ruling directorate if they abuse the Assembly by trying to turn it into a puppet parliament to legalize their dictatorship." Now, without any apology or embarrassment, Sung told me, "No civilian candidate for president has enough prestige to solve South Vietnam's problems. We need someone who would have more direct influence than civilian politicians. Ky is smart and honest."

Sung's overt role in the Assembly was to counsel deliberation. Largely through Sung's efforts, the Assembly postponed the election of its chairman for a month; it would spend nearly ninety days endlessly debating and voting on more than 100 internal rules. It did not actually begin drafting the constitution until mid-December or voting on its provisions until one month before the March 26th deadline decreed by Thieu.

Dr. Dan also favored going slow. "The deputies are so young," he told me. "Always talking about everything and anything." But he added, "We are determined to keep our independence. The constitution we will write and vote will be completely different from what the generals want. If a conflict is allowed to develop between this Assembly and the government, it will be very serious." John Dillin, the Saigon correspondent of the *Christian Science Monitor*, who had also been following the Assembly closely, warned me not to confide in Dr. Dan. Dillin said Dr. Dan had told him and another American newsman that William Colby, a senior-ranking CIA officer, and former Deputy Ambassador U. Alexis Johnson had secretly visited Saigon and proposed making Dr. Dan president if he would support sending 40,000 Tonkinese guerrillas into North Vietnam to try to overthrow the Communist regime. Dillin quoted Dr. Dan as saying, "I have no ambitions to be president of just South Vietnam." Both Dillin and I checked out this story. Qualified American sources said it was untrue; Dr. Dan had made it up.

During the Assembly's first few weeks, I was able to interview nearly half of the 117 members. One of the men I saw often was, of course, Tran Van Van—whose interview begins this book. Van was not alone in his bitterness toward the Ky regime. As tensions rose, more and more of the Assembly members complained that their articles and letters were censored out of Saigon newspapers, while a plethora of cartoons ridiculing the Assembly and patently false reports of the Assembly's proceedings were allowed to appear almost daily. Dr. Sung's newspaper, *Chinh Luan*, printed some of these flagrant falsehoods about the Assembly, and Sung's cartoonist, "Twist," drew scurrilous caricatures of its members. One of Ky's men proposed that the Assembly buy a $90,000 fleet of luxury cars; Tran Van Van and others at once denounced this and said that the Assembly could rent mini-buses if it needed to go anywhere, but Sung's newspaper and others reported only that the Assembly was demanding the luxury cars—without carrying Van's denuciation of the idea. Nguyen Thanh Vinh, a deputy from Quang Tri Province, told me, "The Dai Viets are trying to slander the Assembly. All those stories about salaries and cars."

For nearly two months Ky did not pay the deputies. Those from the rural provinces were initially put up at two third-rate downtown hotels. Soon they were notified by their managements that they had to pay their own daily bills of $10, but this was a clear impossibility to most deputies with families at home to support. On October 22nd, these deputies were evicted. The Assembly asked Ky for $180 a month in salaries, hotel and transportation allowances for each deputy, and a budget of $15,000 to cover running expenses in the opera house and pay a clerical staff. In late November, two months after the election, Ky agreed to "loan" each civilian deputy $110 and each military officer $310. The only Protestant in the Assembly, Do Ai, whom I had met in Danang, proposed increasing a press budget of $1,500 to $20,000 monthly to publish a 200,000-circulation weekly magazine for the villages to inform the peasants "about each deputy's background, issues involved in drafting the constitution and how the democratic process functions." Do Ai told the Assembly, "We must compete with the government radio, which slanders the deputies and the Assembly." Zorthian's information agency, which was spending millions on anti-Communist propaganda, made no offer to underwrite this project, and the Dai Viet deputies were able to defeat it.

One civil servant told me government officials had threatened to reassign him to a remote, insecure province if he did not cooperate. Others claimed they had been offered bribes, import licenses and hard cash to vote with the Dai Viets. They repeatedly asked the American Embassy to come to their assistance, or at least send someone to hear their complaints. Sung, in contrast, was in almost daily contact with senior American officials. In October, twenty-nine deputies, including the Assembly's eighteen military officers, signed a petition asking to be discharged from government service on the grounds that they were being "subjected to undue official pressure." In November, each military officer in the Assembly received a letter bearing the signature of Ky's armed forces chief of staff, ordering them to report for duty within ten days of the Assembly's completion. The letter stated that deputies could not expect to be automatically returned to their old units, but would be reassigned "where national security requires." Most of them interpreted this as a threat of assignment to dangerous, insecure provinces if they refused to cooperate with Sung and Ky.

Several deputies besides Van, including Dr. Dan, received

anonymous assassination threats. Another government circular was then sent to each deputy offering a pistol in "self-protection." One deputy told me, "It was only a funny statement to insult us. They know a civilian has no way of protecting himself in Saigon." One of Ky's men on the floor declared, "If we go too far, there will be terrible trouble for us." He was shouted down with cries of "We don't fear their guns!"

Many deputies expressed misgivings when President Johnson announced that he would meet Ky and the leaders of the allied governments involved in Vietnam at a seven-nation Manila summit conference in late October. They warned that it gave the same impression as the Honolulu meeting: that Johnson was committing his government to Ky and the North Vietnamese military junta. None of the deputies, who fairly reflected the diverse religious, ethnic and political grouping of the South Vietnamese people, were invited to Manila.

As the Manila conference approached, Ky began a new purge of Cochinchinese officials in and around Saigon, replacing them with northern refugees. When the Cochinchinese violently protested the ouster of a Vietnamese navy captain, Ky's police chief, Nguyen Ngoc Loan, arrested the Cochinchinese deputy health minister on announced charges of "plotting a southern separatist movement." Dr. Sung told me and other Americans, "The Viet Cong were behind the Buddhist movement; now they are behind the North-South movement. Political war consists of dividing and weakening the enemy." He suggested to me that Van was consciously collaborating with the Viet Cong.

Seven Cochinchinese ministers who held lesser posts in Ky's Cabinet resigned to protest the arrest. Well-informed Saigonese had by now read Le Duan's just-published article in which he boasted that Hanoi's most "clever tactic" was its application of the Leninist principle of exploiting internal contradictions. In a published interview, Deputy Vinh told me, "The Viet Cong, instead of trying to propagate Communism, have attempted to infiltrate the upper echelon of this government in order to foment division between northerners and southerners." Another deputy told me, "While it is naïve to think there is a Communist under every bed in Saigon; it is more naïve to assume the Viet Cong are not behind this new trouble." One pro-Communist Vietnamese journalist I knew smiled when I asked his opinion. "South Vietnam is like a firecracker. The VC light the fuse and stand back. Now nobody can stop the burning, nobody."

On the eve of Manila, the Saigon University student union held a press conference to charge Ky with using his secret police to "foment disunity and division." They said Ky held "sole responsibility" for "sowing animosity between northerners and southerners." The students claimed that the arrest without warrant of the Cochinchinese minister was "concrete proof of a police-state regime condemned by all." Student spokesmen said the Manila conference would be "beneficial only if it is represented by a government vested with full prestige." They demanded that Ky fire his top two civilian aides: Bui Diem, who also served as deputy foreign minister, and Dinh Trinh Chinh, Ky's *chef de cabinet,* as well as Police Chief Loan. All three were Dai Viets. Habib told me Bui Diem would become ambassador to Washington, and Chinh, ambassador to Bangkok; Habib said both men were "tired and in poor health." In the Assembly, both Van and Dr. Dan, who seemed to have broken with the Dai Viets, accused the Ky regime of practicing "regional divisionism" and "divide and rule" tactics; they charged Loan with "ruthlessness."

Ky reinstated the arrested minister and flew to Manila. In the fiesta atmosphere of Manila, where the Filipinos were mostly concerned with welcoming President Johnson, the crisis back in Saigon seemed forgotten; over cocktails in his hotel suite, Ky told me and several other American reporters from Saigon that he thought peace could come just as soon as the Communists went back north. When I asked if he meant South Vietnamese Communists or North Vietnamese Communists, Ky replied: "I make no distinction between North Vietnamese and the Viet Cong. As you know, in Vietnamese the word Viet Cong means 'Vietnamese Communist.' For me there is only one man, this Communist. We don't want to kill them if they leave *my* country and go back to the Communist country and live there."

After Manila, the Dai Viets had a major setback in the Assembly on October 26th, when they attempted to elect a well-known Dai Viet, Tran Dien, as chairman. Tran Dien, who was from Hue, was notorious in Saigon for having recruited youths to join the anti-Ky rebel forces during the Annam civil revolt of 1966. He had also been eased out of the Vietnamese Boy Scout movement on suspicion of trying to infiltrate Communist agents into its senior leadership ranks. Both Tran Dien and his brother-in-law, Ha Thuc Ky, the Dai Viet boss in Annam, had been arrested by Diem as suspected Communist collaborators in the fifties.

Tran Dien was defeated for the Assembly chairmanship by the elderly ex-president, Phan Khac Suu, who got sixty-one votes to Dien's forty-four. I was out of Saigon at the time, but Ward Just of the Washington *Post* reported that the supposedly secret balloting could be watched from the press gallery, since the deputies went one by one to a table to write out their choice on a slip of paper. Dr. Sung had told me he supported Suu as a "compromise." But, Just reported, "If you leaned over the balustrade far enough, you could see the name of the man the delegate voted for. Sung, for example, voted for Dien." Sung had supported Ky's stand during the Annam revolt, and Dien had been one of Tri Quang's rebel leaders. I interpreted this as further evidence that Ky and Tri Quang had stage-managed the near civil war. (Tran Dien, in the 1968 Tet offensive, would be one of two prominent Dai Viets reportedly buried alive, along with 1,000 others, when the Communists overran Hue. I suspected, however, that he was one of Le Duan's men, and that in the confusion of the mass killings Tran Dien was executed by local Communist military commanders who did not know who he was.)

On November 4th, when the deputies divided into four voting blocs and a fifth group of nonaligned independents, assigning members proportionally to key committees, it finally became apparent that Dr. Sung's other maneuvering had worked. The two largest blocs, together totaling sixty-nine of the Assembly's 117 votes, were led by deputies loyal to Ky. The biggest faction, called the Greater People's bloc, had forty-four deputies and was led by Tran Dien; its membership was composed almost entirely of Montagnard and Cambodian ethnic minorities or deputies on the government payroll—teachers, civil servants and two-thirds of the Assembly's eighteen army officers. The other bloc was formed around deputies from the two regionally strong feudal sects, the Cao Dai and Hoa Hao. It was led by a young Hoa Hao who had briefly served as Ky's secretary of state. Dr. Sung was in this bloc. The Catholics, with thirty-five members, were reduced to a voting bloc of sixteen, and the Cochinchinese, with forty-four members, to a voting bloc of twelve. In this way they received no important committee chairmanships, which went to the Dai Viets.

Ky continued his harassment of the Assembly. He flew Suu and some of the older deputies to a Montagnard ceremony in the highlands and then stranded them there without transport in a dangerous area, a ploy later to be repeated. On November 10th, he threatened to revive public executions of "economic specula-tors." He fired General Quang, the Catholic Delta commander and one of the few Cochinchinese generals left. On November 11th, Viet Cong propagandists began distributing leaflets in Saigon's slums urging Cochinchinese to "Rise up and kill northerners!" Ky announced the closing of half a dozen French *lycées*, where the southern middle class sent its children. When Ky invited thousands of minor civil servants and military men to sit in the reviewing stands at the National Day Parade, but sent only nine deputies invitations, Van with some amusement led the rest of the deputies to stand with the crowd. (During this parade, the Viet Cong shelled Saigon for the first time, aiming at the re-viewing stand half an hour before the scheduled arrival of Thieu and Ky, but directing their fire at a hospital some blocks away during a second volley once Thieu and Ky were in the stands.) Ky released five Catholics imprisoned without trial since Diem's fall; but priests such as Father Tran Du charged that Ky still held more than eighty others in jail and had arbitrarily con-fiscated some of their property.

Dr. Dan began lecturing to student, labor and business groups, drumming up support for a showdown with the Ky regime: "Unless the government reduces its power to simply the right to advise, we will have students, bonzes and priests out in the streets again." Dr. Dan urged that the deputies pledge themselves to "a month of struggle." Some of the deputies accused Dr. Dan himself of delaying the Assembly's work. At Dan's insistence, Chairman Suu met Thieu and Ky. Afterward, Suu called Cochinchinese and Catholic leaders together and told them he was now convinced that Dr. Sung's faction was trying to delay completion of the constitution until the March 26th deadline so Ky could dissolve the Constituent Assembly and hold a national referendum for a constitution his own lawyers had written. The elderly Suu began constantly ringing his bell and even pounding the podium with his fists to cut off Dai Viet filibustering. Some deputies accused Dinh Thanh Chau, the twenty-nine-year-old chairman of the constitution drafting committee, of deliberate inaction. Chau was a cousin of Ky's aide Dinh Trinh Chinh, one of the Dai Viets eventually named by Van. When I asked Chau why he was going so slow, he said, "I cannot predict how fast the constitution will be finished, submitted and promulgated. Some people in the committee and outside are trying to delay and disrupt our work." Many of the committee members, however, told me that Chau himself was to blame.

It was in mid-November that Tran Van Van called me to his home and declared his intention of exposing the northern Dai Viets in the world press. Ten days later, I was standing on the steps of the opera house with John Dillin, talking to Dr. Dan. Dr. Sung approached and, without any preliminary greeting, said to me, "You are the most dangerous American in this country." He added something about "finding out too much," but we couldn't catch exactly what he said because Dr. Dan interrupted loudly to say, "No, he's the nicest." Sung wheeled around and walked off. Dr. Dan, flustered and embarrassed, asked me to dinner at Saigon's Club Nautique just before I was to leave for Christmas holiday. Dillin and I both decided not to cover politics for some days; he went to the Delta and I flew up to Annam to join the South Korean troops. Before leaving Saigon I applied for an exit permit for the midday December 7th Air France flight to Hong Kong and filled out the appropriate police application. When I returned to the Continental a few days later, I found that someone had rifled my files and a number of carbon copies were missing.

At the dinner with Dr. Dan, I was uneasy. There was a third man present whom I had never seen; since he did not appear to know English, Dr. Dan translated everything I said. After Dr. Dan insisted on buying several rounds of drinks, I asked him flatly if he was working with the Dai Viets. He said no, he had quit the organization years ago. He added, however, that he had known Dr. Sung since they had been classmates at the University of Hanoi with Vo Nguyen Giap in the thirties. Dr. Dan said he felt that Dr. Sung was "reasonable and moderate," ending my further trust in Dan. The next morning, on the spur of the moment, I went to the Cathay Pacific office and found they had a seat available on an afternoon flight to Hong Kong, so I cancelled my earlier reservation for a noon flight the next day, December 7th. I hurried back to the Continental and packed, jamming one suitcase full of my most important files, then went directly to the airport. Thus I had already left Saigon when Van was shot to death in the heart of the city some eighteen hours later.

On December 14th, there was a small panic at Tan Son Nhut Airbase when American military police cleared the restaurant-waiting room after a hand grenade, with the pin still intact, was discovered hidden behind some rags and supplies in a locker in the men's room of the restaurant. An attendant said that the grenade could have been there undiscovered for days. From Hong Kong, I cabled my newspaper most of what Van had told me and booked the first flight to Washington.

Just before leaving, I came across notes I had taken at Habib's last press briefing in mid-November, shortly before my interview with Van. Rereading them I was troubled. Habib had described the Assembly as "a damn good cross section of the country" and "a strongly anti-Communist group" which was "moving along at a very good pace." Asked who the most promising deputies were, Habib said, "Sang, Chau, Ngai, Dat and Dien will be looked to." Four were affiliated with Ky and the Dai Viets. When someone voiced doubts about Dr. Sung's performance, Habib replied, "I wouldn't question his strong anti-Communism." He denied Ky was trying to dominate the Assembly: "There is no organized effort on a major scale to influence blocs or to infiltrate and manipulate the Assembly."

Graham Greene was right; innocence should wear a bell.

Fourteen

Toward Negotiations

The true color of the Thieu-Ky clique as country sellers and the puppet government's incompetency and rottenness are revealing themselves in broad daylight.

—Le Duan, March 1966

After Van's murder and his story ran on page one, I did not expect to return to Saigon. And then, after only ten days in Washington, I found myself on a plane crossing the Pacific once more. I remembered once asking Dennis Duncanson what kept the Vietnamese soldiers fighting. "Why does anyone do anything?" he had replied. "For lack of an alternative. The soldier knows that if he goes out on patrol he'll get fed at six o'clock." The Americans were like that, too. You asked an infantryman why he was fighting in Vietnam and he replied, "It's my job." I suppose I felt the same way about Van. I believed him absolutely now, and there was so much left unexplained and undocumented.

But I was not to reach Saigon for another six weeks. Mao Tse-tung's attempt to bring pure Marxism to China had brought the country to the brink of civil war and a possible diplomatic break with Russia, and I was delayed in Hong Kong. When I finally did return, it was just after Red Guards had besieged the Soviet Embassy in Peking and forced Russian women to crawl on their knees under banners proclaiming Chairman Mao's thought. The Russians were enraged and accused the Chinese of blocking rail shipments of arms to Vietnam. There was speculation that Hanoi might finally have to choose between its two big Communist allies.

On my return, I found that Saigon's mood had subtly changed. In January, Ky had made headlines with a seemingly casual remark: "We are getting closer to negotiations every day." In conversations with other Vietnamese, I sensed that they, too, felt this might be true and that everything turned on the coming national elections, that somehow victory or defeat would be decided when the South Vietnamese went to the polls in the fall.

The South Vietnamese I talked to thought that if they could elect a southern president there might be a chance. But Dr. Sung and the Dai Viets also seemed confident. Convinced as I was by Van's death and my subsequent investigations that a Dai Viet election victory would serve Hanoi's interests, I began to speculate about what kind of settlement Le Duan had in mind.

The first hint, which turned out to be far more revealing than I realized at the time, came from Professor Ho Huu Tuong, whom I had known over the years as a white-haired, affable old Trotskyite who had a lunatic scheme to put South Vietnam under United Nations trusteeship. But the day he summoned me to his house, soon after my return to Saigon, he seemed twenty years younger. He was hard-eyed, alert, and briskly businesslike. Without explaining where he got his information, he said that Ho Chi Minh feared the possibility of a Sino-Soviet break in state relations which would force North Vietnam to wind up the war in the south. According to Tuong, Ho Chi Minh, whom he had known some forty years, was convinced that in the event of a break he would have to stand with China, since to do otherwise would risk Chinese intervention and eventual annexation. Tuong told me that Ho had sent instructions to the NLF authorizing its deputy chairman, Huynh Tan Phat, to negotiate on his behalf with the South Vietnamese government and the United States if events took a turn for the worse. Tuong emphasized that everything was contingent on events in China. He then listed from memory what he described as Hanoi's peace terms.

The terms: In return for a cessation of northern air strikes, Hanoi would agree to withdraw 50,000 troops and a substantial number of political cadres timed to an American withdrawal in accordance with the six-month provision in the October 1966 Manila communiqué. The Viet Cong would drop their arms and peacefully collaborate with a non-Communist government in Saigon, the NLF would be dissolved, and the southern wing of the Vietnamese Communist party, called the People's Revolutionary Party, would be disbanded. Instead, these elements would be allowed to form a new popular front to be called the "Alliance of National and Peace Forces" (the organization that Hanoi Radio was to announce as being created in Saigon during the 1968 Tet offensive a year later). If the Saigon government was "reasonably liberal" and led by men who had not served the French or Ngo Dinh Diem, the Front would not demand a coalition government or a U.S. guarantee of safety. If, however, such a government was not installed in Saigon, Hanoi wanted the new front to get 50% of all Cabinet posts, a legalized Communist party that could contest elections, and a guarantee of safety from the United States, which would leave troops garrisoned in the coastal enclaves "subject to negotiation." While North Vietnam would remain Communist, South Vietnam would be neutralized, with diplomatic relations with the United States, the Soviet Union and China.

Later, Assistant Secretary of State William Bundy, on a visit to Saigon, told me similar terms had come from Communist sources in Warsaw. At the time I had no way of knowing whether the terms were genuine or not, and before cabling my story, I sought the advice of General Lansdale. Lansdale exploded in frustration; he said he had no doubt the terms were authentic. "Nobody understands this problem," he said. "President Johnson doesn't. Diem didn't. You don't. Land reform is a gimmick. The military war is a gimmick. It's fundamentally a question of forming a political base. Now these boys come driving right down the middle of the avenue."

Within weeks a Sino-Soviet break had been averted and Peking signed an agreement allowing the Russians to transship military supplies to Vietnam across China. But the Tuong episode was of vital importance, suggesting as it did that Hanoi had already formulated its final peace terms.

As Lansdale said, it was all a question of forming a political base. This was what President Johnson seemed to be trying to do by creating the institutions of constitutional government as fast as possible in 1967. These included the new constitution, hamlet and village elections in the spring and presidential and parliamentary elections in the fall. Johnson's apparent hope was that if the South Vietnamese were allowed to choose freely their own government, a southern non-Communist political base would form naturally and enable the south to negotiate an end to the war from a position of strength.

Le Duan's aim was, of course, to ensure that this did not happen. To prevent the formation of a non-Communist southern political base, it was to his advantage to try to manipulate the movement toward constitutional government so that the South Vietnamese were effectively denied their rightful share of power in Saigon. If the elections legitimatized the continued rule of the North Vietnamese Dai Viets for another four years, the southerners would not only be denied the chance to build a political base of their own but might be attracted to a covertly-led Communist southern popular-front protest movement against northern domination, widening the Communists' own political base.

If Le Duan could do this, Hanoi would be in a position to propose reasonable peace terms, asking only that the southern Viet Cong be allowed to form a legal popular-front opposition. Indeed, this would sound so reasonable that it would be difficult for any American president to refuse. All the Communists would have to do militarily in the meantime was to demonstrate that the Viet Cong were strong enough so that they could not be totally excluded from the postwar political structure of South Vietnam. Hanoi could even agree, as Tuong suggested, to American troops remaining in Vietnam, although back in their bases and camps.

If Ky and the Dai Viets legalized their domination of the south in rigged elections, with the Americans' seeming approval, I believed it would be only a question of time before South Vietnam went Communist. For this reason, I began to see the presidential election as the climax of the long charade. If the northerners won and stayed in power, it would not matter much what happened. The chance for creating a non-Communist political base would have been lost for four more years, which, in an unpopular war, might just as well have been forever.

The true South Vietnamese leaders seemed to understand this, too, and as the weeks wore on, the entire *dramatis personae* of the last five years, when stars rose and fell so quickly, filed back onstage. If Le Duan succeeded, of course, the charade would go on. Not only in Vietnam, but wherever men could be persuaded to accept artificially contrived appearance rather than seek out the truth.

The next act in the charade came in late March 1967 at the meeting between President Johnson and Ky on the American island of Guam. In Saigon, as the March 26th deadline approached, the Dai Viets were still delaying the Assembly's final vote on the new constitution. In Washington, Ambassador Bui Diem made it implicitly clear that the price of the constitution's ratification by the Assembly and the junta was either an invitation to Ky to visit the United States or, at second best, a chance to appear before the American press at a third Pacific conference.

One week before the deadline, the generals harshly rejected a series of Assembly demands. The next day Bui Diem flew back to Saigon. In Washington, Johnson announced the Guam conference. The generals withdrew their objections, the Assembly took its final vote, and within thirty-six hours the junta approved the constitution and Ky brought it to Guam in an orange folder for presentation to Johnson. At the Assembly's final session, defiant Cochinchinese and Catholic deputies carried in a white marble bust of Tran Van Van, and a young member declared, "This constitution was written in blood."

By calling the Guam conference, Johnson saved the constitution. But, according to White House aides, he also wanted to put in plain language to Ky and Thieu that they had to move on the social reforms promised in Honolulu more than a year before and make clear that the American military buildup had reached the limits of political acceptability in the United States.

A few days earlier, Ellsworth G. Bunker, the former ambassador to India who had handled the Dominican Republic crisis for Johnson (earning Walter Lippmann's accolade as "America's most accomplished diplomat"), had succeeded Henry Cabot Lodge as ambassador to Saigon. Westmoreland was to be given direct responsibility for pacification, with Robert Komer, Johnson's controversial White House "other-war" aide, as his deputy, to bring more of a political judgment to bear. Johnson gave Bunker supreme authority over both the American military and political effort in Vietnam; his mission was to build a non-Communist South Vietnamese political base in preparation for a political settlement of the war on terms that would not shatter the American position in Asia or lead to a Communist takeover in Saigon.

In a clean sweep, Philip Habib and other senior officials on Lodge's staff were reassigned to Washington. Habib was soon made Deputy Assistant Secretary of State in charge of the State Department's Vietnam Task Force. When I asked Komer how this had come about, since Habib had been the principal executor of the U.S. policy to support Ky and the ruling generals, Komer told me, "The President's probably never heard of Habib."

Lodge left Saigon defensive about his support of Ky and the North Vietnamese generals. He told me he was genuinely convinced that Ky had sought to carry out the Honolulu plan but lacked a viable administration. He described his contact with Ky as a "self-respecting relationship between two independent men." Lodge was apparently persuaded that no civil political alternative to the Dai Viets existed. A distinguished elder statesman, the Republican vice-presidential candidate on the Nixon ticket and a former ambassador to the United Nations, Lodge had twice accepted dangerous assignments in Vietnam. Yet he was never able to put his ideas into practice and left telling me, "The idea that any American ambassador could assume the powers of a colonial administrator and build a political base is absolutely nuts. The entire Vietnamese population would turn against you." (Other authorities disagreed. Dennis Duncanson, for instance, reached the conclusion in his book that "few foreign observers believe the South Vietnamese can put their house in order by their unaided efforts. . . . So far [South Vietnam] has produced relatively few political leaders and no ideas on government and still depends for ideas even more than for money . . . on foreign countries, Communist or Western. . . ." Lieutenant Colonel Le Xuan Chuyen, the defector I have previously quoted who had commanded the Viet Cong forces around Saigon, once told me, "The war will never end unless the government in Saigon gets the cooperation of all the nationalists in the south. I don't think without this the Americans can make progress. It's the kind of help that should be done frankly and in the open. With me, unless the Americans step in and help South Vietnam to form a broadly based nationalist government, I see no sign of peace at all.")

Unlike Lodge, Bunker saw that it was imperative that an authentically popular Cochinchinese civilian, such as Tran Van Huong, hold the premiership or some other key position of power. He asked Lansdale to stay on and help him. Ky's response to the changeover was to tell Jim Lucas of Scripps-Howard that an entire North Vietnamese battalion had infiltrated south to kill Bunker and other top American officials. In Guam, Ky seemed intent on upstaging President Johnson and on persuading what Americans he could that he was the only man to hold South Vietnam together.

Johnson's official greeting to Ky at Guam Airbase seemed ironic. The President said that "all those who have thoughtfully studied the modern history of Vietnam know that military power alone cannot secure the peace. . . . Any system which stands in the way of democratic processes cannot stand very long before the will of the people—even with terror and assassination."

Ky told the press he believed Hanoi had given up hope of a military victory and sought to win politically, which he defined as bringing about the "collapse of the South Vietnamese regime and a change in public opinion in the United States." He warned that an early negotiated settlement depended upon "how fast and how quick the military situation is resolved and how firm we stand to convince them there's no political trouble, *no political change* in the next few months." Ky then proceeded to grab at world headlines with what was reported as an appeal to mine Haiphong harbor, block the Ho Chi Minh trail in Laos, pursue the Viet Cong into Cambodia and lift restrictions on bombing in North Vietnam. It worked. In private, he assured Johnson, who was furious, that he had been misquoted and had "no concrete suggestions or proposals" to escalate the war.

At a second press conference, Ky and Thieu put on an Alphonse and Gaston act over who would run for president in September. Thieu declared, "We never wished any personal place in government. Prime Minister Ky has stated he will support me if I would be a candidate for the next presidency. Thank you very much, but Prime Minister Ky and I have not yet any intention of it." Ky said he would certainly support Thieu. Thieu said the "same thing" went for him if Ky ran. At the end of the press conference, Ky made what seemed to be a few extemporaneous remarks; it was to be his major speech of the presidential election campaign:

> Before I leave Guam to go back to Vietnam, I would like your help. I think I've tried to help you. Now I would like your help to carry this message to the American people. First, I would like to confirm that the presence of the thousands of American sons fighting in Vietnam is something great. What they are now doing in Vietnam is not just supporting the Johnson administration or the administration of Nguyen Ky. No, what they are doing now is not just fighting and killing. But what they are doing now is really great, really great. They are helping us to write history. They are helping us to build a new nation. They are helping us to bring social justice to millions of people who have suffered from aggression. I am sure that our sons and grandsons will remember the names of the units and the names of the sons you have sent to Vietnam. . . .
>
> We need peace more than any other people. For many years we have suffered in war. I have seen many of my friends die. Please stop blaming us. It's unfair. It's not justice. I'm not a politician. But I try to explain to you here this morning on this small island what's in my heart. Some say there are profiteers who want the war to go on. But look at me. Where do I profit? I would be much happier just being a simple citizen. You have heard much about the black market and corruption. But I am not involved in this. I profit nothing. So there is no reason why we want this war continued. . . .
> But we want freedom, and we are going to fight. I can assure you that millions of Vietnamese will support us in this fight. . . . You will remember the first time we met together in

Honolulu about a year ago. And I am sure the time when I spoke about building democracy in Vietnam by my group of so-called military junta, everyone just laughed and smiled. At that time, not too much trust was placed in what we said. So today, a year after we met in Honolulu, it is our pleasure to come here to meet with your President and tell him here the progress we have made in the last thirteen months concerning building democracy.

No one thought to ask what progress. Ky's voice had choked up toward the end; even some of the veteran White House correspondents said it was a moving speech.

Back in Vietnam, Thieu and Ky chose to promulgate the new constitution on the day the French had celebrated as April Fool's Day. Cannons boomed out a twenty-one-gun salute, Skyraiders streaked the red-and-yellow national colors across a cloudless sky, and 4,000 soldiers, civil servants and deputies listened in silence as Thieu declared from a balcony at Doc Lap Palace that his government had "exerted no pressure whatever" on the Constituent Assembly.

Forty-eight hours later, almost as if on cue, General Vo Nguyen Giap began a two-year offensive to seize the two northernmost provinces of Thua Thien and Quang Tri, and the Annamite capital of Hue. Simultaneously, Giap's North Vietnamese and Viet Cong troops struck every strong point in the northern sector. U.S. Marine positions at Gio Linh, Dong Ha and Con Thien came under heavy shelling; North Vietnamese soldiers were spotted from the air dragging heavy artillery pieces across 8,000-foot mountain passes toward Khe Sanh. Giap's troops stormed into Quang Tri City and two Vietnamese army regimental headquarters near Hue. In many of the attacks there was a pattern of internal subversion and treachery: a regimental commander was wounded by his own bodyguard, and at one headquarters rice rations mysteriously had not arrived and the defending forces were caught scattered throughout nearby villages scrounging for food. Throughout the northern sector the Communists wreaked havoc, mortaring provincial capitals, shelling Danang Airbase with new Russian rockets, attacking and wiping out pacification teams in the hamlets. Bridges were blown, road links cut, civil and military traffic mined, and terror and propaganda teams sent into the towns. I flew north at once and found Hue in a state of near panic. A North Vietnamese regiment had dug into underground fortifications in the Imperial Tombs just outside the city; you could see their campfire smoke at night, but the local authorities, most of them Dai Viets since 1966, refused to allow the U.S. marines to go in after them with preparatory artillery fire.

Until now, like most Americans in Vietnam, I had always loved to visit Hue. For years, untouched by the war, Hue had a dreamlike, hazy serenity. I'll always remember my first evening there in the summer of 1964. Just at sunset I hired a cycle-rickshaw to drive through the deserted ruined courtyards of the Forbidden City. Cushioned sampans floated along the Perfume River, its banks ablaze with iris and geraniums, as we passed over a cobblestone avenue under one towering pagoda-roofed gate after another—past silken Vietnamese girls strolling in their white gowns, past the stone chambers of the palace with its crumbling thrones and gardens choked with grass. There were cannons green with age, moats filled with lotus blossoms, stone temple dragons and ghostly vistas of orange flame trees, huge dynastic urns and white-barked eucalyptus. A university student told me, "Hue's people feel they are chosen by destiny to lead the country." To visit Hue was to understand much about the Vietnamese people. To them, Hue was not a place but a mystique. And now Le Duan wanted to destroy this monument to their proud and mythical past.

The chief concern of Lieutenant General Robert E. Cushman, Jr., the Marine commander, was how to reinforce the northern frontier without abandoning pacification efforts on the populated coastal plain. Cushman told me he thought that Giap's pressure on the marines along the DMZ was "an invasion, not a diversion, but its main objective is to draw marines from the essential task of weeding out the political infrastructure in these hamlets. That's where they're going to win or lose—in those hamlets, and this is primarily a Vietnamese battle. But, obviously, if all I did was just sit here in the rice paddies, the NVA would be at Hai Van Pass north of Danang." Since the Communists were losing men at a seven to one ratio against the marines at the DMZ, Cushman said, "Ho is not gaining anything but time by spending the blood of his country's youth. It looks to me as if Ho Chi Minh is buying time for something."

Communist agitprop teams were moving openly about Hue, telling the people the Americans were plotting a new partition of the country by advancing the frontier of North Vietnam down to the 16th parallel, putting Hue and the two northernmost provinces under Communist control. Robert Kelly, the senior American pacification adviser in Hue, told me, "The Communists are trying to create a situation here so bad—through terror, rumors and commando raids—that the population will write off the Vietnamese and American forces and frenetically look for safety through peace at any price."

The tension in Hue and the other northern towns was partly fed by Ky's government in Saigon. An unidentified government official leaked a story to Associated Press that the entire population of Quang Tri Province—nearly 300,000 people— would be evacuated. Ky subsequently corrected this and said that only 20,000 peasants south of the DMZ would be moved, but the denial failed to catch up with the original report. Back in Saigon, I found Dr. Sung and other Dai Viets spreading the lie that Johnson was secretly plotting a new partition of the country. When Sung told me at a diplomatic reception, "I understand the Americans are considering giving up Thua Thien and Quang Tri and pulling back to Danang," I snapped, "That's just what the VC are telling the people in Hue." I began to see that General Giap's 1965 offensive through the highlands, the 1966 Annam revolt and now the new military-psychological campaign were all part of the same unified Communist plan for getting control of Annam, perhaps to ensure that they at least got a slice of the country if their plans in the south failed.

The height of the panic in Hue was reached in late April. Westmoreland duly rushed reinforcements to Cushman from the south and asked Washington for substantially more troops, up to 200,000 more. Defense Secretary McNamara made his ninth lightning trip to Vietnam; in a conference room code-named "High Noon," McNamara told Westmoreland that 50,000 more troops was the best he could hope for with an American election year just ahead. This would bring American troop strength to only 525,000 by early 1968, not enough for Westmoreland's strategy to drive the Communist main forces back into Laos and Cambodia and still have the manpower needed to shift many American units and nearly half the South Vietnamese Army into pacification, where real progress could be made. Moreover, the heavy fighting on the DMZ, even at a high cost in North Vietnamese lives, would result in high American casualties and help sustain in the American public mind the illusion of a big war with no end in sight.

Ho Chi Minh was buying time with blood, Cushman had said. Time for what? Hanoi could not possibly settle the war on the battlefield. Nor, did I believe, could it try to throw the presidential election to an unpopular North Vietnamese like Ky without its being manifestly rigged and therefore made unaccept- able to world opinion.

It seemed that somebody else was capable of making this analysis. A Thieu-Ky quarrel commenced in June. Ky did not invite Thieu to an elaborate ceremony at Dien Hong Palace commemorating their government's second anniversary. More- over, Ky began flagrantly violating electoral laws prohibiting any presidential campaigning before August. Ky's men painted Saigon's walls with the slogan "The Government of Nguyen Cao Ky Is the Government of the Poor." Thieu's supporters protested to their American contacts that Ky's police chief, Loan, had ordered all the provincial police chiefs to produce 20,000 votes apiece for Ky. The Saigon press corps began speculating about a possible split in the South Vietnamese Army.

Both Thieu and Ky formally filed candidacies. Ky's running mate was a little-known Cochinchinese lawyer and ex-Viet Minh propagandist, Nguyen Van Loc; Thieu's was a politician from the regionally strong Hoa Hao sect in the Delta. In contrast to Ky, Thieu took a stand for high morals and legality. He warned over television that "failure to elect a civilian government" in a "fair and free" contest, would lead to a Communist victory. (Although the constitution prohibited military officers on active duty from contesting or holding public office, both Thieu and Ky appeared to continue to hold the rank of generals, although they began wearing unadorned uniforms. Ky, however, kept control of the air force.)

Thieu seemed plausible and convincing in a two-hour interview

I had with him at the time, and he reiterated the need for free elections. I had expected more of the gung-ho militant anti-Communism Thieu usually voiced to reporters, but instead he described what he thought Hanoi's eventual peace terms would be. They were almost identical to those outlined by Professor Tuong back in February. Ho Chi Minh would agree to pull some 60,-000 North Vietnamese troops home in return for a bombing halt and an American agreement to allow the NLF's remaining supporters to form a legal opposition. "Not as Communists or the NLF," Thieu said. "They can call it the Flower Party, the Royalist Party, the Winston or Salem Party. Then they can win through elections. First the hamlet, then the National Assembly and the government. I tell you frankly, we have already been heavily infiltrated by the Viet Cong—the government, labor unions, Saigon, perhaps less so in the army. But if this happens I believe the Communists will be everywhere." I gathered Thieu meant that with the help of a fifth column within the government, the Communists could use deception and intimidation to win votes wholly disproportionate to their actual popularity.

This conversation, like Thieu himself, puzzled me. In terms of performance, Thieu's record had been almost as damaging as Ky's to American aims in Vietnam. And yet Thieu described exactly how I now believed the Communists wanted to win. Of all the personalities in the charade, Thieu was the most enigmatic. Was he really with the Dai Viets, or like Generals Khanh and Thi, did he simply collaborate with them in hopes of using them to rise to power? He was a lone wolf. Unlike Ky, he had not surrounded himself with an entourage of military cronies and high school classmates. Thieu's American apologists called him "mature"; his critics, "crafty."

His real strength seemed to me to be that nobody could say with any certainty how he stood on anything. Some felt that Thieu was close to his brothers, both of whom were known to be members of the secret Dai Viet brotherhood. Yet during the election campaign one was ambassador to Japan and the other to Italy—removed from the center of power. Thieu's closest personal adviser was said to be a Dai Viet, a onetime Saigon banker viewed with a certain amount of distrust since his jungle imprisonment by the Communists from 1950 to 1954. (Many

Vietnamese felt that no one could be subjected to Viet Cong indoctrination for so long and escape unaffected.)

Hanoi also blasted Thieu daily as an "American puppet and former French servitor." Yet he had been a Viet Minh district chief in 1945 and 1946, a post usually given only to Communist party members. Later, switching to the French side in 1947, Thieu was commissioned a lieutenant at the age of twenty-six, studied in the United States in 1956 and 1960, was commandant of the Dalat Military Academy for four years, rose to a divisional commander under Diem, and was put in charge of the Mekong Delta by General Nguyen Khanh.

In 1958, Thieu had been converted to Catholicism by his wife, who was from a Cochinchinese landowning family in the Delta. But Vietnamese always drew a sharp distinction between converts and born Catholics, and some people believed that Thieu might have converted to Catholicism to gain Diem's favor. Had Thieu been for or against Diem in 1963? His Fifth Division sent a regiment into Saigon on the side of the rebels against Diem, but two hours too late, which many Vietnamese felt was a calculated delay. Still, Thieu carried Diem's personal bamboo cane as a macabre trophy. Because of his association with the Dai Viets, who had persecuted Catholics in Tonkin in the forties, the Roman Catholic hierarchy held Thieu suspect; and such leading Catholic priests from Tonkin as Father Tran Du and Father Hoang Quynh flatly regarded Thieu as a hard-core Dai Viet. During the campaign, however, an impression was created, whether contrived or real, that Thieu might break with Ky and the Dai Viets if he were elected. In one conversation with me, he said that he might appoint the popular Cochinchinese former premier, Tran Van Huong, as his prime minister.

Aside from Thieu and Ky, Huong was the most imposing figure in the presidential race. His candidacy had been quietly explored in early summer by both the Vatican and Ambassador Bunker, who wanted a popular and respected Cochinchinese and non-Catholic to contest. Gradually, Huong became the rallying point of a loose coalition formed by the Cochinchinese educated middle class, organized labor and the Roman Catholic Church. In mid-June, I visited Huong at his Villa Santa Maria in the seaside resort of Cap St. Jacques, where he had been living in forcible retirement under an armed guard since his government fell in early 1965. I found him sitting in an undershirt and eating noodle soup in his small, bare dining room. His wife had died, and he himself had visibly aged in three years; he breathed asthmatically, although he claimed he was in good health. But he seemed as mentally keen and as kindly and soft-spoken as ever. I remembered Sir Robert saying, "We depend very much on the character and integrity of Huong, the one bright spot in the picture."

I asked Huong why he was going back to Saigon politics after barely escaping with his life in 1965. He smiled. "Since they have asked me, as a citizen I must do my duty. I am an old man. I would like to spend the rest of my days writing poetry and—as Candide said—cultivating my garden. But, as you know, things are going very badly. The people do not seem to have faith in anything any more—in law and order, the old Confucian morality, in the government, in the future, in themselves. It is necessary to end the war. But this cannot be done until there is a government in Saigon the people like and will respect." Huong said he feared that President Johnson's policy to try to erect a broad-based democracy in Vietnam had been a grave error, especially through village and hamlet elections, where he felt the Communist underground had determined most of the winners and tightened its grip on the peasantry. At the end of the interview, Huong walked with me to the gate. As we shook hands he said, "Thank you for coming such a long way to listen to an old man with old-fashioned ideas."

Huong had some difficulty reaching Saigon to campaign. His supporters were afraid he would be ambushed on the road by Viet Cong, and the Ky regime offered no air transport. I told Bunker about this and I believe he came to Huong's assistance. Huong's son told me that in the meantime, Ky sent one of his aides, a man named Can, to threaten Huong with physical violence if he did not withdraw.

Another prominent Cochinchinese in the presidential race was Phan Khac Suu, the elderly ex-president and chairman of the Constituent Assembly, who had dismayed and mystified many Saigonese by announcing he would run against Huong, his old friend and ally. Much of the mystery was cleared up when Ky's

Military Security Service, which had a Gestapo-like reputation, filed smuggling charges against Suu's wife before the Saigon Military Tribunal. These were never pressed. Dr. Phan Quang Dan was Suu's running mate. Since Dr. Dan's car had been blown to pieces by a terrorist bomb the previous December, killing two pedestrians, I believed he was once more subject to Dai Viet manipulation, if indeed he had ever escaped it.

When I went to see Suu in his office in the opera house, he was almost apologetic about running. He was extremely myopic and suffered badly from arthritis, but his face, framed by snowy white hair, still had a pink, cherubic look. Despite his decision to run against Huong, he felt it was imperative to have a Cochinchinese civilian president. "Our greatest need," he said, "is to solve the political problem in South Vietnam and have a predominantly southern government, so that the NLF lacks enough popular support around Saigon and the Delta to keep the war going. An elected southern government fully representative of the South Vietnamese people could end the war quickly and honorably." I believed this was Suu's true position, but I did not hear him express it publicly during the campaign, where Dr. Dan did almost all the talking for him.

Aside from the Suu-Dan ticket, Ky appeared to be behind one other important spoiler-candidate to split the civilian vote: Truong Dinh Dzu, a slick Saigon lawyer with a disreputable background who faced embezzlement charges. Some said Dzu had entered the presidential race to escape arrest, but I suspected it was the other way around, that he had been blackmailed, like Suu, into running. Dzu's Saigon campaign headquarters, where I first interviewed him, turned out to be a rundown suburban mansion used as a shrine for the murdered leader of the feudal Cao Dai sect. The rooms were dark and shuttered, but I saw figures moving around the shadowy antechambers. When I asked Dzu about them, he said they were the dead general's colonels and majors. Since he also told me that the general had been dead for a decade, this seemed strange indeed. In such a setting and even in Saigon itself, Dzu was an incongruous figure. A pudgy little man, he always wore a Rotary Club tie and had two children going to college in California. His glib style seemed somehow out of place in Saigon's medieval atmosphere. One could imagine him winning an American local election, but not a Vietnamese one.

That day, as we sat under a gloomy portrait of the Cao Dai hero, Dzu told me cheerily, "I am the only man who can solve all our problems, the Buddhist-Catholic problem, the north-south problem, war and peace. One day it will be me who leads this country." Dzu argued that although he was a native of Annam, he had studied in Hanoi for six years and lived in Saigon for twenty-three, which would make him regionally acceptable to everyone. "Thieu and Ky can never negotiate a peace settlement," he scoffed. "If the Communists go to the conference table, they have to give their political cadres convincing explanations. They have always taken the line the Thieu-Ky regime is a puppet of the Americans. Nobody can talk peace with Thieu or Ky, since the Communists would be caught in their own internal contradiction. But, anyway, Thieu and Ky will destroy themselves with infighting. You will see. Just wait. Nineteen sixty-eight will be the year of Dzu." The next time I passed the Saigon marketplace I asked one of the old soothsayers there what 1968 was on the Lunar Calendar. "The Year of the Monkey," he said. "Playful, clever, joyful and full of hope." Oddly enough, a few days later, Ky contemptuously threatened to put Dzu in a cage on the palace lawn.

I began to wonder if Dzu had another role to play besides that of splitting the civilian vote in what was beginning to look like a stop-Huong movement by Ky and the Dai Viets. The evidence suggested that Ky was really behind Dzu, and yet in speeches and press interviews the fast-talking lawyer was beginning to emerge as the most outspoken critic of the ruling generals and as an advocate of peace at any price.

The northerners themselves provided some valuable clues. Tran Van Tuyen, the Tonkinese lawyer who had accompanied Dr. Sung to Paris in 1965 as a vice-premier in the Quat government, had just returned from another visit to France and Geneva with Foreign Minister Do. Tuyen told me he had met some North Vietnamese diplomats in Paris. "Both Vietnams are preparing for peace," he said. "There's something in the air, but first it will be necessary to create the right atmosphere. It is impossible to deny the National Liberation Front all right to existence and legality. Viet Cong who are not hard-core Communists will have to be allowed to form some sort of popular front. It is a danger, but we must accept this danger if we pretend to be a democracy." (Tuyen, in 1968, would be the first prominent figure to endorse a coalition government with the Communists.)

Dr. Dan sounded much the same theme over a cup of tea at his clinic. "I tell you," he said, "the end of the war can come very soon. We are not for continuing the war at all cost. We are going to open all doors and windows to negotiations but also push vigorously on the military front."

"Do you think a compromise settlement with the Communists is possible?" I asked.

"Why not? Later on, the NLF should be given a chance to organize legally when the government is strong enough."

I next interviewed Dr. Sung, who spelled out the northerners' peace theme most clearly. "I have a hunch Hanoi might be ready to negotiate in the fall of the year," he said, with seeming casualness. "When they are ready, they can change overnight. In the meantime it is best to have *no major political change;* stability in Saigon will be important at a time like that. I think it is best to keep the military in power. Hanoi cannot last very long under the heavy American bombing. I don't think the Viet Cong could stand alone if Hanoi pulled out of the fight. But if the war ends and all Americans go home it would be a catastrophe. *Some American troops must remain to garrison the enclaves on a permanent basis. I know of no instance where Communists could take over without force.*"

As I left Dr. Sung that day, putting his words together with those of Professor Tuong, Thieu, Tuyen, Dr. Dan and the others, I at last understood Le Duan's strategy for winning the war. I also realized that there would be only one military candidate and that would be Thieu. Ky would withdraw but remain in a position of power and rivalry with Thieu.

It happened at noon the day of the midnight filing deadline for presidential tickets. Rumors swept Saigon that morning of a Thieu-Ky showdown. At noon I met Deputy Ambassador Komer and asked him flatly just what was United States policy in the election. Komer replied, "The army's got effective power and the only political base. While the civilians like Huong are charming old men to sit around with talking politics in a drawing room, I can't see any of them running the country. The President wants negotiations. Everybody wants negotiations. Ky is willing to go along. But Thieu is fanatically opposed to negotiations in any form. We want a single military candidate to avoid a split in the Vietnamese Army. So it looks like Ky." I told Komer, who was an old friend of mine, that if the North Vietnamese generals used the elections simply to legitimatize their rule, it would destroy what little political base Johnson had left in Vietnam. Tran Van Van was dead, but many other knowledgeable Vietnamese now suspected that some of the Dai Viets were working for Le Duan. I told Komer what I now believed: that Le Duan wanted to keep Thieu and Ky in power and then get a settlement recognizing the NLF as a legal opposition so that the Communists could take over gradually right under the noses of American troops sitting by helpless in the enclaves. I told him I was convinced Ky, Dr. Sung, Loan, Thang and the rest were working for Hanoi. Komer listened attentively. He finally replied, "That's not what we're getting from the CIA." But, he went on, he was so tied up with the mechanics of pacification, that he didn't have time to properly follow internal Vietnamese politics. Komer did have doubts, though. As I walked down the hall, he came running after me and asked me to meet an American two-star general serving as General Thang's military adviser. Komer asked me to repeat what I had said about the Dai Viets and I did. The general was astonished. He said with some indignation that Thang was "a very able, patriotic young man."

By midafternoon, when Barry Zorthian, the official Embassy spokesman, was still telling American newsmen that Thieu was expected to withdraw from the race, a cigarette vendor in front of the Continental told me Ky had stepped down to become Thieu's vice-presidential running mate. Ky's press secretary told reporters an hour later the generals had decided something had to be done to "consolidate the army's ranks" and that had led to Ky's decision. Ky himself declared in public that "all Vietnamese must make sacrifices in order to achieve unity and maintain the prestige of the armed forces. We can sacrifice our very life . . . or anything, including the renunciation of titles." The

American Embassy did not conceal its surprise, although it was pointed out that Bunker had warned the generals at a luncheon at his house earlier in the week that any rivalry between Thieu and Ky leading to a split in the army would have very serious consequences in terms of American domestic support for the war effort. Bunker's warning was seized on by the press to explain Ky's withdrawal.

There was one more brief stir of excitement that day when the wife of Lieutenant General Duong Van ("Big") Minh filed her husband's candidacy before a cheering Constituent Assembly, which was to supervise the election. Minh was promptly forbidden to return by Thieu and Ky on grounds of "national security." Au Truong Thanh, Ky's onetime economics minister, also announced plans to enter the race on a "Stop the Bombing" and "Call an Immediate Ceasefire" platform, but he was barred from running by the Assembly for having held "pro-Communist sympathies." While interest in Minh and Thanh soon faded, their disqualification helped to discredit the election abroad.

Tran Van Van's widow had also filed that day as a candidate in the election for the new Senate, entering her dead husband's name, not her own. (The Senate election was to be held the same day as the presidential election; the lower house would be elected six weeks later.) I knew I would have to see her, but I did not want to go back to that house again. When I finally did, the street in the old quarter of Dakow was empty, but I felt as if eyes were following me to the gate. Nothing had changed. There was the same smell of incense, the same dim yellow light, the same room with all its Chinese antiquities, and Madame Van was sitting on the same sofa where Van had sat. She smiled politely, but her face was haggard and she wore mourning white. Beside her sat a pretty girl with upswept hair and an expensive white linen frock. The girl said she had just arrived from France to interpret for her mother during the campaign. She seemed to me a very sheltered debutante; I felt Madame Van should not have brought her back to Saigon. "My mother is running for the Senate to carry on the beliefs my father fought and died for," the girl said in stilted, convent English. "She says until my father's death she did not share his interest in politics. But because he continued to struggle for what he believed, even after threats of death and her own pleading, she feels she must try to fill his place." The girl smiled and folded her hands in her lap, waiting for me to speak. The two of them looked pathetic, sitting there side by side.

"Ask her who killed your father."

As she started to translate, I explained that I had seen Madame Van accuse Ky on television in Washington. Madame Van nodded that she understood. She had her daughter explain that while she had named Ky, since his name would be familiar to Americans, she actually blamed Ky, Loan, Dr. Sung, Bui Diem, Ky's foster father, Le Van Thai, and all the senior Dai Viets. "It was all of them acting together," the daughter said.

I cabled my newspaper, "Madame Van charges Ky's powerful northern political advisers with collective guilt for her husband's murder." Some days later, Le Van Thai, whom I had never met before, called me to his house. At the end of a conversation on the election, he told me he had heard rumors that I might be arrested by Loan's Military Security Service. Since Thai was a man who started rumors, not a man who "heard" them, I reported the threat to the American Embassy. I was told, should anything develop, to try to reach, or telephone, the nearest American installation. My friends in the press corps advised doing nothing precipitous and, above all, to avoid any outward show of fear, so I flew north and spent some days with the U.S. marines. In Vietnam, it sometimes felt safer covering the war.

Fifteen

A Choice Denied

*Democracy is not elections and voting; it is the liberty of the
individual and his protection by law, not just against the Viet
Cong but against all the local factional secret society cliques,
so that he can make a free choice.*

—Sir Robert Thompson, April 1968

Dr. Dan captured American headlines on the opening day
of the formal campaign, August 3rd, with a catchy phrase; he
appealed for early peace talks, "a shouting war and not a
shooting war." Ky, who invited a large number of American
newsmen to tour the countryside with him, said he thought the
Communists were demoralized. "I don't think they can sustain the
war very long."

To me, this was simply more of the charade. But reality, when
it came, was unmistakable and magnificent. That morning in the
ballroom of the Continental, the educated southern middle class,
South Vietnam's disinherited political leadership, gathered to
hear Tran Van Huong's first public speech since his government
had been overthrown and he had fled to the British ambassador's
residence almost three years before. In the stately old ballroom,
with its sodden palm court and air of musty elegance, I
recognized the faces of Roman Catholic leaders and orthodox

southern Buddhists, members of the Cochinchinese landed gentry, many professional men, lawyers, doctors, professors from the university.

Beside Huong stood the elderly leader of South Vietnamese Buddhist orthodoxy, Dr. Mai Tho Truyen, who was Huong's vice-presidential running mate. Truyen, a distinguished Buddhist scholar and retired civil administrator, owned Saigon's big Xa Loi Pagoda and spoke for Vietnamese Buddhist orthodoxy. Dr. Truyen had banned Tri Quang from his pagoda in 1964. Just behind them, to Huong's right, stood Madame Tran Van Van, her face pale and tense, wearing the white silk gown of mourning. By now, the Tran Van Van posters, bearing a flaming-torch emblem, had appeared on shops and walls all over Saigon. (Thieu and Ky's were defaced almost as soon as they were posted, and fresh ones had to be pasted up each day.) At a table to Huong's left sat Ton That Thien, the editor of the *Vietnamese Guardian,* the independent English-language newspaper in Saigon until Loan's police closed it after Van's assassination the year before. The room was full of purged military officers, civil servants and former ministers, all prominent anti-Communist figures.

Huong, with his close-cropped grey hair and kindly peasant face, rose and faced the crowd. He nodded with a smile toward the press, saying he was "glad and moved, after three years of absence and silence, to resume the dialogue" with them. He said he regretted that South Vietnam's movement toward democratic government had been delayed since 1965, but that now the country was moving toward a new stage on this path. "But before entering it," he went on, "we should look back on the road traveled and remember all those, known and unknown, who have accepted sacrifices, including the sacrifice of their lives, to struggle for democracy in this country." Madame Van bent her head, her mouth trembling.

"Drawing from our experience of the past years to assess the situation today, what do we see?"

Huong put his glasses on and began reading from a prepared text. As in my talk with him at Cap St. Jacques, he stressed that South Vietnam was in a state of crisis, not only economic but moral:

> The signs of depravation are more obvious each day and constitute a bleak vision for future generations. . . . Disci-

pline and moral and spiritual values are shaken to their foundations by grave and blatant evils . . . factionalism, division and deep conflict within the various groups have weakened the nation. . . .

Encompassing these crises, there is the war, whose intensity and whose destructive effects have grown to frightful proportions, bringing upheaval, dispersion, death and mourning to nearly every Vietnamese family. In all our history, the Vietnamese people have never been faced with such a deep and total crisis.

But these are only symptoms of a still more terrible crisis, the crisis of confidence: the people have been deceived too much, day after day they had to hear fine words which are nothing but lies, noisy statements which had neither meaning nor consistency. For this reason the general attitude is one of mistrust of everything: mistrust of the spiritual legacy of our ancestors, mistrust of the effectiveness and sincerity of their elders, and especially mistrust of the government.

Once the people have lost confidence, the government has no more authority and must count on force. If the government must count on force because it has lost authority, then the state will have lost the moral foundations of self-defense, development and self-determination; such is the basic psychological fact concerning Vietnam today. Only Communism can move into such a moral vacuum.

Huong was using the words of modern politics, but he was appealing to the most important aspect of a Vietnamese citizen's attitude toward his government. Thieu and Ky had lost the "mandate of heaven." Confucian teachings maintained that if the sovereign oppressed the people, he no longer deserved to be treated as the sovereign. Huong, then and in his later speeches, seemed close to paraphrasing the Confucianist scripture: "Advance the upright and set aside the crooked, then the people will submit . . . when one by force subdues men, they do not submit to him in heart; but when one subdues men by virtue, then in the heart's core they are pleased, and sincerely submit." It was the fundamental principle of Confucianism; Huong was making a moving and dignified appeal for a restoration of traditional Vietnamese values as the only way left to save the country.

My friends, this confidence is the internal strength we must possess. It is the essential condition for the solution of the problems of our country, for disentangling the chaotic political situation. To restore confidence, the leaders of government must clearly possess dignity and virtue; *their past must bear witness to their integrity;* they must have a clear, rational and realistic policy and they must have the courage and determination to implement it.

General Thieu's platform consisted of nine words: "To build democracy, solve the war and reorganize society." Huong's ran to several thousand words and was the most impressive document on social reform I had seen in Vietnam. On peace, it said that no treaty or international guarantee could be as secure as "the strength and vigilance of the people when they live in a healthy social order established by themselves and worthy of their sacrifices to protect and develop it." There was a strong section on rule of law to protect individual liberty. An economic section centered on labor legislation and changes in the tax system. Huong promised to give land to the tiller and "absolute priority to agricultural development, to give a strong impulse to land banks, cooperatives, land development, rural electrification, mechanization and diversification of agriculture." A comprehensive program of changes in the educational system was included. The document was more detailed and all-embracing than anything produced by American drafters at either the Honolulu or Manila conferences.

The platform concluded:

> We have deliberately avoided using the word "revolution" because it has been so much abused in recent years. . . . We have only assessed the concrete demands of the population and have endeavored to find solutions which can meet them rationally. . . . If we can meet that challenge successfully, we shall become a dragnet attracting all Vietnam, north and south, and the country will be united according to the popular wish.

Huong told his audience that he considered his platform to be "a contract concluded by us with the nation if we are elected." Thien, the editor standing next to me, muttered, "It has come just about five years too late. Huong doesn't have a chance in hell of winning against Thieu and Ky." Although he was Tonkinese, Thien later wept the night election returns came in.

Reporters asked if Huong would accept the premiership under Thieu.

"Yes, if I felt I could serve the people with the policies in my platform. I would never accept if I would play the role of a puppet."

Huong was a tough-minded man with immense warmth and kindness, but now he was too clearly aware of what was going on; he seemed to carry a private burden of near resignation and hopelessness. It was not surprising that Huong at once got on well with Bunker; both were good and wise old men who had arrived perhaps too late. Huong's concern transcended the long charade; he sought to alert an entire society to the danger facing its moral and social foundations, which were being systematically destroyed by an enemy perhaps best described by the French journalist Lucien Bodard in his book *L'Enlisement:*

> Guerrilla warfare is not merely one aspect of the art of fighting. It is in the first place a pitiless logic—the logic of the utter want of compassion. It is the mathematics of "persuasion," into which there enter precisely weighed doses of brainwashing and atrocity. It is a matter of arriving at "correct solutions" by means of dialectic reasoning, solutions that will allow one to dominate human beings completely and turn them into perfect tools for the cause. It requires a total dehumanization; all civilized society's feelings vanish; individuals no longer exist. The goal is the creation of the People, the politically worked-over mass that acts as the supporting basis for the guerrilla, the mass that is to be urged and drawn to a higher fate and that is to be sacrificed to that fate.

Huong knew he had almost no chance of winning the election, but the campaign gave him a platform to try to reawaken civilized Vietnam's feelings and warn the world why the war was being lost.

With Huong's words fresh in my mind, I flew to Vung Tau that evening. Ky was to attend a graduation ceremony of the "Revolutionary Development Cadre." Six thousand black-clad young peasants with flaming torches were massed in formation on a large open plain; in the distance a gigantic urn spouted orange flames, artillery rumbled, and fireworks exploded against the sky. A group of American officials from the CIA, which financed the training center, sat stiffly in the front row, incongruously dressed in neat dark business suits. I also recognized Lansdale. Ky marched onto the field, flanked by most of the ranking generals and his usual entourage of bodyguards. As Ky stood on a raised dais, the shadows of the flames flickering on his face, thousands of youths marched past with clenched fists and rigidly swinging arms, their voices raised in martial songs. One of them spoke on behalf of the graduating class, vowing that they would "accept the long-term struggle to bring a new life to the peasantry." The youth stood at attention as he spoke, uttering his words in sharp, shrill phrases: "Along with the military, political and specialized training, we were taught to have a strong will, to like community life. Every night, we spent two hours in criticism and self-criticism at cell, squad, group, inter-group and battalion levels, in order to improve our work and ourselves. . . . These emulation campaigns brought our community an inspiring atmosphere, developing our sense of responsibility and strengthening our fighting spirit." Watching this human sea, with its upraised torches and martial young voice, I caught a glimpse down that vista of Le Duan's fanaticized, homogenized mass.

A countrywide barnstorming campaign by all the candidates from the eleven presidential tickets finally approved by the Assembly was to be kicked off August 5th, followed by a whistle-stop tour of twenty-one other cities and towns. But Thieu and Ky did not show up, the candidates had trouble finding their promised two C-47s at Tan Son Nhut Airbase and, after a turbulent flight during which many of the elderly candidates became airsick, they finally landed at Dong Ha, the heavily shelled U.S. Marine airstrip just south of the DMZ. After waiting in vain for forty-five minutes under the wings of the planes in 98-degree heat and a near duststorm, they flew off again to Danang. When nobody met them there, either (an aide said the local military commander was having his siesta and could not be disturbed, and the mayor could not be found), the candidates returned to Saigon. On arrival at Tan Son Nhut Airbase, Dzu told a waiting group of reporters, "The government sabotaged our trip!"

Ky later cracked to newsmen, "What do they want? Mercedes and Cadillacs?" Thieu called it "a technical error over the airstrip and time of arrival of the plane . . . a very rare incident, a minor incident." For the next twelve days, the election campaign was called off. By demanding that the government apologize and promise to provide adequate security and transport before they would agree to campaign again, Dzu, Dr. Dan and some of the others managed to delay the whole campaign tour; as a result the number of towns to be visited was eventually cut to nine.

In Washington, as Congress demanded some explanation, Assistant Secretary of State William Bundy publicly endorsed the Ky regime's official explanation that the planes had originally been expected to land at Quang Tri City, where the rally was to be held, but had to proceed to Dong Ha, nine miles north and a twenty-minute drive away, because of heavy crosswinds. President Johnson cautioned Americans not to impose "impossible standards" on a "nation, racked by a war of insurgency and beset by its neighbors in the north."

The facts, however, indicated that the Ky regime had deliberately created the incident to disrupt the campaign. Much of the Saigon press corps had flown up to Quang Tri in lighter aircraft, which, unlike the candidates' C-47s, could land at the city's small dirt strip. We were driven to the province chief's villa for cold drinks; there he told us he did not know where or when the candidates were arriving. Fortunately, I met a young American officer, Lieutenant Gary Loveridge of San Francisco, who had been assigned to handle press arrangements. He said he and the province chief had been told a week before that the candidates and press party would arrive at Dong Ha. Accordingly, he had asked the marines to have two trucks and an escort party standing by. That day he made the drive to Dong Ha twice, and the second time found the candidates waiting at its airstrip. Loveridge offered them the press trucks, which were noisily rejected by Dzu and some others. He then telephoned the province chief. When Loveridge went back and told the candidates the welcoming party was on the way, the Vietnamese air force pilots of the two planes insisted on taking off for Danang at once. Loveridge said the welcoming party arrived at Dong Ha just after the candidates' planes were airborne.

The press, which spent the day milling around Quang Tri, discovered that the province chief first called the city's population to the rally at eight o'clock in the morning and then did not inform them that the candidates were not coming until three o'clock that afternoon. All day long, an old town crier with a megaphone made from American beer cans had been going through Quang Tri calling, "Hello, hello. I would like to invite all the people to come to hear the candidates for the presidency. There is no reason you should stay at home." Announcement of the rally's cancellation brought the expected reaction. One woman told me indignantly, "As a voter I have been waiting more than five hours. If they don't arrive, it will mean they broke their promise with the voters in Quang Tri and then how can we believe what they say?" A thirteen-year-old boy, whose father, a military doctor, had been killed in action, said he had memorized the names of all eleven presidential candidates and their running mates. He said that he had heard adults talking about how the current government only bluffed the people and exploited them. "This time they say we can choose to get sincere and good people." I asked him what an election was. "It's to choose a good man to run the country," he said. Many of those in the crowd had walked in from outlying villages, some ten and fifteen miles away. They had been cruelly deceived.

Washington's attempt to paper over the Dong Ha incident, even though most politically conscious Vietnamese realized that Thieu or Ky had staged it, put the United States in the posture of seeming to condone a rigged campaign; Johnson's twenty-two member observer team of prominent Americans later fell into this same error. Everyone in Saigon by now expected the generals to win but was critical of Washington for not insisting that Thieu and Ky observe the decencies and not subject the civilian candidates to this kind of humiliation. Yet it kept up. Ky and the Dai Viets began defaming Huong with vulgar obscenities in their conversations with Americans. President Johnson continued to make the mistake of defending the farce; he said the election was not "without blemishes," but that it represented a serious effort to conduct an "election in a nation under fire." But Johnson also warned that he took the "solemn pledge" by Thieu and Ky for fair elections "most seriously."

On August 15th, Huong called a second press conference in the Continental ballroom and threatened to withdraw from the race. He criticized Thieu and Ky for their "lack of sincerity and good will" as evidenced by the Dong Ha incident; he then revealed that his supporters in the Mekong Delta, most of them schoolteachers and students, were increasingly the "victims of heavy pressures and intimidation." Huong was visibly angry:

> They are all young, they still have a long future ahead of them, and they live in the countryside. They realize that to speak up means to risk danger. But they consider that it is their duty to speak up, because they are deeply attached to the establishment of a genuine democracy in this country. . . . We conclude that when the people in power continue to apply intimidation, and put pressure throughout the country on the electors and on the campaigners for civilian tickets, then our contribution to the establishment of democracy becomes ineffective and there is not the slightest hope of a direct dialogue between the people and future government. . . . I fear, if this is not brought to an end very soon . . . many unexpected reactions may take place, and the people will not know where to look for a democratic government which is honest and strong, capable of pulling this country out of its sufferings and hardships. . . . As far as my ticket is concerned, if this warning does not lead to any concrete action, we shall be compelled to reconsider our participation in the election.

Huong got a roaring ovation from the packed ballroom. Then one young speaker after another got up to tell of being beaten up by Ky's thugs and threatened with reprisals by the police unless they voted for Thieu and Ky; many army troops, they said, were being issued two and three voting cards to help elect Ky and Thieu. Almost all the speakers were young teachers or students; the entire educational community in the Mekong Delta was out campaigning for Huong. During the question period, Huong declared, "I want to state formally now that after what has happened, I should absolutely refuse to accept the premiership if offered it by General Thieu. I would rather go back to Vinh Long and read books."

On August 17th, two weeks late and only eighteen days before the actual polling, the campaign finally got under way with the abbreviated nine-town tour of the countryside. Ky attended only one rally; oddly, he chose Hue, where he was drowned out by chants of "Lanh Dao Cowboy [Down with the Cowboy]!" When

Ky declared, "The government must, of course, fight inflation, but we still have not had time," he drew a storm of jeers and shouts of "No, no, stop!" Thieu's two appearances were more decorous. But even he, as he stood in the drizzling rain in his wife's native town of My Tho in the Delta, was heckled by soldiers in the crowd. One cried out, "Stop talking and let us ask questions!" A private shouted, "You talk a lot about democracy and justice. But I am a private who has spent five years in the army and we still have injustices. You say you increase our wages and we still cannot cope with rising food prices. *You are turning the soldiers into thieves!*" The crowd roared with laughter and applause. One felt the Vietnamese had marvelous political potential for a genuine election.

After that, the future president's only other appearance on a platform with his civilian rivals was at a military training center for draftees near Saigon; officers kept strict order and discipline. Neither Thieu nor Ky dared face the people whose aspirations they claimed to represent. In the highland town of Ban Me Thuot, 5,000 Vietnamese soldiers and Montagnard tribals hissed and jeered when it was announced that Thieu and Ky were too busy with "pressing military commitments" to appear with the other candidates. Even Nguyen Van Loc, Ky's short-lived running mate, drew boos and derisive laughter at two rallies where he attempted to speak on behalf of the military ticket. Loc was a pallid, round-faced Cochinchinese who wore rimless glasses and chain-smoked nervously; he was virtually unknown except as an ex-Viet Minh propagandist who had written novels with such titles as *Rebellion* and *Social Classes*. His prepared speeches plugged direct Saigon-Hanoi negotiations: "We Vietnamese have the same blood, the same language, the same history and the same ancestors. Why must we kill each other?"

Truong Dinh Dzu and Dr. Dan provided comic relief in the campaign with their rapid, often funny speeches and denunciations of Ky and Thieu, coupled with demands for instant peace. Dzu's main role was to stand in front of American television cameras and proclaim with florid gestures, "I will soon unveil specific charges of fraud against Thieu and Ky. I shall take every opportunity to denounce before national and international opinion the maneuvers of Thieu and Ky to get votes." At a series of press conferences in the Continental ballroom, where liquor flowed lavishly, Dzu claimed that he was in contact with both Hanoi and the Viet Cong and could achieve immediate peace if he were elected. Dr. Dan was more moderate. He attacked the generals and hit the peace issue hard but also criticized the United States: "American aid is not going to the people. Instead, we are importing lots of luxury goods—Hondas and Suzuki motor scooters, TV sets and transistor radios—while garbage piles up in Saigon's streets and our children become bar girls and shoeshine boys."

The role of Dzu and Dr. Dan in the election, I believed, was to dramatize the unpopularity of the generals and the desire for peace, and to upstage and take away votes from Huong, the rightful winner. Le Duan wanted the generals to win but look unpopular, and to create an impression that the Vietnamese wanted peace, even at the Communist price. Huong wanted peace, but with terms a non-Communist South Vietnam could hope to survive under. And he wanted to defeat the generals, not merely tarnish their image. Both Dzu and Dan were Annamites; neither had any real popular following among the Cochinchinese masses. If either man had really wanted to defeat Thieu and Ky, they would have stayed out of the race and supported Huong.

There was only one "hawk" candidate, Dr. Pham Huy Co, a former Parisian exile who was roundly booed every time he declared, "I advocate we invade the north. The South Vietnamese flag should fly over Hanoi, and South Vietnamese generals, not foreigners, should lead the invasion." There were rumors the CIA had put Co up to it. At one rally a soldier shouted back at Co, "Do you want to wipe out the entire Vietnamese race?"

But the crowd usually grew silent when Huong would say, "After twenty-five years of war, thousands of homes destroyed, thousands dead, rice lands uncultivated and the roar of cannon shells even as we stand here, we want peace. But what kind of peace? Nobody wants war. But before talking we must create conditions to become politically strong enough to have peace talks. Military victories are not enough." As Dr. Sung cynically put it in conversation with me, "Huong's all right; he supplies the moral quotient to the campaign."

Huong took a progressively harder line on peace talks as Election Day approached. In his last press conference at the Continental, he said, "This is not the moment to sit down and discuss peace." He categorically rejected talking with the NLF, saying, "Although many members are true nationalists, they are under strict control of the Communists and North Vietnamese."

An army colonel speaking to soldiers at a highlands rally declared his support of Huong: "Thieu and Ky cannot bring peace because they do not represent a majority of the people in this country and are not qualified to speak on their behalf with the Communists." He received a standing ovation.

Eight days before the election, Thieu announced for the first time that he was willing to talk to representatives of the NLF, offering them safe passage to and from Saigon if they wished to confer with him on a possible settlement. Two days before the election, Radio Hanoi broadcast the first new political program of the NLF since it was formed in 1960. The Front's new program, according to Hanoi, promised to hold "free general elections" and made pledges of land to the tiller, expansion of trade and aid with all countries and even to "give state encouragement to capitalists in industry and trade." Many felt it was primarily directed to the embittered southern middle class. Election Day was also preceded by an intense eleventh-hour Communist terrorism campaign in which more than 2,000 persons were killed, wounded or abducted. This inevitably invoked the image, in American eyes, of a contest between ballots and bullets. It also tended to discourage speculation that the Communists might try to infiltrate and control the elections.

Just before the election, Huong's supporters gathered one last time in the ballroom of the Continental Palace. A monsoon storm drenched the palm garden as white-jacketed waiters scurried around with cocktail trays. In the crowd of Cochinchinese, I saw Huong and Madame Van. It was a solemn and private Vietnamese scene and I did not stay long. As I came out and crossed the Continental terrace, I found one of Ky's journalists slumped over a table, getting drunk. He gestured scornfully toward the ballroom, "Look at them. They'll all get their heads cut off when the VC take over."

At dusk on election eve in the heart of Saigon, the last colors of

the sunset were as green and golden as Delta rice fields, as red as
the blood of fallen dead. Little black figures were silhouetted
against the rooftops; the windows of the old French opera house,
the Caravelle and Continental balconies, the Rex officers' billet,
the Eden Cinema building, all around the central square, were
packed with people. The great mass in the square itself had
already surged past the police cordons and wooden barriers and
up to the speaker's platform when Tran Van Huong rose to make
the last speech of his presidential campaign. Beggar children and
street boys climbed trees and statuary for a better look.
Prominent Americans sent by President Johnson to observe the
election leaned over the railing of the rooftop Rex officers' club,
glasses in their hands. A lone figure, his arms resting on a balcony
of a building above the speaker's platform, waved to someone in
the crowd. The gesture was familiar; it was Dr. Sung.

For a moment Huong stood there motionless. He was wearing
a grey suit and stood very straight. Over the entire square silence
fell, and Huong began to speak: "Soldiers, do not sacrifice your
lives for a few ambitious generals . . ." His voice was amplified
on loudspeakers installed throughout the square, and his words
echoed and re-echoed off the tall buildings. "You must choose
worthy leaders who can save the country and restore peace to our
people. This is not a contest between soldiers and civilians but
between only worthy and unworthy Vietnamese. If the election is
honest, there is no doubt those elected will be worthy men and
we will be given a chance to bring peace. If this does not
happen . . ."

The echo came back, *not happen . . . not happen . . . this
terrible crisis will go on . . . go on . . . go on . . . and lead to
the total disintegration of our society . . .*

All at once hecklers seemed to be shouting and pushing
everywhere in the crowd. Policemen started swinging their sticks
and I could not hear Huong. I tried to push forward, but others
were crowding to get out and the way was impassable. One of
the hecklers was shouting at Huong like a maniac, but his voice
was lost in the general din. The heat of the pushing, tightly
packed bodies was suffocating, distorting sight and sound. Dr.
Sung was still standing alone on the balcony, but now his arms
were outstretched against the railing. Some of the Americans on

the roof of the officers' club had turned away. I could see Huong's lips still moving, but he was engulfed now in the surging mass of people as the crowd in the square went out of control. It seemed for a moment that we stood on the edge of a whirlpool, and that if Huong were swept in, the whole mass of us—newsmen, soldiers and police, the Vietnamese and the Americans, if not South Vietnam itself and even the United States—would be swirled into the vortex after him . . .

General Nguyen Van Thieu was elected president of South Vietnam for a four-year term, along with his vice president, Ky. In what the world press generally referred to as a major surprise, Dzu, with his campaign for immediate peace and bitter denunciations of Thieu and Ky, came in second. More than 83% of the registered voters in the country cast ballots. The final results could not have better suited Hanoi. Thieu with only 1,649,561 votes, or less than 35% of the total cast, looked like a pretty unpopular winner, but the military junta that had ruled the country since early 1965 stayed in power. Dzu's 817,120, or 17.2%, appeared to be a strong peace and protest vote. According to the returns, Suu got 513,374 votes, or 10.8%, and Huong polled 474,100 votes, or 10% of the total presidential vote of 4,735,404.

Few of us could believe the results. On election eve I had visited Huong's native village in the Delta; the old Confucian schoolmaster was revered there and was expected to win by a landslide. Yet the results gave Thieu 1,288 votes, Dzu 940 and Huong 594. I could find no one in this village, before or after the election, who had ever heard of Dzu. Moreover, Dzu had never been in national politics before. He was known only in Saigon and there as a shady lawyer who was briefly imprisoned by Diem for passing a bad check. Some Saigonese called his showing "a national disgrace." Dzu visited only seven cities during the abbreviated eighteen-day campaign; perhaps a total of 50,000 people heard his glib and sometimes funny speeches. But his vote came not from these seven cities or even from the country towns, but from the remotest areas of the countryside. It was just not credible that his, or anyone's, campaign had made any real impact in the villages. Election-eve polls by the wire services and others indicated that the majority of village voters had never even heard of most of the candidates. In one poll Ky's name was familiar to only 26%, although he had been premier for more than two years. Another disturbing aspect was that Dzu, an Annamite, got most of his vote in the southern Delta, while Suu, a Cochinchinese with a demonstrated following in the Delta, ran strongly only in Annam, where he carried the cities of Hue and Danang. Huong, furthermore, had carried the city of Saigon itself, where the voting was most closely observed, by an officially announced margin of 2,000 votes. Some weeks later, civil servants who had taken part in the counting told me that Huong's actual lead over Thieu in Saigon was more than 200,000 and that initially they had received orders from Ky's dreaded police chief, Loan, that Thieu was to win Saigon by a narrow margin. The higher Huong vote was much more likely, based on the pattern in precincts where I and other newsmen had actually observed the tally and Huong had a strong lead.

Most of the world press duly described the election as a success. The New York *Times* said it was the "first presidential election that was even reasonably fair in the 13 years since Vietnam was partitioned." *Le Monde* in Paris commented somewhat sardonically that the elections, in which "the results were known in advance, certainly render homage to democracy by the military power." In London, the *Economist,* whose confident editorials on the election differed markedly from the troubled dispatches of their correspondent in Saigon, contended that President Johnson "now has a reasonably solid political base in South Vietnam, in the shape of a government there with a claim to legitimacy." Despite his victory in Saigon, Huong's 10% showing, the *Economist* felt, "may well mark the political death of Mr. Huong." The Washington *Post* noted that "Huong and Suu are the major losers." In Washington, the State Department called the election "a major step forward" and said that "the consensus of the American and other foreign observers was that the election was conducted remarkably smoothly and fairly in the light of wartime conditions and Viet Cong harassment."

The interpretations of sophisticated and informed Saigonese were very different. The results gave many a chilling sense of how strong the Communists' political underground had now become. That hundreds of thousands of peasants had cast ballots for Dzu suggested to many of my friends that the Communists were now capable of mobilizing a large minority of the population into massive collusion action. Since June, the Viet Cong had been telling their political cadres to prepare for a "general offensive, general uprising." In September, the American military command had released a captured political commissar's diary, which noted, in connection with the planned uprising, "Despite the existence of a central government the governmental infrastructure should be in our hands." Vietnamese took this to mean that Communist penetration agents would by then control many of the key posts in the provincial administrations.

Ky and his allies in the police were thought to have blackmailed Dzu into running by filing charges of embezzlement against him in the Saigon military court, just as they had done against Suu's wife. But only Viet Cong support could explain Dzu's vote. Had Ky planned it that way? Shortly after the election, some of the wealthy middle class and intelligent Vietnamese began leaving the country, either buying expensive visas to Paris or just packing up their cars and driving to the Cambodian frontier.

A Dai Viet journalist who over the years had been a reliable informant told me Thieu would be sworn in only if he made an extra-constitutional arrangement to give real power to Ky. The deal, as he described it, was that Thieu would get Saigon and Ky the provinces. Thieu was supposed to be in charge of setting up the democratic institutions envisaged in the constitution and establishing a national political organization. Ky, seconded by General Thang, the pacification chief, would run a program to purge "corrupt" officials from the army and administration. My source said Ky demanded that his man, Nguyen Van Loc, be made premier, but that Loc's actual role would be as a "messenger boy," in the event of talks with the NLF. When I pointed out that the constitution specified that the vice president "shall have no other powers" than a few prescribed ceremonial functions, my friend was amused.

Although balloting for the new Senate took place the same day as Thieu's election, the results were not officially announced for two weeks, during which the winners changed several times. As in the House election, which followed on October 21, 1967, there was virtually no campaigning. In the countryside Senate election, peasant voters were asked to choose six out of forty-eight lists of ten candidates, most of them without having any idea who or what they were choosing. While House elections were conducted in local constituencies, there were almost no public rallies as in the Constituent Assembly election the year before. In Saigon, except for three-minute radio speeches by the candidates, there was no sign of a political campaign.

The final Senate results gave half of sixty seats to Roman Catholics, although some of these belonged to a new Tonkinese refugee group led by Nguyen Gia Hien, a petroleum engineer loyal to Ky. Dr. Sung got in as the tenth man on a list headed by General Tran Van Don, a suave St. Cyr-trained former defense minister and Cochinchinese who seemed willing to work with the Dai Viets to get back in power. Dr. Sung's developing alignment with a group of French-oriented Cochinchinese military men such as Don appeared to me as a fall-back position should Ky and the northern generals ever fall from power. Several other senior Dai Viets were elected. Also in the Senate was Tran Chanh Thanh, an ex-Communist who had once run "people's courts" and Tonkin's economic-affairs committee for Ho Chi Minh. He later served as Ngo Dinh Diem's information minister and ambassador to Tunisia, but dropped out of government after Diem began to distrust him. No one was really sure where Thanh stood, but there was universal agreement he was one of the smartest men in the country. Just as in the Constituent Assembly, Sung's men soon appeared on the key committee to draw up internal regulations and debating rules. Madame Van was defeated.

The House membership was regarded by many responsible Vietnamese as unrepresentative by any standard. Nearly twenty-five of the 137 members were men who had figured prominently in the Communist-penetrated Buddhist-led revolt in Annam; some of these had afterward mysteriously escaped arrest. There were also candidates who had been badly beaten in the 1966 election after running on pro-Ky planks, such as Captain Khieu Thien Ke, a Tonkinese air force pilot from Danang. The two biggest pluralities in Saigon went to pro-Communists: Professor Ho Huu Tuong, the man who had given me Hanoi's peace terms the previous February, and Ho Ngoc Cu, a Saigon businessman disqualified from the 1966 election by virtue of his Communist sympathies; he had been caught visiting a Viet Cong jungle camp. Tuong became the dominant backstage figure in the House, as Dr. Sung was in the Senate.

The Constituent Assembly, which had stayed on as a provisional legislature, was to ratify Thieu's election in late October as its last major act before dissolution. In the weeks that followed the election, Dzu and Tri Quang launched an ugly anti-American campaign with the visible cooperation of Ky's police. Rumors spread that the Assembly would vote for invalidation; there was an impression that Ky was blackmailing Thieu and the American Embassy to accept his continued power or face an invalidated election.

As the Assembly's deadline approached, mobs of student agitators rioted outside the opera house, pelting paint and rocks at a billboard announcing the Thieu-Ky victory. Tri Quang launched a hunger strike, and Dzu declared that unless the United States "immediately stops this bloody war" it would be considered "not as an ally but as an invading country." In some of the street demonstrations, American newsmen were brutally beaten by Ky's police. Since most of the agitators had the familiar faces of Ky's Anti-Fraud and Youth Forces, his attempt to blackmail Bunker and Thieu grew more obvious. At Bunker's urging, Thieu, enigmatic as ever, three times asked Huong to be his premier and was refused. Huong, instead, once more fled into hiding, telling me, "When the generals are fighting, it is not the time to talk politics."

By early evening on October 2nd, the ratification deadline, green police jeeps ringed the opera house. A monsoon rain lashed the deserted downtown streets, cordoned off by the police for blocks around. Plainclothes detectives sat on the entrance steps of the opera house barking orders into walkie-talkies. Truckloads of bayonet-carrying combat police parked in readiness around the side streets.

Inside, the opera house was brilliantly lit, its horseshoe-shaped tiers of balconies jammed once again with diplomats, government dignitaries, police and newsmen. Nguyen Ngoc Loan, Ky's police chief, sat in a box overhanging the stage; a pistol dangled from one hand as he sipped from the ever-present beer bottle. Rumors swept back and forth like shudders through the press galleries. The vote would be tied, and Suu, the elderly chairman and defeated candidate, would cast the decisive ballot to invalidate. The generals would prorogue the Assembly and arrest the deputies. Another rumor was that the police planned to pile the deputies into trucks and then, at a signal, attack the American cameramen when they tried to film it. My interpreter was almost hysterical and refused to stay inside the building once voting began.

The clerk began calling the roll, and the deputies filed forward one by one to cast secret ballots; there was a stir as Loan rose and left his seat. Another ripple of excitement followed when fourteen deputies, who had been missing throughout the debate, suddenly walked in the door. Neither Dr. Sung nor Dr. Dan appeared, a bad sign. At ten minutes to midnight, Suu read the results: fifty-eight for validation and forty-three against; four ballots invalid and one abstention. There was a roar as everybody began talking at once and moving up the aisles. Through a balcony door I saw that the rainswept square outside was empty. All the police jeeps, detectives and trucks full of troops had vanished.

The opera house was half empty when Suu rose to his feet. He stood there for some minutes, motionless, a frail, tired old man. To his right on the dais was the white marble bust of Tran Van Van. Together with Van and Huong, Suu had put together the civil government that led South Vietnam out of the anarchy of late 1964; with their help he had forced the Quat government to resign in mid-1965 when it tried to prepare for a sellout peace. Now it was all over.

When Suu finally spoke, his voice was so weak it was barely audible. He leaned against the podium nodding his snowy-white head and said, "I will add my vote against Thieu and Ky. I believe this election was fraudulent. I also resign as chairman of this Assembly as of this minute." He looked up once more and stared out at the empty seats. Somewhere an electrician began switching off the lights. "I am not responsible before history," Suu whispered.

It was raining hard as I left the opera house and hurried down to the bar on Rue Catinat. Along the dark street, gusts whipped at black wet branches, glistening in the rain. A lone cycle-rickshaw man pedaled by, his bell ringing like a telephone in an empty house. He was soaked to the skin, his thin shirt plastered against emaciated ribs.

The bar was dark and grimy with a dusty pink light. I asked Gio, the bar girl, what she thought about the election. Her smile faded and she looked stale and sad. She put her hand across mine. "All the girls want to marry Americans now. Yes, even me."

"Why?"

"Because I want to leave this country. It is what these generals are doing. No one likes it. In America, if you do not like your president you can say so. Here everyone is afraid. If the Americans are here, the Viet Cong cannot win. But if they go, the VC will take over in one night."

The Chinese piano player had seen me sit down at the bar and he began playing "Charade." Although it was no longer Saigon's favorite song, he still played it whenever I came in. I had asked for it so many times.

> *When we played our charade,*
> *We were like children posing.*
> *Playing at games,*
> *Acting out names,*
> *Guessing the parts we played . . .*

The bar mirrors reflected the black hair of the girls and their pale faces, cheeks pink with rouge, the sunburned faces of American soldiers, glasses of beer, dominoes and stained cards. Out in the doorway a crippled child held out a grimy hand to passing soldiers. Black-winged bats darted through the wet tamarind branches. Soon it would be curfew time.

> *Oh, what a hit we made . . .*

The birdlike voices of the girls rose above the piano, some cajoling and scolding, some sensual, others merry. "Sure I like Joe. I have to like. I no like, I no work here." "All G.I. same-same. He buy house, he buy girl. Then he go Danang, maybe America. No say byebye." The dialogue was always the same. The girls would say, "What is your name? Where do you live? What is your job?" The Americans would say they worked too hard, they killed VC, they wanted to go home.

We came on next to closing . . .

Gio deftly replaced a fallen wisp of hair. "Nobody wanted these elections. When the generals make trouble, people are afraid."
"Have you been here a long time, Gio?"
"Yes, I have been here a long time."
"I, too. Too long. I am going home soon."

Millions saw President Thieu's inauguration on television. It was, in its way, a spectacular.

Downtown Saigon was a mass of flags and brilliantly colored bunting, balloons and uniforms. The dying trees were festooned with the national colors. The whole front of the opera house was draped with red-and-yellow cloth. A big wooden stand built over the opera-house steps held crowds of foreign delegations, members of the new legislature, military commanders and lesser dignitaries. Tall cardboard petards with yellow standards proclaimed, "Long Live the Second Republic of Vietnam."

A saluting base was erected in the street facing a big ancestral urn and a tall cardboard monument to one of the ancient national heroes. A red-and-green-carpeted staircase, flanked by military cadets, led to the presidential dais. Ramrod-stiff honor guards with sabres and white gloves lined the Rue Catinat. The façades of the Caravelle and Continental hotels were pale yellow, but all the soldiers wore white; in the bright morning sunshine the effect was dazzling.

Two military bands played as honored guests arrived in their black cars to set the stage. There was an American vice president, a Korean prime minister, the commander of Thailand's army, a prince of the Laotian royal house. Thieu and Ky arrived in two black Mercedes; they wore identical neat black suits. Ky's bodyguards, in grey suits, marched by the side of his car. At an order, the honor guards drew their swords and a single bugle note sounded. Thieu, with Ky a pace behind, advanced to the saluting base. With a crash the bands began the national anthem. All those who had seats rose to their feet. Thieu administered the oath of president, or *tong thong*, to himself. Then, with another crash of music and sounding trumpets, troops raised thirty gold-fringed red standards of the army regiments at Thieu's command. A judge in a long red satin cape trimmed with ermine advanced with Thieu to the urn. Thieu bowed ceremoniously and lit joss sticks. Orange flames and thick black smoke rose from the urn. Thieu returned to the speaker's dais, Ky just behind him.

He stood there motionless for a moment. I had read an advance English text of his inauguration speech. It was the expected oration endowing the new president with unchallengeable authority: Thieu setting himself up as the sole protector of the people; stressing that the army was the country's firmest foundation; promising that his "major preoccupation" would be to "eradicate corruption in the government machinery and armed forces"; declaring that while South Vietnam was ready to have friendly relations with any country that respected its sovereignty, peace talks should be directly between Saigon and Hanoi, without American involvement, so that "the government of the south and north can directly seek together ways and means to end the war."

A hush fell over the square as Thieu began to speak in his own oddly musical language: "My fellow countrymen. Three months ago, in order to continue to serve the ideals of freedom and democracy and restore peace and prosperity to all of you, we stood for an election. . . . *On September third, you placed your confidence in us through a free, democratic, fair and honest election. . . . Today in taking office, amidst this sacred atmosphere, in communion with our ancestors and our heroes, before the entire nation I solemnly pledge to . . ."*

Sixteen

The End of the Charade

*On seven November, 1917, like a bugle sounding a charge, the
first salvoes of the October Revolution shook the world. . . .
Ever since, communism is no longer the specter which haunted
Europe and has, instead, become the reason of life and hope of
people of all continents. In Europe as in Asia and Latin America, in Moscow as in Peking, in Hanoi as in Pyongyang, in
Berlin as in Havana, over a billion people are advancing toward communism with differing methods. . . . The October
Revolution . . . awakened the Oriental peoples and paved the
way for the introduction of Marxism-Leninism in Vietnam.
. . . Following Lenin's teachings on revolution in the Orient,
the Vietnamese revolutionaries have applied Marxist-Leninist
principles to the concrete and specific conditions of Vietnamese society. . . . There is no other way than to use revolutionary violence. . . . The time has gone forever when the
imperialists could do as they pleased.*

—Le Duan, November 1967

In the early morning hours of January 31st, during the
1968 celebration of Tet, the first wave of Communist attacks on
the cities began. It was to be the beginning of the great battle of
the Vietnam war, a battle that would come in many bloody waves
in the months ahead. But the truly decisive battle—as I have tried
to show—was the political struggle, especially since mid-1963, of
the South Vietnamese people to choose their own government and
prevent a North Vietnamese seizure of power in Saigon. The people's greatest handicap was that their principal foreign supporter,
the United States, had the resources and the will but did not
understand the nature of the struggle. This was especially true of
the two most important segments of the American population
involved in the war, the U.S. military establishment and the
liberal intellectual community.

The struggle's major turning points were the murder of Ngo

Dinh Diem in 1963, the fall of the Huong government in early
1965, the murder of Tran Van Van in late 1966, and, finally, the
political suppression of Huong, the symbolic South Vietnamese
leader, and the legalization of the North Vietnamese rule through
the constitution and presidential and parliamentary elections of
1967. Thus the political battle had already been lost three months
before the Tet offensive, making General Vo Nguyen Giap's
attacks on the towns both possible and inevitable. The true South
Vietnamese leaders understood this so thoroughly that, based on
their analysis, I wrote my newspaper just after the elections to
expect imminent armed attacks against urban population centers
and American civilians in the provinces.

My story might have ended with President Thieu beginning his
inaugural address in Saigon's Lam Son Square on October 31,
1967, or even with Huong's last campaign speech two months
earlier. To many South Vietnamese these events publicly ratified
their defeat in a political struggle that had gone on for more than
five years, what I have attempted to chronicle as the long
charade. But the measure of that defeat would be how much or
how little the South Vietnamese and the Americans learned from
it and how they acted on that knowledge.

The heart of the matter in the Vietnam war was who would
run Saigon when the fighting stopped. Sometimes it can happen
in history that a rebel movement has to be recognized as a
legitimate political opposition if not a rightful claimant to the
government itself. There comes a moment when a state of affairs,
however unpalatable, has to be accepted as reality. Le Duan's
aim, from Thieu's inauguration on, was to create the impression
that this point had been reached—that the Viet Cong could no
longer be denied a place in South Vietnam's political future.

As men like Huong and Suu saw clearly, there could be no
compromise solution in South Vietnam. The country would be
run after the war either under a Communist system, dominated
by North Vietnamese, or under a non-Communist one, dominated
by South Vietnamese. If the Communists succeeded in imposing
their system, having beaten the United States by the technique of
subversion and guerrilla war, the revolutionary tactics of Le
Duan and Giap would gain a validity they did not before possess.
Le Duan's political charade knew no geographical boundaries;

nor was he only interested in the fate of a few million South Vietnamese. There were already Communist insurrections in Laos, Cambodia, Thailand, Malaysia, Burma and Indonesia, all in some degree controlled by Hanoi, Peking or Moscow. The thinking of the men leading ·these insurrections and those opposing them would be affected by the outcome in Vietnam. The Soviet Union would be tempted to adopt a more adventurous foreign policy and would continue to except support of "wars of national liberation" from its policy of peaceful coexistence. China would claim Mao's theories were valid everywhere. In the United States it would be folly to assume there would not be would-be Le Duans from Harlem to Berkeley. The real danger of an American defeat in Vietnam is that it would not end with Vietnam.

Le Duan himself has put the challenge better than anyone else. In his March 1966 letter, captured by American forces in the Duong Minh Chau Forest near Cambodia in January 1967, he wrote:

> Southeast Asia is the center of the world revolutionary storm and is the convergence point of the most acute contradictions in the world. . . . If the proletarian revolution is successful in this region, and if the densely populated countries—such as India and Pakistan with nearly 550 million people and Indonesia with more than 100 million people—also move toward socialism, then, as Lenin predicted, "There is no doubt about the conclusion of the struggle on a world scale." It is for this reason that the U.S. imperialists set foot on the region with the hope of checking the revolutionary tide there. But do they have adequate strength to successfully check this revolutionary tide? Definitely not . . .
>
> Our country is small. . . . it is even more difficult and complicated for us to evaluate U.S. imperialism . . . [but] in the world today, the evaluation of U.S. imperialism is an extremely important matter. . . . Previously, to understand and evaluate U.S. imperialism, we had to discuss it with fraternal countries. Today through our collision with U.S. imperialists . . . we have been able to evaluate their schemes and capabilities on our territory . . . more and more accurately. . . . Our party has clearly identified the strong and weak points of the U.S. imperialists. . . . In war as well as in the

formulation of strategy and tactics of the world revolution in general, and of each country in particular, the problem of prime importance is to know the enemy and ourselves. . . . Our aim is to defeat the enemy at all costs. As for restricting the war within the limits of the south, it is aimed at defeating the enemy in a way that is most advantageous to the revolution in our country and in the world. . . . This war must be won by all means, at any price. . . .

The countries in the socialist camp, the communist parties, the proletarian movements and the national liberation movement in the world are increasingly cooperating with us in the common cause against U.S. imperialism. . . . The more the U.S. imperialists escalate, intensify and expand the war, the more they will be defeated and isolated, and at length they must fail. Faced with two failures, either small or big, they must choose the one which costs them less. . . . If they are bold enough to widen the war to a larger scale and to convert the present war into an ideological conflict, our resources can never be exhausted, considering we have on our side the socialist bloc [and] the full potentiality of the Chinese people. . . .

Le Duan does not speak the language of a movement fighting a local civil war for internal reasons, as Hanoi's propagandists and diplomats claim. (And in November 1967 in Moscow, Le Duan went so far as to claim that the antiwar movement in the United States had become part of the world Communist revolutionary movement. "The peace movement," he said, "is not merely an antiwar movement with a democratic character, as it used to be, but one that takes on a new, really revolutionary and offensive significance. It can be said that the struggle for peace is one of the spearheads poised against imperialism.")

But beyond understanding the nature of the struggle, perhaps even more important is to understand the tactics, most notably the Leninist tactic of "exploiting internal contradictions in the enemy camp." In this sense, what happened just before and after the Tet offensive was crucial. As I hope to suggest, the moment of defeat coincided with the moment of understanding by President Johnson and some of the key men in his government. Whatever happened in Vietnam would no longer be because the American President and his top advisers did not understand the problem. I would define "understanding" as the full realization that the United States could only win if it did what it said it had been doing right along: fighting for the right of the South Vietnamese people to choose their own government. This would mean fighting not only on the battlefield but also in the corridors of power and hidden backrooms of persuasion in Saigon. President Johnson and Ambassador Bunker had to insist that Thieu, who despite his Dai Viet affiliation was a native-born South Vietnamese, restore a proportionate share of power in his government to the Cochinchinese majority. Necessarily most of Ky's Dai Viet North Vietnamese would have to be dropped.

The day Tran Van Van had shown me his last testament, I had asked him, "Do you think Ky is working for Hanoi?" Van's indirect reply—that there were two wars in South Vietnam, the North Vietnamese against the South Vietnamese and the Communists against the non-Communists, and that the United States could not win one without the other—implied that the question of conscious collaboration with the Communists was basically irrelevant.

In my own case, suspicion gradually hardened into conviction after Van's murder until finally it became an article of faith with me that Dr. Sung, Ky, Thang, Loan, Bui Diem and the others were not only working for Le Duan but had been sent south for this express purpose. But as time wore on, I despaired of ever being able to provide absolute proof. It is probably one of those things that will never be known. To me their records, going back two decades in most cases, were enough. In effect, it scarcely mattered. Dr. Sung, Ky and the rest, by clinging to power and denying the South Vietnamese their free choice of government over a period of more than three years, had shown themselves to be the enemies of everything the United States was trying to accomplish in Southeast Asia.

The Dai Viets could be opportunistic power seekers, or they could be Le Duan's collaborators—the actors he required on the Saigon stage to exploit inner contradictions and carry on the charade. We did not know and probably never would, even if Ky suddenly turned on the Americans and declared that he and his fellow North Vietnamese were throwing in their lot with the Viet Cong. Ky's justification could simply be anticolonialism. Probably Americans could be found—and historians, too—who would say we drove him to it.

In 1966, I took my newspaper's military editor, Richard Fryklund, to meet Dr. Sung. Fryklund, who subsequently became a Deputy Assistant Secretary of Defense, was impressed by Dr. Sung's Western rationalism and disbelieving when I told him Sung had been lying to us throughout the conversation. Later, in an interview on pacification with Deputy Ambassador William Porter, Fryklund brought the matter up. Porter agreed with me and said, "In Vietnam we listen to what people say, but we pay more attention to their past and present associations and what they actually do."

Dr. Sung was a highly sophisticated politician; he repeatedly revealed his grasp of Le Duan's tactic of exploiting internal contradictions and more than once told me, "Political warfare consists of dividing and weakening the enemy." He was fully capable of realizing that continued North Vietnamese domination in Saigon was helping the Communists to win. In my mind, he must assume responsibility for this. Ky, as the military head of a war government, might have seen his power position threatened by a peace settlement or the creation of a rival political base through social and land reform among the peasantry. But, I think, a case can be made that Ky stood to gain more by cooperating with the United States; his only choice for postwar political survival was to work for the United States or Le Duan, who did have a powerful rice-roots political organization in the south. Johnson, at Honolulu, seemed willing to sponsor Ky as another Park Chung Hee. But seemingly, with much to lose and little to gain, Ky chose inaction. In my mind, there can be only one explanation for Ky's behavior; he was not a free agent.

The role of men like Dr. Dan was much more ambiguous. At times Dr. Dan seemed to strike out on his own; at others, as when he helped delay the drafting of the constitution or joined Suu's ticket in the presidential race, supporting Ky's tactic to split the civilian vote and deprive Huong of his natural victory, Dan was subject to Dai Viet manipulation. And yet I believe Dr. Dan was essentially the Western-style liberal he appeared to be, but one who found himself caught in a merciless power struggle and compromised to survive.

But the record should speak for itself.

To examine both Giap and Le Duan's interpretation of the various stages of the war and, at the same time, to trace the simultaneous performance of the Dai Viets and Tri Quang is to discover a consistent pattern of congruent action over a five-year period. In his famous 1961 treatise, *People's War, People's Army,* General Giap observed, "If insurrection is an art, its main content is to know how to give the struggle the forms appropriate to the political situation at each stage. At the beginning, the political struggle was our main task, the armed struggle secondary. Gradually both became of equal importance. Later we went forward to the stage in which armed struggle occupied the key role."

As Le Duan described it, from the creation of South Vietnam in 1954 until midsummer 1965, political struggle was the main task. First, a Communist-led rice-roots popular front whose rank and file genuinely considered themselves part of a peasant movement for land and independence had to be patiently constructed. By 1959, that movement was strong enough to support an armed Viet Cong insurrection in the Mekong Delta. The second task, which Le Duan does not treat in specific terms, was to penetrate Saigon in order to weaken and divide the enemy's political center. In 1963, Tri Quang's artificially contrived Buddhist organization began its agitation against Diem for alleged "religious persecution." At the same time, Dai Viet leaders in Paris and Saigon started complaining publicly and privately (to American officials and journalists) that Diem's alleged incapacity as a leader and reformist was responsible for the growth of Communist power in the Delta. (The Communists took this one step farther and said that Diem's "dictatorial repression" was the *reason* for armed insurrection in the countryside.)

After Diem was discredited and murdered, armed and political struggle assumed equal importance. Diem's rural administration was systematically destroyed, both in Viet Cong terror attacks and in the disintegration that followed the dizzying succession of post-Diem governments in 1964. Tri Quang and his street rioters and propaganda apparatus were the prime movers in toppling each regime and the Dai Viets were the main beneficiaries, using each change of government as a rung up the ladder to power.

In January 1965, the Dai Viet-Tri Quang alliance succeeded in seizing effective power in Saigon by deposing Tran Van Huong's southern civil government. By Le Duan's own admission, the political struggle had moved faster than anticipated. In his captured March 1966 letter, Le Duan wrote, "Since the Binh Gia battle [three weeks before Huong was overthrown], it was obvious that the situation of the war developed more rapidly than we had anticipated. At that time, we had not yet acquired adequate conditions to cope with the rapid development of the situation, and make the puppet army disintegrate, really disintegrate, in an irretrievable manner. And once the puppet army had disintegrated to such an extent, the U.S. imperialists' massive introduction of troops into the south would undoubtedly have met with many difficulties." Le Duan was blaming the Communists' failure to achieve final political victory in early 1965 before American troops could come ashore *not on political shortcomings,* but on Giap's failure to defeat the South Vietnamese Army in time. He also cited as secondary reasons for failure President Johnson's unexpectedly "obstinate" stand and the Sino-Soviet split.

With political struggle in hand, armed struggle—as Giap noted—was to play the dominant role from the fall of Huong in early 1965 until Giap's offensive was decisively defeated in the battle of Ia Drang the following November. It was during this period that Westmoreland criticized the army's command—in which Dai Viets ran intelligence and operations—for committing units to battle piecemeal; thrown into battle in insufficient numbers, they were ambushed and wiped out. At the same time, the premier handpicked by Tri Quang and the Dai Viets, Phan Huy Quat, allowed the wholesale purge of anti-Communist elements in his army and administration, and sent Dr. Sung and his North Vietnamese vice-premier on the diplomatic tour to Paris that opposition leaders claimed was to arrange a settlement with capitulatory terms. When it became evident that President Johnson intended to commit American soldiers to the fight and that this would turn the military tide, Giap's role receded once more. The Quat government was publicly charged by Catholic leaders of favoring peace on Communist terms and forced to resign. Quat handed power back to the army—by now controlled by North Vietnamese Dai Viets—and the first phase of the Vietnam war, what Giap has called the "special war," was over. What Giap described as a conventional "local war," whose aim was to bog down and stalemate the Americans, began, then, sometime between the November 1965 battle of Ia Drang and early 1966.

But it seems reasonable to assume that the men in Hanoi, despite the bravado of their internal and external propaganda, were realists. Far from Giap's envisaged stalemate, it would have been only a question of time before superior American firepower began to eat deeper and deeper into the Communist hold on the back country. Some might argue that Giap always had the option of going back to protracted guerrilla warfare—as the Chinese kept urging Hanoi to do. Le Duan apparently did not agree. In March 1966, he wrote General Nguyen Chi Thanh, the Viet Cong commander, "Tremendous efforts are to be made to obtain decisive victory within a relatively short period of time."

My own feeling is that once the United States became directly involved, Hanoi had only one option: to stake everything on an attempt to rattle the South Vietnamese and American people into making concessions before the military war had time to yield its own verdict—a verdict which, without Chinese intervention, seemed certain to go to the United States. Hanoi's only chance of victory from late 1965 on lay in a complex combination of legal, constitutional maneuvering, subversion and intimidation, massive mobilization, global agitation and propaganda, and, at the right moment, spectacular armed struggle geared to its maximum effect on the American living-room TV screen.

The first step was to win the five-year political struggle, pursuing the course I have described through most of 1966 and 1967. But having won politically, Le Duan then had to have a fairly rapid settlement to ratify his covert victory before it slipped from his grasp. It would require a tremendous military gamble, in Westmoreland's phrase, "going for broke." As I saw it, after Thieu's inauguration, this was what Le Duan had to do to get the peace terms he wanted: First, get the United States to a negotiating table during a presidential campaign, while keeping up American casualties and making it appear that all the pacification gains since 1965 had been wiped out so the Americans would seek to wash their hands of Vietnam. Second, in South Vietnam itself, demoralize the key southern middle class, create a new, more broadly based southern popular front, use the political underground to split the army and bring the government to near collapse, and then have the already-penetrated legislature prepared to accept his terms in direct Saigon-Hanoi negotiations. (The 1967 constitution specifically gave the power "to determine declarations of war and the holding of peace talks" to the new two-house legislature, not to the executive. It also made the lower house the ultimate repository of Vietnamese sovereignty. While the Senate could veto legislation initiated in the House, the House could override it by a two-thirds vote, thus giving it the final say on peace. The president himself could veto such an action, but could be overridden by a simple majority of both houses meeting in joint session.)

Le Duan's only hope of succeeding, of course, lay in creating an illusion of defeat in the minds of the actual military victors. He had to conceal the reality that the United States, if it could replace northerners in the Saigon government with southerners, was itself on the brink of victory against an enemy close to cracking. Why did Le Duan stake everything on such a gamble? The answer, I think, is best provided by the words of a Viet Cong defector who once told Douglas Pike that the Communists could not retreat to purely guerrilla warfare since that would mean "trying to slow down a typhoon." "There is no such thing as a slow typhoon; for when a typhoon slows down it breaks up," the Viet Cong had said. I believed that Le Duan and the rest of them were compelled to press on, whether to victory or ruin.

Immediately after Thieu's election was ratified in late October 1967, according to Indian Communist sources, Hanoi spread word along its networks in the Communist world, especially to Cuba and North Korea, that it could not sustain the war and heavy American bombing for more than twelve months. According to East European Communist sources, Hanoi also alerted the Communist world to its general lines of strategy. Moscow, after Le Duan's November visit, notified Communist-bloc countries and its satellite parties in the West to prepare for a maximum agitprop effort against U.S. policy in Vietnam in 1968. In late January, the North Koreans attempted to assassinate South Korea's President Park and kidnaped the American intelligence ship *Pueblo* in the Sea of Japan.

Also in October, General Giap published a 25,000-word thesis, *The Big Victory and the Great Task,* calling for an all-out "1968 winter and spring campaign," with hit-and-run attacks from Laotian and Cambodian sanctuaries and wave after wave of shock attacks on the cities, military enclaves and communications. In December, Giap launched North Vietnamese and Viet Cong infantry, from jumping-off points in Cambodia and Laos, into a series of attacks starting from the south and moving north: at Loc Ninh, Dak To and eventually Khe Sanh. In mid-January, two provincial towns just north of Saigon were seized and shot up by the Viet Cong after troops of the Vietnamese Army's 25th Division failed to rescue them; at that time the 25th Division had provided the sole protection on Saigon's western flanks since November 1964. At Westmoreland's insistence, General Phan Trong Chinh, a Tonkinese Dai Viet, was relieved of the 25th Division's command, almost three years to the day since Lieutenant Reach had been killed at Tan Buu. The Associated Press reported that under the three-year command of Chinh, who had demanded the dismissal of his American adviser the year before, the 25th Division had suffered fewer casualties in a year than the nearby American 25th Division often had in a single day.

Then came the Tet offensive. As Viet Cong suicide squads penetrated the American Embassy and rocket and mortar fire ripped through Saigon and the cities, Liberation Radio called for a popular uprising. "Compatriots," it appealed, "the general offensive against the Thieu-Ky clique you have waited for so long has arrived." Hanoi's *Nhan Dan* newspaper declared, "The people in the countryside and in the towns are rising to overthrow the puppet administration, smash the puppet grip and wrest power in many areas."

Sir Robert Thompson called the Tet offensive Giap's "masterstroke." Analyzing it in the London *Times,* he wrote:

> The immediate military object of the simultaneous attacks on Saigon and the other leading cities of Vietnam was not to

capture them but to cause a complete dislocation of the American and South Vietnamese war effort and a breakdown of government. . . . If the immediate military objective was dislocation, the real long-term objective of the attacks on the towns is psychological and political. The North Vietnamese channels to victory, after the commitment of American combat troops in 1965, have never been strictly military. This is not in the nature of a people's revolutionary war.

The four inter-related channels to victory have always been the failure of American resolution at home, the failure of South Vietnamese resolution, the failure of the Americans to develop a successful counter-insurgency strategy and the failure of the South Vietnamese to build, with American help, a stable nation. It is not difficult to see how decisively these channels have now been widened. While no one should expect American resolution or valour to be weakened by setbacks, it must be recognized this is not solely an American military war against North Vietnam. Where American resolution may now falter is in continuing to support a government and people for whom it may no longer appear to be worth fighting.

Sir Robert concluded that Giap "has served notice on every South Vietnamese that no one can be protected, even in the towns or the Armed Forces, that this is a ruthless war and that all who oppose him in the future will be mercilessly executed. The stage has been set for a campaign of massive mobilization."

To achieve this, Giap threw something like 60,000 men into the attacks, roughly half his available main-force units, including at least 10,000 North Vietnamese regulars. Military observers estimated that half this attacking force very likely never made it back to base. In one week, Hanoi lost a quarter of its regular troops in the south, equivalent to a year's supply of recruits. This slaughter would continue; in mid-May the Americans officially would claim 85,000 enemy killed in 1968; in April a record 20,000 North Vietnamese reinforcements reportedly poured down the Ho Chi Minh trail or across the DMZ. At Khe Sanh, whether diversion or attempted second Dien Bien Phu, Giap's forces took a severe beating from the U.S. marines and airpower before withdrawing. Only in Hue did Hanoi try to set up a "people's government"; the Communists surged through the old city, executing or burying alive more than 1,000 officials and members of the educated middle class, including two Dai Viet senators, in nineteen mass graves. It took twenty-five days, 490 allied lives and 2,252 wounded to take Hue back, and when the fight was over, the imperial capital, symbol of Vietnam's heroic past and national identity, lay in ruins. But in the rest of the country, the grinding began to tell on the Communists' ability to hold on to recaptured areas in the countryside as well as their ability to move back into areas lost.

Viet Cong prisoners told Douglas Pike, who flew in from Hong Kong, that they had been briefed to expect some degree of unsolicited support from the population. Instead, only 2% of several hundred prisoners screened said that people had voluntarily helped them; 90% said they had not. In Saigon, where NLF political cadres knocked on doors to announce, "We have come to liberate Saigon," the population remained impassive. There was no uprising, no troop units defected. The army did not fall apart at the seams; it fought back. Ambassador Bunker pointedly declared that the Vietnamese Army's soldiers had "demonstrated their ability" and "gained confidence in themselves." In turn, he said, "the people have gained confidence in them." Bunker asserted that the idea of a non-Communist government in Saigon has "probably wider support today than it had before the Tet offensive."

Most of the Dai Viets were not in Saigon the night of the attack. Ky was skin-diving off the coast from Nha Trang; Dr. Dan was vacationing at the seaside resort of Cap St. Jacques. President Thieu was visiting his wife's family in the Delta town of My Tho; he rushed back to Saigon to declare on television that "in order to save time" in clearing the Viet Cong from Saigon, the army would have to "act ruthlessly." Many Vietnamese blamed much of the destruction in Saigon and its greatest number of civilian casualties on Ky's Skyraider bombers, as well as American planes and armed helicopters called in by Ky's local authorities.

Don Tate of the Scripps-Howard newspapers reported from Saigon, "The most baffling aspect of the last dramatic days was the behavior of the South Vietnamese government. The allied officials say they knew weeks in advance of the enemy's plan for mass urban attacks during the Tet holiday; yet the street-jammed celebrations, the night-and-day firecracker orgy, were allowed to go on uninhibited. . . . Many government officials were reported to have been vacationing out of town when the attack came—strange tactics to prepare for the most pervasive onslaught of the war." Peter Arnett of the Associated Press reported, "With all their planning and careful execution, the Communists managed to carry out their Saigon assault only with the unintentional assistance of the Saigon authorities." Arnett said that despite police interrogations of Viet Cong prisoners, the Viet Cong underground in Saigon survived "in perfect shape." He concluded, "The success of the Communists in gaining easy access to the city and staying for at least three days [before the attack] also throws into doubt the effectiveness of Vietnamese security in and around Saigon."

Other reporters filed critical dispatches, saying that Ky's police chief, Loan, had led an attack on Tri Quang's An Quang Pagoda, after telling newsmen it was the Viet Cong's command center in Saigon. But rather than a Viet Cong stronghold, the pagoda only held a hundred terrified civilians who had taken refuge there; some of them were wounded, others dead. During this attack, Loan dragged a young Vietnamese before an American press photographer and shot him in the head as a suspected Viet Cong officer in a by-now historic horror picture.

The London *Economist* noted that Thieu's government "has made a point of keeping all refugee operations and plans under its firm control," refusing to allow "foreign voluntary agencies . . . to make direct contact with Vietnamese religious and social groups involved in relief work." As refugees poured in from the bombed suburbs, Thieu appointed Ky and General Thang to run an emergency relief program. When they were accused of doing little but gather statistics, Ky and Thang resigned, citing Ky's "rivalry" with Thieu as the pretext. (This rivalry, whether genuine or contrived, worried American officials, who feared that it could at any time degenerate into a split in the army between Ky and Thieu factions.)

Some American newsmen were shocked to find that a rumor was being spread openly by Dai Viet members of the House and Senate that President Johnson was secretly plotting an election-year "sellout" deal with Hanoi and that American forces had colluded with Hanoi in the Tet attack. In a dispatch from Saigon, the Washington *Star* reported, "Perhaps the most bizarre and incredibly widespread Saigon interpretation of the Communist attacks is that the Americans actually supported the Viet Cong."

Dr. Sung declared to the Senate, "Why should Vietnamese die for Americans?" And a Tonkinese Dai Viet House member said, "I have two enemies, the Communists and the United States, whose stupidity prompts me to tell them to go home."

This anti-American campaign was fed by the Thieu government's seeming impotence in a moment of crisis and its use of indiscriminate force in pushing back the Viet Cong from the cities, often calling in American airpower. Thieu, once the "crafty" or "mature" general, now became the weak and vacillating ruler. Twice the House and Senate rejected his pleas for emergency powers, eroding his government's authority still further.

But Thieu remained firm on the two main pledges of his inaugural address: his support for direct Saigon-Hanoi peace talks, without American participation, and his pledge to "eradicate corruption in the government machinery and armed forces." He declared, "We will not hesitate to oppose the Americans if they want to negotiate unilaterally with the Communists on peace in Vietnam," and said that if the Americans ever withdrew military support, "we can withdraw to the underbrush and fight it out."

In the weeks immediately after Tet, Thieu, pushed by Ky and Thang, began his promised purge of "corrupt" officers from the army and administration. Prime Minister Nguyen Van Loc, who had done little except appear at ceremonial functions, publicly denigrated the South Vietnamese bureaucracy as a "haven for the lazy" and vowed to cut the number of civil servants from 220,000 to 50,000. Thieu fired the last two remaining non-Dai Viet corps commanders and replaced them with brotherhood members, appointing Thang to run Fourth Corps, the first Tonkinese ever to command either the government or Viet Cong forces in the wholly Cochinchinese Mekong Delta.

Twelve province chiefs were fired; Dai Viet sources let it be known that Ky had drawn up a list of twenty-six young officers personally loyal to himself who would soon take over all but eighteen of the country's forty-four provinces. This would take place despite the collapse of pacification in Binh Dinh (the only province where real headway had ever been made) after the purge of its chief for "corruption" the previous October. The chief, Lieutenant Colonel Tran Dinh Vong, had been convicted by a special Saigon military tribunal of extorting and misappropriating funds, and sentenced to die by firing squad. The sentence, given the day before Thieu's inauguration, was never carried out, but the day Vong was sentenced Peter Lisagor of the Chicago *News* was told by a Vietnamese journalist close to Ky that Vong's real crime had been to pacify twenty-six more hamlets than the modest number Thang had officially scheduled for Binh Dinh. "He wasn't corrupt," the journalist had told Lisagor, "he was stupid." Lisagor, who was only visiting Saigon for the inauguration, said that such cynicism had to be heard to be believed. That was in October.

Three weeks after the Tet offensive, the New York *Times* reported in an article on setbacks to pacification that Binh Dinh Province had been one of the hardest hit by the Tet offensive. Bernard Weinraub of the *Times* quoted an American official in the province as saying, "I was here in 1964, and you couldn't move out of town without an escort. You could expect to get ambushed at any time. Then in 1965, when allied troops came in, things began changing and they kept getting better and better until the middle of 1967." It was then, the official was quoted as saying, that Vong and several other high officials in the province were arrested on graft charges. "Everything just came to a halt. Lacking guidance, the Vietnamese in the field just failed to react." Weinraub said other Americans in the province began hearing reports in mid-December, more than a month before the Tet offensive, that the Viet Cong and North Vietnamese were slipping into villages north of Qui Nhon, the province capital, that were already considered pacified. Binh Dinh, with a large garrison of American and South Korean troops, had been considered the pacification showpiece of South Vietnam.

From other provinces as well, word was flowing back to Saigon of suspected local fifth columns in the police or army. Some

American journalists, such as Flora Lewis of the Washington *Post,* noted that "the atmosphere in official places is peculiar." Writing about the Delta, Miss Lewis said, "The administrative machine seems to be there. But nothing much gets done. It's like an overturned car with the wheels still spinning furiously, but getting nowhere. Most people are scared and don't mind saying so, more scared than angry . . . The loss you hear most about in Can Tho is the new science annex of the University. It had just been built and was the pride and joy of the Delta, two attractive modern buildings. Now they are gutted shells. The Viet Cong went in, and artillery and bombardment was ordered. It was said that afterwards, when the damage was complete, three bodies were found inside, not the well-armed company that had been reported."

At the height of the Tet fighting, Radio Hanoi had announced the formation of a new southern popular front, the Alliance of National and Peace Forces (the exact name Professor Tuong had used in outlining Hanoi's peace terms more than a year before). Although Hanoi claimed that many prominent Cochinchinese belonged to the new front, most of the Saigonese who slipped into the jungle and eventually emerged as its members were North Vietnamese refugees. In mid-February, the Saigon government's official press agency distributed an article to Saigon newspapers hinting that the popular exiled Cochinchinese general Duong Van ("Big") Minh was the Alliance's chairman. Minh promptly denied this in Bangkok. The government's story also hinted that Dzu, the presidential runner-up, and ex-economics minister Thanh and Tri Quang were Alliance members, and they were hauled in and out of jail several times. Dzu publicly endorsed a coalition government with the Communists, and Tri Quang warned that any peace settlement by the Americans "should not betray us Vietnamese who have been the victims of this cruel struggle." A Buddhist communiqué declared that Buddhists "did not want to follow the same path created by Communists, colonialists and imperialists."

In late February, Loan, the police chief, held a press conference to play taped Buddhist confessions implicating Tri Quang in the Tet attack on Saigon. Loan's police also closed Dr. Sung's paper, *Chinh Luan,* for three days for criticizing the government. (I interpreted this as a ploy to try to disassociate Sung from the now-suspect Dai Viet generals in the government. My belief was that Le Duan would try to protect Sung from suspicion and attack at all costs. The others, such as Tri Quang, were more expendable.) Then, in Washington, Senator Ernest Gruening, a critic of the war, revealed that the Vietnamese customs director in Saigon had been caught dealing in gold and opium smuggling "in the interest of certain high government of Vietnam officials." Pentagon sources confirmed that an investigation was under way of Loan's possible involvement in the 1967 murders of three American military investigators, a colonel, major and captain. Loan's suspected activities involved the rapid transit of American aid dollars to France on behalf of a number of generals and officials, where they were exchanged for gold. This was believed to have significantly affected the international monetary crisis and the gold drain.

In early March, Ky and Thang proposed forming a new citizens' army to march north; the State Department at once issued a repudiation citing the Manila communiqué's pledge that South Vietnam had "no desire to threaten or harm the people of the north, or invade their country." Ky continued handing out thousands of rifles to peasants and students. On March 14th, the Associated Press reported Ky telling a Tonkinese Catholic peasant audience, "Down with the Communists is not enough. You have to say, 'Down with Communists, Communist henchmen and colonialists.' We will kill all of them and not let one remain alive." In an interview with the West German magazine *Stern*, Ky was quoted: "The Americans are here to defend their interests, which do not always correspond with those of Vietnam. . . . Always it is those countries who talk of democracy and freedom in order to carry on colonialism." Ky told other reporters he might favor a peace settlement in which Saigon controlled the cities and let the Viet Cong administer the countryside they already held. A few weeks earlier, the Communist revolutionary committee in Hue had issued a decree saying that Hanoi's real aim was to isolate the American forces in their camps and bases.

That same month, Johnson sent a high-level team of State Department and CIA officers to Saigon. The team, led by George Carver, first met Thieu alone and then Ky and Loan together.

According to authoritative Pentagon sources, Thieu told the Americans he was on the ragged edge and believed Ky and Loan were going to kill him, probably during another wave of attacks on the cities in June or July. The Americans flatly confronted Ky with Thieu's charge. He did not deny it but reportedly replied, "I am not yet ready, but when I am I will take over. Your President has reason to be afraid." Ky said that if anyone reached an accommodation with Hanoi, it would be Ky, not the United States, and that he would do it from a position of power. At the same time, William Colby, a senior CIA Far East hand who had been working for some time at the White House, was assigned to Saigon on a permanent basis, his mission unstated. Johnson also assigned to Saigon Samuel D. Berger, a former ambassador to South Korea from 1961 to 1964, as Bunker's deputy. The White House, in announcing the appointment, noted that Berger was remembered in South Korea for "his effective work in support of President Park Chung Hee's efforts to establish constitutional government after the military coup of 1961."

Although there was no published comment by Le Duan on the Tet offensive, an editorial that appeared in the official Communist party journal in Hanoi seemed to reflect his thinking. As the editorial put it, the Tet fighting had achieved "a military success which will have important strategic significance" in that it had created "favorable prerequisites to carry on the fight to still greater victories." These prerequisites were spelled out. All were political:

> The internal contradictions in the United States are much more strongly felt. Government authorities have been criticizing one another. The United States people are angry at their government's policy. The United States imperialists are now at the turning point and are doomed to failure. They have been witnessing a series of contradictions that are developing at a critical stage and cannot be resolved: the contradictions between the United States global strategy and the local war they are waging in Vietnam; between the strategy of fighting and occupying areas quickly and the realities that compel them to lengthen the war with vague hopes.

The political impact of the Tet offensive had produced a near chain-reaction in the United States. Senator Eugene McCarthy won the March New Hampshire primary with 42% of the vote. Senator Robert F. Kennedy challenged Johnson's leadership of the country and his Democratic nomination for a second term. McCarthy endorsed a "coalition government" in Saigon. The Hanoi editorial spoke of "vague hopes." Kennedy accused Johnson of harboring "false hopes." He contended that the Tet offensive was an American failure, that the Saigon government was "a government without supporters," and that the war should be settled "by the Vietnamese themselves."

And then on Sunday evening, March 31, 1968, President Johnson made his historic announcement that he would not seek renomination for a second presidential term, but would devote his last nine months in office toward bringing an honorable peace to Vietnam. In his speech, Johnson stressed that the Tet attack had failed to achieve its principal objectives. These he enumerated:

> It did not collapse the elected government of South Vietnam or shatter its army—as the Communists had hoped. It did not produce a "general uprising" among the people of the cities. The Communists were unable to maintain control of any city. And they took very heavy casualties. But they did compel the South Vietnamese and their allies to move certain forces from the countryside, into the cities. They caused widespread disruption and suffering. Their attacks, and the battles that followed, made refugees of half a million human beings. The Communists may renew their attack. They are, it appears, trying to make 1968 the year of decision in South Vietnam— the year that brings, if not final victory or defeat, at least a turning point in the struggle.

It was a long speech, lasting more than an hour. Johnson reviewed his entire Vietnam policy, going back to the Johns Hopkins promise of aid for all Southeast Asia, the American troop commitment, the Pacific conferences at Honolulu, Manila and Guam. Then he announced he was extending a new peace offer to Hanoi based on a reduction of the bombing.

Finally, the President concluded:

> This I believe very deeply. . . . In these times, as in times before, it is true that a house divided against itself by the spirit of faction, of party, of region, of religion, of race, is a

house that cannot stand. . . . There is division in the American house now. . . . There is divisiveness among us all tonight. . . . Accordingly, I will not seek and I will not accept the nomination of my party for another term as your President. But let men everywhere know, however, that a strong and a confident, and a vigilant America stands ready to seek an honorable peace and stands ready tonight to defend an honored cause, whatever the price, whatever the burden, whatever the sacrifices that duty may require.

A cable was sent to Thieu inviting him to a meeting in Honolulu the first week of April to be followed by a state visit to the United States. Thieu declined both invitations, saying that to do so at the moment would make him appear an "American puppet."

The same day that Johnson spoke to the nation, March 31st, the Associated Press cabled a brief political story from Saigon. It appeared on the inside pages, if at all, in most American newspapers. The story began:

> President Nguyen Van Thieu was reported today to be planning a top-level overhaul of his government, including the dismissal of Premier Nguyen Van Loc and Police Chief Nguyen Ngoc Loan. Others said to be facing ouster are the mayor of Saigon, four or five cabinet members and the commander of the III Corps area, which includes Saigon. Government informants said high-level changes are in the works, but that nothing is definite. There have been reports of contention between Thieu and Vice-President Nguyen Cao Ky, who was top man before last September's elections. Informants said Premier Loc has not performed as well as expected. Reports are that he will be replaced by Tran Van Huong. . . .

Besides Huong, the story named some of the new men Thieu planned to appoint. The outgoing civil and military officers, with the exception of Loc, were all North Vietnamese and members of the Dai Viet. The incoming men were all South Vietnamese and included not only Huong but the last Cochinchinese police chief, a respected and tough-minded anti-Communist who would be certain to initiate a wholesale purge of Loan's men from the police.

It meant the Dai Viets would lose control of the police and

troops in Saigon; their whole structure would come crashing down.

For seven weeks nothing happened. Only a brief news item appeared reporting that Huong had gone into hiding "to avoid the press." Dai Viet sources denied the possibility of a major government shakeup. Then, the commander of Tan Son Nhut Airbase and General Loan's deputy police chief, two of Ky's closest lieutenants, were killed in separate Viet Cong attacks. Loan himself was wounded and hospitalized. Although there were rumors of American involvement, the London *Economist* dismissed "the ludicrous story that the CIA helped to get General Loan wounded."

In the United States, Vietnam faded as the principal campaign issue and, as Vice President Humphrey and Governor Nelson Rockefeller joined the presidential race, the mood in American politics became one of unity and the search for national reconciliation.

Finally, after weeks of rejecting U.S.-proposed negotiation sites, Hanoi agreed to Paris. On May 13th, W. Averell Harriman, the chief American delegate, and Xuan Thuy, the leader of the North Vietnamese team, shook hands in the elegant, chandeliered ballroom of the old Hotel Majestic. "Good morning. How do you do?" Harriman said. Then, as photographers clicked away, recording the scene for posterity, the United States and North Vietnam at last sat down to a conference table.

Harriman's deputy was Cyrus Vance, who had visited Vietnam, although in a military capacity, as Deputy Secretary of Defense. Third on the U.S. delegation was Philip Habib, now Deputy Assistant Secretary of State in charge of Vietnam affairs, who was expected to prepare the position papers if it came to a political settlement.

But it would not be in Paris but in Saigon that the peace terms would be decided.

The end of the charade came on a Saturday morning in Washington, May 19th; a news bulletin from Saigon announced that Thieu had just accepted the resignation of Loc and his Cabinet and had appointed Tran Van Huong as the new prime minister. It was reported that prior to accepting the post, Huong had asked that he, with Thieu's support, control the army and administration, and that Ky's power be limited to those few ceremonial duties prescribed for the vice president by the constitution. Huong's running mate in the September election, Dr. Mai Tho Truyen, perhaps South Vietnam's most respected Buddhist leader, would be his deputy. General Tran Thien Khiem, a Catholic former defense minister, was named interior minister, which included running the police. Dr. Dan got the ministry dealing with defectors. The new information minister was Ton That Thien, the editor whose newspaper was closed for challenging the government's version of Van's assassination. A number of exiled Cochinchinese and Catholic generals were expected to be recalled home.

It was reported that the United States welcomed the change and warmly supported the new government. Ambassador Bunker was known to be especially pleased. Ky was quoted in the press as telling a student force that the new government was "a gang of slaves" who had sold themselves to the Americans. Ky declared, "We must rid the country of these traitors. If necessary, they must be destroyed. If necessary, I am ready to resort to blood and fire to sweep everything away." In another statement, Ky said, "If the Americans want to withdraw, they can go ahead. We only want people who want to stay." He asked one audience, "Why has South Vietnam not been able to produce a Ho Chi Minh or Vo Nguyen Giap whom the world admires and respects? Why have we been unable to produce such people? Isn't it because our leaders are merely a bunch of servile and corrupt officials?" As his pronouncements took on distinctly anti-American tones, Ky no longer appeared in public in his old Captain Midnight flight suit with its lavender ascot, but instead took to wearing the coarse Mao jackets of China's Red Guard, an outfit equally un-Vietnamese. Moodily brooding at his luxurious seaside summer home at Nha Trang, Ky told Peter Arnett of the Associated Press, "I could launch a *coup d'état* any time I liked, any time I wanted to, and the Americans could not stop me."

But Ky's power apparatus was crumbling fast. In Saigon in early June, a rocket hit a command post, killing the police chiefs of Saigon and its Cholon district, the director of Saigon's port, who was Ky's brother-in-law, and three other chief aides of Ky. All were Tonkinese Dai Viets. The U.S. command at first denied reports that the missile had come from an American helicopter, witnessed circling over the post for two minutes before the explosion, but later confirmed that one of its gunships had fired a round in error. Later, the Saigon police claimed that some of the bodies had been riddled with machine-gun fire. The Ky-controlled Saigon *News* front-paged a story headlined "One Accident Too Many," which charged that the attack had been deliberate. Dai Viets in the Saigon parliament spoke of a "liquidation plot," and a visiting Buddhist monk in Washington, Thich Tam Chau, told me he believed that the rocket incident had been "an American plot to kill Ky's people."

Within one month, eight of Ky's men were killed, either in the rocket incident or in other Saigon skirmishes. Coincidentally, eight more were fired from important posts running the Vietnamese Army's Saigon military district and the Fourth Corps in the Mekong Delta, Saigon's municipal government and port, the Information Ministry and censorship bureau, and the national police and internal security apparatus. One Saigon newspaper claimed that more than 150 secret policemen had quietly been sacked and some of them arrested. Generals losing their commands included Le Nguyen Khang, Nguyen Duc Thang, Nguyen Ngoc Loan and Nguyen Bao Tri, the four other generals besides Ky named by Tran Van Van as the Dai Viet hard-core leadership in the Vietnamese Army. Ky himself was forced to resign command of his newly armed Tonkinese student and peasant force. Huong's friend, Ton That Thien, the new information minister, began issuing permits to Cochinchinese publishers to reopen newspapers closed by Ky since 1965. Thien also closed *Song*, a newspaper dominated by Dr. Sung, for trying to "sow hatred" between Vietnamese and Americans.

The Viet Cong, who throughout the war had avoided using indiscriminate force against Saigon, began pounding the capital nightly with 100-lb Russian rockets—what the Vietnamese called "whispering death," a random form of terror that killed and maimed government and Communist sympathizers alike.

In Hanoi, there were now clear signs of disarray. Le Duc Tho, the sixth-ranking member of the Politburo and an ally of Le Duan, suddenly flew to Paris, reportedly to press for a more rapid settlement. In North Vietnam, this mission was attacked by Truong Chinh, the leader of the Politburo's pro-Chinese faction who ranked just below Ho Chi Minh and Le Duan. In an interview published in Hanoi, Chinh demanded that the talks drag out until after the American presidential elections, arguing that any new president would have to make the concessions Hanoi needed to win. Chinh said that the "antiwar movement" in the United States, combined with the "Afro-American movement," would develop "prodigious strength" in the five months before November and have a "profound effect."

In far-off San Francisco, Dr. Dan, on an AFL-CIO-sponsored speaking tour, told an audience that the Saigon government should "take the initiative" to talk with the Viet Cong, since "killing all of them is impossible." From Saigon, Premier Huong sternly reprimanded Dr. Dan for misrepresenting the views of the South Vietnamese government. When Dan in another speech again called for "direct talks" with the National Liberation Front, Huong dismissed him from his Cabinet. Voices in the Vietnamese press and parliament demanded that Dr. Dan be arrested for treason; his wife cabled him to remain in the United States. I, too, urged Dr. Dan to stay and send for his family, but he was adamant about returning to Saigon. In late June, just before his departure, as we sat in his suite in Washington's Lafayette Hotel, I decided to tell Dr. Dan about the book I was writing and what I believed about the Dai Viets and his own role. When I had finished, Dr. Dan said nothing for some moments but stared out impassively across the treetops of the park at the White House, floodlit and glistening in a summer rain. Finally, Dr. Dan turned back to me and asked, "Do *they* believe this, too?"

Le Duan had his answer.

There could no longer be any doubt that Johnson at last understood Le Duan and his "most clever tactic." In one stroke, by renouncing a second term and restoring Huong to power to end the Dai Viet subversion, the President had done all he could to reunite two divided societies, the American and the South Vietnamese. He had gone very far toward eliminating the internal contradictions Le Duan had depended on to win the war.

Ironically, it was Russia, fighting its war by proxy with the United States, that was now faced with an acute internal contradiction. The Russians, since Khrushchev's 1961 declaration of full support for wars of national liberation, had shown that they sought to preside over a revolutionary movement dedicated to expanding the Communist world's area at the non-Communist world's expense. But there were also men in Moscow who wanted peace with the West, so they could get on with the modernization of Russia, men who for reasons of national security and economic need wanted to consolidate their relationship with the greatest non-Communist power.

Since Moscow's decision to supply arms to North Vietnam after the United States abandoned Ngo Dinh Diem, Soviet foreign policy had been a five-year record of the Russians' attempt to operate these two incompatible policies side by side. As long as the United States failed to understand the political struggle in Vietnam, as long as the futile attempt to find a military solution continued to weaken and divide the United States, the Russians could pull it off. But once President Johnson answered Le Duan's strategy, he brought the United States much closer to the point where an American president, possibly Johnson's immediate successor, could push the Russians to choose between *détente* or continued support for wars of national liberation. As President Kennedy had realized in 1963, the insurmountable obstacle to an American-Russian *détente* was not strategic-weapons control, which he viewed as manageable, but Khrushchev's policy of supporting wars of national liberation. As both Kennedy and Johnson saw, once Moscow gave the word, the war in Vietnam would be over.

The Soviet decision depended on what happened in Vietnam and how events there affected the Paris talks and American elections. Russia's announced willingness in the last week of June 1968 to "exchange opinions" on a mutual reduction in offensive and defensive missiles and its agreement to sign the long-delayed treaty banning the spread of nuclear weapons did not mean that Russia had yet made its choice; the movement toward *détente* could be a purely psychological gambit. But it did indicate that Russia was moving to change the atmosphere in which that historic decision would be taken.

Whether it was too late for Vietnam, whether the charade had already done its work, only time would tell. The end of the charade in the minds of Johnson, Bunker and other senior American leaders had, I believed, denied Hanoi total victory, a coalition government or a return to protracted guerrilla warfare. But the typhoon could not stop.

As Johnson had predicted in March, Hanoi seemed determined to make 1968 its year of decision. From the Tet offensive at the end of January to mid-July, 35,000 additional American troops came ashore. By then, 25,000 Americans had died in Vietnam, and they continued to fall by the hundreds each week. But the North Vietnamese and Viet Cong losses had been a staggering 100,-000 in the first six months of the year. With pitiless logic, Giap continued to pour into the south 20,000 more men each month to be virtually slaughtered; Giap's total force of men under arms in the south was expected to surpass the pre-Tet level of 280,000 by August. Beyond that, much of the Communist political infrastructure of 65,000 to 80,000 largely covert cadres still survived intact, although once Loan was ousted, arrests began rising to 1,000 a month.

As spring turned to summer and the days moved rapidly toward the American election and Johnson's anticipated departure from power on January 20th, Le Duan continued to pursue the only option he had left: to destroy or neutralize Huong and persuade Thieu's government to accept a postwar political party system which Hanoi could once again gradually come to dominate—one in which a Communist-penetrated popular front could organize legal political activities, even if American troops were garrisoning the coastal enclaves. To achieve this, it was essential for Le Duan to obtain direct negotiations between the governments of Saigon and Hanoi—in other words, to exclude Washington from participation in the political settlement.

A significant blow to pacification came in June when President Thieu refused to deal with Lansdale on the unsubstantiated grounds that he was too closely identified with Ky. This appeared to end the quiet American's long and legendary stay in Vietnam. In Washington, I asked Lansdale, "Will we win it?" "Yes, we will," he replied. "Someday, in our way, muddling through."

American casualties dropped dramatically during a summer lull before the expected storm, as Giap pulled his forces back to the jungles to regroup. Prime Minister Huong, in expectation of bitter fighting in the months ahead, tried to stiffen the morale of what he described as an "invaded, dependent and divided nation," warning that the capital city must be defended at all costs: "If we lose Saigon, we lose everything." Huong vowed he would never accept any settlement save "peace with honor, with real guarantees." And the people believed him. The Dai Viets no longer dared call him senile or "not very bright"; instead, in a move to neutralize him, they told the Americans he was "honest and good but ineffectual," a Confucian moralist who could not "administer" or "organize."

Gradually, the Dai Viets fall-back position emerged: a cynical posture of despair that no end of the war was in sight, that despite the Communists' military losses, they were still winning politically. Eventually, it was said, South Vietnam would have to work out an accommodation with Hanoi and become a neutralist state. Such arguments were coupled with stronger anti-Communist avowals than ever and appeals for direct Saigon-Hanoi negotiations and the exclusion of the United States from the bargaining table.

In the midst of this, President Thieu remained an enigma. In his inaugural address he, too, had said that peace talks should be between Saigon and Hanoi, without American involvement, so that "the governments of the south and north can directly seek together ways and means to end the war." But Thieu had also bowed to pressure from Johnson and Ambassador Bunker to appoint Huong as his prime minister. He had purged the Tonkinese generals. He had allowed Huong to choose his own Cabinet members, with one important exception: Thieu's personal choice as the new foreign minister, made despite Huong's misgivings, was Senator Tran Chanh Thanh, the ex-Communist who had once run "people's courts" for Ho Chi Minh in the north and was distrusted by many knowledgeable South Vietnamese. In July, Thieu gave amnesty to Tri Quang while inexplicably putting the monk's ally, Lawyer Dzu, on trial for advocating a coalition government. Dzu's arbitrary sentence by a military tribunal—suggesting that he was being groomed as a neutralist martyr—heightened American distaste for the Saigon government. Thieu was also reportedly in touch with the North Vietnamese delegation in Paris through several neutralist emissaries. Le Duan, in March, had informed French Communist Jacques Duclos that the future

Saigon government could include "pro-French and pro-American neutralist elements," and the Russians had floated a rumor that Thieu might agree to head a neutralist front government with Communist participation. And as the war reached its climax, Thieu had still made no move against Dr. Sung or Bui Diem; the two most powerful Dai Viet figures named by Tran Van Van remained in positions of prominence and influence. The constitutionally elected president of South Vietnam—a natural-born South Vietnamese who rose to power through collaboration with North Vietnamese Dai Viets—remained a man whose true loyalties no one, perhaps not even he himself, really knew.

In Washington by July, the question began being raised with increasing frequency in the Senate, in letters from Huong's Cabinet ministers and by such old Vietnam hands as Lansdale and William Corson, whether Philip Habib, who had been principal executor of the policy to support Ky and the other Tonkinese generals, was an appropriate choice as the third-ranking member and senior political offcer of the American delegation in Paris.

On July 8th, Thieu suddenly appealed publicly to Johnson to meet him in Honolulu for a fourth mid-Pacific conference. The following day, Dr. Sung's newly emergent bloc of thirty-seven of the Vietnamese Senate's sixty members issued an anti-Communist declaration advocating a policy of "protracted war against Communist aggression" that would be "arduous and long-term." In Paris that same day, Bui Diem, who was now serving both as ambassador to Washington and as South Vietnam's official observer at the peace talks, called for direct Saigon-Hanoi "political" negotiations, drawing a distinction between such talks and those already under way between Hanoi and Washington, which, Diem said, solely concerned a bombing halt and concessions by North Vietnam in return.

President Johnson met Thieu in Honolulu July 20th. The President sent away his advisers and even an interpreter and spent ten hours alone with Thieu, talking until midnight and resuming the dialogue at breakfast. That afternoon, speaking briefly at a press conference held by Thieu, Johnson dismissed as "pure, absolute tommyrot and fiction" press speculation that he would compromise to get an early peace settlement. In a communiqué,

Johnson stated that he agreed with Thieu that South Vietnam should play "a leading role" in any political settlement; Thieu said nothing about direct Saigon-Hanoi talks.

Then, just before this book went to press, I learned from an official with White House and Pentagon connections that the U.S. government had conclusive evidence of Dr. Sung's involvement in the December 1965 assassination of his deputy editor, Tu Chung, and also evidence implicating Dr. Sung, Ky's foster father-in-law, Le Van Thai, and other Dai Viets in Tran Van Van's murder. Van's personal papers and diaries, he said, including the article Van had shown me, had been recovered and were in American possession. Further confirmation was provided by a private American citizen in Washington who had friends in British intelligence. The British version, as he remembered hearing it "over a year ago," was that Tu Chung's murder had been arranged by Dr. Sung and a person he had heard described as the Dai Viet party whip. Tu Chung's death in December 1965 had followed his attempt the previous spring to expose the involvement of the Dai Viets in a massive opium-smuggling operation from northern Thailand and Laos into Saigon in which Vietnamese air force planes had figured. According to this source, Tu Chung first went to French and British intelligence and then, in May 1965, to Washington, where he was reportedly given a sympathetic hearing but offered no protection. Subsequent American efforts to investigate the smuggling ring had led to the 1967 murders of three U.S. military counterintelligence officers, two in Saigon and one in Thailand. Ky's police chief, Loan, at the time had claimed the two in Saigon were Viet Cong terrorist victims shot by a girl sniper from a motor scooter; her subsequent capture and confession was widely publicized. Pierre Ferri-Pisani, a Corsican who had committed suicide in Paris in 1967, had allegedly also been involved in the ring.

Finally, just a few hours before he was leaving the country, I reached a Vietnamese who had known Tu Chung well. "He was my close friend," the man said. "My friends told me afterward that Dr. Sung and Le Van Thai killed him, just as they did Tran Van Van. I remember how unhappy he was that summer. 'I am in trouble,' he told me. 'What can I do?' He said he had evidence of smuggling, that Ky was smuggling opium from Laos. I told him to go to the American journalists. 'No,' he said, 'it all depends on the American Embassy.'"

"What about Dr. Sung?"

"He said there was some kind of business . . . that Dr. Sung was not anti-Communist . . ."

I interrupted him. "Did he say anything about Dr. Sung and Le Duan?"

"Yes." He seemed shocked, but the answer came instantaneously. "Tu Chung said that Dr. Sung had some dealing with Le Duan."

The Dai Viets, it seemed clear, would never give up without a fight, even if they had to retreat and wait. It was their survival and probably Le Duan's, too.

And in the United States, by midsummer of 1968, it seemed as if political assassination and violence had become a way of life in a great democracy. Many would search their hearts for some dark sick flaw in the American national character.

But there was no intrinsic American sickness, only a failure to understand the nature of the challenge that Le Duan and his allies in Peking and Moscow represented. Latent contradictions, the divisions between blacks and whites, the military establishment and the liberal community, right and left, already existed in America, just as divisions had between Buddhists and Catholics, northerners and southerners in Vietnam. But it was the exploitation of them that created the poisonous hatreds—what President Johnson called "a climate of extremism," a divisiveness among the many that seemed to turn into paranoia among the few.

The cure lay in understanding. In America, it would take time, and both compassion and common sense, to achieve a national reconciliation. But now there was a chance the South Vietnamese would understand what Johnson and Bunker were trying to do before American society was torn any farther apart. For once the South Vietnamese understood, really understood, they, too, would act.

That was the hope of it.

Index of Persons

Vietnamese names appear under the first, or given, name rather than under the family name. Thus Nguyen Cao Ky, whose family name is Nguyen, is entered under his given name, Ky. Chinese names appear under the family name, which precedes the hyphenated prename.

Ai, Do, 271, 314
Anh, Truong Tan, 33
Arnett, Peter, 377, 386

Ba, Hoang Trong, 65, 68
Ball, Al, 273
Bao Dai, Emperor, viii, ix, 4, 19, 20, 35, 46, 189, 190, 200, 294
Berger, Samuel D., 382
Binh, Nguyen, 46, 49
Bissell, Richard, 165
Blum, Léon, 44
Bodard, Lucien, 346
Bong, Pham Van (see Tri Quang)
Brezhnev, Leonid, 134
Buck, Pearl, 187, 243
Buddha, Gautama, 67
Bundy, McGeorge, 125, 126, 128, 132, 218
Bundy, William P., 125, 215, 323, 348
Bunker, Ellsworth G., 9, 10, 170, 325, 326, 327, 334, 335, 340, 346, 359, 368, 376, 382, 386, 389, 391, 394
Burdick, Eugene, 164
Burke, Father Patrick, 307
Burke, John, 301
Buu, Tran Quoc, 79

Caesar, Julius, 278, 279
Can (a Ky aide), 335
Can, Ngo Dinh, 68, 76
Cang, Chung Tan, 139, 140, 141, 142

Cao, Huynh Van, 249
Carver, George, 82, 381
Castillo, Manolito, 136
Chau, Dinh Thanh, 319
Chau, Thich Tam, 387
Chen Yi, 114
Chiang Kai-shek, 37, 40, 192, 240, 247, 292
Chieu, Thich Minh, 258
Chinh, Dinh Trinh, 36, 39, 316, 319
Chinh, Phan Trong, 374
Chinh, Truong, 52, 190, 191, 388
Chou En-lai, 134
Chung, Tu, 41, 42, 393, 394
Church, Frank, 74
Chuyen, Le Xuan, 80, 327
Clement, David, 278
Co, Nguyen Huu, 94, 98, 142, 229
Co, Pham Huy, 352
Co, Tran Van, 201–04, 208
Colby, William, 313, 382
Connick, Major, 106–10
Corson, William, 283, 392
Cronkite, Walter, 73
Cu, Ho Ngoc, 359
Cuong, Le Chi, 269
Cushman, Robert E., Jr., 330, 331, 332

Dai, Mai Van, 36
Dan, Phan Quang, 4, 27, 32, 36, 37, 40, 292–94, 301, 311, 312, 313, 314, 316, 318, 319, 320, 336, 338, 342, 348, 351, 352, 360, 369, 376, 386, 388

395

Dang, Nguyen, 65, 68, 69
De, Cuong, 33
De Castries, General Christian, 222
De Gaulle, Charles, 31, 74, 126, 301
De Lattre de Tassigny, Marshal, 39
De Puy, William, 144
De Rhodes, Alexander, ix
Deepe, Beverly, 95
Diem, Bui, 4, 23, 29, 36, 39, 77, 130, 140, 151, 295, 316, 325, 368, 392
Diem, Ngo Dinh, ix, x, xi, 6, 7, 10, 19, 20, 21, 35, 38, 42, 43, 45, 47, 48, 51, 52, 59, 62, 68, 69, 71, 72, 73, 74, 75, 76, 77, 78, 81, 84, 85, 87, 92, 105, 120, 137, 138, 160, 162, 165, 167, 170, 177, 178, 186, 188, 192, 194, 204, 207, 219, 227, 275, 278, 279, 282, 292, 293, 294, 296, 297, 298, 300, 306, 307, 317, 318, 323, 334, 341, 355, 358, 365, 389
Dien, Tran, 316–17
Dillin, John, 313, 319
Do, Dr. Tran Van, 337
Do, Thich Tri, 64, 65
Don, Tran Van, 358
Dong, Do Quoc, 254
Dong, General Pham Van, 6, 88, 89, 90, 94, 100, 138, 139, 140, 141, 142, 199–201, 217
Dong, Premier Pham Van, 49, 134
Dong, Phan Lac Giang (alias), 246–48
Du, Father Tran, 17, 239, 318, 334
Duc, Duong Van, 81
Duc, Thich Quang, 69
Duclos, Jacques, 391
Dulles, Allen, 91
Dulles, John Foster, 165
Duncanson, Dennis J., x, 10, 33, 34, 35, 37, 39, 70, 97, 161, 163, 209, 219, 240, 263, 264, 282, 283, 321, 326
Dzu, Truong Dinh, x, 8, 336–37, 347, 348, 351, 352, 355, 356, 357, 359, 380, 391

Eisenhower, Dwight D., 91
Em, Vo Van, 26
Emacio, Captain, 104
Etherington-Smith, Gordon, 128

Fall, Bernard, 82, 191, 209
Ferri-Pisano, Pierre, 393
Flynn, Sean, 249
Freeman, Orville, 218
Fryklund, Richard, 369
Fulbright, William J., 28, 29, 181, 182

Giai, Bui Van, 271
Gia Long, Emperor, 17, 18
Giap, Vo Nguyen, x, 4, 34, 37, 44, 45, 49, 53, 54, 55, 85, 93, 101, 143, 144, 146, 157, 158, 179, 182, 269, 298, 320, 329, 330, 331, 365, 372, 374, 375, 386, 390
Gilpatric, Roswell, 165
Gio, 61, 361–62
Gray, John, 126
Greene, Graham, 103, 164, 165, 166, 167, 320
Gromyko, Andrei, 114
Gruening, Ernest, 381
Gyaltso, Shirob, 67

Habib, Philip, 9, 25, 168, 169, 170, 213, 227, 229, 311, 312, 316, 320, 326, 385, 392
Harbridge, Kenneth, 250
Hart, John, 43

Harriman, W. Averell, 75, 385
Hien, Nguyen Gia, 358
Hiep, Nguyen Van, 184
Higgins, Marguerite, xi, 75, 76, 89
Hilsman, Roger, 73, 75, 82
Hoan, Nguyen Ton, 40, 71
Ho Chi Minh, viii, x, 3, 7, 18, 19, 34, 37, 39, 40, 44, 45, 46, 49, 54, 64, 65, 133, 156, 158, 167, 190, 191, 200, 206, 210, 212, 236, 241, 242, 244, 292, 300, 322, 330, 331, 332, 333, 358, 386, 388, 391
Honey, P. J., 191
Hughes, Emmet John, 242
Humphrey, Hubert H., 168, 219, 220, 385
Humphreys, James W., 173
Huong, Nguyen Van, 36
Huong, Tran Van, x, 7, 8, 59, 76, 81, 82, 83–102, 114, 123, 124, 125, 128, 129, 130, 132, 138, 151, 160, 199, 205, 210, 303, 308, 327, 334–35, 336, 337, 339, 342, 343–46, 349, 350, 352, 353, 354, 355, 356, 359, 360, 365, 369, 384, 385, 386, 387, 388, 390, 391, 392

Johnson, Lyndon B., 9, 22, 28, 53, 58, 76, 91, 93, 125, 126, 134, 135, 137, 138, 146, 159, 161, 184, 192, 194, 196, 209, 210, 211, 212, 214, 215, 216, 217, 218, 219, 225, 230, 237, 239, 241, 242, 246, 249, 264, 265, 266, 305, 306, 315, 316, 323, 324, 325, 326, 327, 329, 331, 335, 339, 348, 349, 354, 356, 367, 368, 369, 377, 381, 382, 383–84, 388, 389, 390, 391, 392, 393, 394
Johnson, U. Alexis, 95, 96, 136, 218, 260, 313
Just, Ward, 267, 307, 317

Karch, Frederick, 275
Karen, Sister, 175
Ke, Khieu Thien, 358
Kelly, Robert, 331
Kennedy, John F., 51, 53, 71, 73, 74, 75, 76, 91, 92, 165, 211, 389
Kennedy, Robert, 91, 168, 383
Khang, Le Nguyen, 5, 23, 36, 38, 39, 59, 237, 248, 387
Khanh, Nguyen, 8, 21, 76, 77, 78, 79, 80, 81, 84, 87, 89, 92, 93, 94, 95, 96, 97, 98, 100, 114, 124, 125, 128, 129, 130, 139, 142, 147, 229, 333, 334
Khiem, Tran Thien, 81, 142, 386
Khoi, Dang Duc, 36
Khrushchev, Nikita, 50, 51, 52, 55, 338, 388
Kiem, Mrs. (see Yen, Pham Thi)
Kiem, Tran Buu, 47, 48
Killen, James S., 177
Komer, Robert W., 9, 27, 28, 169, 184, 237, 326, 338, 339
Kosygin, Aleksei, 55, 125
Ky, Ha Thuc, 36, 317
Ky, Mme. (Mai), 241
Ky, Nguyen Cao, x, 4, 5, 7, 8, 9, 12, 15, 16, 20, 22, 23, 27, 28, 29, 32, 36, 38, 39, 48, 49, 59, 77, 81, 94, 95, 98, 99, 101, 125, 127, 128, 130, 139, 142, 147, 150, 151, 152, 159, 161, 162, 166, 167, 168, 169, 180, 181, 182, 184, 185, 186, 193, 194, 195, 197, 198, 205, 207, 208, 212, 213, 214, 215, 216, 217, 218, 219, 220, 227, 228, 229, 230, 231, 232, 233, 234, 235, 236, 237, 238, 239, 240, 241, 242, 244, 248, 249, 250, 251, 252, 253, 254, 257, 258, 259, 260, 261, 262, 263, 264, 265, 266, 267, 269, 283, 293, 295, 297, 298, 299, 300, 301, 302, 303, 304, 306, 308, 309, 310, 311, 312, 313, 314, 315,

Ky, Nguyen Cao (*continued*)
316, 317, 318, 319, 320, 321,
322, 324, 325, 326, 327, 328,
329, 331, 332, 333, 334, 335,
336, 337, 338, 339, 340, 341,
342, 343, 344, 345, 346, 347,
349, 350, 351, 352, 353, 355,
356, 357, 358, 359, 360, 362,
363, 368, 369, 374, 376, 377,
378, 379, 381, 382, 384, 385,
386, 387, 390, 392, 393, 394

Lansdale, Edward, xi, 10, 25, 41,
43, 82, 160, 163–70, 174, 211,
216, 217, 218, 219, 228, 301,
323, 324, 327, 347, 390, 392
Larson, Stanley R., 157
Lederer, William J., 164
Le Duan, x, 4, 11, 23, 27, 30, 43,
44–60, 61, 62, 64, 66, 71, 80,
81, 82, 86, 103, 156, 163, 171,
177, 187, 189, 196, 207, 208,
212, 213, 217, 225, 240, 245,
265, 266, 268, 274, 292, 298,
315, 317, 321, 322, 324, 325,
330, 338, 339, 347, 352, 364,
365, 366–67, 368, 369, 372,
373, 381, 382, 387, 388, 389,
390, 391, 394
Lenin, Nikolai, 39, 57, 247, 268,
366
Lewis, Flora, 380
Lien, Thich Quang, 130, 131
Lieu, Pham Van, 5, 36, 38, 39,
94, 139, 150, 226, 227, 228
Lin Piao, 54–55
Linh, Nguyen Ngoc, 38
Lippmann, Walter, 28, 216, 326
Lisagor, Peter, 379
Liu Shao-chi, 50, 55
Loan, Nguyen Ngoc, 5, 23, 26,
36, 38, 39, 207, 208, 249, 254,
315, 316, 332, 339, 341, 343,
356, 359, 360, 368, 377, 380,
381, 382, 384, 385, 387, 390,
393

Loc, Nguyen Van, 8, 332, 351,
357, 378, 384, 385
Lodge, Henry Cabot, 9, 10, 15,
16, 25, 27, 73, 74, 75, 76, 91,
159, 160, 164, 166, 167, 168,
169, 170, 184, 189, 193, 194,
205, 216, 218, 219, 231, 233,
234, 254, 266, 283, 326, 327
Loi, Mrs. Ho Thi, 155
Loveridge, Gary, 348
Lucas, Jim, 327

MacArthur, Douglas, 192, 195
Magsaysay, Ramon, 10, 160, 165
Malik, Adam, 191
Manh, Nguyen Van, 236
Mao Tse-tung, 37, 44, 50, 53, 54,
56, 66, 106, 109, 133, 161,
191, 247, 321, 322, 366
Markbreiter, Mrs. Tuyet Nguyet,
131
Marshall, Robert, 127
May, Jim, 175
McCarthy, Eugene, 28, 382, 383
McCone, John, 75
McDowell, Harris B., Jr., 259
McNamara, Robert S., 75, 92,
132, 146, 165, 210, 212, 217,
278, 279, 331
Minh, Duong Van, 8, 21, 59, 76,
79, 81, 142, 340, 380
Minh, Thien, 64
Minh, Tran Van, 128, 142
Minh, Vo Cong, 41
"Mr. Moto," 31, 260
Mohr, Charles, 230, 307
Murphy, Mr., 273

Nehru, Jawaharlal, 292
Nessen, Ronald, 257, 258
Nghe, La Thanh, 206, 207
Nhu, Mme., 74, 76
Nhu, Ngo Dinh, 68, 72, 74, 75,
76, 293, 297, 298
Nhu Phong (*see* Tien, Le Van)

Nixon, Richard M., 326
Nolting, Frederick E., Jr., 71, 72

Oanh, Nguyen Xoan, 59
Oberdorfer, Don, 307
Oka, Takashi, 140

Page, Tim, 256, 257
Park Chung Hee, 25, 369, 374, 382
Paul VI, Pope, 126
Pearson, Lester B., 134
Peng Chen, 50, 55
Phat, Huynh Tan, 47, 48, 322
Phat, Mrs. Huynh Tan, 48
Phat, Lam Van, 81
Pike, Douglas, xi, 32, 33, 34, 40, 47, 163, 164, 209, 309, 373, 376
Poos, Robert, 258
Porter, William, 169, 170, 218, 369
Prager, Karsten, 256, 258

Quach, Mrs. Le Thi, x, 9, 269–74, 285
Quang, Dan Van, 142, 318
Quang, Mme. Dan Van, 296
Quang, Dinh Xuan, 294
Quat, Phan Huy, 4, 5, 6, 20, 23, 38–39, 40, 42, 43, 48, 59, 71, 130, 131, 133, 140, 141, 148, 149, 150, 151, 180, 261, 262, 263, 264, 300, 372
Quy, Nguyen Van, 153–55
Quyen, Le Khac, 78
Quynh, Father Hoang, 17, 334

Reach, Bill, 110–12, 114, 117, 118, 122, 123, 374
Reach, Rosemary, 111
Reston, James, 211
Richardson, John, 72, 75

Robbins, Barbara, 136
Rockefeller, Nelson, 385
Rose, Jerry, 167, 262, 263
Rostow, Walt, 82, 165
Rusk, Dean, 75, 96, 100, 101, 131, 231, 249
Russell, Richard, 239

Sanders, Sol, 141
Say, Henri, 48
Schlesinger, Arthur M., 210
Scotton, Frank, 42
Shaplen, Robert, 32, 42, 43, 81, 82
Sharp, William, 185
Smith, Edith, 136
Solis, Antonio, 110–17, 122
Stout, William, 257
Sun Tzu, 53, 226
Sung, Dang Van, 4, 5, 20, 22, 23, 24, 25, 27, 32, 36–39, 40, 41, 42, 43, 45, 47, 48, 70, 71, 74, 77, 83, 130, 131, 133, 140, 149, 150, 151, 167, 170, 210, 214, 241, 261, 262, 264, 265, 267, 295–300, 301, 302, 305, 306, 309, 311, 312, 313, 314, 315, 317, 318, 319, 320, 322, 331, 337, 338, 339, 341, 352, 354, 358, 359, 360, 368, 369, 378, 380, 381, 387, 392, 393, 394
Suslov, Mikhail, 50
Suu, Phan Khac, 7, 8, 81, 84, 94, 148, 150, 295, 299, 301, 303, 317, 318, 319, 335, 336, 355, 356, 357, 360, 365, 369
Sy, Dang, 69, 79

Tam, Nguyen Tuong, 40
Tan, Le Van (pseudonym), 242–45
Tate, Don, 376
Taylor, Maxwell D., 10, 75, 91, 92, 93, 94, 95, 96, 97, 98, 101, 125, 126, 131, 136, 141, 151,

Taylor, Maxwell D. (*continued*)
156, 159, 160, 161, 163, 165,
177, 205, 211, 217, 218, 260
Teng Hsaio-ping, 50, 55
Thai, Le Van, 5, 36, 241, 341, 393
Thang, Le, 40
Thang, Nguyen Duc, 6, 23, 36,
39, 161, 162, 167, 168, 169,
198, 339, 357, 368, 377, 378,
379, 381, 387
Thanh, Au Truong, 8, 340
Thanh, Nguyen Chi, 47, 54, 58,
184, 185, 372, 380
Thanh, Tran Chanh, 358, 391
Thant, U, 126, 134
Thao, Phan Ngoc, 150
Thi, Nguyen Chanh, 9, 81, 94,
95, 98, 99, 125, 128, 130, 139,
149, 151, 226–30, 233, 234,
235, 238, 239, 240, 249, 261,
262, 263, 264, 265, 333
Thien, Ton That, 343, 345, 386,
387
Thieu, Nguyen Van, x, 7, 8, 9,
36, 128, 150, 151, 194, 214,
230, 231, 236, 239, 244, 248,
249, 261, 262, 267, 300, 301,
306, 308, 310, 311, 312, 318,
321, 325, 328, 329, 332, 333–
34, 337, 338, 339, 340, 343,
344, 345, 346, 347, 349, 350,
351, 352, 353, 355, 356, 357,
359, 360, 362, 363, 365, 368,
372, 373, 374, 376, 377, 378,
379, 381, 382, 384, 385, 390,
391, 392, 393
Tho, Le Duc, 387
Tho, Nguyen Huu, 47
Thompson, Sir Robert, x, 10, 33,
72, 73, 87, 97, 98, 105, 128,
131, 137, 138, 142, 160, 162,
163, 170, 205, 213, 219, 265,
282, 293, 335, 342, 374–75
Thuan, Tran Quang, 234, 237
Thuc, Archbishop Ngo Dinh, 68,
76
Thuy, Xuan, 385

Tien, Le Van, 36
Tien, Nguyen Van, 47
Ton, Truong Thai, 182, 185
Tri, Nguyen Bao, 5, 6, 17, 23,
36, 38, 39, 387
Tri, Nguyen Huu, 34
Tri Quang, Thich, x, 6, 20, 22,
27, 32, 45, 48, 61, 62–81, 84,
87, 88, 89, 90, 91, 94, 98, 99,
101, 124, 125, 130, 131, 132,
133, 139, 141, 149, 152, 169,
174, 225, 226, 227, 228, 229,
230, 231, 234, 235, 236, 237,
238, 239, 242, 243, 245, 246,
249, 259, 260, 261, 262, 263,
264, 265, 266, 270, 293, 294,
305, 306, 308, 317, 343, 359,
377, 380, 381, 391
Truyen, Mai Tho, 77, 343, 386
Tuong, Ho Huu, 9, 48, 322, 323,
324, 333, 338, 358, 359, 380
Turchik Steve, 287
Tuyen, Tran Van, 131, 149, 150,
337–38

Van, Mme. Tran Van, 9, 14, 27,
340–41, 343, 358
Van, Tran Van, 8, 12–29, 31, 32,
35, 36, 41, 42, 43, 45, 59, 61,
73, 78, 81, 84, 94, 95, 148,
150, 151, 162, 184, 210, 229,
237, 248, 295, 299, 301, 303,
311, 312, 313, 314, 315, 316,
319, 321, 322, 325, 339, 340,
343, 353, 360, 365, 368, 387,
392, 393
Vance, Cyrus, 385
Vinh, Nguyen Thanh, 313, 315
Vinh, Ta, 9, 230–32, 233, 302
Vong, Tran Dinh, 379

Walker, Patrick Gordon, 134
Walt, Lewis W., 249, 251, 254

Ward, Lyttleton T., Jr., 287–88, 290, 291
Wehrlie, Roy, 184
Weinraub, Bernard, 379
Westmoreland, William C., 10, 47, 85, 92, 126, 139, 140, 141, 142, 143, 144, 145, 146, 156, 157, 158, 159, 169, 173, 176, 189, 212, 218, 230, 234, 283, 326, 331, 372, 374
Wheeler, Earl, 148
White, Theodore H., 196

Wilson, Sam, 193, 218
Wilson, Tom, 136

Xa, Mme., 15

Yen, Pham Thi, 48, 49

Zorthian, Barry, 10, 91, 124, 169, 192, 227, 303, 307, 314, 339